AF768259

The Challenges of Collaboration in Environmental Governance

NEW HORIZONS IN ENVIRONMENTAL POLITICS

Series Editor: Arthur Mol, *Chair and Professor in Environmental Policy, Director, Wageningen School of Social Sciences, Wageningen University, the Netherlands, Professor in Environmental Policy, Renmin University, Beijing*

The New Horizons in Environmental Politics series provides a platform for in-depth critical assessments of how we understand the many changes in the politics of nature, the environment and natural resources that have occurred over the last 50 years. Books in the series question how the environment is (re)defined, debated and protected; explore differences between countries and regions in environmental politics; analyse how actors do and do not collaborate around environment and natural resource conflicts; describe who wins and who loses and in what ways; and detail how to better study, analyse and theorize such developments and outcomes.

The series is designed to promote innovative cross-disciplinary analysis of the contemporary issues and debates influencing the various dimensions of environmental politics. Covering a diverse range of topics, the series will examine the political, economic and ethical aspects of environmental policy, governance and regulation. It brings together cutting edge research on environmental politics worldwide in order to shed light on, and explain current trends and developments.

With oversight from the Series Editor, Professor Arthur Mol – a noted specialist in the field of environmental politics at Wageningen University, the Netherlands – the New Horizons in Environmental Politics series comprises carefully commissioned projects from experts in the field including both academics and professionals. The audience for the series is global, and books in the series are essential reading for students, academics and professionals – in short, anyone with an interest in understanding the vital issues affecting environmental politics in the twenty-first century.

Titles in the series include:

Russia and the Politics of International Environmental Regimes
Environmental Encounters or Foreign Policy?
Anna Korppoo, Nina Tynkkynen and Geir Hønneland

American Environmental Policy
The Failures of Compliance, Abatement and Mitigation
Daniel Press

Environmental Governance through Partnerships
A Discourse Theoretical Study
Ayşem Mert

The Domestic Politics of Global Climate Change
Key Actors in International Climate Cooperation
Edited by Guri Bang, Steinar Andresen and Arild Underdal

Linking EU Climate and Energy Policies
Decision-making, Implementation and Reform
Jon Birger Skjærseth, Lars H. Gulbrandsen, Per Ove Eikeland and Torbjørg Jevnaker

The Challenges of Collaboration in Environmental Governance
Barriers and Responses
Edited by Richard D. Margerum and Cathy J. Robinson

The Challenges of Collaboration in Environmental Governance

Barriers and Responses

Edited by

Richard D. Margerum

Professor, University of Oregon, USA

Cathy J. Robinson

Principal Research Scientist, Commonwealth Scientific and Industrial Research Organisation (CSIRO), Australia; University Fellow, Northern Institute, Charles Darwin University, Australia

NEW HORIZONS IN ENVIRONMENTAL POLITICS

EE Edward Elgar PUBLISHING

Cheltenham, UK • Northampton, MA, USA

© Richard D. Margerum and Cathy J. Robinson 2016

All rights reserved. No part of this publication may be reproduced, stored in a retrieval system or transmitted in any form or by any means, electronic, mechanical or photocopying, recording, or otherwise without the prior permission of the publisher.

Published by
Edward Elgar Publishing Limited
The Lypiatts
15 Lansdown Road
Cheltenham
Glos GL50 2JA
UK

Edward Elgar Publishing, Inc.
William Pratt House
9 Dewey Court
Northampton
Massachusetts 01060
USA

A catalogue record for this book
is available from the British Library

Library of Congress Control Number: 2016938608

This book is available electronically in the **Elgar**online
Social and Political Science subject collection
DOI 10.4337/9781785360411

MIX
Paper from
responsible sources
FSC® C013056

ISBN 978 1 78536 040 4 (cased)
ISBN 978 1 78536 041 1 (eBook)

Typeset by Servis Filmsetting Ltd, Stockport, Cheshire
Printed and bound in Great Britain by TJ International Ltd, Padstow

A special thank you to all of the authors who contributed to this book and all of the reviewers who provided valuable assessment and feedback. This book is dedicated to our families.

Richard D. Margerum, University of Oregon
Cathy J. Robinson, CSIRO and Charles Darwin University

Contents

Figures

Tables

Boxes

Contributors

Robert Agranoff is Professor Emeritus in the School of Public and Environmental Affairs, Indiana University Bloomington, and Professor in the Government and Public Administration Program at the Instituto Universitario Ortega y Gasset, Madrid. His most recent book is *Collaborating to Manage: A Primer for the Public Sector* (Georgetown University Press, 2012). He is currently working on a book on the historical development of intergovernmental management in the United States.

Jennifer Bellamy is an Honorary Senior Fellow in the School of Agriculture and Food Sciences and the Institute of Social Science Research at the University of Queensland. She has held senior research positions in Australian national scientific research and academic institutions for over 30 years, leading interdisciplinary research projects and publishing widely on natural resources management, water resources governance and evaluation of related collaborative policy and planning processes. Much of her research has bridged the social, environmental and policy sciences and focused systemically at the regional scale.

Jurian Edelenbos is Professor in the Department of Public Administration and Sociology, Erasmus University Rotterdam. His focal areas for research and education are: trust, interactive governance, community engagement, network management and water governance.

Jan M. Fliervoet is a PhD candidate at the Institute for Science, Innovation and Society, Radboud University. He studied Environmental Sciences (MSc) at Radboud University and followed the science communication track during his Master's degree. His research focuses on river governance, especially on collaborative initiatives of stakeholders related to management of floodplains. Currently, Jan is involved in the national research program RiverCare (http://www.ncr-web.org/rivercare/about).

John Forester is Professor of City and Regional Planning at Cornell University. His best-known works include: *Planning in the Face of Power* (University of California Press, 1989), *Making Equity Planning Work* (with Norman Krumholz, Temple, 1990) and *The Deliberative Practitioner* (The

MIT Press, 1999). His recent work focuses on multi-stakeholder problem solving including collaboration and mediated negotiations: *Dealing with Differences: Dramas of Mediating Public Disputes* (Oxford, 2009), *Planning in the Face of Conflict* (American Planning Association Press, 2013) and (with David Laws) *Conflict, Improvisation, Governance* (Routledge RTPI, 2015). He is currently working on improvisation in planning and public life.

Ken Genskow is an Associate Professor, extension water resources specialist, and Chair of the University of Wisconsin-Madison Department of Urban and Regional Planning. His research, teaching and outreach focus on environmental planning and policy, watershed planning, and collaborative and participatory approaches to resource management, including the influence of collaboration, technical assistance and outreach on voluntary actions by private landowners. Ken also directs a statewide network of extension educators interacting with agency and organizational partners to address priority resource management needs.

Mat Gilfedder is a Senior Research Scientist and hydrologist with CSIRO, specializing in the development and application of models to better understand groundwater-surface water interactions at large scales, and to provide tools that improve our ability to predict the impact of catchment changes on stream flow and salt export. His work is often focused on regional or watershed-scale approaches which seek to bring together regional datasets, expert knowledge, and robust science to explore the links and feedbacks between changes in vegetation on groundwater processes and the implications for stream flow and for mobilizing salt stores to streams.

Misty Grayer is a PhD candidate in the School of Public Affairs at the University of Kansas. Her research focuses on law and public policy, as well as contracting out.

Mike Grundy is the Research Director leading the Agricultural Soil and Landscape Program in CSIRO, Australia's national research agency. The program observes and predicts trends across agricultural landscapes and seeks to understand the interconnection with the wider economy and environment. Mike has a long-standing personal interest in soil science and its application to agricultural and forest production, environmental protection and systems approaches to complex problems. He is a Fellow and Honorary Life Member of the Australian Institute of Agricultural Science and Technology.

Brian Head is Professor of Policy Analysis at the University of Queensland. He has also held several senior roles in government. He has published widely on public policy, public management, governance, social issues and environmental policy. He has won funding for projects on research utilization, research impacts, wicked problems, policy innovation, natural resources management and social program evaluation. He is a Fellow of the Academy of Social Sciences in Australia, and a past-President of the Australian Political Studies Association.

Tomas M. Koontz is an Associate Professor in Environmental Studies at the University of Washington Tacoma, in the School of Interdisciplinary Arts and Sciences. Following a PhD from Indiana University in Public Policy, he served on the faculty at The Ohio State University School of Environment and Natural Resources. A scholar of environmental policy and collaborative management, Koontz has published over 20 journal articles on collaboration along with a book on government roles in collaborative environmental management. His recent work focuses on collaborative implementation, use of science, and sustainability.

Susan D. Lurie is an Adjunct Research Associate with the Community Service Center in the Department of Planning, Public Policy and Management at the University of Oregon. Her professional interests include network organizations in natural resource planning and policy, institutions for community-level problem solving and sustainability, The New Natural Resource Economy for rural economic development, and ecosystem services markets at the local level.

Richard D. Margerum is a Professor and Head of the Department of Planning, Public Policy and Management at the University of Oregon. He holds a PhD in urban and regional planning and Master's degrees in water resources management and urban planning. For the past 20 years, his research has focused on collaborative approaches to planning and management in Wisconsin, Australia and the Pacific Northwest. He has published over 25 articles and book chapters and his book entitled *Beyond Consensus* (The MIT Press, 2011) examines the research and theory related to collaboration, focusing in particular on the approaches to implementation.

Daniel H. Nelson is the Director of the Syracuse University Maxwell School Executive Education training and research programs with the Government of India. Daniel is responsible for designing and developing these programs and establishing working collaborations with domestic and international partners from the government, private and nonprofit sectors. His research focuses on public policy analysis, policy implementation and human resource management.

Rosemary O'Leary is the Edwin O. Stene Distinguished Professor of Public Administration at the University of Kansas. She has published more than two dozen research articles and book chapters on collaboration as a management and leadership strategy, and trains practitioners in collaborative problem-solving processes. In 2014 O'Leary won the Dwight Waldo Award for "persons who have made outstanding contributions to the professional literature of public administration over an extended career." O'Leary is an elected member of the National Academy of Public Administration.

Jill M. Purdy is interim Dean and an Associate Professor at the Milgard School of Business, University of Washington Tacoma. She earned her doctorate in Business Administration at the Pennsylvania State University. Her research, published in such journals as *Academy of Management Journal*, *Academy of Management Review* and *Public Administration Review*, focuses on multi-level institutional dynamics and cross-sector collaboration. She is currently studying the emerging ecology for social enterprise and stakeholder perceptions of corporate social responsibility projects.

Cathy J. Robinson is a Principal Research Scientist at CSIRO and a University Fellow at Charles Darwin University in Australia. Cathy's work with government agencies, Indigenous Australians and local farmers enables scientific, Indigenous and local knowledge to respond to conservation, climate change and biosecurity risks facing Northern Australia. She leads a research program that is enabling Australia to design climate mitigation innovations that benefit Indigenous Australians. She has also worked on water-quality risks facing the Great Barrier Reef and a collaborative approach to biosecurity risk assessment and management. Cathy is also an IUCN Commissioner for the World Commission on Protected Areas.

Jane Rongerude is an Assistant Professor in the Department of Community and Regional Planning at Iowa State University, where she teaches courses in planning theory, community and urban revitalization, housing, and neighborhood planning. Her research interests focus on the potential of planning as a tool to interrupt local systems of poverty management. She is especially interested in how housing policy and planning practices shape and maintain poverty places. She earned her PhD in city and regional planning from the University of California at Berkeley.

Helen Ross is Professor of Rural Development in the School of Agriculture and Food Sciences, the University of Queensland. She is an interdisciplinary social scientist specializing in social aspects of sustainable rural development and resilience. In research she focuses particularly on people-environment relationships, collaboration processes for natural resource management, social aspects of water management, and climate change adaptation. She is co-editor of the *Australasian Journal of Environmental Management*, Chair of Healthy Waterways Social Science Experts Panel, and a member of the Australian Psychological Society's Climate Change Reference Group and UNESCO's International Experts Group on Urban Futures.

Gerardo Francisco Sandoval is an Associate Professor in the Department of Planning, Public Policy and Management at the University of Oregon and co-directs the Center for Latino/a and Latin American Studies. His research focuses on the roles of immigrants in community regeneration, the responses of governments to the presence of immigrants, and the ways that transnational relationships shape spaces that immigrants inhabit. He earned his PhD in city and regional planning from the University of California at Berkeley.

Larry D. Schroeder is Emeritus Professor of Public Administration and International Affairs at the Syracuse University Maxwell School. He is a public finance economist with primary interest in state and local public finance and financial management both in the United States and in developing and transition economies. His specific research issues include decentralization, intergovernmental fiscal relations, and the effects of institutional arrangements on the provision of public services.

Antoine J. M. Smits occupies a chair at Radboud University Nijmegen (Sustainable Water Management) and a chair at Van Hall Larenstein University of Applied Sciences (Delta Areas and Resources). Prior to his academic career Toine was Head of the Department of Integrated Water Management with the Ministry of Infrastructure and the Environment (East Netherlands division). His main fields of interest are innovative governance and finance, smart engineering and CleanTech in water resources management.

Arwin van Buuren is an Associate Professor in the Department of Public Administration at the Erasmus University Rotterdam. His research focuses on the governance of climate change adaptation, water and spatial planning. He is especially interested in issues of collaboration, innovation, institutional change and governance capacity. He publishes extensively in peer-reviewed journals, has contributed to a number of renowned handbooks and has also published several edited volumes. In addition, he is frequently asked to be an advisor and evaluator in the Dutch flood risk and adaptation domain.

Ingmar van Meerkerk is a postdoctoral student in the Department of Public Administration and Sociology, Erasmus University Rotterdam. His focal areas for research and education are boundary spanners, legitimacy, self-organization and governance networks.

Jitske van Popering-Verkerk is a PhD student in the Department of Public Administration at the Erasmus University Rotterdam. In her research she studies how in multi-level governance actors at different levels could synchronize their actions in concrete water management projects. Jitske pays special attention to the kinds of rules, interactions and management strategies that foster successful multi-level governance. In addition to her PhD research, she has conducted many studies to design and evaluate collaborative governance processes in the field of water management and spatial planning.

Nidhi Vij is a PhD candidate in the Department of Public Administration and International Affairs at the Syracuse University Maxwell School. Her research focuses on use of information communication technologies in public management, collaborative governance and community public participation.

Jeroen F. Warner teaches and publishes on disaster studies at Wageningen University, where he also earned his PhD degree and is now Associate Professor. He currently coordinates a European-funded European network on disaster, culture and social networks (EDUCEN) and has a Brazilian CAPES scholarship as Special Visiting Professor related to the same domain. In the water domain Jeroen works on domestic and transboundary water conflict, participatory resource management and governance issues. He is a co-editor of the *International Journal of Water Governance*, and an editor of *Ambiente e Sociedade*. A founder member of the London Water Research Group, he also sits on the Netherlands UNESCO Water Commission.

Edward P. Weber is the Ulysses G. Dubach Professor of Political Science in the School of Public Policy at Oregon State University. He is the former Director of the Thomas S. Foley Public Policy Institute at Washington State University. Edward specializes in the role of bureaucracy in a democracy, and the idea of, and institutional mechanisms for, bringing society back into the governing process. He also is the author of *Bringing Society Back In: Grass-Roots Ecosystem Management, Accountability, and Sustainable Communities* (The MIT Press, 2003) and *Pluralism by the Rules: Conflict and Cooperation in Environmental Regulation* (Georgetown University Press, 1998), and has published more than 45 refereed journal articles and book chapters.

Julia M. Wondolleck is an Associate Professor in the School of Natural Resources and Environment at the University of Michigan where she conducts research and teaches courses addressing the multiple dimensions of collaboration in ecosystem management. Among her other work she has authored or co-authored *Public Lands Conflict and Resolution: Managing National Forest Disputes* (Springer, 1988), *Environmental Disputes: Community Involvement in Conflict Resolution* (Island Press, 2012) and *Making Collaboration Work: Lessons from Innovation in Natural Resource Management* (Island Press, 2000).

1. Introduction: the challenges of collaboration in environmental governance

Richard D. Margerum and Cathy J. Robinson

Around the world a host of collaborative strategies and approaches have been initiated to address some of the most complex, contentious and difficult environmental issues facing society today. Although there are now diverse purposes, forms and functions of collaborative approaches to environmental governance, each share mechanisms to enable the integration of knowledge, activities and perspectives of diverse actors to improve management decisions. They have been initiated because long-standing conflict and competition over resources has led to untenable situations and pressures for change. They have also been initiated because the types of problems and solutions have changed.

This book encompasses a diversity of experiences and scholarship focused on collaborative approaches to environmental governance and shows that collaboration has rapidly evolved from an emerging concept to a leading practice and paradigm. The rationale behind collaboration is clear. Collaboration between institutions at multiple jurisdictional levels, and with multiple perspectives and epistemologies, can lead to benefits of shared responsibility for management decisions, trust and social learning to create adaptive, innovative and mutually agreed solutions. It can also produce institutional flexibility to manage multiple stakeholder interests and knowledge that can respond to the interconnectedness of social-ecological systems which shape and are shaped by the context and nature of environmental decisions.

Over the past few decades the theoretical pedigree of collaboration has grown based on academic roots in governance, public participation, planning, conflict resolution, resilience and public management to create theories and principles that not only reflect disciplinary foci but also the countries in which this scholarship has grown. Just as importantly, rapid application and experimentation has propelled collaboration to the forefront of governance and management practice. With or without the theories to guide them, practitioners have been engaged in collaboration on an increasing basis. Stakeholders, decision makers and scientists alike recognized that at the heart of the collaborative governance imperative has been the need to strengthen the link between the diversity of knowledge and the range of actions for addressing some of the most complex and wicked environmental issues of our era.

As this body of scholarship and practice matures, it is timely to consider the challenges of collaborative approaches to environmental governance. This volume highlights how these challenges reflect the variety of perspectives and experiences that are brought together. Conflict is the prelude to consensus and debate about the efficacy of collaboration is rarely fully resolved. It is within this debate that these chapters focus on new innovations and adaptations needed for collaboration to create the social and institutional conditions for changes needed for sustainability.

THE CHALLENGE OF COLLABORATION

This book grew out of an ongoing conversation among researchers addressing collaborative governance and practitioners working to make collaboration more effective. As chapters in this volume highlight, the empirical research on the practice of collaboration is increasing in sophistication, breadth and detail. Models, evaluation frameworks and principles to examine collaborative environmental governance now exist based on a range of methods, academic traditions and settings. The success of collaboration has been celebrated, but there is less research on the difficulties and challenges of collaborative planning and policy.

In recent years there is a small but growing body of literature that takes a more critical view of collaboration (Echeverria, 2001; Hanemann and Dyckman, 2009; Layzer, 2008; Lubell, 2004). In part this reflects the increased complexity and competition over the management of natural resources that is demanding more of collaborative processes and partnerships. It also reflects the diversity of purposes, decision-making levels and types of collaborative governance arrangements that influence the types of barriers that collaborative partners will face (Margerum and Robinson, 2014). This research highlights significant hurdles that collaborators face because different stakeholders have different needs, missions and mandates. Thus, from the outset, collaborative processes and arrangements confront barriers and challenges related to power sharing and consensus building, particularly when the issues and context offer more trade-offs and fewer opportunities for joint gains.

Our goal with this book is to bring together a wide range of researchers from different disciplines and different countries to examine the challenges of collaboration from a variety of perspectives. We have sought out authors who have explored these challenges in theory, those engaged in empirical research, and those exploring new ways of practicing collaboration. We did not start this book with a pre-identified set of challenges, but instead sought out a range of authors who could offer different perspectives. All the authors approached the task of unpacking the challenges facing collaboration with a view that the combined work will lead to better collaborative approaches and strategies.

In this chapter, we seek to set the context for collaborative approaches to governing environmental problems by presenting the emergence of the concept and academic traditions from Europe, the United States and post-colonial countries like Australia and India. We follow this with a brief summary of three terms that form the themes for this book: challenges, collaboration and governance. This is followed by an overview of the book structure and summary of the chapters.

THE EMERGENCE OF COLLABORATION

The collaborative approach to planning, management and governance has a deep history in political science, public administration, planning, sociology, resilience theory and natural resources management. The concept has evolved from a range of concepts and ideas related to public participation, conflict resolution, democratic governance and increasingly complex problems that belied traditional solutions (Arnstein, 1969; Gildea, 1959; Godschalk and Mills, 1966; Lindblom, 1965; Litwak and Hylton, 1962; March and Simon, 1958).

However, as updated concepts of public roles, stakeholder involvement, networked governance, ecosystem management, conflict resolution and consensus-based processes took hold in the 1980s and 1990s, collaboration became increasingly touted as a new and emerging paradigm (Agranoff, 1990; Gray, 1989; Grumbine, 1994; Innes, 1995; Johnson and Agee, 1988; Rainey and Milward, 1983). In describing the emergence of collaboration, we cast a wide net over a range of literature. In the environmental field, integrated environmental management, watershed management and ecosystem management all incorporated many of the core elements of collaboration (Cortner and Moote, 1999; Loh and Rykiel, 1992; U.S. EPA, 1992). In public administration, collaboration is related to inter-organizational coordination and networks, which has been a growing theme in how governments and organizations work more effectively together to solve complex problems (Agranoff, 1990; Knoke, 1990; O'Toole, 1990; Rainey and Milward, 1983). Finally, in planning and public policy, collaboration, consensus building and collaborative planning were all used to describe this emerging approach (Healey, 1992; Innes and Booher, 1999; Susskind and Cruikshank, 1987).

Just as important to the emergence of collaboration as a theoretical concept was the increasing use of collaboration in practice. Through necessity imposed by problem complexity, conflict, interjurisdictional interaction or simply pressure for results, practitioners began experimenting with strategies and approaches that researchers eventually coined "collaborative governance" (Born and Genskow, 1999; Born and Margerum, 1993; Curtis, 1998; NPCC, 2006; Robinson et al., 2014; Ross et al., 2009; U.S. EPA, 1992). This on-the-ground experimentation quickly provided findings about effective practice that helped test existing theory and build new theory.

As several authors in this volume point out, the research on collaboration has shifted over the years from presenting the normative claims of collaboration, to defining best practices, to developing typologies and frameworks (Margerum, Chapter 2; Koontz, Chapter 3; Agranoff, Chapter 4). A significant literature has emerged on the capacity and possibilities of collaboration but note that mechanisms to build consensus and paradigms under which collaborative governance are institutionalized can marginalize some stakeholders, ignore different types of knowledge throughout the planning process and empower some perspectives over others (Gilfedder et al., Chapter 6; Nelson et al., Chapter 12; Robinson, Chapter 16).

The history of collaborative practice throughout the world could be a book by itself, but it is worthwhile to consider some context and examples of where these concepts have emerged. We focus on its development in the United States, Europe and beyond, but as several chapters in this book demonstrate, it's a concept being adopted in countries throughout the world.

United States

In the United States, concepts such as integrated environmental management, ecosystem management and watershed management were becoming increasingly applied in practice in the 1980s and 1990s (Born and Genskow, 2000; Born and Sonzogni, 1995; Cairns and Crawford, 1991; Cortner and Moote, 1999; Gardiner et al., 1994; Grumbine, 1994; Hooper, 1995; Mitchell and Pigram, 1989). These approaches were responding to complex problems that crossed multiple boundaries and generated difficult tensions and conflict. The heart of these concepts was the concept of collaborative interaction among a range of participants.

In the area of water quality management, it was becoming increasingly apparent that goals could not be achieved without an approach that addressed both point and nonpoint sources (Born and Genskow, 2000; Dixon and Easter, 1986). The US Environmental Protection Agency (EPA) promoted a watershed approach that encouraged broad based stakeholder engagement due to the range of implementation actions, but particularly because many nonpoint source pollution goals required community and landowner participation (U.S. EPA, 1992).

In the management of water quantity and water flow, legal challenges to existing arrangements empowered environmentalists and other users. As the long-term effects of historical management practices became more apparent, these groups used policies such as the US Endangered Species Act to force agencies to reconsider policies and management approaches (Layzer, 2008; Margerum, 2011; Weber, 2000). These policies have been particularly powerful as environmental impact reviews and hydroelectric license renewals raise new issues not considered when projects were constructed 40–50 years ago. As a result, in places such as the Florida Everglades, Columbia Basin and San Francisco Bay Delta, these challenges have led to significant collaborative efforts and ongoing conflict about long-term management approaches (Benson et al., 2013; Dutterer and Margerum, 2015; Heikkila, 2006; Innes et al., 2007; Lurie, 2011).

In forestry and natural resources management, agencies such as the US Forest Service were increasingly facing ecological questions that challenged their traditional production approach (Koontz et al., 2004; Weber, 2003). The competing uses for public lands and increasing concern about endangered species led to legal challenges and conflict that stalled plans and timber projects (Thomas, 2003). Managers began experimenting with negotiated and collaborative strategies, while community-based efforts emerged to bring the range of perspectives together using more collaborative approaches (Carr et al., 1998; Moseley and KenCairn, 2001).

Europe

The emergence of collaborative governance in Europe has been influenced by a range of national and regional trends, including the increased role in public-private partnerships and new models promoting more interactive governance (Skelcher et al., 2013; Sørensen and Torfing, 2008; Sullivan and Skelcher, 2002; Wesseling, 2011). In the UK, the increased use of public-private partnerships spawned a wide range of collaborative efforts across government sectors (Vangen et al., 2014) which prompted scholars to examine the various interactive and adaptive dimensions of collaborative planning regimes (e.g. Healey, 1997; Prager et al., 2012; Van Buuren,

2009). Across Europe, reductions in the size of government and an increased focus on performance has resulted in governance more focused on effectiveness and efficiency (Voets et al., 2008). With the increasing recognition that problems span organizational boundaries, there has been increasing attention on the performance across the network of collaborating organizations (Arnouts et al., 2012; Voets et al., 2008). Resilience thinking has also considered how the design of collaborative governance systems can enhance system attributes for resilience in different planning contexts (e.g. natural resource management) and for different planning purposes (e.g. Olsson et al., 2004; Wilkinson, 2012).

One important recent influence on environmental governance has been the European Union's Water Directive Framework and Common Implementation Strategy, which has promoted a river basin approach and a more participatory planning model (Moss, 2012; Newig and Koontz, 2014; Wesseling, 2011). This has led to a range of approaches ranging from agency-led basin initiatives in England and Wales, river basin agency-led efforts in France and the Netherlands, and a more collaborative structure in Germany (Moss, 2012; Newig and Koontz, 2014; Warner, 2007). Each country has faced its own set of implementation challenges, including complications from multi-level implementation, distrust of public agencies with less participatory traditions, and the complications of international boundaries (Bréthaut and Pflieger, 2013; Newig and Koontz, 2014; Warner, 2007).

And Beyond

The experiment with collaboration has also been tried in a number of countries in a wide range of cultural, institutional and economic contexts, including Australia, New Zealand, Canada, South America and Southeast Asia (Curtis et al., 2014; Robinson et al., 2011; Taylor and de Loe, 2012; Warner, 2007). While much of this scholarship reinforces European and North American traditions, researchers have also added to this scholarship based on lessons learned from the context of collaborative practice. This includes the role of collaboration to reconcile the relationships between Indigenous peoples and Europeans, including rights to territory, its uses and derived resources (e.g. Hill et al., 2012; Lane and Hibbard, 2005; Maclean et al., 2015; Robinson and Lane, 2013; Ross et al., 2009). Intellectual frameworks from planning, geography, resilience, sociology, public policy and economics have also been used to critically examine national and regional policy attempts to refashion collaborative governance as a means of reinvigorating democracy, improving the fidelity and efficacy of government and achieving diverse and complex environmental policy goals (e.g. Lane et al., 2009). This includes modifications of collaborative approaches to resolve complex water quality and resource sharing issues (e.g. Kroon et al., 2009; Robinson et al., 2014) including comparative case-study analysis with Northern Hemisphere experiences (e.g. Margerum and Robinson, 2014). Theoretical approaches from geography, resilience theory and planning have also explored collaborative approaches to conservation planning and practice (Armitage et al., 2012; Hill et al., 2015). Sub-disciplines from ecology have also added to the debate by highlighting the potential and challenges of collaborative approaches to natural resource management including forestry and fisheries (e.g. Maclean et al., 2015; Pinkerton, 1989).

DEFINING THE THEMES OF THIS BOOK

As highlighted above there are many excellent publications on multiple facets of collaborative governance. Our goal in this book is not to provide an overview of the collaboration concept, but to explore key challenges as the theory and practice of collaboration matures. Therefore, this book is focused around three themes reflected in the title: collaboration, challenges and governance.

Collaboration

Collaboration has rapidly evolved from an emerging concept to common practice and a dominant theme in the governance literature. The concept of working across boundaries, a regional focus and public consultation have all been long-standing themes in governance (Advisory Commission on Interstate Relations, 1972; Arnstein, 1969; Dworsky and Allee, 1981; Healey, 1997; Rogers and Whetten, 1982). More recently these concepts were updated to reflect the need to examine problems in a more holistic and integrated approach through terminology such as co-management, integrated management, and watershed and ecosystem management (Berkes, 2009; Born and Sonzogni, 1995; Cortner and Moote, 1999; Johnson and Agee, 1988; Loh and Rykiel, 1992; Margerum, 1999). Collaboration is broad and diverse drawing from multiple academic lenses to examine how real-world collaborative arrangements and practice achieve inclusive participation, consensus-based approaches, knowledge sharing, integrated management and supporting networks (Gray, 1989; Innes and Booher, 2009; Margerum, 2011; Robinson et al., 2011). Concepts surrounding co-management, networks and inter-organizational collaboration are often used interchangeably to describe consensus-based approaches to managing cross-boundary problems through formal and informal structures (Agranoff, 2007; Goldsmith and Eggers, 2004; Mandell, 1990; McAllister et al., 2015; Provan and Milward, 1995).

Collaboration is broadly defined as a consensus-based approach to management and governance involving a wide range of stakeholders in an ongoing role. However, it is not limited to government-initiated or government-led efforts. As researchers note, consensus is often an ongoing and political process that can engage, disengage, contain or even block certain stakeholders. There are now examples of community-based collaboration efforts that have mobilized local stakeholders yet can have limited roles for government, collaborations where non-government organizations play a central convening and facilitation role, and consensus-building efforts that are targeted for particular environmental management outcomes and/or stakeholder groups (Gray, 1989; Linden, 2002; Warner, 2007; Weber, 2000). Common to all these manifestations of collaboration is that power is shared so that collaborators can agree on solutions to share responsibility for common and often complex environmental issues.

Some collaborative efforts have emerged to promote voluntary action, such as motivating landowners to adopt conservation actions to improve water quality or habitat (Robinson et al., 2014). However, there are many examples of collaborative efforts that have emerged without top-down authority, such as collaborative efforts to manage air quality and metropolitan growth (Barbour and Teitz, 2009; Margerum, 2005). It could be argued that some of these collaboration efforts have effectively expanded the role of government where state or regional governance was not willing to address these issues. There are also examples of collaborative efforts that have led to new policy, different policy interpretations or new management programs (Margerum, 2007; Robinson et al., 2011). In many cases, there are collaborative efforts to developing policy or management plans, but implementation follows traditional hierarchical approaches.

These different views of collaboration are often distinguished by differences in the focus of collaboration. In some cases, the collaboration operates at the highest levels of governance. In these settings, the topics of collaboration are the policies themselves and how policies and programs should be implemented. These policy-level collaboration efforts often involve elected officials, policy stakeholders and interest groups that work at this policy level (Lurie, 2011; Margerum, 2011; McAllister et al., 2015; Robinson et al., 2011). For example, much of the collaboration efforts in the Sacramento-San Joaquin Delta case study, commonly referred to as CALFED (Wondolleck and Lurie, Chapter 9), have involved deliberation about state and federal water quality and quantity—and the programs and activities to achieve collective goals.

In contrast, some efforts occur within the existing policies, and collaboration is more focused on the integration of governance among the array of government and non-government organizations. These organizational-level collaboration efforts involve individuals representing organizations as well as other stakeholders that may contribute important perspectives (Imperial, 2005; Margerum, 2011). For example, Thomas (2003) examines the roles of agencies such as the National Park Service and Bureau of Land Management in coordinating the management of public lands for biodiversity.

Finally, some collaboration efforts are focused more on direct actions, such as restoration and best management practices. These action-level collaboration efforts tend to be community-based or grass-roots-level efforts that involve an array of individuals who can help promote collective actions and community support (Curtis and Lockwood, 2000; Margerum, 2011). These efforts may also involve government participants, but they tend to be involved as technical advisors or program funders. As a result these efforts are less likely to involve the sharing of power by organizational participants, because the focus is more upon on-the-ground delivery. Some of these efforts may also be led and carried out without government involvement (Koontz et al., 2004).

Clearly, collaboration activities don't always fit neatly into this policy–organizational–action typology. There are many examples of efforts that span these categories, shift focus over time or present nested approaches. However, it is important to carefully define the topic that is the focus of collaboration so that there is a logical comparison of findings across different contexts. Using research and examples from around the world along with theories from a range of disciplines this book proposes to explore the challenges of collaboration. Challenges are defined in terms of the structural, procedural and substantive aspects of collaborative governance. These limitations may be barriers that cannot be overcome; they may be the boundaries of collaboration effectiveness; in some cases they may be able to overcome with innovative strategies and responses.

Challenges

Challenges with respect to collaboration can be described as limitations, weaknesses or difficulties which affect the efficacy of consensus building efforts to negotiate and deliver agreed goals. There is a range of ways in which these challenges have been examined.

First, some challenges relate to the limitations of collaborative governance in the face of deep-seated conflict, culture or power barriers (Hill et al., 2012; Leach and Pelkey, 2001). For example, several researchers note the difficulty of applying collaborative management in developing countries with authoritarian governments and deep-seated regional animosities (Dore, 2007; Wegerich, 2007) or in cross-cultural contexts where democratic approaches to stakeholder engagement and building consensus is not appropriate (Robinson and Wallington, 2012). It is also important to note that these are also limitations of traditional governance approaches.

Second, there are challenges that can be classified as weaknesses of the collaboration model. These are the vulnerable points where failure is more likely to occur. There are examples of how these weaknesses can be overcome, but they are often not occurring in practice because they are difficult or complex. For example, collaborative efforts that rely heavily on stakeholder perspectives are sometimes criticized for failing to include a diversity of views and perspectives (Healey, 1997; Leach, 2006; Purdy, 2012; Sousa and Klyza, 2007). Participants are more likely to include organized interests, and those with the education, time and resources to participate (Kroon et al., 2009; Leach, 2006). There are examples of strategies for overcoming these representation weaknesses, but they involve additional time and resources, and different strategies to reach a more diverse set of voices (see Rongerude and Sandoval, Chapter 14).

Third, some challenges relate to the difficulties of applying the collaborative model. These are the components of the design that shouldn't fail if people are paying attention to how it is operating. It may require training, experience and careful attention to best practices. For example, much has been written about the issue of collaborative leaders, brokers and facilitators (Edelenbos et al., 2013; Lejano and Ingram, 2010). There are many accounts of the key principles, strategies and innovative examples of practice (Chrislip and Larson, 1994; Crosby and Bryson, 2010; Linden, 2008). However, these roles can be difficult and delicate (see Forester, Chapter 15). Mistakes and poor practice can unravel good sound principles.

It is important to acknowledge that all of the challenges outlined in this book also appear in other forms of governance—including hierarchical, non-consultative approaches. For example, authoritarian governance, representation diversity and leadership are challenges for governance generally. However, these issues have also been scrutinized by researchers over the years. If collaborative governance is to be promoted as an alternative to traditional decision making, it must be able to undergo the same level of assessment. It is only through this scrutiny that the theory and practice of collaboration will improve.

Governance

The final term that comprises a major theme in this book is governance, which has a wide range of definitions. Environmental planning and decision making in many countries around the world has undergone a fundamental shift in which actors from civil society and the market are participating more directly in environmental policy formation and implementation. There are now different governance regimes that exist around the world each of which provide various institutional mechanisms for sectors of society to engage in environmental decisions through formal and informal structures (Provan and Kenis, 2008; Vangen et al., 2014). These terms are often associated with networks, which emphasizes horizontal relationships in contrast to more traditional, hierarchical relationships (Arnouts et al., 2012; Lange et al., 2013; Provan and Kenis, 2008; Vangen et al., 2014). One of the debates appearing in the public administration and planning literature is whether there is a shift from government to governance, or whether the change is towards new governance that reflects increased interdependencies (Lange et al., 2013; Lindquist, 2004). These increased interdependencies include increased participation of non-state actors that supplement bureaucratic authority rather than replace it (Head, 2008; Lange et al., 2013).

While some confine the definition of governance to those initiated or sanctioned by formal government (Ansell and Gash, 2007), many view governance more broadly to include a range of decision makers (Emerson et al., 2012). This may include community-based or self-determined approaches to governance, which may occur without formal government roles (Arnouts et al., 2012; Kooiman, 2003). However, one of the common defining characteristics of governance is collective action (Ansell and Gash, 2007), which requires key participants to interact on an ongoing basis through formal and informal networks (Emerson et al., 2012).

By using the term governance, we recognize the various types of consensus-based efforts. Some of the literature on collaborative planning and conflict resolution views collaborative processes in terms of reaching an agreement, completing a contract or finalizing a plan. This approach implies a more cooperative approach in which negotiated plans and agreements are the primary guide for future decision making. Collaborative governance implies that stakeholders play an ongoing role in decision making in which there is a need for coordination of management and adjustment in response to new information and changing conditions (Agranoff, 2007; Bingham and O'Leary, 2008).

OVERVIEW OF CHAPTERS

The chapters in this book offer contributions from a range of disciplines and contexts. Our goal in seeking out leading authors in this field is to identify those who have been exploring the cutting edge of conceptual thinking and empirical research. We also sought authors working across the world to allow a shared comparison of trends and differences. The book is divided into six sections addressing:

1. Theory and context
2. Problems and context
3. Policy, politics and power
4. Organizations, stakeholders and governance
5. Process and participation
6. Conclusions.

Theory and Context

Chapter 2 by Richard D. Margerum reviews the literature from areas such as collaboration, consensus building, conflict resolution and network theory to examine some of the underlying themes about the challenges of collaboration. The goal of this chapter is not to confirm or deny these challenges, but to document the range of researchers who have raised collaboration challenges as a significant issue and organize them into themes. The challenges are grouped into the following themes: (a) problems and societal context; (b) policy and political setting; (c) power; (d) collaborative ability and capacity; (e) participant factors; and (f) costs and benefits. In reviewing these themes, he also seeks to identify the theoretical underpinnings of these challenges to help guide future research.

Tomas M. Koontz draws on the American context to review the evolution of collaboration in environmental governance over time in Chapter 3. He examines the origins of ecosystem management, its focus on a holistic, interdisciplinary approach and its gradual expansion to address social concerns and stakeholder and organizational roles. He also traces the early origins in community-based, collaborative environmental management. With origins in Elinor Ostrom's work on self-governance in response to the failures of centralized government control, collaborative partnerships emerged to fill important gaps and voids. The early scholarship in this realm focused on the failures of top-down practice and best practices and the second generation scholarship began to propose typologies, models, and to take a more critical examination of outcomes. Finally, he examines the research on collaborative public management in response to reduced government roles, resulting in more networked forms of governance. His comparison of these fields and their evolution over time reveals some important common themes and differences, and the tensions between theory and practice.

In Chapter 4, Robert Agranoff examines the limitations of networks as a form of collaborative management by looking deeper into issues related to their internal operational processes. First, he highlights the complexities involved when agencies and organizations work collaboratively including challenges of governing bodies, statutory constraints, turf battles and the management of network processes. Second, he highlights the overlooked issue of mission incompatibility and the challenges it creates in working collaboratively. Third, there is the issue of "big P" politics; or the role of elective leaders in supporting or constraining collaborative efforts. Fourth, there are the "small p" politics of process, power and operational barriers in the collaboration process. Fifth, there is the array of processing barriers or transaction costs. Sixth, he notes the issue of process fatigue created by the complexity of multiple collaboration efforts. Finally, there are the perils of operational localism, or the gap between policy and delivery. Agranoff suggests that these limitations can be more effectively addressed by applying continuous improvement functions that suggest more systematic approaches to improving collaborative practice.

In Chapter 5, Jurian Edelenbos and Ingmar van Meerkerk introduce the phrase "vitality mechanisms" which support interactive and collaborative governance and discuss the challenges associated with applying them in practice. Vitality mechanisms refer to the procedural and relational capacity among actors in a network, which they suggest is strongly related to governance capacity and relational capacity. Vitality is supported by informal structures or settings that promote interaction among actors, boundary spanning activities that build and activate relationships among actors, constructive dialogue and deliberation among actors, trust to enhance the performance of networks, and institutionalization of relationships that allow ongoing interaction. However, these conditions necessary for supporting vitality also confront challenges related to the interplay between the conditions, the impacts of the evolution of networks over time, and the contextual effects on these conditions.

Problems and Context

In Chapter 6, Mat Gilfedder, Cathy J. Robinson and Mike Grundy critically evaluate how scientific evidence is used to guide and evaluate collaboration. Drawing on expertise in collaborative planning, hydrology and soil systems science, they trace the challenges in Australia of translating scientific data into informed and sustained on-ground, voluntary responses. They highlight the challenges of introducing complex and uncertain scientific information into real-world collaborative decisions and on-ground actions. The chapter also highlights the importance of considering and debating science at the collaborative planning table, even if the information challenges fluctuating support for long-term, on-ground efforts to address broad and undesirable environmental change.

In Chapter 7, Arwin van Buuren and Jitske van Popering-Verkerk address the challenges of utilizing collaboration to address one of the most challenging issues facing society today—climate change adaptation. Drawing on an analysis of Dutch efforts to manage their Delta Programme, they found that consensus efforts were able to overcome deep uncertainties and value controversies. However, they also found significant challenges, including the need to develop more powerful political leadership, trade-offs between scientific depth and negotiated knowledge and trade-offs between consensus and decisiveness. They conclude that the approach in the Dutch Delta Programme has been successful in introducing new ways of working, but can't determine whether this has been sufficient to adjust standard routines in the water domain.

In Chapter 8, Helen Ross, Jennifer Bellamy and Brian Head examine the challenges of using collaboration on a regional scale to address wicked problems in Australia. Their research examines four diverse collaborative efforts: salinity management in an important irrigated agricultural region, dryland salinity in a landscape with high biodiversity values, water quantity management in inland Australia, and water quality in the urbanized South East Queensland region. Their comparative work reveals five consistent challenges. First, the complexity and difficulty associated with solving the problems creates significant resistance that requires major problems or crises to develop political will. Second, building and maintaining collaborative arrangements with continuous policy adjustments and changing stakeholders has generated a constantly adapting governance environment. Third, a diverse range of collaborative scientific research of unique relevance to each region may be available, but needs to be well linked with local knowledge systems and management needs in order to gain acceptance. Fourth, there has been a mismatch between political and policy time frames and the timescales needed to address long-term resource decision making. Finally, there has been the difficulty of managing in a multi-level context; ranging from national- and state-level policy to community engagement and local participation.

Policy, Politics and Power

In Chapter 9, Julia M. Wondolleck and Susan D. Lurie examine the issue of mandated collaboration, which contradicts the long-standing central tenet of voluntary participation that emerged from the field of alternative dispute resolution. They examine this issue using thorough research on the CALFED case. They note that collaboration was essentially mandated through instilling a sense of urgency, developing a need to work together through procedural and political means, developing the recognition that the CALFED approach was the preferred alternative, and creating procedures that ensured greater fairness. However, they identify three significant process challenges that weakened this mandated approach: faltering political support that undermined the mandate, resistance within the agencies among those not directly involved, and the difficulty of shared accountability.

In Chapter 10, Edward P. Weber examines the issue of political support for collaborative governance and the logic of support that spans both liberal and conservative politicians in the western United States. For liberal politicians, collaborative governance is viewed as a way to achieve environmental goals such as species recovery. From their perspective, the national environmental superstructure of environmental laws provides enough security that their preferred environmental protection outcomes will be reached that they are willing to loosen the reins of discretion in order to produce better outcomes. For conservative politicians, the place-based collaboration approach matches the conservative ideas of small government and governance close to home. This support continues to be challenged by lawsuits from the left and right, but broad-based public interest outcomes offer policy solutions that are often hard for elected officials to oppose. In response to these trends, Weber notes that politicians have been granting more discretion to agencies, which also have been lending more support to collaboration due to declining budgets and more emphasis on collaboration.

Jill M. Purdy examines the issue of power in collaborative governance in Chapter 11. She notes that the use of episodic power in everyday interactions is more easily managed than structural power, which is rooted in the institutional order of society and is often invisible. She discusses forms of power, orientations toward power, and power dynamics stemming from the desire for legitimacy within one's institutional order. She identifies two challenges for managing power in environmental collaborations. First, the context for interaction may not insulate participants from the demands of their institutional logics, preventing the creation of a shared logic that allows a robust and equitable process. Second, the legitimacy of collaboration as a governance system may be insufficient, particularly when collaborations may identify solutions that challenge the basis and order of the inter-institutional system. She concludes that power issues may impose barriers on the meaningful participation of diverse groups in environmental decision making and planning that are difficult to overcome.

Organizations, Stakeholders and Governance

In Chapter 12, Daniel H. Nelson, Rosemary O'Leary, Larry D. Schroeder, Misty Grayer and Nidhi Vij examine the adoption and challenges of using collaboration in the Indian Forest Service. Their findings revealed surprisingly high rates of collaboration support and use within the agency, and participants were strongly motivated by leveraging resources, common purpose and improving outcomes. The challenges of collaborating in India include hierarchical structure, misalignment of interests, different organization cultures, clashing time horizons, numerous stakeholders, low accountability, complex political environments, frequent transfers of personnel, low trust and lack of transparency. The authors present a new three-part Need-Attitude-Skillset theory of collaboration.

Jeroen F. Warner, Jan M. Fliervoet and Antoine J. M. Smits examine the challenges facing the Netherlands' approach to collaborative governance in Chapter 13. They compare three case studies of mono- or multi-functional floodplain maintenance, to assess the scope for a Joint Maintenance Approach (JMA) in a Dutch context in light of the actor configuration, changing role of the public sector in land-use planning and the fragmented maintenance activities. Exploring JMA revealed several collaborative challenges. An important challenge is how to sustain multi-stakeholder collaboration established in the planning and implementation phase. Additionally, there are complications related to multi-stakeholder leadership, conflicting policies and fragmentation of powers within organizations. Finally, the Dutch experience highlights challenges in integrating public and non-governmental roles in land-use planning.

Process and Participation

In Chapter 14, Jane Rongerude and Gerardo Francisco Sandoval examine the issue of participation through the lens of an intensive, grass-roots engagement strategy. Through direct experimentation, they have been able to demonstrate and refine techniques for engaging some of the least powerful and most marginalized communities. Their approach seeks to address the long-standing weakness of collaboration that relates to stakeholder-based processes. However, they also identify significant challenges to this approach that relate to the difficulty of creating an ongoing role for marginalized communities, the costs and time involved in undertaking this approach, and the difficulty of finding third parties who can take the lead role in implementing the outreach approach.

In Chapter 15, John Forester explores the challenges of facilitators' roles in collaborative processes and the ways that researchers can learn from such facilitators' experiences. By examining a rich practice story detailing a facilitator's collaborative work, the chapter focuses upon facilitators' professional expertise, their concerns about inefficiency and the complexities of convening, guiding and intervening. Forester also highlights the challenges for researchers to define and explain collaborative approaches, which often do not fit traditional labels of facilitation, collaboration or dispute resolution. He challenges researchers to do a better job of exploring grounded accounts of collaborative work by practitioners to help readers better understand the complexities of collaborative efforts. Forester argues that researchers and practitioners alike must think carefully about the challenges of building relationships, framing contentious issues, responding to participants' demands, and understanding the processes of dialogue, debate and negotiation—along with the corresponding intervening roles that each of these three processes require.

In Chapter 16, Cathy J. Robinson reviews the context for Indigenous collaborative partnerships in Australia. She highlights the history of disempowerment through Australian colonization, and the emerging collaborative management efforts evolving in the Northern Territory. These joint efforts have exposed several challenges, including tensions between wildlife conservation goals and Indigenous hunting that is important for both culture and subsistence, and the tensions between traditional environmental knowledge and scientific knowledge. These challenges along with the concepts of nature and culture that underpinned Northern Australian settlement have challenged contemporary cross-cultural collaborative efforts.

Conclusions

In Chapter 17, Richard D. Margerum, Cathy J. Robinson and Ken Genskow summarize some of the major issues confronting collaborative governance across the authors of this book. Using a peer-review process involving the book authors and other researchers examining collaboration, they also present a research agenda for collaboration. This agenda highlights the need for more longitudinal research, studies of politics and governance, work that addresses the art and nuance of collaborative processes, studies of the role of community and the public, research on the role of individual participants, studies examining science and problem complexity, research on the role of external pressures, and work that addresses issues of management relationships.

REFERENCES

Advisory Commission on Interstate Relations. (1972). *Multistate Regionalism*. Washington, D.C.: U.S. Government Printing Office.

Agranoff, R. (1990). Responding to human crises: intergovernmental policy networks. In R. W. Gage and M. P. Mandell (eds.), *Strategies for managing intergovernmental policies and networks*. New York: Praeger.

Agranoff, R. (2007). *Managing within networks: adding value to public organizations*. Washington, D.C.: Georgetown University Press. Retrieved from http://www.loc.gov/catdir/toc/ecip071/2006031171.html.

Ansell, C. and Gash, A. (2007). Collaborative governance in theory and practice. *Journal of Public Administration Research and Theory*, *18*(4), 543–571.

Armitage, D., de Loë, R. and Plummer, R. (2012). Environmental governance and its implications for conservation practice. *Conservation Letters*, *5*, 245–255.

Arnouts, R., van der Zouwen, M. and Arts, B. (2012). Analysing governance modes and shifts—governance arrangements in Dutch nature policy. *Forest Policy and Economics*, *16*, 43–50. http://doi.org/10.1016/j.forpol.2011.04.001.

Arnstein, S. R. (1969). A ladder of citizen participation. *Journal of the American Institute of Planners*, *35*(4), 216–224.

Barbour, E. and Teitz, M. B. (2009). Blueprint planning in California: an experiment in regional planning for sustainable development. In D. A. Mazmanian and M. E. Kraft (eds.), *Toward sustainable communities: transition and transformations in environmental policy* (2nd edn., pp. 171–200). Cambridge, MA: The MIT Press.

Benson, D., Jordan, A., Cook, H. and Smith, L. (2013). Collaborative environmental governance: are watershed partnerships swimming or are they sinking? *Land Use Policy*, *30*, 748–757.

Berkes, F. (2009). Evolution of co-management: role of knowledge generation, bridging organizations and social learning. *Journal of Environmental Management*, *90*, 1692–1702.

Bingham, L. and O'Leary, R. (eds.). (2008). *Big ideas in collaborative public management*. Armonk, N.Y.: M. E. Sharpe.

Born, S. M. and Genskow, K. D. (1999). *Exploring the "watershed approach" – critical dimensions of state-local partnerships*. Madison, WI: University of Wisconsin Extension, Report No. 99-1.

Born, S. M. and Genskow, K. D. (2000). *The watershed approach: an empirical assessment of innovation in environmental management* (p. 70). Washington, D.C.: National Academy of Public Administration.

Born, S. M. and Margerum, R. D. (1993). *Integrated environmental management: improving the practice in Wisconsin*. Madison, WI: Wisconsin Department of Natural Resources.

Born, S. M. and Sonzogni, W. (1995). Towards integrated environmental management: strengthening the conceptualization. *Environmental Management*, *19*(2), 167–183.

Bréthaut, C. and Pflieger, G. (2013). The shifting territorialities of the Rhone River's transboundary governance: a historical analysis of the evolution of the functions, uses and spatiality of river basin governance. *Regional Environmental Change*, *15*(3), 549–558.

Cairns, J., Jr. and Crawford, T. V. (eds.). (1991). *Integrated Environmental Management*. Chelsea, MI: Lewis Publishers.

Carr, D. S., Selin, S. W. and Schuett, M. A. (1998). Managing public forests: understanding the role of collaborative planning. *Environmental Management*, *22*(5), 767–776.

Chrislip, D. D. and Larson, C. E. (1994). *Collaborative leadership: how citizens and civic leaders can make a difference*. San Francisco, CA: Jossey-Bass Publishers.

Cortner, H. J. and Moote, M. A. (1999). *The politics of ecosystem management*. Washington, D.C.: Island Press.

Crosby, B. C. and Bryson, J. M. (2010). Integrative leadership and the creation and maintenance of cross-sector collaborations. *The Leadership Quarterly*, *21*(2), 211–230.

Curtis, A. (1998). Agency-community partnerships in landcare: lessons for state-sponsored resource management. *Environmental Management*, *22*(4), 563–574.

Curtis, A. and Lockwood, M. (2000). Landcare and catchment management in Australia: lessons for state-sponsored community participation. *Society & Natural Resources*, *13*(1), 61–73.

Curtis, A., Ross, H., Marshall, G. R., Baldwin, C., Cavaye, J., Freeman, C., Carr, A. and Syme, G. (2014). The great experiment with devolved NRM governance: lessons from community engagement in Australia and New Zealand since the 1980s. *Australasian Journal of Environmental Management*, *21*(2), 175–199.

Dixon, J. A. and Easter, K. W. (1986). Integrated watershed management: an approach to resource management. In K. W. Easton, J. Dixon and M. M. Hufschmidt (eds.), *Watershed resources management: an integrated framework with studies from Asia and the Pacific* (pp. 3–16). Honolulu, HI: Westview Press, East-West Center.

Dore, J. (2007). Mekong region water-related MSPs–unfilled potential. In J. Warner (ed.), *Multi-stakeholder platforms for integrated water management* (pp. 205–234). Aldershot, England: Ashgate.

Dutterer, A. D. and Margerum, R. D. (2015). The limitations of policy-level collaboration: a meta-analysis of CALFED. *Society and Natural Resources*, *28*(1). http://doi.org/10.1080/08941920.2014.945054.

Dworsky, L. B. and Allee, D. J. (1981). Unified/integrated river basin management: evolution of organizational arrangements. In D. J. Allee, L. B. Dworsky and R. M. North (eds.), *Unified river basin management, symposium proceedings*. Minneapolis, MN: American Water Resources Association.

Echeverria, J. D. (2001). No success like failure: the Platte River collaborative watershed planning process. *William and Mary Environmental Law and Policy Review*, *25*(3), 559–604.

Edelenbos, J., Bressers, N. and Scholten, P. (eds.). (2013). *Water governance as connective capacity*. Aldershot, England: Ashgate.

Emerson, K., Nabatchi, T. and Balogh, S. (2012). An integrative framework for collaborative governance. *Journal of Public Administration Research and Theory*, *22*(1), 1–29.

Gardiner, J., Thomson, K. and Newson, M. (1994). Integrated watershed/river catchment planning and management: a comparison of selected Canadian and United Kingdom experiences. *Journal of Environmental Planning and Management*, *37*(1), 53–67.

Gildea, R. J. (1959). Watershed management: past and present. *The Journal of Geography*, *58*(1), 14–20.

Godschalk, D. R. and Mills, W. E. (1966). A collaborative approach to planning through urban activities. *Journal of the American Institute of Planners*, *32*(2), 86–95.

Goldsmith, S. and Eggers, W. D. (2004). *Governing by network : the new shape of the public sector*. Washington, D.C.: Brookings Institution Press. Retrieved from http://www.loc.gov/catdir/toc/ecip0421/2004019411.html.

Gray, B. (1989). *Collaborating: finding common ground for multiparty problems*. San Francisco, CA: Jossey-Bass, Inc.

Grumbine, R. E. (1994). What is ecosystem management? *Conservation Biology*, *8*(1), 27–38.

Hanemann, M. and Dyckman, C. (2009). The San Francisco Bay-Delta: a failure in decision making capacity. *Environmental Science and Policy*, *12*(6), 710–725.

Head, B. W. (2008). Assessing network-based collaborations: effectiveness for whom? *Public Management Review*, *10*(6), 733–749.

Healey, P. (1992). Planning through debate: the communicative turn in planning theory. *Town Planning Review*, *63*(2), 143–162.

Healey, P. (1997). *Collaborative planning*. Vancouver, Canada: University of British Columbia Press.

Heikkila, T. (2006). Comparing collaborative mechanisms in large-scale ecosystem governance. *Natural Resources Journal*, *46*(3), 51.

Hill, R., Grant, C., George, M., Robinson, C. J., Jackson, S. and Abel, N. (2012). A typology of Indigenous engagement in Australian environmental management: implications for knowledge integration and social-ecological system sustainability. *Ecology and Society*, *17*(1), 23.

Hill, R., Davies, J., Bohnet, I., Robinson, C. J., Maclean, K. and Pert, P. L. (2015) (on line). Collaboration mobilises institutions with scale-dependent comparative advantage in landscape-scale biodiversity conservation. *Environmental Science & Policy*, *51*, 267–277.

Hooper, B. (1995). Integrated resource management – a national vision for Australia. *Australian Journal of Soil and Water Conservation*, *8*(1), 9–12.

Imperial, M. T. (2005). Lessons from six watershed management programs. *Administration & Society*, *37*(3), 281–320.

Innes, J. E. (1995). Planning theory's emerging paradigm: communicative action and interactive practice. *Journal of Planning Education and Research*, *14*(3), 183–189. http://doi.org/10.1177/0739456X9501400307.

Innes, J. E. and Booher, D. E. (1999). Consensus building and complex adaptive systems: a framework for evaluating collaborative planning. *Journal of the American Planning Association*, *65*(4), 412–423.

Innes, J. E. and Booher, D. E. (2009). *Planning with complexity: an introduction to collaborative rationality for public policy*. New York: Routledge.

Innes, J. E., Connick, S. and Booher, D. (2007). Informality as a planning strategy – Collaborative water management in the CALFED Bay-Delta Program. *Journal of the American Planning Association*, *73*(2), 195–210.

Johnson, D. R. and Agee, J. K. (1988). Introduction to Ecosystem Management. In J. K. Agee and D. R. Johnson (eds.), *Ecosystem management for parks and wilderness*. Seattle, WA: University of Washington Press.

Knoke, D. (1990). *Political networks: the structural perspective*. Cambridge, England and New York: Cambridge University Press.

Kooiman, J. (2003). *Governing as governance*. London: Sage Publications.

Koontz, T. M., Steelman, T. A., Carmin, J., Korfmacher, K. S., Moseley, C. and Thomas, C. W. (2004). *Collaborative environmental management: what roles for government?* Washington, D.C.: Resources for the Future. Retrieved from http://www.loc.gov/catdir/toc/ecip0419/2004014207.html.

Kroon, F. J., Robinson, C. J. and Dale, A. P. (2009). Integrating knowledge to inform water quality planning in the Tully-Murray Basin, Australia. *Marine & Freshwater Research*, *60*(11), 1183–1188.

Lane, M. B. and Hibbard, M. (2005). Doing it for themselves. Transformative planning by Indigenous peoples. *Journal of Planning Education and Research*, *25*(2), 172–184.

Lane, M. B., Robinson, C. J. and Taylor, B. (eds.). (2009). *Contested country: local and regional environmental management in Australia*. Melbourne: CSIRO Publishing.

Lange, P., Driessen, P. P. J., Sauer, A., Bornemann, B. and Burger, P. (2013). Governing towards sustainability—conceptualizing modes of governance. *Journal of Environmental Policy & Planning*, *15*(3), 403–425. http://doi.org/10.1080/1523908X.2013.769414.

Layzer, J. A. (2008). *Natural experiments: ecosystem-based management and the environment*. Cambridge, MA: The MIT Press.

Leach, W. D. (2006). Collaborative public management and democracy: evidence from western watershed partnerships. *Public Administration Review*, *66*(s1), 100–110.

Leach, W. D. and Pelkey, N. W. (2001). Making watershed partnerships work: a review of the empirical literature. *Journal of Water Resources Planning and Management*, *127*(6), 378–385.

Lejano, R. P. and Ingram, H. (2010). Collaborative networks and new ways of knowing. *Environmental Science and Policy*, *12*(6), 653–662.

Lindblom, C. E. (1965). *The intelligence of democracy*. New York: Free Press.

Linden, R. (2008). Collaborating across organizational boundaries. In T. Newell, G. Reeher and P. Ronayne (eds.), *The trusted leader: building the relationships that make government work* (pp. 156–180). Washington, D.C.: CQ Press.

Linden, R. M. (2002). *Working across boundaries: making collaboration work in government and nonprofit organizations* (1st edn.). San Francisco, CA: Jossey-Bass. Retrieved from http://www.loc.gov/catdir/toc/wiley031/2002011933.html.

Lindquist, E. (2004). Strategy, capacity and horizontal governance: perspectives from Australia and Canada. *Optimum: Journal of Public Sector Management*, *34*(4), 2–12.

Litwak, E. and Hylton, L. F. (1962). Interorganizational analysis: a hypothesis on co-ordinating agencies. *Administrative Science Quarterly*, *6*(March/April), 395–420.

Loh, D. K. and Rykiel, E. J., Jr. (1992). Integrated resource management systems: coupling expert systems with data-base management and geographic information systems. *Environmental Management*, *16*(2), 167–177.

Lubell, M. (2004). Collaborative environmental institutions: all talk and no action. *Journal of Policy Analysis and Management*, *23*(3), 549–573.

Lurie, S. D. (2011). The CALFED Bay-Delta Program: lessons from the rise and fall of a large-scale ecosystem management network. *Journal of Natural Resources Policy Research*, *3*(3), 251–262.

Maclean, K., Robinson, C. J., Natcher, D. (2015). Consensus building or constructive conflict? Aboriginal discursive strategies to enhance participation in natural resource management in Australia and Canada. *Society and Natural Resources*, *28*(2), 197–211.

Mandell, M. P. (1990). Network management: strategic behavior in the public sector. In R. W. Gage and M. P. Mandell (eds.), *Strategies for Managing Intergovernmental Policies and Networks*. New York: Praeger.
March, J. G. and Simon, H. A. (1958). *Organizations*. New York: Wiley.
Margerum, R. D. (1999). Integrated environmental management: the elements critical to success. *Environmental Management*, *65*(2), 181–192.
Margerum, R. D. (2005). Collaborative growth management in metropolitan Denver: "fig leaf or valiant effort?" *Land Use Policy*, *22*(4), 373–386.
Margerum, R. D. (2007). Overcoming locally based collaboration constraints. *Society & Natural Resources*, *20*(2), 135–152.
Margerum, R. D. (2011). *Beyond consensus: improving collaborative planning and management*. Boston, MA: The MIT Press.
Margerum, R. D. and Robinson, C. J. (2014). Limitations of collaborative partnerships for sustainable water management. *Current Opinion in Environmental Sustainability*, *12*, 53–58.
McAllister, R., Robinson, C. J., Maclean, K., Guerrero, A., Collins, K., Taylor, B. and De Barro, P. (2015). From local to central: a network analysis of who manages plant pest and disease outbreaks across scales. *Ecology and Society*, *20*(1), 67.
Mitchell, B. and Pigram, J. J. (1989). Integrated resource management and the Hunter Valley conservation trust, NSW, Australia. *Applied Geography*, *9*(3), 196–211.
Moseley, C. and KenCairn, B. (2001). Problem solving or social change? The Applegate and Grand Canyon forest partnerships. In R. K. Vance, C. B. Edminster, W. W. Covington and J. A. Blake (eds.), (Vol. proceedings RMRS-P-22, pp. 121–129). *Ponderosa pine ecosystems restoration and conservation: steps toward stewardship*, Ogden, Utah: Department of Agriculture, Forest Service.
Moss, T. (2012). Spatial fit, from panacea to practice: implementing the EU Water Framework Directive. *Ecology and Society*, *17*(3), 2.
Newig, J. and Koontz, T. M. (2014). Multi-level governance, policy implementation and participation: the EU's mandated participatory planning approach to implementing environmental policy. *Journal of European Public Policy*, *21*(2), 248–267. http://doi.org/10.1080/13501763.2013.834070
NPCC. (2006). *Transportation collaboration in the States*. (Report prepared by the National Policy Consensus Center for the Federal Highway Administration Office of Project Development and Environmental Review.) (p. 38). Portland, OR: National Policy Consensus Center.
Olsson, P., Folke, C. and Berkes, F. (2004). Adaptive co-management for building social-ecological resilience. *Environmental Management*, *34*, 75–90.
O'Toole, L. J., Jr. (1990). Multiorganizational implementation: comparative analysis for wastewater treatment. In R. W. Gage and M. P. Mandell (eds.), *Strategies for managing intergovernmental policies and networks* (pp. 81–111). New York: Praeger.
Pinkerton, E. (ed.). (1989). *Co-operative management of local fisheries: new directions for improvement management and community development*. Vancouver: University of British Columbia Press.
Prager, K., Reed, M. and Scott, A. (2012). Encouraging collaboration for the provision of ecosystem services at a landscape scale—rethinking agri-environmental payments. *Land Use Policy*, *29*, 244–249.

Provan, K. G. and Kenis, P. (2008). Modes of network governance: structure, management and effectiveness. *Journal of Public Administration Research and Theory*, *18*, 229–252.

Provan, K. G. and Milward, H. B. (1995). A preliminary theory of interorganizational network effectiveness: a comparative study of four community mental health systems. *Administrative Science Quarterly*, *40*(1), 1–33. http://doi.org/10.2307/2393698.

Purdy, J. M. (2012). A framework for assessing power in collaborative governance processes. *Public Administration Review*, *72*(3), 409–417. http://doi.org/10.1111/j.1540-6210.2011.02525.x.

Rainey, H. G. and Milward, H. B. (1983). *Public organizations: policy networks and environments*. Newbury Park, CA: Sage Publications.

Robinson, C. J. and Lane, M. B. (2013). Boundary riding Indigenous knowledge contributions for natural resource decision-making in Northern Australian regions. In B. Walker, T. Jojola and D. Natcher (eds.), *Reclaiming Indigenous Approaches to Community and Land-use Planning in the Twenty-first Century* (pp. 396–413). Montreal: McGill-Queen's University Press.

Robinson, C. J. and Wallington, T. J. (2012). Boundary work: engaging knowledge systems in co-management of feral animals on Indigenous lands. *Ecology and Society*, *17*(2), 16.

Robinson, C., Margerum, R., Koontz, T., Moseley, C. and Lurie, S. (2011). Policy-level collaboratives for environmental management at the regional scale: lessons and challenges from Australia and the United States. *Society & Natural Resources*, *24*(8), 849–859.

Robinson, C. J., Taylor, B., Vella, K. and Wallington, T. (2014). Working knowledge for collaborative water planning. *International Journal of Water Governance*, *2*(1), 43–60.

Rogers, D. L. and Whetten, D. A. (1982). *Interorganizational coordination: theory, research and implementation*. Ames, IA: Iowa State University Press.

Ross, H., Grant, C., Robinson, C. J., Izurieta, A., Smyth, D. and Rist, P. (2009). Co-management and Indigenous protected areas in Australia: achievements and ways forward. *Australasian Journal of Environmental Management*, *16*(4), 242–252.

Skelcher, C., Sullivan, H. and Jeffares, S. (2013). *Hybrid governance in European cities*. Basingstoke: Palgrave Macmillan.

Sørensen, E. and Torfing, J. (2008). *Theories of democratic network governance*. New York: Palgrave Macmillan.

Sousa, D. J. and Klyza, C. M. (2007). New directions in environmental policy making: an emerging collaborative regime or reinventing interest group liberalism. *Natural Resources Journal*, *47*, 377.

Sullivan, H. and Skelcher, C. (2002). *Working across boundaries: collaboration in public services*. Basingstoke: Palgrave Macmillan.

Susskind, L. and Cruikshank, J. (1987). *Breaking the impasse: consensual approaches to resolving public disputes*. New York: Basic Books.

Taylor, B. and de Loe, R. C. (2012). Conceptualizations of local knowledge in collaborative governance. *Geoforum*, *43*(6), 1207–1217.

Thomas, C. W. (2003). *Bureaucratic landscapes: interagency cooperation and the preservation of biodiversity*. Cambridge, MA: The MIT Press. Retrieved from http://www.loc.gov/catdir/toc/fy035/2002071779.html.

U.S. EPA. (1992). *The Watershed Protection Approach: Annual Report 1991* (No. EPA 840-S-93-001). Washington, D.C.: U.S. Environmental Protection Agency.

van Buuren, A. (2009). Knowledge for governance, governance of knowledge: inclusive knowledge management in collaborative governance processes. *International Public Management Journal, 12*(2), 208–235.
Vangen, S., Hayes, J. P. and Cornforth, C. (2014). Governing cross-sector, inter-organizational collaborations. *Public Management Review, 17*(9), 1–24.
Voets, J., Van Dooren, W. and De Rynck, F. (2008). A framework for assessing the performance of policy networks. *Public Management Review, 10*(6), 773–790.
Warner, J. (2007). *Multi-stakeholder platforms for integrated water management.* Aldershot, England and Burlington, VT: Ashgate. Retrieved from http://www.loc.gov/catdir/toc/ecip078/2006103144.html.
Weber, E. P. (2000). A new vanguard for the environment: grass-roots ecosystem management as a new environmental movement. *Society and Natural Resources, 2000*, 237–259.
Weber, E. P. (2003). *Bringing society back in: grassroots ecosystem management, accountability, and sustainable communities.* Cambridge, MA: The MIT Press.
Wegerich, K. (2007). Chapter 14: Multiplatform platforms in Uzbekistan. In J. Warner (ed.), *Multi-stakeholder platforms for integrated water management* (pp. xvi, 281). Aldershot, England: Ashgate. Retrieved from http://www.loc.gov/catdir/toc/ecip078/2006103144.html.
Wesseling, R. (2011). *Transnational transformations of governance: the European Union and beyond.* Amsterdam, NLD: Amsterdam University Press. Retrieved from http://site.ebrary.com/lib/alltitles/docDetail.action?docID=10459445.
Wilkinson, C. (2012). Social-ecological resilience: insights and issues for planning theory. *Planning Theory, 11*, 148–169.

PART I

Theory and context

2. Theoretical perspectives on the challenges of collaboration

Richard D. Margerum

INTRODUCTION

Collaborative approaches to planning, management and governance are increasingly becoming standard practice throughout the world today. It has emerged in response to increased problem complexity, competition and conflict, and recognition of interconnectedness that has led a range of decision makers to see the benefits of making decisions more collaboratively. At the same time, it is becoming increasingly apparent that collaboration faces challenges, complications and limitations. Many of these are not unique to collaboration. In fact, collaboration has often emerged because traditional management and governance approaches have not been successful. However, it is important for the maturation of collaboration to go beyond best practices and exemplary cases to interrogate the shortcomings and challenges. As Innes and Booher outline (Innes and Booher, 2014) the critiques of collaboration need to be transformed into key tensions and opportunities for deliberation that would allow an improved understanding of effective practice.

The goal of this chapter is to review a wide range of literature to lay out the range of theoretical arguments related to challenges facing collaboration. Some challenges are unique to collaborative governance—such as the need for collaborative leadership skills. Others are challenges to governance generally—such as the difficulty of addressing problems that are highly complex and not well understood. Because collaboration is billed as both an emerging paradigm and an alternative to traditional approaches, it is important to examine this full range of tensions and challenges. Failure to explore the challenges of collaboration can present three important risks. First, collaborative approaches may be attempted when other strategies could be more effective or when conditions are not yet ripe. Huxham (2003, 421) goes so far as to assert that when there is a choice, collaboration should be avoided. Second, collaboration may overlook challenges leading to less than optimal outcomes. This could lead to increasing reluctance to apply the collaborative model when it may be the most appropriate approach. Third, failure to explore these challenges may ignore conceptual weaknesses. Thus, challenges may be blamed on practice when in fact these consistent difficulties reveal underlying weaknesses in how collaborative models are conceived.

In the following sections, I define the concept of challenges and review my approach to identifying these themes from the literature. This chapter clearly does not cover every challenge presented in research and practice. My objective is to highlight the challenges that are deeper, more complex, more difficult to overcome, and more likely to result in failure or suboptimal outcomes. The ultimate goal in presenting these themes is to describe them as clear statements that can then be interrogated, tested, evaluated and refined by a range of researchers studying collaboration in practice.

DEFINING CHALLENGES

Over the past several decades, a substantial literature has emerged on best practices and lessons learned, which has been important for providing guidance for how collaboration can be practiced effectively. As the number of cases and breadth of experiences have increased, researchers and practitioners have compiled a rich set of strategies, rules and best practices from case studies, empirical studies and meta-analyses (Agranoff, 2012; Agranoff and McGuire, 2003; Beierle, 2002; Bingham and O'Leary, 2008; Huxham and Vangen, 2005; Imperial, 1999; Innes and Booher, 2009; Kallis et al., 2010; Leach and Sabatier, 2005; Leach et al., 2002; Margerum, 1999a, 2002b; Mattessich et al., 2004; O'Leary and Bingham, 2009; Wondolleck and Yaffee, 2000).

Researchers typically argue that when these kinds of conditions are not met, the collaborative effort is more likely to fall short or fail (Margerum, 1999b). Over time these kinds of problems have become well documented, and the solutions or strategies for overcoming them are well known. Thus, these issues are less about the challenges and more about effective practice for how collaboration should work in a typical practice setting. For example, having an effective facilitator or coordinator that allows a diverse set of stakeholders to openly communicate has long been cited as a key to effective practice (Elliott, 1999; Forester, 2013).

In contrast, some challenges associated with collaboration may have "deeper roots." They are societal, structural, or related to the broader policy and political setting. They are more than just the day-to-day difficulties faced by participants. They are the challenges that often lead to stalled efforts, less-than optimal outcomes or failure.

For example, a common lesson learned in convening a collaborative group is to assemble a diverse stakeholder group that represents the full range of perspectives (Edelenbos and Klijn, 2007; Margerum, 1999b). However, the expectations for stakeholder participation can be difficult for some individuals and unorganized interests. This can place them at a significant disadvantage because they lack leaders to represent them and networks to support them. There are structural barriers to the intense participation demanded of a stakeholder related to issues such as time, access, awareness, education, socioeconomic status and social connections (Depoe, 2004; Hamilton, 2004; Lubell, 2005; Newig et al., 2005; Newman et al., 2004; Samuelson et al., 2005). As a result, stakeholder groups are more likely to consistently under-represent minorities, minority viewpoints, the economically disadvantaged, and even younger participants. Thus, diverse representation may be a challenge not because a diverse array of participants was not invited. It may be a limitation because structural, societal, political and other factors make it very difficult for them to participate.

Many of the challenges reviewed in this chapter are present under other forms of governance, but traditional governance has been exposed to more critique and examination. Practitioners and researchers have developed deliberative and participatory strategies for involving the community in decision making that consciously avoids dependence on representative leaders (Dryzek, 2000; Weeks, 2000). Other researchers suggest that less powerful interests may be more successful focusing their efforts on administrative and judicial decision making forums rather than collaborative venues (Layzer, 2008). However, there has been little exploration in the literature of how stakeholder-driven efforts may mesh with these alternative strategies. This chapter seeks to review the range of challenges facing collaboration, to explore their significance and articulate the challenges for research and practice.

THEMES RELATED TO CHALLENGES

This chapter is based on a review of a range of sources representing many fields and disciplines. I began the research with a review of articles specifically focusing on the challenges, problems and shortcomings of collaboration (Echeverria, 2001; Hanemann and Dyckman, 2009; Kenney, 2000; Lane, 1997; Layzer, 2008). I conducted literature searches to identify authors that address challenges in fields such as alternative dispute resolution, integrated resources management, network governance and community-based natural resources management. I also examined a number of comprehensive research studies related to collaborative governance that covered lessons learned and challenges. Finally, additional sources were recommended to me when I presented a preliminary review of this literature at conferences in Canada, Europe, Australia and the United States.

With all of these works, I noted major themes related to challenges and compiled them into a table organized by sub-themes and relevant authors (see Table 2.1). I don't attempt to evaluate or validate all of the themes, but tried to uncover the underlying challenges as distinct from the cases of poor practice. This compilation clearly has weaknesses, including missing contributions, the cursory nature of this review and my own biases and interpretations. Furthermore, the summaries below don't even fully cover all of the topics that I compiled in Table 2.1. Ultimately, this is a work in progress and my goal is to refine the dialogue and research around collaboration rather than to present a conclusive contribution. These themes are broad categorizations with some overlap of ideas and concepts; they could be grouped or parsed out more, but this provides a starting point for this discussion.

The Problem and its Context

Some governance and management problems are more difficult to solve than others. In fact, collaborative responses often emerge because traditional governance and management approaches have not worked. Problems cross jurisdictional boundaries; they don't have a clear intervention point; they involve multiple policies; they require an extensive range of intervention efforts; they are caused by highly diffuse actions. When stakeholders collaborate they are sometimes able to find creative solutions that overcome a difficult context, but some problems and their societal context may create very problematic challenges.

Nature of the problem

Sabatier et al. (2005) and Lubell et al. (2002) cite the political contracting framework as the basis for the calculus stakeholders use for determining whether to collaborate. When scientific knowledge is not good, when there is a high likelihood of constant adaptation, and when the problems are highly complex, the anticipated costs of deliberation may limit the willingness to collaborate (Kallis et al., 2010; Lubell et al., 2002; Sabatier et al., 2005).

Alternatively, exchange theory argues that one of the drivers of collaboration is the attraction of altruistic purposes and better results. This tends to motivate actors to develop collaborative networks and empower them to

Table 2.1 Literature on challenges related to collaboration

Challenge	Description
A. Problem and societal context	
Nature of the problem	• Problems are not homogeneous or not severe (Sabatier et al., 2005) • Costs and benefits are not spread evenly (Sabatier et al., 2005) • High technical complexity, multi-scaled problem settings and interconnectedness (Gray, 1989; Irvin and Stansbury, 2004; Wyborn and Bixler, 2013) • Zero sum problem with lack of win-win scenarios (Amy, 1987; Putnam and Wondolleck, 2003; Stanley, 1995; Sullivan and Skelcher, 2002) • Issues that are highly difficult, present discursive divides or require transformational responses (Gallemore et al., 2014; Layzer, 2008; Stanley, 1995) • Scientific knowledge is not good or the authority of science is unstable (Davis et al., 2013; Sabatier et al., 2005) • Problem complexity creates high transaction costs (Lubell et al., 2002) • Adaptive management creates significant uncertainty (Kallis et al., 2010) • Unclear there will be better results or lack of altruistic purpose (Layzer, 2008)
Societal or community context	• Societal and cultural limits on decision making (Wegerich, 2007) • Low trust, social cohesion, local knowledge or social capital in a community (Benson et al., 2013; Bradshaw, 2003; Gray, 1989; Sabatier et al., 2005; Samuelson et al., 2005) • High cultural or belief heterogeneity (Gallemore et al., 2014; Sabatier et al., 2005) • History of conflict, mistrust or factions (Ansell and Gash, 2007; Barry, 2011; Connelly et al., 2008; Gray, 1989; Sørensen, 2014) • Limited community orientation, history of prior collaboration or response to collaborative strategies (Curtis et al., 2014; Gray, 1989; Irvin and Stansbury, 2004; Wegerich, 2007) • High number of low-income residents or those with limited access to governance limits participation (Ghose, 2005; Huxley and Yiftachel, 2000; Irvin and Stansbury, 2004) • Locally focused collaboration in community highly dependent on resource outcomes (Bradshaw, 2003; Kenney, 2000)

Table 2.1 (continued)

Challenge	Description
B. Policy and political setting	
Policy context	• Requires strong driver agency or legislative mandate (Layzer, 2008) • Policy limits implementation to voluntary and non-regulatory approaches (Layzer, 2008) • Narrow or single-issue policy constraints (Agranoff, 2007; Benham et al., 2015; Margerum, 2011) • Lack of higher-level policy integration and policy complexity makes lower-level integration very difficult (de Boer and Krantzberg, 2013; O'Leary and Vij, 2012; Rigg and O'Mahony, 2013) • Policy fragmentation restricts leeway to optimize joint results (de Boer and Krantzberg, 2013)
Political context	• Policy makers curtail options or undermine capacity (Curtis et al., 2014; Layzer, 2008; Weir et al., 2009) • Political leaders support competing venues over collaborative ones (Head, 2008; O'Leary and Vij, 2012; Weir et al., 2009) • Lack of a political champion to support collaboration (Hanemann and Dyckman, 2009; Ingram and Fraser, 2006; Lurie, 2011; Weir et al., 2009) • Government restrictions on collaborative groups in developing countries (Brinkerhoff, 1999; Dore, 2007; Ratner et al., 2014)
C. Power	
External power and pressure	• Environmentalists have had more success using litigation and public campaigns than through collaboration (Echeverria, 2001; Kenney, 2000; Layzer, 2008; McCloskey, 2001) • External pressures (courts, regulation, public pressure, political action) affect participation positively and negatively (Heikkila and Gerlak, 2005; Sabatier et al., 2005; Thomas, 2003) • Lack of a "hurting stalemate" makes status quo acceptable (McCarthy and Shorett, 1984; Sabatier et al., 2005)
Power within the process	• Power of existing stakeholders and power elite (Echeverria, 2001; Lane, 2003; Layzer, 2008) • Power disparities (Gray, 1989; McGuire, 2006; O'Leary and Vij, 2012; Purdy, 2012) • Communicative rationality fails to adequately address the issues of power, conflict and partisanship (Flyvbjerg, 2012)

	• Ability to increase power by participation in the process (Benjamin et al., 2011) • Concern among interest groups of expectation to compromise (Gray, 1989) • Bias towards economic interests (Bradshaw, 2003; Reed and McIlveen, 2006) • Lack of participants to represent key perspectives (Dore, 2007; Ghose, 2005)
D. Collaborative network capacity	
Collaborative leadership	• Collaborative leadership demands for facilitative, supportive and consultative skills (Ansell and Gash, 2007; Connelly et al., 2008; Huxham, 2003; Kettl, 2006; Sullivan et al., 2012) • Leaders need key interpersonal skills (O'Leary and Vij, 2012; O'Leary et al., 2012) • Need for person or entity (collaborative superagency) to maintain functioning (Leach and Sabatier, 2005; Parker et al., 2010) • Leadership challenges of balancing expectations, autonomy and independence, participation and authoritative versus voluntary strategies (Connelly et al., 2008; Huxham and Beech, 2003)
Collective capacity and legitimacy	• Need for entity to maintain ongoing collaborative relationships (Goldsmith and Eggers, 2004; Velez et al., 2014) • Willingness to invest in ongoing structures for collaboration (Agranoff, 2007; Imperial, 2005) • Inability to handle downloaded responsibilities (Bradshaw, 2003; Reed and McIlveen, 2006) • Inertia resulting in negligible or low rates of output (Huxham, 2003) • Recognition of network as an entity and a legitimate form of governance (Human and Provan, 2000; Provan et al., 2008) • Need for goal congruence, shared motivation, and complimentary roles and missions (Emerson et al., 2012; Goldsmith and Eggers, 2004; Head, 2008; Irvin, 2010) • Complexity of maintaining trust among a high number of diverse and potentially competing organizations (Connelly et al., 2008; Huxham, 2003; Irvin, 2010; O'Leary and Vij, 2012; Provan and Milward, 2001)

Table 2.1 (continued)

Challenge	Description
E. Participant factors	
Organizational operations	• Organizational demands for time, resources and attention outweigh the needs of the network or collaborative (Alford and O'Flynn, 2012; Benjamin et al., 2011) • Interorganizational systems make performance accountability difficult (Kettl, 2006; Provan and Milward, 2001) • Organizational constraints in relation to culture, operation, funding, power and forms of decision making (Lubell, 2004; McGuire, 2006; O'Leary and Bingham, 2009; O'Leary and Vij, 2012; Thomas, 2003) • Competition between collaborative problems and "core business" of organizations (Agranoff, 2007; Margerum, 2011; Thomas, 2003)
Support	• Collaborative activities are not durable and tend to attenuate over time without a strong driver agency (Layzer, 2008) • Stability to network relationships and maintenance of participation (Blackman, 2014; Goldsmith and Eggers, 2004; O'Flynn et al., 2013; Robins and Kanowski, 2011) • Collaboration can produce gridlock, which favors interests wanting to prevent action (Echeverria, 2001) • Organizations can't complete tasks on own; have to collaborate (Benjamin et al., 2011) • Network legitimacy and formal recognition (Provan and Kenis, 2008; Provan et al., 2008) • Ongoing collaboration networks experience challenges with sustaining support from individuals within organizations (Connelly et al., 2008; O'Leary and Vij, 2012)

F. Costs and benefits	
Costs and benefits	• Immediate costs and long-term benefits limit willingness to collaborate (Linden, 2002) • Stakeholders not convinced that solutions will be implemented or will achieve the outcomes they seek (Velez et al., 2014) • Diffuse, dispersed and cross-cutting problems being addressed through collaboration have less immediacy and relevance to other narrow problems (Koontz et al., 2004; Margerum, 2011) • Some groups may benefit more from collaborative activity (O'Toole and Meier, 2004)
Transaction costs	• Impact on human relations processing makes cost of collaboration too high (Agranoff, 2007; Lubell, 2004) • Collaboration increases transaction costs making alternative venues more attractive (Huxham et al., 2000; Lubell, 2004; Voets et al., 2008) • Agencies, organizations and individuals don't have the capacity to participate—particularly with multiple collaborative efforts demanding their time (Dukes and Firehock, 2001; Ghose, 2005; Goldsmith and Eggers, 2004; Huxham et al., 2000; Margerum, 2011; Mattessich et al., 2004; Rigg and O'Mahony, 2013; Voets et al., 2008) • Ongoing and stable funding is available to support the transaction costs of collaboration and maintaining collaborative networks (Agranoff, 2007; Margerum, 2011) • Stakeholder funders are less tolerant of developing shared goals and perspectives through collaboration (O'Leary and Bingham, 2007; O'Leary and Vij, 2012)

produce better results (Sullivan and Skelcher, 2002). Conversely, when the problem issue and context does not generate a clear altruistic purpose or the promise of better results, organizational actors are less likely to commit to solving problems collaboratively. For example, environmental problems that have clear goals, iconic species and clear opportunities for impact often generate greater commitment (Dukes and Firehock, 2001). Thus, salmon restoration generates more widespread commitment than nutrient reduction. Efforts to improve surface water are more likely to generate participation than efforts to address groundwater.

The conflict resolution literature also highlights the barriers that emerge when stakeholders have limited ability to transform a problem from a zero sum scenario to a win-win scenario. Putnam and Wondelleck (2003) point out that when issues are high-stake and distributional in nature this leads to situations in which the cost of settling is higher than the cost of fighting. These high stakes may lead participants to use power plays, threats, pressure and other forces before they accept defeat.

Other problems involve fundamental moral and value differences (such as abortion or nuclear power) that cannot be easily mediated (Amy, 1987; Campbell, 2006; Flyvbjerg, 2012; LeBaron and Carstarphen, 1999; Putnam and Wondolleck, 2003). Douglas Amy (1987) points out that mediators sometimes attempt to translate conflicts of values into conflicts of interest, which suggests that values are negotiable. The redistribution of costs and benefits can also be very disruptive or cannot account for non-monetary concerns (Amy, 1987). For example, compensating indigenous groups for the monetary value of land may address the economic impact, but not the cultural, spiritual and social impacts.

Finally, several authors point out that the need to maintain consensus among participating stakeholders may limit options, lead to risk-averse agendas or produce lowest common denominator solutions (Agranoff, 2007; Layzer, 2008). Agranoff (2007, 180) points out that one of the prices of holding stakeholders together "is keeping issues off the agenda that are threatening or contrary to consensus building." Similarly, in Layzer's (2008, 275) study of collaborative efforts she concluded, "stakeholder groups tended to avoid issues likely to provoke serious disagreement and to mask such differences using vague language—a decision that ultimately haunted implementation." Layzer (2008) and Stanley (1995) contend that stakeholder-driven processes have not resulted in major transformations in ecosystem management, and the win-win solutions developed by participants have not altered the fundamental consumption patterns that prompted the problem solving efforts in the first place.

Societal context

Another set of challenges relates to the societal and community context within which collaboration operates. Some authors suggest that certain characteristics about a community may make a collaborative effort likely—or less likely—to emerge. For example, in states that have created voluntary programs for community based natural resources management—why do collaborative groups emerge in some places but not others? Leadership is often critical to initiating these efforts, but is there something about the community limiting the willingness to collaborate?

Samuelson et al. (2005) argue that community assessment of participation relates to trust. When people trust other participants they anticipate that their involvement will require less investment than a process involving participants they don't trust. This trust assessment view can be translated into a community-wide condition, such as communities that experience low levels of trust, low social capital, lack of a community orientation or a history of conflict and disagreements (Ansell and Gash, 2007; Connelly et al., 2008; Gray, 1989).

Community capacity can also relate to the resources and capability of community members to participate (Huxley and Yiftachel, 2000; Sullivan and Skelcher, 2002). Bradshaw (2003) highlights the importance of social cohesion, leadership and local ecological knowledge to support community participation in collaborative decision making. There has been limited examination of this issue in the United States, but some research has found that community-based collaboration requires not only solving resource problems, but also repairing community social networks (Flitcroft et al., 2009).

The challenges of social context are more obvious from the international literature, particularly developing countries. Wegerich (2007) examines attempts to convene collaborative water management efforts in Uzbekistan. He found that the country's Soviet policies and structures persisted after independence and government authorities exhibit a strong top-down influence. More horizontal management is not encouraged, because that would challenge the current vertical structure of political decision making (Wegerich, 2007, 243). Similarly, Dore (2007) examined a wide range of collaborative water management efforts in the Mekong Delta and found significant tensions between the concept of multi-stakeholder participation and the dominance of one-party or military states that resist dissenting views. Finally, Faysse et al. (2007) conclude that collaborative efforts in Bolivia confront fundamental power asymmetries that present a significant challenge.

Policy and Political Context

A second set of challenges relates to the policy and political context, which refers to the policies and political activities that may enable or constrain effective collaboration.

Policy context

Some researchers suggest that the effectiveness of collaboration is reduced when implementation is limited to voluntary and non-regulatory approaches. Under these settings, collaboration can be effective when implementation involves voluntary actions such as ecosystem restoration, but encounters more difficulty with distributional problems (Connell, 2007; Hanemann and Dyckman, 2009; Lurie, 2011; O'Leary and Vij, 2012). Legislative mandates, such as those created by federal environmental legislation, can create pressure for agencies and stakeholders to engage in deliberation (Thomas, 2003; Weber, 2003). However, in the absence of these pressures, the ability to engage more powerful and controversial implementation tools can be difficult (Echeverria, 2001; Layzer, 2008).

When there is a high level of policy complexity and fragmentation, the deliberative process of collaboration also confronts challenges (de Boer and Krantzberg, 2013; Rigg and O'Mahony, 2013). In de Boer and Krantzberg's (2013) analysis of water governance in the Great Lakes they note that there are too many levels and scales for effective negotiation and policy fragmentation restricts the leeway of stakeholders to develop integrated strategies. Layzer (2008) contends that cooperation and commitment to collaborative management tends to decline over time unless there is a landscape scale focus and or clear goal. A "landscape scale focus" is important because narrow or single-issue policies may act to constrain collaboration (Margerum, 2002a; Thomas, 2003). In other words, single-objective policies (e.g., flood control, hydropower, traffic congestion) can constrain the ability of stakeholders to define a problem and develop creative solutions.

Implementation flexibility is often cited as a key issue for successful collaboration (Agranoff, 2007; Cortner and Moote, 1999; Wondolleck and Yaffee, 2000). Conversely, policy barriers can become a significant obstacle. Agranoff (2007, 182) found in several local government collaborations that stakeholders were constrained by legislation and policy that was out of their hands.

Political context

For issues that involve policy-level deliberations, the actions of elected officials relative to a collaborative effort have a significant effect. It can be challenges by policy makers that curtail options and close out certain negotiation options (Layzer, 2008; Weir et al., 2009). Policy makers and political leaders also need to support a collaborative forum as a venue for problem solving in contrast to other venues (Hanemann and Dyckman, 2009; Ingram and Fraser, 2006; Lurie, 2011; Weir et al., 2009). For example, in their analysis of the Sacramento-San Joaquin Delta case (CALFED), both Lurie (2011, 259) and Ingram and Fraser (2006, 96) note that Interior Secretary Bruce Babbitt "cracked the whip" over the participating stakeholders, and his stake in the process prevented the effort from languishing. In contrast, later federal and state administrations showed far less interest and support—resulting in the dissipation of commitment (Ingram and Fraser, 2006; Lurie, 2011).

Power

Power is a significant issue in all forms of governance, and the challenges faced by collaborative processes are often similar to traditional governance settings. However, collaboration is often championed for its ability to empower a wider range of stakeholders and induce greater power sharing. Thus the challenges of power sharing demand particular attention.

External powers and pressures

A number of power issues relate to the broader social, economic and political powers of society (Benjamin et al., 2011; Bradshaw, 2003; McGuire, 2006; Reed and McIlveen, 2006). Collaboration operates side-by-side with other forums and venues, including the political, administrative and legal systems. Stakeholders are likely to "forum shop" to seek the best venue to utilize external powers to influence collaboration. Thus, collaborative forums are competing against other venues for decision making (Hanemann and Dyckman, 2009; Ingram and Fraser, 2006; O'Leary and Vij, 2012; Weir et al., 2009). Some researchers argue that stakeholders may be able to achieve "better" outcomes through traditional legal and legislative venues (Kenney, 2000; Layzer, 2008).

Another theme emerging from the literature on collaboration in natural resources management is the need for societal pressure or severe problems to create pressure for collaboration or make alternative management approaches less desirable (Imperial and Kauneckis, 2003; Sabatier et al., 2005; Thomas, 2003). The conflict resolution literature cites this as "problem ripeness" or a "hurting stalemate" that can bring participants to the negotiating table (McCarthy and Shorett, 1984; Sabatier et al., 2005; Susskind and Cruikshank, 1987). A hurting stalemate can occur when the status quo or potential outcomes are viewed as unacceptable (McCarthy and Shorett, 1984; Sabatier et al., 2005). When individuals are satisfied with the status quo they have little incentive to give up anything, "thus negotiating with them is probably a waste of time" (Sabatier et al., 2005, 195). For example, a widely cited example of policy creating a hurting stalemate is the US Endangered Species Act (ESA). In many parts of the western United States, coalitions of diverse stakeholders have agreed to work together on restoration and management efforts because the ESA offered a looming threat to autonomy and a clear goal upon which to focus (Margerum, 2011; Weber, 2003). In Thomas' (2003, 267) study of federal agency involvement in collaborative efforts, he found that "without the impending threat of a lawsuit that might constrain management authority, the presence of listed species [under the Endangered Species Act] did not prompt cooperation from line managers."

Finally, support and opinions about collaboration can wane over time, particularly as turnover among elected officials produces different levels of commitment (Heikkila and Gerlak, 2005; Kallis et al., 2010; Owen, 2007). Interest groups are sometimes able to use the power of the press and public opinion to assert their influence on collaboration, or simply to bring other stakeholders to the table. However, if public and political opinion shifts or wanes, the pressure to collaborate can dissipate.

Power within the process

In most collaboration settings the assembled stakeholders will have different types of powers, such as experience, expertise, resources, time, timeline (the power of delay) and autonomous decision making power. In most settings there will be differences in these powers, and some researchers contend that significant differences in power among stakeholders can limit collaboration effectiveness, disadvantage certain stakeholders or undermine the capacity of a group to act (Dukes and Firehock, 2001; Gray, 1989; Sullivan and Skelcher, 2002).

Differential power at the table may allow some stakeholders to gain more through the process, because they have access to data or expertise. This can result in fewer options being explored or weight given to some options over others. This may also limit participation in collaboration if stakeholders become wary of participating in processes in which they feel they will be at a disadvantage (Amy, 1987; Dukes and Firehock, 2001; Kenney, 2000). In their guide to environmental interest groups Dukes and Firehock (2001) present a "continuum of caution" that lists issues like power differentials as a factor that may lead stakeholder groups to not participate. Similarly, Layzer (2008) argues that there is an inherent disadvantage to environmental groups engaged in collaborative processes because they are expected to make compromises that result in less successful outcomes than they could achieve through political and legal action.

Some researchers contend that economic interests have substantially more power in a collaborative process, which may skew outcomes and make them more acceptable because they are achieved through consensus (Bradshaw, 2003; Kenney, 2000). In particular, researchers have argued that community-based efforts may favor resource-dependent interests, because local representatives are more likely to participate and align with this perspective. Other interests (recreation, ecological health) may be located outside the immediate area and not have access to representation in the process (Bradshaw, 2003; Echeverria, 2001; Kenney, 2000). Flyvbjerg (2012) contends that the power of particular interests can be substantial, subtle and hidden—requiring explicit strategies and an active role in balancing the debate.

Capacity

Another important limitation is the capacity of the collaborative effort to be sustained over time. Many collaborative management and governance problems are not resolved by agreements or legislation. They require an ongoing entity or network, and there are many challenges in sustaining these efforts.

Collaborative leadership

While collaboration is often described in terms of a collection of actors and organizations participating in a network, there is often a person or organization at the center of that network. Their role is to support the activities of the network, coordinate network implementation efforts, carry out specific network assignments and represent the network in other forums and settings.

For smaller and simpler networks, this role may be assigned to a coordinator who works directly for the network. In some cases this function is assigned to a nonprofit organization with multiple staff. For larger and more complex networks, the coordination role may be assigned to an organization created to act as a kind of collaborative agency (Provan and Kenis, 2008; Sabatier et al., 2005). For example, the International Joint Commission and CALFED were both created to support collaborative governance activities in the Great Lakes and the San Francisco Bay Delta regions.

There has been excellent scholarship on collaborative leadership, but less attention has been paid to the challenges created by the absence of collaborative leadership. Researchers point out that collaborative leadership requires very different types of leadership skills and strategies that may not be present in some settings (Huxham, 2003; Kettl, 2006; O'Leary et al., 2012; Sullivan et al., 2012). Leaders are confronted with a challenging set of expectations, including the ability to work with both autonomy and independence, balance common and diverse goals, the need for both participative and authoritative strategies, the need to see both the forest and the trees, and the ability to balance advocacy and inquiry (Connelly et al., 2008; O'Leary and Bingham, 2009). Bradshaw (2003) contends that it is not sufficient for government to simply download authority and responsibility to a collaborative group if there is not the leadership capabilities and local capacity to make it effective.

Network collective capacity

Another potential challenge of collaboration—particularly when it depends upon an ongoing network of decision makers—is the capacity of the network to sustain its efforts. This requires a person or entity with the capacity to maintain coordination relationships and ongoing operations (Goldsmith and Eggers, 2004; Parker et al., 2010). This extends Lubell et al.'s (2002) political contracting framework from a formation subsidy to an ongoing subsidy of transaction costs. Because the costs for maintaining networks are typically not solely the responsibility of one entity, they also become hard to support financially.

Goldsmith and Eggers (2004) point out that the flexibility and adaptability of networks also creates uncertainty about whether they will be sustained. Some of the very attributes that make networks adaptable and creative may also make them vulnerable (Booher and Innes, 2010; Ingram and Fraser, 2006; Lurie, 2011). Collaboration through contracts and grants can add an additional layer of instability because the stability of the relationship may disintegrate once the contract or grant is completed (Agranoff, 2007; Goldsmith and Eggers, 2004; Linden, 2002).

Sullivan and Skelcher (2002) identify several types of capacity required for effective networks, including: collaborative vision (strategic capacity); structures and processes (operational capacity) and upwards accountability. Researchers translate this issue of capacity into the need for networks defined by norms or rules (Imperial, 2005; Margerum, 2011). These networks can evolve incrementally over time or they might require a concerted effort by participants to develop them (Agranoff, 2007; Emerson et al., 2012; Margerum, 2011). However, this network development process can take considerable time and energy. Agranoff (2007, 118) notes that this process of structuring "resembles herding cats," and "with their governing boards/executive committees, committees and subgroups, and contacts with other networks, they look very much like nonprofit organizations" (Agranoff, 2007, 111).

Participant Factors

Another set of challenges relate to the factors that affect the ability of participants to engage and sustain their involvement in collaborative governance. These participants include both individuals and organizations that represent themselves, organized interests, private organizations, government entities and types of interests (farmers, residents).

Operations

A commonly cited challenge relating to organizational participation is the tension between the collective goals of the collaborative and the priorities of an organization. Collaboration works at the interface and boundaries of organizations and policies, sometimes described as the interstices of governance (Koontz et al., 2004). Organizational demands for time, resources and attention often outweigh the needs of the collaboration (Benjamin et al., 2011). As a result, when organizations face budget constraints, changing priorities, leadership turnover and other changes a collaborative network is at risk of losing to internal priorities (Margerum, 2011; Weiss, 1987).

In practice, this is often described in terms of the tensions between the activities of the collaborative network and the "core business" of each agency (Koontz et al., 2004; Margerum, 2011; Thomas, 2003). Core business includes those things most central to the missions and mandates of an agency, and they may be reinforced by administrative directives, budget allocations and even judicial action. When resources are limited, there is often a tendency for agencies to focus on "core business" and the "cost" of collaborative efforts is often viewed as a luxury (Agranoff, 2007). Management approaches are also challenged by the expectations for accountability, which often get diffused in a shared governance setting (Agranoff, 2007).

Another limitation relates to internal appraisals and rewards, which are often geared towards the outputs and outcomes of the organization. As a result, appraisal systems within organizations may not reward people for their work on collaborative efforts (Cortner and Moote, 1999; Linden, 2002). Goldsmith and Eggers (2004) point out that personnel systems generally tend to be more hierarchical rather than networked, making it hard to recognize and reward interorganizational activities. Interorganizational arrangements also make performance accountability difficult (Kettl, 2006), which may create challenges with assessing agency performance or personnel performance within an organization.

Finally, the culture and managerial flexibility within an organization is cited by many as having an effect on whether individuals from those organizations can support a collaborative effort (O'Leary and Vij, 2012; Thomas, 2003). Thomas (2003) cites the degree of agency discretion as one important determinant of interagency coordination. He notes that when collaborative groups decide on a course of action, participants often need clearance from higher-level managers. In some agencies this authority is highly centralized, while in others there is far more discretion at the line manager and field staff level (Thomas, 2003, 274–275).

Support

Implementation in most collaborative settings requires ongoing interaction among participants in the collaborative. While capacity addresses the ability of a collaboration network to sustain itself with adequate leadership and network capacity, the policies, approaches and culture of participating organizations can also present challenges for collaboration. Layzer (2008) contends that collaboratives tend to attenuate over time and implementation is often not durable.

Provan et al. (2008) note that collaborative structures or networks are a relatively new form of organizing and thus the concept itself may not always be legitimized the way a formal organization might be recognized. This means it must be recognized as a forum, requiring an organization to commit to being a member at the table (Agranoff, 2007; Human and Provan, 2000; Margerum, 2011; Provan et al., 2008). Legitimacy also requires goal congruence among participating organizations. Goldsmith and Eggers (2004) point out that this is often not clear in the public sector, because outcomes are often unclear, difficult to measure and can take years to realize. Furthermore, collaboration is likely to bring together actors whose goals simultaneously overlap and differ, all of which makes it difficult for organizations to maintain their commitment (Goldsmith and Eggers, 2004).

The support for collaboration also revolves around the tension of effectiveness and results. The deliberative nature of the process can create gridlock, which favors those in the status quo (Echeverria, 2001). As noted below, collaboration can be a time-consuming process and the lack of intermediate results can lead to weakening support (Margerum, 2011). Conversely, the interrelationships and interdependencies among actors may also encourage collaboration when it's not possible to act individually (Benjamin et al., 2011).

Collaboration Costs and Benefits

The final set of challenges relates to the costs and benefits of collaboration. While these overlap with some of the others discussed above, I believe they are significant enough to warrant specific mention.

Costs and benefits

First, collaboration involves immediate and ongoing transaction costs (time, money, staff resources) while the benefits are usually long term (Linden, 2002). Consensus takes time, and significant human relations processing is part of the price that most networks pay for collaborative results (Agranoff, 2007, 179). A commitment of resources is not always limited by transaction costs per se, but on the delayed returns from investing in the collaborative effort (Margerum, 2011). For example, Ivery (2008) found that organizations which obtained clear benefits for participating were more likely to stay involved over time.

Second, in many contexts, collaborative efforts are dealing with problems that are diffuse, dispersed and at the margins of traditional policies and programs (Koontz et al., 2004). As a result, it is more difficult to direct resources from traditional programs and budgets unless there is sufficient flexibility in administrative rules or legislation. For example, policy changes over the years have increased the ability of federal land management agencies (BLM and US Forest Service) to operate more collaboratively, because they are able to use funds in more flexible ways (Thomas, 2003). This includes changes that allow expenditures on non-federal land management efforts when they have benefits to water quality or ecosystem health (Koontz et al., 2004). Collaboration has been more challenging for organizations such as the National Park Service and Bureau of Reclamation, which work under narrower mandates and have fewer mandates to collaborate (McPadden and Margerum, 2014; Thomas, 2003).

Transaction costs

Because collaboration incurs ongoing transaction costs to support and maintain interaction, ongoing and sustainable sources of funding are critical to effectiveness (Agranoff, 2007; Huxham, 2003; Lubell et al., 2002). This support may come in the form of funding from one or more of the participating organizations; it may derive from direct budget allocations at the state or national level; it may depend on grants, donations and fundraising. In any of these cases, resource support for this collaboration function is often precarious. Grant-dependent entities suffer from instability and high input costs for grant writing. Entities supported by participating organizations or direct budget allocations often suffer in times of funding shortfalls, because other issues take priority. They also don't typically have a built-in constituency the way other agencies and initiatives may have interest groups, lobby groups or other beneficiaries advocating for their funding (Koontz et al., 2004; Parker et al., 2010; Thomas, 2003). Different stakeholders may also have different funders with varying tolerance for embracing different perspectives in a collaborative setting (O'Leary and Bingham, 2007; O'Leary and Vij, 2012).

For individuals participating in collaborative efforts, capacity is also a consideration. Many locally based collaborative efforts desire the participation of people who are leaders and well networked in their community. These same attributes make them sought out by every other government, nongovernment and nonprofit organization in the community. This makes it a challenge to sustain efforts in a way that don't burn out participants or involve people who can't adequately participate (Byron et al., 2001; Parker et al., 2010).

CONCLUSION

Given this litany of challenges, it would be easy to argue that these are barriers to effective collaboration or collaboration effectiveness. Yet, many of these challenges have always been prominent challenges in traditional governance and management. Complex problems, difficult political settings, power issues, governance capacity, participant barriers and the costs and benefits of various governance strategies are all persistent governance and management themes.

As collaboration becomes increasingly applied in practice to address an array of management and governance issues, we are learning more about best approaches and practices. These lessons are helping practitioners improve collaborative structures, processes and implementation. However, best practices may overlook the significance of collaboration challenges outlined in this chapter.

Many of these challenges require new research and new methods that go beyond current description and conceptualization. As collaboration matures as a concept it is time to take a harder and deeper look at these challenges to improve practice and articulate its challenges. Some of these challenges may be limitations of the collaborative model, and thus future research may point to new or hybrid strategies. Other challenges are weaknesses of practice that may require better articulation of concepts, clearer implications for training and education, and better translation of concepts to guide practice. Finally, other challenges are consistent difficulties that require more scrutiny and careful research. In particular, there is an increasing need to look at these issues through interdisciplinary lenses, which requires researchers, funders and journals to move out of their comfortable silos and embrace a research agenda that is itself more collaborative.

REFERENCES

Agranoff, R. (2007). *Managing within networks: adding value to public organizations*. Washington, D.C.: Georgetown University Press.
Agranoff, R. (2012). *Collaborating to manage: a primer for the public sector*. Washington, D.C.: Georgetown University Press.
Agranoff, R., and McGuire, M. (2003). *Collaborative public management: new strategies for local governments*. Washington, D.C.: Georgetown University Press.
Alford, J., and O'Flynn, J. (2012). *Rethinking public service delivery: Managing with external providers*. Basingstoke, England: Palgrave Macmillan.
Amy, D. (1987). The politics of environmental mediation. *Ecology Law Quarterly*, *11*(1), 1–19.
Ansell, C., and Gash, A. (2007). Collaborative governance in theory and practice. *Journal of Public Administration Research and Theory*, *18*(4), 543–571.
Barry, J. M. (2011). Mobilized bias and multistakeholder protected-area planning: a socio-institutional perspective on collaboration. *Society and Natural Resources*, *24*(10), 1116–1126. http://doi.org/10.1080/08941920.2010.550083
Beierle, T. C. (2002). The quality of stakeholder-based decisions. *Risk Analysis*, *22*(4), 739–749.
Benham, C. F., Beavis, S. G., and Hussey, K. E. (2015). The cost of collaboration: how caring for our country has shaped regional natural resource management in an Australian river catchment. *Australasian Journal of Environmental Management*, *22*(3), 285–297. http://doi.org/10.1080/14486563.2014.976847
Benjamin, C. E., Brechin, S. R., and Thoms, C. A. (2011). Introduction to the special issue: organizational networks and environmental governance. *Journal of Natural Resources Policy Research*, *3*(3), 211–222.
Benson, D., Jordan, A., Cook, H., and Smith, L. (2013). Collaborative environmental governance: are watershed partnerships swimming or are they sinking? *Land Use Policy*, *30*(1), 748–757. http://doi.org/10.1016/j.landusepol.2012.05.016
Bingham, L., and O'Leary, R. (eds.). (2008). *Big ideas in collaborative public management*. Armonk, N.Y.: M. E. Sharpe.
Blackman, D. (2014). The diagnostic solution? Gauging readiness for cross-boundary working. In J. O'Flynn, D. Blackman, and J. Halligan (eds.), *Crossing boundaries in public management and policy* (pp. 172–189). New York: Routledge.
Booher, D. E., and Innes, J. E. (2010). Governance for resilience: CALFED as a complex adaptive network for resource management. *Ecology and Society*, *15*(3), 35 [online].
Bradshaw, B. (2003). Questioning the credibility and capacity of community-based resource management. *The Canadian Geographer*, *47*(2), 137–150.
Brinkerhoff, D. W. (1999). Exploring state—civil society collaboration: policy partnerships in developing countries. *Nonprofit and Voluntary Sector Quarterly*, *28*(suppl 1), 59–86.

Byron, I., Curtis, A., and Lockwood, M. (2001). Exploring burnout in Australia's Landcare program: a case study in the Shepparton region. *Society and Natural Resources*, *14*(10), 901–910.
Campbell, H. (2006). Just planning the art of situated ethical judgment. *Journal of Planning Education and Research*, *26*(1), 92–106. http://doi.org/10.1177/0739456X06288090
Connell, D. (2007). *Water politics in the Murray-Darling Basin*. Annandale, N.S.W.: Federation Press.
Connelly, D. R., Zhang, J., and Faerman, S. (2008). The paradoxical nature of collaboration. In L. Bingham and R. O'Leary (eds.), *Big ideas in collaborative public management* (pp. 17–35). Armonk, N.Y.: M. E. Sharpe.
Cortner, H. J., and Moote, M. A. (1999). *The politics of ecosystem management*. Washington, D.C.: Island Press.
Curtis, A., Ross, H., Marshall, G. R., Baldwin, C., Cavaye, J., Freeman, C., Syme, G. J. (2014). The great experiment with devolved NRM governance: lessons from community engagement in Australia and New Zealand since the 1980s. *Australasian Journal of Environmental Management*, *21*(2), 175–199.
Davis, E. J., Moseley, C., Olsen, C., Abrams, J., and Creighton, J. (2013). Diversity and dynamism of fire science user needs. *Journal of Forestry*, *111*(2), 101–107. http://doi.org/10.5849/jof.12-037
de Boer, C., and Krantzberg, G. (2013). Great Lakes water governance: a transboundary inter-regime analysis. In J. Edelenbos, N. Bressers, and P. Scholten (eds.), *Water governance as connective capacity* (pp. 315–332). Burlington, VT: Ashgate.
Depoe, S. P. (2004). Public involvement, civil discovery, and the formation of environmental policy: a comparative analysis of the Fernald Citizens Task Force and the Fernald Health Effects Subcommittee. In S. P. Depoe, J. W. Delicath, and M.-F. A. Elensbeer (eds.), *Communication and public participation in environmental decision making* (pp. 157–173). Albany, NY: State University of New York Press.
Dore, J. (2007). Mekong region water-related MSPs–unfilled potential. In J. Warner (ed.), *Multi-stakeholder platforms for integrated water management* (pp. 205–234). Aldershot, England: Ashgate Publishing Ltd.
Dryzek, J. S. (2000). *Deliberative democracy and beyond : liberals, critics, contestations*. Oxford and New York: Oxford University Press.
Dukes, E. F., and Firehock, K. E. (2001). *Collaboration: a guide for environmental advocates*. Charlottesville, VA: University of Virginia.
Echeverria, J. D. (2001). No success like failure: the Platte River collaborative watershed planning process. *William and Mary Environmental Law and Policy Review*, *25*(3), 559–604.
Edelenbos, J., and Klijn, E. (2007). Managing stakeholder involvement in decision making: a comparative analysis of six interactive processes in the Netherlands. *SAGE Public Administration Abstracts*, *34*(1), 3.
Elliott, M. L. P. (1999). The role of facilitators, mediators, and other consensus building practitioners. In L. Susskind, S. McKearnon, and S. Carpenter (eds.), *Consensus building handbook* (pp. 199–239). Thousand Oaks, CA: Sage.
Emerson, K., Nabatchi, T., and Balogh, S. (2012). An integrative framework for collaborative governance. *Journal of Public Administration Research and Theory*, *22*(1), 1–29.
Faysse, N., Cossøo, V., Ampuero, R., Quiroz, F., and Paz, B. (2007). Less tension,

limited decision: a multi-stakeholder platform to review a contested sanitation project in Tiquipaya, Bolivia. In J. Warner (ed.), *Multi-stakeholder platforms for integrated water management* (pp. 165–190). Aldershot, England: Ashgate Publishing Ltd.

Flitcroft, R. L., Dedrick, D. C., Smith, C. L., Thieman, C. A., and Bolte, J. P. (2009). Social infrastructure to integrate science and practice: the experience of the Long Tom Watershed Council. *Ecology and Society*, *14*(2), 36 [online].

Flyvbjerg, B. (2012). Bringing power to planning research: one researcher's praxis story. In S. S. Fainstein and S. Campbell (eds.), *Planning Theory: Prospects for the 1980s* (3rd edn.). Malden, MA: Wiley-Blackwell.

Forester, J. F. (2013). *Planning in the face of conflict: the surprising possibilities of facilitative leadership* (1st edn.). Chicago, IL: APA Planners Press.

Gallemore, C. T., Prasti H., R. D., and Moeliono, M. (2014). Discursive barriers and cross-scale forest governance in Central Kalimantan, Indonesia. *Ecology and Society*, *19*(2), 18. http://doi.org/10.5751/ES-06418-190218

Ghose, R. (2005). The complexities of citizen participation through collaborative governance. *Space and Polity*, *9*(1), 61–75. http://doi.org/10.1080/13562570500078733

Goldsmith, S., and Eggers, W. D. (2004). *Governing by network: the new shape of the public sector*. Washington, D.C.: Brookings Institution Press.

Gray, B. (1989). *Collaborating: finding common ground for multiparty problems*. San Francisco, CA: Jossey-Bass, Inc.

Hamilton, J. D. (2004). Competing and converging values of public participation: a case study of participant views in Department of Energy nuclear weapons cleanup. In S. P. Depoe, J. W. Delicath, and M.-F. A. Elensbeer (eds.), *Communication and public participation in environmental decision making* (pp. 59–81). Albany, NY: State University of New York Press.

Hanemann, M., and Dyckman, C. (2009). The San Francisco Bay-Delta: a failure in decision making capacity. *Environmental Science and Policy*, *12*(6), 710–725.

Head, B. W. (2008). Assessing network-based collaborations: effectiveness for whom? *Public Management Review*, *10*(6), 733–749.

Heikkila, T., and Gerlak, A. K. (2005). The formation of large-scale collaborative resource management institutions: Clarifying the roles of stakeholders, science, and institutions. *Policy Studies Journal*, *33*(4), 583–612.

Human, S. E., and Provan, K. G. (2000). Legitimacy building in the evolution of small-firm multilateral networks: a comparative study of success and demise. *Administrative Science Quarterly*, *45*(2), 327–365. http://doi.org/10.2307/2667074

Huxham, C. (2003). Theorizing collaboration practice. *Public Management Review*, *5*(3), 401–423.

Huxham, C., and Beech, N. (2003). Contrary prescriptions: recognizing good practice tensions in management. *Organization Studies*, *24*(1), 69–93. http://doi.org/10.1177/0170840603024001678

Huxham, C., and Vangen, S. (2005). *Managing to collaborate: the theory and practice of collaborative advantage*. London and New York: Routledge.

Huxham, C., Vangen, S., Huxham, C., and Eden, C. (2000). The challenge of collaborative governance. *Public Management: An International Journal of Research and Theory*, *2*(3), 337–358. http://doi.org/10.1080/14719030000000021

Huxley, M., and Yiftachel, O. (2000). New paradigm or old myopia? Unsettling the communicative turn in planning theory. *Journal of Planning Education and Research, 19*(4), 333–342. http://doi.org/10.1177/0739456X0001900402

Imperial, M. T. (1999). Institutional analysis and ecosystem-based management: the institutional analysis and development framework. *Environmental Management, 24*(4), 449–465.

Imperial, M. T. (2005). Lessons from six watershed management programs. *Administration and Society, 37*(3), 281–320.

Imperial, M. T., and Kauneckis, D. (2003). Moving from conflict to collaboration: watershed governance in Lake Tahoe. *Natural Resources Journal, 43*(4), 1009–1055.

Ingram, H., and Fraser, L. (2006). Path dependency and adroit innovation: the case of California water. In R. Repetto (ed.), *Punctuated equilibrium and the dynamics of U.S. environmental policy* (pp. 78–109). New Haven, CT: Yale University Press.

Innes, J. E., and Booher, D. E. (2009). *Planning with complexity: an introduction to collaborative rationality for public policy*. New York: Routledge.

Innes, J. E., and Booher, D. E. (2014). A turning point for planning theory? Overcoming dividing discourses. *Planning Theory, 14*(2), 195–213. http://doi.org/10.1177/1473095213519356

Irvin, R. A. (2010). Collaboration versus competition in the third sector. Retrieved from http://EconPapers.repec.org/RePEc:elg:eechap:12757_6

Irvin, R. A., and Stansbury, J. (2004). Citizen participation in decision making: is it worth the effort? *Public Administration Review, 64*(1), 55–65.

Ivery, J. (2008). Policy mandated collaboration. *Journal of Sociology and Social Welfare, 35*(4), 53–70.

Kallis, G., Kiparsky, M., and Norgaard, R. (2010). Collaborative governance and adaptive management: lessons from California's CALFED water program. *Environmental Science and Policy, 12*(6), 631–643.

Kenney, D. S. (2000). *Arguing about consensus: examining the case against Western watershed initiatives and other collaborative groups active in natural resources management* (p. 72). Boulder, CO: Natural Resources Law Center, University of Colorado.

Kettl, D. F. (2006). Managing boundaries in American administration: the collaboration imperative. *Public Administration Review, 66*, 10–19. http://doi.org/10.1111/j.1540-6210.2006.00662.x

Koontz, T. M., Steelman, T. A., Carmin, J., Korfmacher, K. S., Moseley, C., and Thomas, C. W. (2004). *Collaborative environmental management: what roles for government?* Washington, D.C.: Resources for the Future.

Lane, M. B. (1997). Aboriginal participation in environmental planning. *Australian Geographical Studies, 35*(3), 308–323.

Lane, M. B. (2003). Participation, decentralization, and civil society: indigenous rights and democracy in environmental planning. *Journal of Planning Education and Research, 22*(4), 360–373.

Layzer, J. A. (2008). *Natural experiments: ecosystem-based management and the environment*. Cambridge, MA: The MIT Press.

Leach, W. D., and Sabatier, P. (2005). Are trust and social capital the keys to success? Watershed partnerships in California and Washington. In P. Sabatier, W. Focht, M. Lubell, Z. Trachtenberg, A. Vedlitz, and M. Matlock (eds.), *Swimming upstream: collaborative approaches to watershed management* (pp. 231–258). Cambridge, MA: The MIT Press.

Leach, W. D., Pelkey, N. W., and Sabatier, P. A. (2002). Stakeholder partnerships as collaborative policymaking: evaluation criteria applied to watershed management in California and Washington. *Journal of Policy Analysis and Management, 21*(4), 645–670.
LeBaron, M., and Carstarphen, N. (1999). Finding common ground on abortion. In L. Susskind, S. McKearnon, and S. Carpenter (eds.), *Consensus building handbook: a comprehensive guide to reaching agreement* (pp. 1031–1050). Thousand Oaks, CA: Sage.
Linden, R. M. (2002). *Working across boundaries: making collaboration work in government and nonprofit organizations* (1st edn.). San Francisco, CA: Jossey-Bass. Retrieved from http://www.loc.gov/catdir/toc/wiley031/2002011933.html
Lubell, M. (2004). Collaborative environmental institutions: all talk and no action. *Journal of Policy Analysis and Management, 23*(3), 549–573.
Lubell, M. (2005). Do watershed partnerships enhance beliefs conducive to collective action? In P. Sabatier, W. Focht, M. Lubell, Z. Trachtenberg, A. Vedlitz, and M. Matlock (eds.), *Swimming upstream: collaborative approaches to watershed management* (pp. 201–232). Cambridge, MA: The MIT Press.
Lubell, M., Schneider, M., Scholz, J. T., and Mete, M. (2002). Watershed partnerships and the emergence of collective action institutions. *American Journal of Political Science, 46*(1), 148–163.
Lurie, S. D. (2011). The CALFED Bay-Delta Program: lessons from the rise and fall of a large-scale ecosystem management network. *Journal of Natural Resources Policy Research, 3*(3), 251–262.
Margerum, R. D. (1999a). Getting past yes: from capital creation to action. *Journal of the American Planning Association, 65*(2), 181–192. http://doi.org/10.1080/01944369908976046
Margerum, R. D. (1999b). Integrated environmental management: the elements critical to success. *Environmental Management, 65*(2), 181–192.
Margerum, R. D. (2002a). Collaborative planning: building consensus and building a distinct model for practice. *Journal of Planning Education and Research, 21*(3), 237–253.
Margerum, R. D. (2002b). Evaluating collaborative planning—implications from an empirical analysis of growth management. *Journal of the American Planning Association, 68*(2), 179–193.
Margerum, R. D. (2011). *Beyond consensus: improving collaborative planning and management.* Boston, MA: The MIT Press.
Mattessich, P. W., Murray-Close, M., and Monsey, B. R. (2004). *Collaboration: what makes it work* (2nd edn.). Saint Paul, MN: Amherst H. Wilder Foundation.
McCarthy, J., and Shorett, A. (1984). *Negotiating settlements: a guide to environmental mediation.* New York: American Arbitration Association.
McCloskey, M. (2001). Is this the course you want to be on? *Society and Natural Resources, 14*(4), 627–634.
McGuire, M. (2006). Collaborative public management: assessing what we know and how we know it. *Public Administration Review, 66*(S1), 33–43.
McPadden, R., and Margerum, R. D. (2014). Improving National Park Service and nonprofit partnerships—lessons from the National Trail System. *Society and Natural Resources, 27*(12), 1321–1330. doi: 10.1080/08941920.2014.970738
Newig, J., Pahl-Wostl, C., and Sigel, K. (2005). The role of public participation in managing uncertainty in the implementation of the Water Framework Directive. *European Environment, 15*, 333–343.

Newman, J., Barnes, M., Sullivan, H., and Knops, A. (2004). Public participation and collaborative governance. *Journal of Social Policy*, *33*(2), 203–223.

O'Flynn, J., Blackman, D., and Halligan, J. (2013). *Crossing boundaries in public management and policy: the international experience*. New York: Routledge.

O'Leary, R., and Bingham, L. B. (2007). *A manager's guide to resolving conflicts in collaborative networks*. Arlington, VA: Center for the Business of Government.

O'Leary, R., and Bingham, L. (2009). *The collaborative public manager: new ideas for the twenty-first century*. Washington, D.C.: Georgetown University Press.

O'Leary, R., and Vij, N. (2012). Collaborative public management: where have we been and where are we going? *The American Review of Public Administration*, *42*(5), 507–522. http://doi.org/10.1177/0275074012445780

O'Leary, R., Choi, Y., and Gerard, C. M. (2012). The skill set of the successful collaborator. *Public Administration Review*, *72*(s1), S70–S83. http://doi.org/10.1111/j.1540-6210.2012.02667.x

O'Toole, L. J., and Meier, K. J. (2004). Public management in intergovernmental networks: matching structural networks and managerial networking. *Journal of Public Administration Research and Theory*, *14*(4), 469–494.

Owen, D. (2007). Law, environmental dynamism, reliability: the rise and fall of CALFED. *Environmental Law*, *37*, 1145–1204.

Parker, K. B., Margerum, R. D., Dedrick, D. C., and Dedrick, J. P. (2010). Sustaining watershed councils: the issue of coordinator-board relationships. *Society and Natural Resources*, *23*(5), 469–484.

Provan, K. G., and Kenis, P. (2008). Modes of network governance: structure, management and effectiveness. *Journal of Public Administration Research and Theory*, *18*, 229–252.

Provan, K. G., and Milward, H. B. (2001). Do networks really work? A framework for evaluating public-sector organizational networks. *Public Administration Review*, *61*(4), 414–423.

Provan, K. G., Kenis, P., and Human, S. E. (2008). *Legitimacy building in organizational networks* (pp. 121–137). Armonk, NY: M. E. Sharpe.

Purdy, J. M. (2012). A framework for assessing power in collaborative governance processes. *Public Administration Review*, *72*(3), 409–417. http://doi.org/10.1111/j.1540-6210.2011.02525.x

Putnam, L. L., and Wondolleck, J. M. (2003). Intractability: definitions, dimensions, and distinctions. In R. J. Lewicki, B. Gray, and M. Elliot (eds.), *Making sense of intractable environmental conflicts: concepts and cases* (pp. 35–59). Washington, D.C.: Island Press.

Ratner, B. D., Mam, K., and Halpern, G. (2014). Collaborating for resilience: conflict, collective action, and transformation on Cambodia's Tonle Sap Lake. *Ecology and Society*, *19*(3), 31.

Reed, M. G., and McIlveen, K. (2006). Toward a pluralistic civic science?: Assessing community forestry. *Society and Natural Resources*, *19*(7), 591–607. http://doi.org/10.1080/08941920600742344

Rigg, C., and O'Mahony, N. (2013). Frustrations in collaborative working: insights from institutional theory. *Public Management Review*, *15*(1), 83–108.

Robins, L., and Kanowski, P. (2011). "Crying for our Country": eight ways in which "Caring for our Country" has undermined Australia's regional model for natural resource management. *Australasian Journal of Environmental Management*, *18*(2), 88–108.

Sabatier, P. A., Leach, W. D., Lubell, M., and Pelkey, N. W. (2005). Theoretical frameworks explaining partnership success. In P. A. Sabatier, W. Focht, M. Lubell, Z. Trachtenberg, A. Vedlitz, and M. Matlock (eds.), *Swimming upstream: collaborative approaches to watershed management* (pp. 173–199). Cambridge, MA: The MIT Press.

Samuelson, C. D., Vedlitz, A., Whitten, G. D., Matlock, M., Alston, L. T., Peterson, T. R., and Gilbertz, S. J. (2005). Citizen participation and representation in collaborative engagement processes. In P. A. Sabatier, W. Focht, M. Lubell, Z. Trachtenberg, A. Vedlitz, and M. Matlock (eds.), *Swimming upstream: collaborative approaches to watershed management* (pp. 137–169). Cambridge, MA: The MIT Press.

Sørensen, E. (2014). Conflict as driver of pluricentric coordination. *Planning Theory*, *13*(2), 152–169. http://doi.org/10.1177/1473095213496099

Stanley, T. R., Jr. (1995). Ecosystem management and the arrogance of humanism. *Conservation Biology*, *9*(2), 255–262.

Sullivan, H., and Skelcher, C. (2002). *Working across boundaries: collaboration in public services*. Basingstoke, England: Palgrave Macmillan.

Sullivan, H., Williams, P., and Jeffares, S. (2012). Leadership for collaboration. *Public Management Review*, *14*(1), 41–66. http://doi.org/10.1080/14719037.2011.589617

Susskind, L., and Cruikshank, J. (1987). *Breaking the impasse: consensual approaches to resolving public disputes*. New York: Basic Books.

Thomas, C. W. (2003). *Bureaucratic landscapes: interagency cooperation and the preservation of biodiversity*. Cambridge, MA: The MIT Press.

Velez, M., Adlerstein, S., and Wondolleck, J. (2014). Fishers' perceptions, facilitating factors and challenges of community-based no-take zones in the Sian Ka'an Biosphere Reserve, Quintana Roo, Mexico. *Marine Policy*, *45*, 171–181. http://doi.org/10.1016/j.marpol.2013.12.003

Voets, J., Van Dooren, W., and De Rynck, F. (2008). A framework for assessing the performance of policy networks. *Public Management Review*, *10*(6), 773–790.

Weber, E. P. (2003). *Bringing society back in: grassroots ecosystem management, accountability, and sustainable communities*. Cambridge, MA: The MIT Press.

Weeks, E. C. (2000). The practice of deliberative democracy: results from four large-scale trials. *Public Administration Review*, *60*(4), 360–372.

Wegerich. (2007). Chapter 14: Multiplatform platforms in Uzbekistan. In J. Warner (ed.), *Multi-stakeholder platforms for integrated water management* (pp. xvi, 281). Aldershot, England: Ashgate.

Weir, M., Rongerude, J., and Ansell, C. K. (2009). Collaboration is not enough: virtuous cycles of reform in transportation policy. *Urban Affairs Review*, *44*(4), 455–489.

Weiss, J. A. (1987). Pathways to cooperation among public agencies. *Journal of Policy Analysis and Management*, *7*(1), 94–117.

Wondolleck, J. M., and Yaffee, S. L. (2000). *Making collaboration work: lessons from innovation in natural resource management*. Washington, D.C.: Island Press.

Wyborn, C., and Bixler, R. P. (2013). Collaboration and nested environmental governance: scale dependency, scale framing, and cross-scale interactions in collaborative conservation. *Journal of Environmental Management*, *123*, 58–67. http://doi.org/10.1016/j.jenvman.2013.03.014

3. Back to the future? Collaborative environmental governance theory and practice

Tomas M. Koontz

Although "collaborative environmental governance" is a relatively new term, the concept is firmly rooted in the past. Following World War II, observers noticed that natural resource management had grown increasingly specialized and fragmented. In 1955 the Ohio Forestry Association published a report advocating a new, integrated approach for watershed management:

> Within recent years there has emerged from the many programs and projects being used to develop and conserve our natural resources a new ally known as the watershed movement . . . [T]he potential force of the new conservation movement promises to bring to the people in many sections of this country a new unity, integration of effort, and recognition of local responsibility which has for the most part sadly declined with the growing separation of conservation effort into so many different activities. (Ohio Forestry Association, 1955, p. 4)

This "new" approach called for management by hydrological boundaries and across political jurisdictions:

> [T]he watershed movement offers an opportunity for molding into a common purpose the earnest endeavors and skills of many groups . . . [in] a newly-defined arena for solving our resource problems – a unit of the earth's surface, bounded by the ridges and valleys as Nature made them – rather than by the political boundaries as drawn by men. (Ohio Forestry Association, 1955, p. 4)

Moreover, it called for engaging multiple stakeholders, both expert and non-expert, for watershed management:

> By unity of purpose, there can be joined in new understanding the efforts of the man in town with the man on the land, those of the industrialist with the farmer, the merchant with conservationist, the banker with engineer, the mayor with forester, all to provide a new leadership toward a better way of life in the watersheds of this land. (Ohio Forestry Association, 1955, p. 4)

This description, now 60 years old, resonates with many collaborative environmental governance themes: using natural boundaries rather than political boundaries, integrating various conservation disciplines, cooperating across multiple organizations, drawing on perspectives of multiple stakeholders, and having a local focus. The report went on to provide prescriptions for how to carry out watershed management. As a practical guide, it lacked theoretical development or empirical justifications for its advice, yet over the years its concepts have been taken up and examined by scholars in several research fields, including ecosystem management, community-based collaborative environmental management, and collaborative public management. Understanding these three fields will position us to think about the challenges, and unfinished puzzles, that lie ahead for collaborative environmental governance.

ECOSYSTEM MANAGEMENT

In practice, the idea of managing on an ecosystem basis in the U.S. context has roots that extend back to the 19th century. For example, John Wesley Powell advocated in 1879 for demarcating states in the newly acquired western territories according to watershed boundaries (Powell, 1879). While his focus on watersheds didn't embrace the full biotic and abiotic systems with which we associate the term "ecosystem," it was a call for management based on landscapes rather than straight lines. This idea was not politically viable at the time – witness the boxy state borders created in Wyoming, Colorado, Utah, and the Dakotas. However, in the early 1900s Theodore Roosevelt did designate large Forest Reserves based partly on topographical features and watershed boundaries (Sabatier et al., 2005a). Ecologists picked up the banner with The Ecological Society of America's 1932 call for a system of nature sanctuaries based on ecosystem boundaries to be managed for natural disturbances and with inter-organizational cooperation (principally the National Park Service, U.S. Forest Service, and states) (Shelford, 1933; Grumbine, 1994). In 1933 three National Park Service ecologists argued that park boundaries should coincide with meaningful physical processes and biological communities, such as watershed boundaries (Shafer, 2001). This was a time when the wildlife biologist and nature philosopher Aldo Leopold was gaining expertise in wildlife management, advocating for science-based management of wildlife habitat to promote a variety of species rather than just game species. In *A Sand County Almanac* (1949), Leopold described a land ethic emphasizing ecological communities that included humans, urging people to extend care to ecosystems. By 1994, 18 federal agencies and more at the state level had adopted "ecosystem management" to guide their actions (Malone, 2000).

Ecosystem management places a premium on natural science to understand complex ecosystem interactions. The Hubbard Brook studies in the 1960s and 1970s established ecosystem ecology as a multidisciplinary field where interrelated chemical, biological, and physical components could be studied for interactions, system properties, and responses to disturbance (Cortner and Moote, 1999). The trans-disciplinary fields of ecological economics and conservation biology developed in the 1980s with a normative commitment to promoting environmental protection alongside investigation of interrelated ecological and human systems (Costanza, 1991; Primack, 1993).

In his *Conservation Biology* synthesis essay drawing on over 30 definitions of the term, Grumbine (1994) described 10 "dominant themes" of ecosystem management. These themes included a systems perspective, ecological boundaries, ecological integrity, data collection, monitoring, adaptive management, interagency cooperation, agency organizational change, humans embedded in nature, and paying attention to human values. Natural scientists in academia and government have a strong role to play in at least the first seven of these themes. Grumbine listed five goals of ecosystem management, four of which depend on ecological science to drive management: maintain viable populations of native species, represent all native ecosystem types, maintain ecological processes, and maintain evolutionary potential.

Ecosystem management's focus on scientific expertise is related to, yet different from, a tradition of science-based management dating back to the turn of the 20th century. The Progressive Era of bringing science to bear on solving society's ills included faith in natural science and engineering to provide the best solutions. From Gifford Pinchot's scientific forestry to optimization models in fisheries, the environment was seen as something to be managed at peak productivity for human needs. As Pinchot famously described, the vision of conservation forestry was to attain the greatest good for the greatest number of people in the long run. This arrangement put scientists and managers in charge, relying on their expertise to engineer the best decisions on behalf of the people who enjoyed use of the resource. In fact Pinchot was reacting to the wasteful exploitation of forest resources at the hands of the private market, with wealthy individuals and firms practicing "cut and run" timbering that left lands severely degraded. Government control, through scientific management, was thought to be a better approach.

It is important to note that the science that emerged from the Progressive Era to drive natural resource management was qualitatively different from the science associated with ecosystem management. In traditional natural resource management, scientific models treated phenomena as linear and predictable, approaching steady-state equilibria, where managers attempted to "freeze" an ecosystem to produce maximum outputs for human use (Crossley, 1996; Holling and Bocking, 1991). Resource systems were assumed to be predictable and controllable (Cortner and Moote, 1999). In contrast, ecosystem management science views ecosystems as stochastic, nonlinear, and reaching only temporary equilibria. Resource systems are unpredictable and uncontrollable, and seeking to freeze an ecosystem at its point of maximum production for human uses increases its fragility (Crossley, 1996; Holling and Bocking, 1991). Thus adaptive management is recommended, where management actions are treated as experiments with a goal of maximizing learning about the system rather than as attempts to optimize resource production (Lee, 1994).

By the turn of the 21st century, the concept of ecosystem management was being broadened to include more social concerns. In 1999 Cortner and Moote described the four principles of ecosystem management as socially defined goals and objectives that privilege protection of ecological processes; holistic, integrated science; adaptable institutions with a capacity to learn and adjust based on evidence; and collaborative decision making across a broad cross-section of society. Hobbs et al. (2004) argued for the careful articulation of societal goals before undertaking ecological restoration efforts. While natural science still played a key role, this attention to stakeholder interests was in line with the tenets of what would later emerge as collaborative environmental governance.

Recognition of the stakeholder and organizational components of ecosystem management encouraged social scientists to join the conversation. In contrast to a conceptualization of social considerations as the purview of politicians and managers (Grumbine, 1994; Noss and Cooperrider, 1994), Endter-Wada et al. (1998) challenged scientists and practitioners in this field to recognize the role of social science in informing ecosystem management. They argued that social science can provide empirical data and analyses to understand public involvement in ecosystem management decision processes, and how humans affect and are affected by ecosystems. Social scientists also studied organizational adoption of ecosystem management practices (Butler and Koontz, 2005; Kellogg, 1998; Koontz and Bodine, 2008; Olsson et al., 2008; Rigg, 2001), the institutional challenges of ecosystem management (Cortner et al., 1998; Imperial, 1999), stakeholder participation (Brody, 2003; Raedeke et al., 2003; Smith et al., 1999), and stakeholder valuation of ecosystems (Randhir and Shriver, 2009). Such work overlaps squarely with research on community-based collaborative environmental management (see below). In fact, Keough and Blahna (2006) synthesized ecosystem management and collaboration literature to develop the blended concept of "integrative, collaborative ecosystem management."

More recently, social scientists have developed mechanisms to explicitly incorporate the objectives of particular stakeholders, such as indigenous peoples, into water asset assessments (Jackson et al., 2015; Mooney and Tan, 2012).

Over time, the theory and practice of ecosystem management has yielded numerous challenges for this approach:

- Managing natural resources to enhance biodiversity while providing for human demands and experimenting with practices to maximize learning about natural resource systems.
- Coordinating landscape management across human communities and political jurisdictions.
- Understanding the complex ecosystem interactions at play in social-ecological systems.
- Balancing public participation with science-based determination of management practices.

While use of the term "ecosystem management" has diminished in practice as well as scientific research (Breckler, 2006; Predmore et al., 2008), the components of integrated, locally based management that works across boundaries are evident in the concept of collaborative environmental governance. Another set of collaborative environmental governance components emerged from the field of community-based collaborative environmental management.

COMMUNITY-BASED COLLABORATIVE ENVIRONMENTAL MANAGEMENT

Tragedy of the Commons and Self-governance of Common-pool Resources

As described above, scientific expertise played a prominent role in both traditional natural resource management and the ecosystem management approach. To privilege science, a strong government authority was needed to carefully plan and manage with a long-term view, in order to avoid the destruction caused by profit-maximizing actors making short-term decisions. But a competing approach supported relying on the free market and individual actions. Economists argued that secure property rights would incentivize owners to manage their natural resources sustainably instead of wastefully. Where waste occurred, it was due not to lack of scientific information, but rather to insecure property rights and transaction costs that were too high to encourage the free market exchanges that would move natural resources towards their most efficient uses (Coase, 1960). Thus when Garret Hardin wrote his seminal article on "The tragedy of the commons" in 1968, he prescribed two solutions to overcome what he saw as the inevitable tragedy of humans degrading the natural resource that they depended on: centralized government management or free market incentives. The centralized government management solution relied on scientific knowledge to determine appropriate harvest levels, and government authority to establish rules based on these levels and enforce the rules against resource users. The free market solution relied on privatizing the commons (e.g., by fencing-off portions) so that costs of resource withdrawals accrued to an individual's particular stake in the resource rather than to the resource in its entirety.

But Hardin's analysis was incomplete. He relied not on empirical scientific work, but rather on a stylized example whose assumptions led to his conclusions. His first solution, centralized government management, could be effective if the government had accurate information about the natural resource system and about user behavior, and had resources to monitor and sanction violators (including personnel who faithfully upheld the rules), and if the costs to do so were sufficiently low. His second solution, free market privatization, could be effective if resource conditions were uniform across time and space, individual costs to establish and defend property rights were low, and transaction costs for market exchanges were also low. As Elinor Ostrom described in her foundational work, *Governing the commons* (1990), these assumptions often do not hold in field settings. In fact, she argued, communities around the world have experimented with a wide range of natural resource management systems over time, many of which do not rely on either centralized government management or free market privatization. These user-based approaches can sometimes lead to successful governance. Although she did not call it "collaborative environmental governance," Ostrom described stakeholder-based processes that, in successful cases, involved self-governing institutions to match practices to the local context, learn and adapt to changing human and ecological conditions, and interact with resource systems across scales. Here science was less important than local time-and-place knowledge.

Ostrom's contribution was not only in identifying a self-governance approach to common-pool resource management as an alternative to centralized government or free market solutions. By developing and testing theoretical propositions about common-pool resource management, she brought interdisciplinary scientific methods to bear on building knowledge.

In so doing, she developed a conceptual vocabulary that enabled scholars working in specialized fields of study based on a particular resource type (e.g., forests, irrigation systems, fisheries, watersheds) to work together to understand the complex, interconnected human and natural systems involved in collaborative environmental governance. That vocabulary included the concepts of appropriation, provision, collective choice actions, resource attributes, community attributes, rules-in-use, institutional arrangements, mutual monitoring, heterogeneity, accountability, and adaptive institutions.

COLLABORATIVE ENVIRONMENTAL PARTNERSHIPS

Much of Ostrom's self-governance arguments criticized centralized government control, practice and scholarship. Collaborative environmental partnerships in the U.S. began with the notion that local stakeholder-developed solutions could succeed where government policies had failed. In a collaborative environmental partnership, conflicting interests work together to develop a mutually agreed-upon plan of action to address issues that neither stakeholder could achieve alone. This approach had a growing appeal in the 1980s and 1990s, particularly in the western U.S. In this setting federal lands management was seen as creating a stalemate among competing interests at a time of declining public resources and growing distrust of government (Sabatier et al., 2005a; Snow, 2001; Wondolleck and Yaffee, 2000). Early examples such as the Quincy Library Group and the Upper Clark Fork Steering Committee featured conflicting interests coming together to create a consensus-based plan that went around conventional policy channels (Marston, 2001; Olson, 2002). Since that time, scholarship in collaborative environmental partnerships has shifted from a first generation of studies focused on making a case for why collaborative partnerships were needed and sharing "lessons learned" regarding how to foster successful partnerships, to a second generation of more theoretical works developing typologies and testing propositions with empirical data to understand collaborative partnership inputs, processes, outputs, and outcomes in different contexts.

First Generation Scholarship

As collaborative environmental governance gained popularity in practice in the early 1990s, scholars generated work that was largely normative and prescriptive. Some writers argued for a collaborative approach by highlighting the failings of top-down approaches. These failings included harm to the environment and to communities that relied on natural resources for their livelihood, growing conflicts over resource use and preservation, failure to promote the common interest, and distrust in government (e.g., Brunner, 2002; Kemmis, 1990; Weber, 1998). Proponents argued that collaborative governance provided greater accountability, strengthened communities, fostered civic engagement, and ensured environmental conservation (Bernard and Young, 1997; Cortner and Moote, 1999; Innes, 1996; Wondolleck and Yaffee, 2000). Others articulated normative claims about what criteria should be used to judge collaborative processes and outcomes, based on democratic or discourse principles as well as human and environmental conditions (e.g., Kenney, 2001; Renn et al., 1995; for a review see Conley and Moote, 2003). Some developed "best practices" and handbooks giving advice for managing successful collaborations (Moote, 1995; Shindler and Neburka, 1997; U.S. Environmental Protection Agency, 1997; Wondolleck and Yaffee, 2000).

In the late 1990s, empirical research describing these collaborative processes began to appear, demonstrating that there are many unique cases (e.g., Kenney, 1997; Yaffee et al., 1996). Some studies sought to identify the keys to collaborative partnership effectiveness, by distilling "lessons learned" from examining partnerships in action (e.g., Born and Genskow, 2000; Chess et al., 2000; Mullen and Allison, 1999; Thomas, 1999). Studies in this vein provided data on partnership composition, goals, resources, activities, and outputs, which varied tremendously across partnerships. They also suggested a number of key factors thought to affect collaborative processes and, subsequently, results. These factors included resources, organization age, membership diversity, scope of activities, local context, organizational structure, and institutions (Born and Genskow, 2000; Leach and Pelkey, 2001; Koontz, 2003; Koontz and Johnson, 2004; Leach and Sabatier, 2005; Steelman and Carmin, 2002; Thomas, 1999; Wondolleck and Yaffee, 2000).

In fact this empirically based set of key factors resembled factors suggested for practitioners nearly a half century prior. The *How to develop watersheds* guide (Ohio Forestry Association, 1955) advised would-be collaborative watershed organizers to select a dedicated and trusted leader with a broad perspective; scale the effort to be inclusive enough to cover the scope of the problem yet small enough to foster a sense of local ownership; obtain sufficient funding; collect data to identify problems of concern; draw on the resources of existing organizations without threatening their turf; invite stakeholder participation from all affected interests; structure the organization around task-oriented committees; and develop an action plan that prioritizes tasks, assigns responsibilities, and secures funding.

While providing useful descriptive information and identifying some of the key variables affecting collaborative environmental efforts, studies of "success factors" did not foster much systematic understanding. In a comprehensive review of 37 such empirical studies, Leach and Pelkey (2001) identified 210 "lessons learned." They concluded that these studies did not promote knowledge accumulation, as most lacked rigorous multi-case comparisons and none analyzed data over long time frames. Sabatier et al. (2005b) discussed similar limitations with this first generation of collaborative watershed management research, including a lack of attention to how various factors interact in complex causal pathways. Analyzing interactions is important if we are to explain why key factors don't always operate as expected. For example, studies of two different grant programs in support of collaborative efforts in Ohio indicated that a given program, providing the same amount of funding to a number of collaborative partnerships, did not generate consistent impacts across those partnerships. Differences were attributed to interactions with intervening variables that affected results (Koontz, 2003; Nikolic, 2005). These limitations in understanding set the stage for a second generation of scholarship in collaborative environmental partnerships.

Second Generation Scholarship

At the start of the millennium, more research on collaborative environmental partnerships explicitly included multiple interacting variables through development of typologies and theoretical frameworks. Such research included relatively simple typologies that grouped collaborative efforts along a single dimension, such as partnership membership (Moore and Koontz, 2003), scale (Cheng and Daniels, 2005), or relationship with existing organizations (Bidwell and Ryan, 2006). It also included typologies based on a broader set of characteristics, such as Margerum's (2008) action/organizational/policy classification which took into account institutional levels, scope of effort, activity types, and number and types of participants. These typologies helped organize many unique partnerships into observable patterns of partnership strategies and accomplishments. For example, Moore and Koontz (2003) found that collaborative partnerships composed primarily of government employees focused their efforts on creating collaborative land management plans, whereas those composed primarily of citizens focused more on pressuring government agencies to change their policies. Bidwell and Ryan (2006) concluded that partnerships operating independently of existing agencies spent more time developing goals and plans, which resulted in slower progress but also innovative ideas;

whereas partnerships operating closely with existing agencies were faster to generate results but these yielded less innovation.

Alongside these typologies, scholars tackled new research questions revolving around collaborative environmental partnerships. For example, what catalyzes the creation of collaborative partnerships? In analyzing a national sample of watershed partnerships, Lubell et al. (2002) found partnership creation was positively associated with nonpoint source pollution severity, lack of regulatory enforcement, and sufficient resources to cover start-up costs. Similarly Prokopy et al. (2014) described the importance of different kinds of catalyst events. Another question was: Whose voices are included in collaborative partnerships? Citizen participants tended to be individuals of higher socio-economic status, rather than a true cross-section of the local population (Samuelson et al., 2005; Koehler and Koontz, 2008; Larson and Lach, 2008). In addition, different participatory technologies can marginalize different social groups and knowledge bases (Kouw, 2014). Other researchers asked how facilitation affects partnership processes. While professional facilitators following best practices can help produce results through "authentic dialogue" (Innes and Booher, 2010), some studies suggest stakeholders themselves may be better positioned to facilitate (Leach and Sabatier, 2003).

Another process question is: How does spatial scale affect collaborative processes? Studies indicate that large-scale efforts privilege science more than do small-scale efforts, and they are more likely to rely on existing, formal government programs to implement their plans (Heikkila and Gerlak, 2005; Margerum, 2008; Robinson et al., 2011). In a study of Australian cases, Hill et al. (2015) found that collaborative efforts effectively matched the problem scale with appropriate institutional responses.

Since collaborative processes presumably aim to produce outputs, scholars asked what the partnerships produce, and what factors affect these outputs. Partnerships often produce plans, assessments, agreements, and policy recommendations, based on science as well as local knowledge, and they may generate information/education campaigns and projects on the ground. Types of outputs were found to correlate with factors such as group age, member composition, affiliation with external organizations, and level of concern about the problem (Koontz, 2003; Moore and Koontz, 2003; Sabatier et al., 2005b; Bidwell and Ryan, 2006).

Perhaps the most important question, from a practitioner perspective, centers on what outcomes collaborative partnership generate. Several studies have identified economic and social benefits, including grant leveraging, networking, and human and social capital (Connick and Innes, 2003; Hibbard and Lurie, 2006; Mandarano, 2008; Stedman et al., 2009; Koebele, 2015). Much less has been done to examine ecological conditions resulting from collaboration. Those that do include on-the-ground actions typically focus on outputs as proxies for outcomes, for example counting watershed projects completed (Sabatier et al., 2005b), wetland plans and permits (Meyer and Konisky, 2007), hydroelectric dam license operational requirements (Ulibarri, 2015), and implementation of collaborative plan recommendations (Mandarano, 2008; Koontz and Newig, 2014). Measuring ecological outcomes is challenging for many reasons, including a lack of over-time data measuring ecological conditions, a long time horizon between implementing actions and seeing ecological change, and the presence of many confounding factors other than collaborative partnership efforts that affect ecological conditions (Koontz and Thomas, 2006).

Two recent analyses tackle the challenges of explaining ecological outcomes, examining how various collaborative factors affect water quality. Biddle and Koontz (2014) compare attainment of water quality goals across 26 paired watersheds, one with a collaborative partnership and one without. Results from this quasi-experimental design indicate that a key collaborative process, sustained stakeholder participation over time, leads to setting specific pollutant reduction goals, which in turn leads to greater environmental improvement. In a study of 357 cases in the U.S. EPA's National Rivers and Streams Assessment and Wadeable Streams Assessment at two time points, Scott (2015) compares six measures of watershed conditions in watersheds with and without collaborative partnerships. He finds that several factors are significantly associated with improved ecological conditions over time, including the presence of a collaborative watershed partnership with land management responsibility and a dedicated coordinator. In contrast to Biddle and Koontz (2014), Scott does not find evidence that setting specific goals improves watershed conditions.

Studies of collaborative partnerships in this "second generation" of scholarship explicitly link research to broader research traditions, beyond the environmental issue area. Researchers have employed such theoretical frameworks as institutional rational choice, institutional analysis and development, social capital, alternative dispute resolution, and advocacy coalitions to understand collaborative partnerships (Leach and Pelkey, 2001; Koontz, 2005; Leach and Sabatier, 2005). In addition, three books developed theoretical frameworks for collaborative partnerships in the environmental arena, one focusing on watershed management (Sabatier et al., 2005b), another focusing on government roles in collaborative environmental management (Koontz et al., 2004), and the third focusing on how different types of collaborative partnerships move from plans to actions (Margerum, 2011).

The Dynamic Framework for Watershed Management (Sabatier et al., 2005b) provided a conceptual framework for understanding factors thought to affect collaborative watershed management. The framework arose from a need to foster systematic methods of conceptualizing, measuring, and conducting multifactor analysis across a variety of empirical settings. This framework included five categories of variables: context, process rules, civic community, policy outputs, and watershed outcomes. With feedback loops from watershed outcomes to context and process rules, the framework captured reciprocal relationships among several variables. The authors drew on and tested this framework in case studies examining links between process rules and civic community, as well as the effects of context, process rules, and civic community on policy outputs and watershed outcomes.

The Governmental Impacts Framework (Koontz et al., 2004) responded to a gap in understanding collaborative governance that grew out of common-pool resource self-governance theory, as well as 1990s scholarship focusing on collaboration as an alternative to government management of natural resources. First, common-pool resource self-governance theory emphasized the role of community, rather than government. Ostrom's (1990) design principles for common-pool resource self-governance were developed from analyses of collective action problems where communities developed self-governance systems apart from centralized government. But in many collaborative situations, government involvement is critical for success, either as a provider of resources or an authority that motivates by supplying alternative regulatory action should collaboration fail. Similarly, 1990s scholarship arguing that collaboration was an effective alternative to government often neglected to examine how collaborative efforts occurred alongside or within government efforts and institutions. The Governmental Impacts Framework proposed that governments can affect collaboration through both the actors of government (e.g., agency employees) and the institutions of government (e.g., laws, regulations, and programs). Like the Dynamic Framework for Watershed Management, it included process variables and outcomes, as well as contextual variables (including issue definition). More recent work focusing on government roles indicates the importance of links between collaborative environmental partnerships and existing governance regimes (Watson, 2015), as well as the potential for existing governments to block collaboration (Matthews and Schmidt, 2014).

Margerum's (2011) book drew on case studies and prior literature to develop a theory of collaborative planning and management theoretically grounded in institutional analysis and network theory. He organized concepts via a typology of partnerships: action, organizational, and policy level. Margerum described differences in how these three partnership types move through processes of convening, deliberating, deciding, and implementing. In particular, implementation through social, organizational, and political networks varies by partnership type.

Over time, the theory and practice of community-based collaborative environmental management has yielded numerous challenges for this approach:

- Promoting collective action among self-interested individuals.
- Allowing local community members to self-organize for environmental management while respecting legal authority that is often vested elsewhere.
- Fostering a constructive role for government across different contexts.
- Securing the necessary human, technical, and financial resources to allow collaborative processes to unfold over time.
- Encouraging and enabling participation from diverse stakeholders.
- Balancing small-scale, face-to-face interactions conducive to trust building with large-scale interactions conducive to addressing larger environmental problems.
- Creating plans that are stringent enough to protect the environment without generating opposition that slows implementation.
- Measuring the ecological and social performance of collaborative efforts.

The theoretical frameworks developed by Sabatier et al. (2005b), Koontz et al. (2004), and Margerum (2011) represented evolving thought on community-based collaborative environmental management. From an earlier emphasis on how this approach was *not* governmental, explanations of how it worked came to include government as a key factor in such efforts. At the same time, conceptual development in the opposite direction was occurring in the field of public management: starting from a focus on government, collaborative public management came to describe how, across issue areas, government shifted from the role of an authority commanding action to that of a facilitator steering action. This evolution is described next.

COLLABORATIVE PUBLIC MANAGEMENT

Public management, which emerged from the broader field of public administration, has a rich tradition of scholarship that seeks to explain how government delivers goods and services. By placing government administrators, typically in agencies, at the center of inquiry, scholars seek to explain the translation of laws and programs into practice. Although not limited to the environment, this field has relevance for collaborative environmental governance, especially as it has evolved to include a focus on stakeholder participation and cross-jurisdictional cooperation.

In the 1980s and 1990s, research began to focus on the phenomenon of the federal government increasingly relying on actors in state and local governments, private companies, and non-profit organizations to deliver public programs. The impetus for this phenomenon, scholars argued, was the appearance of increasingly complex, interconnected problems for which government alone was unlikely to have solutions. Some termed this the "hollowing out" of the state, as the key activities of central government actors moved from directly producing the goods and services, to instead providing for the goods and services to be produced through partial pre-emption, cooperative agreements, and contracts (Milward et al., 1993; Stoker, 1998). Others termed this "third-party government" (Salamon, 1981), "network governance" (Rhodes, 1996), "governance" (Stoker, 1998), or "polycentric governance" (McGinnis, 1999). In this new approach, challenges arose from public managers attempting to steer the behavior of others through interpersonal relations and exchanges rather than formal power (Keast et al., 2004). Challenges to inter-organizational collaboration included power disparities, agency cultures, and different organizational imperatives (Gray, 1989), as well as agency turf battles (Bardach, 1998).

Scholarship in this field grew to identify patterns across many instances of collaborative public management. Much of this work involved human services and other issue areas outside of the environment. Researchers conceptualized collaboration as upward, downward, and outward, as administrators interacted with actors and organizations at higher, lower, or parallel levels of government, as well as those in private and non-profit sectors (O'Toole et al., 2005). Typologies of collaborative public management included frequency of interactions (Mandell and Steelman, 2003), scope of activities (Agranoff, 2003), and core mission (Agranoff, 2007).

Alongside studies that conceptualized this trend and described it across various issue areas and locations, scholars sought to identify which factors were associated with its effectiveness. Similar to the development of collaborative environmental partnership literature (described above), scholars sought to draw lessons from these varied cases. Results indicated the importance of funding, network structure, stability through long-term contracts, and trust (Milward and Provan, 2000). Authors focusing on the role of collaborative managers identified a number of key skills for success, including the ability to recruit the right participants (Agranoff, 2003), build support from partners (Innes and Booher, 1999), resolve conflicts (Williams, 2002), establish formal and informal communication channels (Goldsmith and Eggers, 2004), and build trust through small tasks (Vangen and Huxham, 2003).

The first book-length treatment of the concept using the term "collaborative public management" appeared in 2003. Agranoff and McGuire (2003) conceptualized collaborative public management as "the process of facilitating and operating in multiorganizational arrangements to solve problems that cannot be solved or easily solved by single organizations." In a special issue symposium on collaborative public management in the journal *Public Administration Review*, O'Leary et al. (2006, p. 7) defined it as involving government "steering the process that influences decisions and actions within the private, public, and civic sectors." Bingham and O'Leary (2008) described collaborative public management as encompassing "not only collaboration between and among organizations but also the role of the public and citizens in governance" (p. 3). In each of these definitions, public managers work across agency boundaries, where they have less control in public administration.

Two broad theoretical frameworks for collaborative public management recognize the shift from commanding to steering, which they term "collaborative governance." The framework developed by Ansell and Gash (2008) examines collaborative governance as "A governing arrangement where one or more public agencies directly engage non-state stakeholders in a collective decision-making process that is formal, consensus-oriented, and deliberative and that aims to make or implement public policy or manage public programs or assets." This framework includes four broad variables: starting conditions, institutional design, leadership, and collaborative process. The authors argue that a "virtuous cycle" of success can occur when these efforts generate "small wins" which promote trust, commitment, and shared understanding that, in turn, generate further success.

The framework developed by Emerson et al. (2012) focuses on internal process characteristics (principled engagement, shared motivation, and capacity for joint action) and actions that constitute a "collaborative governance regime," which is nested within a broader socio-political context, or "system context," that includes networks, legal frameworks, power relationships, trust, and socio-economic health, along with resource conditions. The authors also suggest a "virtuous cycle" whereby principled engagement and shared motivation are mutually reinforcing and, when coupled with capacity for joint action, lead to collaborative action with measurable outcomes. An important distinction in this framework is that, unlike much of collaborative public management literature, the collaboration need not be formal and state-initiated. Thus the government is not necessarily at the center (hollow or not) of the system.

Recent work in collaborative public management identifies an emerging approach based on "public value." Here the citizens are expected to generate public values through inclusive deliberation. Working together, they solve common problems while developing civic learning and capacity (Boyte, 2011; Bryson et al., 2014).

Over time, the theory and practice of collaborative public management has yielded numerous challenges for this approach:

- Keeping public administrators accountable for public program delivery while relying on third parties to provide goods and services.
- Managing horizontal and vertical networked relationships.
- Building trust and cooperating across multiple organizations with different goals, resources, and constraints.
- Engaging citizens in deliberative processes that promote public values while providing public goods and services.

The collaborative public management literature, while starting from a different place as the other two fields described above (ecosystem management and community-based collaborative environmental management), arrived at a similar destination. All three fields examine key questions relevant for collaborative environmental governance, including the primary goal, sources and uses of knowledge, ontology, role of central government and stakeholders, and decision making (see Table 3.1).

TENSIONS BETWEEN THEORY AND PRACTICE: KEY CHALLENGES FOR SCIENTISTS, STAKEHOLDERS, AND LEADERS

The key challenges facing participants at the collaborative environmental governance table depend on where they sit. Scientists, stakeholders, and leaders face distinct challenges. A key challenge for scientists engaged in collaborative environmental governance stems from a desire for their scientific conclusions to be taken seriously by policy makers and managers, to inform policies and actions. Collaborative efforts draw on science but must include other considerations in order to be successful. Thus we need to better understand what factors affect how and how much scientific conclusions are incorporated into practice. Does collaborative governance tend to increase or decrease the role of science in policy making and management, compared to other approaches? The role of science and expert

Table 3.1 Three research streams converging on collaborative environmental governance

Key component	Ecosystem management	Community-based collaborative environmental management	Collaborative public management
Primary goal	Ecological integrity	Sustainable human and natural systems	Address public problems no single agency can adequately address
Privileged source of knowledge	Mainly natural science	Science + local knowledge	Managerial expertise
Use of knowledge	Adaptation and learning	Adaptation and learning	Problem solving
Ontology	Integrated human and ecological systems; must work across ecosystem and jurisdiction boundaries	Integrated human and ecological systems; must work across ecosystem and societal boundaries	Networks; must work across jurisdictional boundaries
Role of stakeholders	Managers are constrained by stakeholders	Stakeholder engagement is key for solutions	Stakeholder engagement is key for solutions
Role of central government	Retains decision making authority	Not necessarily the decision authority	Steers others to achieve public goals
Decision making	Mainly government and scientists decide, within societal constraints	Consensus oriented and deliberative	Consensus oriented and deliberative

knowledge is a key theme running throughout fields of collaborative environmental management scholarship, yet it has been little studied. For example, studies of collaborative environmental partnerships have examined the role of scale, noting that science is more privileged at larger scales (Heikkila and Gerlak, 2005), but we do not know how scientific research agendas and results might affect collaborative processes and outputs, and how this may differ by context (Massaua et al., forthcoming).

A key challenge for stakeholder participants in collaborative environmental governance comes from a desire to have their voices heard by others and their preferences taken into account. Collaborative efforts are just one type of forum in which citizens of a democracy can seek a voice. The challenge of participation is to address issues of representation and equity. Moreover, if participation is to play a constructive role in society, we need to understand the conditions under which collaboration fosters social learning and community building for participants. A related challenge is understanding how partnerships decide which activities to pursue, whom to include, and how to structure their work.

A key challenge for leaders of collaborative partnerships is how to energize participants, manage discussions, generate actionable plans, and follow through to solve problems. Advice for these leaders is never scarce, but empirical evidence supporting it may be lacking (e.g., Ohio Forestry Association, 1955). Such advice may be based on intuition, experience, or collected "lessons learned," and its utility depends on the degree to which it is applicable in new situations that differ from those from which it is derived. It is here that social scientists can play a critical role in developing understanding of complex interactions in different settings. An applied social science study can provide a theoretical underpinning that explains causal mechanisms as well as the range of settings over which the causal mechanisms of collaborative environmental governance are expected to work. Prior studies in this vein point to two key areas ripe for future inquiry: (1) what kinds of plans and recommendations do partnerships produce and what factors affect implementation of their recommendations; and (2) what kinds of ecological outcomes does collaborative governance generate under which circumstances?

Finally, there is the broad challenge of scaling up to address the pressing, international- or global-scale environmental challenges facing humanity. If nonpoint source pollution poses a lack of authoritative commanding force at smaller scales, then surely this problem is even greater at larger scales. The United Nations has neither authority nor resources to force compliance with its policies; rather it relies on powers of persuasion, norms, and resource provision to steer action in member nations. Can collaborative approaches yield success in combating global climate change or ocean resource depletion?

CONCLUSION

This journey through the conceptual development of collaborative environmental governance has made it clear that scholars often work in parallel worlds, even when writing on similar topics. As much as we might like clear narrative arcs, there are few clean temporal breaks in lines of inquiry. Inherently interdisciplinary topics such as this are difficult to grab hold of, as studies and experiences are shared across many outlets, often using different terms for the same phenomenon. Such is the messy, evolving, complexifying world of social science.

Collaborative environmental governance has long held a dual attraction, for both practitioners and theoreticians. This duality has led to fertile grounds for scholars interested in applied theory, with opportunities to propose and test ideas about how to be successful in collaborative governance. At the same time it has raised fundamental questions about what it means to live in a democracy; build divergent viewpoints into broad consensus; blend scientific and local knowledge; manage across physical, political, and community boundaries; and live sustainably within the limits of our resources even as we seek to extend them with human ingenuity. It is not surprising that key fields of study engaging in such inquiry include those with a rich tradition of applied theory across diverse fields: ecosystem management (rooted in ecology), community-based collaborative environmental management (rooted in political science and economics), and collaborative public management (rooted in public administration and public management).

The story, as I've told it, highlights some common themes around these three loosely organized fields of study. Each features research that, first, has focused on describing and documenting a new (or perceived to be new) phenomenon. Early scholars have described key dimensions or characteristics of the phenomenon, contrasting it with what came before (often as an advocate for the phenomenon), and providing examples of the phenomenon across diverse settings. In the process they have used different terms to describe similar concepts, making it harder to compare across cases. As interest in the topic has continued, scholars and practitioners have sought lessons learned for how to make the phenomenon effective, which often highlights measurement challenges. Theoretically, there is interest in developing typologies to find patterns across diverse cases, and these typologies can be used to provide empirical evidence for understanding what factors foster effective outcomes, thus adding rigor and systematization to loose collections of lessons learned. Further development has assembled variables into theoretical frameworks and investigated combinations of variables interacting in causal mechanisms.

As in all areas of knowledge, the more we uncover about collaborative environmental governance, the more puzzles we see lying before us. The current state of knowledge points to several key areas for future research, including the role of science and expert knowledge, stakeholder representation and action within collaborative processes, implementation of collaborative plans, causal mechanisms linking processes and outputs to implementation and the end outcomes of ecological conditions, and possibilities of scaling up international- and global-level environmental problems. Each of these research areas represents a host of challenges posed by collaborative environmental management. As scholarship continues to expand, we may find that it circles back to the earlier motivating questions of interest to both theoreticians and practitioners: How can we include multiple stakeholders in designing and carrying out actions that address pressing environmental problems? In other words, how to "join in new understanding" by a "unity of purpose" for a "better way of life in the watersheds [and other ecosystems] of this land" (Ohio Forestry Association, 1955).

REFERENCES

Agranoff, R. (2003). *Leveraging networks: A guide for public managers working across organizations*. IBM Endowment for the Business of Government.

Agranoff, R. (2007). *Managing within networks: Adding value to public organizations*. Washington, DC: Georgetown University Press.

Agranoff, R., and McGuire, M. (2003). *Collaborative public management*. Washington, DC: Georgetown University Press.

Ansell, C., and Gash, A. (2008). Collaborative governance in theory and practice. *Journal of Public Administration Research and Theory* 18(4), 543–571.

Bardach, E. (1998). *Getting agencies to work together: The practice and theory of managerial craftsmanship*. Washington, DC: Brookings.

Bernard, T., and Young, J. (1997). *The ecology of hope: Communities collaborate for sustainability*. Gabriola Island, BC: New Society.

Biddle, J.C., and Koontz, T.M. (2014). Goal specificity: A proxy measure for improvements in environmental outcomes in collaborative governance. *Journal of Environmental Management* 145, 268–276.

Bidwell, R.D., and Ryan, C.M. (2006). Collaborative partnership design: The implications of organizational affiliation for watershed partnerships. *Society and Natural Resources* 19(9), 827–842.

Bingham, L.B., and O'Leary, R. (eds.). (2008). *Big ideas in collaborative public management*. Armonk, NY: M.E. Sharpe.

Born, S.M., and Genskow, K.D. (2000). *The watershed approach: An empirical assessment of innovation in environmental management*. Washington, DC: National Academy of Public Administration, Research Paper Number 7.

Boyte, H.C. (2011). Constructive politics as public work organizing the literature. *Political Theory* 39(5), 630–660.

Breckler, M. (2006). The evolving face of ecosystem management. B.S. Honors Thesis, The Ohio State University School of Environment and Natural Resources, Columbus, OH.

Brody, S.D. (2003). Measuring the effects of stakeholder participation on the

quality of local plans based on the principles of collaborative ecosystem management. *Journal of Planning Education and Research* 22(4), 407–419.
Brunner, R.D. (2002). Problems of governance. In Ronald D. Brunner, Christine H. Colburn, Christina M. Cromley, Roberta A. Klein, and Elizabeth A. Olson (eds.), *Finding common ground: Governance and natural resources in the American West* (pp. 1–47). New Haven, CT: Yale University Press.
Bryson, J.M., Crosby, B.C., and Bloomberg, L. (2014). Public value governance: Moving beyond traditional public administration and the new public management. *Public Administration Review* 74(4), 445–456.
Butler, K., and Koontz, T.M. (2005). Theory into practice: Implementing ecosystem management objectives in the USDA Forest Service. *Environmental Management* 35(2), 138–150.
Cheng, A.S., and Daniels, S.E. (2005). Getting to the 'we': examining the relationship between geographic scale and ingroup emergence in collaborative watershed planning. *Human Ecology Review* 12(1), 30–43.
Chess, C., Hance, B.J., and Gibson, G. (2000). Adaptive participation in watershed management. *Journal of Soil and Water Conservation* Third Quarter, 248–252.
Coase, R.H. (1960). The problem of social cost. *Journal of Law & Economics* 3, 1–44.
Conley, A., and Moote, A. (2003). Evaluating collaborative natural resource management. *Society and Natural Resources* 16, 371–386.
Connick, S., and Innes, J. (2003). Outcomes of collaborative water policy making: Applying complexity thinking to evaluation. *Journal of Environmental Planning and Management* 46(2), 177–197.
Cortner, H.J., and Moote, M.A. (1999). *The politics of ecosystem management*. Washington, DC: Island Press.
Cortner, H.J., Wallace, M.G., Burke, S., and Moote, M.A. (1998). Institutions matter: the need to address the institutional challenges of ecosystem management. *Landscape and Urban Planning* 40(1), 159–166.
Costanza, R. (ed.). (1991). *Ecological economics: The science and management of sustainability*. New York: Columbia University Press.
Crossley, J.W. (1996). Managing ecosystems for integrity: Theoretical considerations for resource and environmental managers. *Society and Natural Resources* 9, 465–481.
Emerson, K., Nabatchi, T., and Balogh, S. (2012). An integrative framework for collaborative governance. *Journal of Public Administration Research and Theory* 22(1), 1–29.
Endter-Wada, J., Blahna, D., Krannich, R., and Brunson, M. (1998). A framework for understanding social science contributions to ecosystem management. *Ecological Applications* 8(3), 891–904.
Goldsmith, S., and Eggers, W.D. (2004). *Governing by network: The new shape of the public sector*. Washington, DC: Brookings Institution Press.
Gray, B. (1989). *Collaborating: Finding common ground for multiparty problems*. San Francisco, CA: Jossey-Bass.
Grumbine, R.E. (1994). What is ecosystem management? *Conservation Biology* 8(1), 27–38.
Hardin, G. (1968). The tragedy of the commons. *Science* 162(3859), 1243–1248.
Heikkila, T., and Gerlak, A.K. (2005). The formation of large-scale collaborative resource management institutions: Clarifying the roles of stakeholders, science, and institutions. *Policy Studies Journal* 33, 583–612.

Hibbard, M., and Lurie, S. (2006). Some community socio-economic benefits of watershed councils: A case study from Oregon. *Journal of Environmental Planning and Management* 49(6), 891–908.
Hill, R., Davies, J., Bohnet, I.C., Robinson, C.J., Maclean, K., and Pert, P.L. (2015). Collaboration mobilises institutions with scale-dependent comparative advantage in landscape-scale biodiversity conservation. *Environmental Science & Policy* 51, 267–277.
Hobbs, R.J., Davis, M.A., Slobodkin, L.B., Lackey, R.T., Halvorson, W., and Throop, W. (2004). Restoration ecology: The challenge of social values and expectations. *Frontiers in Ecology and the Environment* 2, 43–48.
Holling, C.S., and Bocking, S. (1991). Surprise and opportunity: In evolution, in ecosystems, in society. In C. Mungall and D.L. McLaren (eds.), *Planet under stress: The challenge of global change* (pp. 285–300). Toronto: Oxford University Press.
Imperial, M. (1999). Institutional analysis and ecosystem-based management: The Institutional Analysis and Development Framework. *Environmental Management* 24(4), 449–465.
Innes, J.E. (1996). Planning through consensus building: A new view of the comprehensive planning ideal. *American Planning Association Journal* 62(4), 460–472.
Innes, J.E., and Booher, D.E. (1999). Consensus building and complex adaptive systems: A framework for evaluating collaborative planning. *Journal of the American Planning Association* 65(4), 412–423.
Innes, J.E., and Booher, D.E. (2010). *Planning with complexity: An introduction to collaborative rationality for public policy*. London: Routledge.
Jackson, S., Pollino, C., Maclean, K., Bark, R., and Moggridge, B. (2015). Meeting indigenous peoples' objectives in environmental flow assessments: Case studies from an Australian multi-jurisdictional water sharing initiative. *Journal of Hydrology* 522, 141–151.
Keast, R., Mandell, M.P., Brown, K., and Wolcock, G.W. (2004). Network structures: Working differently and changing expectations. *Public Administration Review* 64(3), 363–371.
Kellogg, W.A. (1998). Adopting an ecosystem approach: Local variability in remedial action planning. *Society and Natural Resources* 11, 465–483.
Kemmis, D. (1990). *Community and the politics of place*. Norman, OK: University of Oklahoma Press.
Kenney, D.S. (1997). *Resource management at the watershed level: An assessment of the changing federal role in the emerging era of community-based watershed management*. Report to the Western Water Policy Review Advisory Commission. Boulder, CO: Natural Resources Law Center, University of Colorado School of Law.
Kenney, D.S. (2001). Are community watershed groups effective? Confronting the thorny issue of measuring success. In Philip Brick, Donald Snow, and Sarah Van De Wetering (eds.), *Across the Great Divide: Explorations in collaborative conservation and the American West* (pp. 188–193). Washington, DC: Island Press.
Keough, H.L., and Blahna, D.J. (2006). Achieving integrative, collaborative ecosystem management. *Conservation Biology* 20(5), 1373–1382.
Koebele, E.A. (2015). Assessing outputs, outcomes, and barriers in collaborative water governance: A case study. *Journal of Contemporary Water Research & Education* 155(1), 63–72.

Koehler, B., and Koontz, T.M. (2008). Citizen participation in collaborative watershed partnerships. *Environmental Management* 41(2), 143–154.
Koontz, T.M. (2003). The farmer, the planner, and the local citizen in the dell: How collaborative groups plan for farmland preservation. *Landscape and Urban Planning* 66(1), 19–34.
Koontz, T.M. (2005). We finished the plan, so now what? Impacts of collaborative stakeholder participation on land use policy. *Policy Studies Journal* 33(3), 459–481.
Koontz, T.M., and Bodine, J. (2008). Implementing ecosystem management in public agencies: Lessons from the U.S. Bureau of Land Management and the Forest Service. *Conservation Biology* 22(1), 60–69.
Koontz, T.M., and Moore Johnson, E. (2004). One size does not fit all: Matching breadth of citizen participation to watershed group accomplishments. *Policy Sciences* 37(2), 185–204.
Koontz, T.M., and Newig, J. (2014). From planning to implementation: Top down and bottom up approaches for collaborative watershed management. *Policy Studies Journal* 42(3), 416–442.
Koontz, T.M., and Thomas, C.W. (2006). What do we know and need to know about the environmental outcomes of collaborative management? *Public Administration Review* 66 (supp.), 111–121.
Koontz, T.M., Steelman, T.A., Carmin, J., Korfmacher, K.S., Moseley, C., and Thomas, C.W. (2004). *Collaborative environmental management: What roles for government?* Washington, DC: Resources for the Future Press.
Kouw, M. (2014). Designing communication: Politics and practices of participatory water quality governance. *International Journal of Water Governance* 4, 37–52.
Larson, K.L., and Lach, D. (2008). Participants and non-participants of place-based groups: An assessment of attitudes and implications for public participation in water resource management. *Journal of Environmental Management* 88, 817–830.
Leach, W.D., and Pelkey, N.W. (2001). Making watershed partnerships work: A review of the empirical literature. *Journal of Water Resources Planning and Management* 127(6), 378–385.
Leach, W.D., and Sabatier, P.A. (2003). Facilitators, coordinators, and outcomes. In R. O'Leary, and L.B. Bingham (eds.), *The promise and performance of environmental conflict resolution* (pp. 148–171). Washington, DC: Resources for the Future.
Leach, W.D., and Sabatier, P.A. (2005). Are trust and social capital the keys to success? Watershed partnerships in California and Washington. In Paul A. Sabatier, Will Focht, Mark Lubell, Zev Trachtenberg, Arnold Vedlitz, and Marty Matlock (eds.), *Swimming upstream: collaborative approaches to watershed management* (pp. 233–258). Cambridge, MA: The MIT Press.
Lee, K.N. (1994). *Compass and gyroscope: integrating science and politics for the environment*. Washington, DC: Island Press.
Leopold, A. 1949 (1970). *A Sand County Almanac*. New York: Ballantine.
Lubell, M., Schneider, M., Scholz, J.T., and Mete, M. (2002). Watershed partnerships and the emergence of collective action institutions. *American Journal of Political Science* 46(1), 148–163.
Malone, C.R. (2000). Ecosystem management policies in state government of the USA. *Landscape and Urban Planning* 48, 57–64.
Mandarano, L.A. (2008). Evaluating collaborative environmental planning outputs

and outcomes: Restoring and protecting habitat and the New York-New Jersey harbor estuary program. *Journal of Planning Education and Research* 27, 456–468.

Mandell, M., and Steelman, T. (2003). Understanding what can be accomplished through interorganizational innovations: The importance of typologies, context and management strategies. *Public Management Review* 5(2), 197–224.

Margerum, R.D. (2008). A typology of collaboration efforts in environmental management. *Environmental Management* 41(4), 487–500.

Margerum, R.D. (2011). *Beyond consensus: improving collaborative planning and management*. Boston, MA: The MIT Press.

Marston, E. (2001). The Quincy Library Group: A divisive attempt at peace. In Philip Brick, Donald Snow, and Sarah Van de Wetering (eds.), *Across the great divide: Explorations in collaborative conservation and the American West* (pp. 79–90). Washington, DC: Island Press.

Massaua, M.J., Thomas, C.W., and Klinger, T. (forthcoming). The use of science in collaborative management of marine environments. *Coastal Management*.

Matthews, N., and Schmidt, J. (2014). False promises: The contours, contexts and contestation of good water governance in Lao PDR and Alberta, Canada. *International Journal of Water Governance* 2(3), DOI: 10.7564/14-IJWG61.

McGinnis, M.D. (ed.). (1999). *Polycentricity and local public economies: Readings from the Workshop in Political Theory and Policy Analysis*. Ann Arbor, MI: University of Michigan Press.

Meyer, S.M., and Konisky, D.M. (2007). Local institutions and environmental outcomes: Evidence from wetlands protection in Massachusetts. *Policy Studies Journal* 35(3), 481–502.

Milward, H.B., and Provan, K.G. (2000). Governing the hollow state. *Journal of Public Administration Research and Theory* 10(2), 359–380.

Milward, H.B., Provan, K.G., and Else, B.A. (1993). *What does the hollow state look like? Public management: The state of the art* (pp. 309–332). San Francisco, CA: Jossey-Bass.

Mooney, C., and Tan, P.L. (2012). South Australia's River Murray: social and cultural values in water planning. *Journal of Hydrology* 474, 29–37.

Moore, E.A., and Koontz, T.M. (2003). A typology of collaborative watershed groups: citizen-based, agency-based, and mixed partnerships. *Society and Natural Resources* 16(5), 451–460.

Moote, A. (1995). *Partnership handbook: A resource and guidebook for local community-based groups addressing natural resource, land use, or environmental issues*. Report, Water Resources Research Center, College of Agriculture, University of Arizona, Tucson.

Mullen, M.W., and Allison, B.E. (1999). Stakeholder involvement and social capital: Keys to watershed management success in Alabama. *Journal of the American Water Resources Association* 35(3), 655–662.

Nikolic, S. (2005). Impacts of state involvement on community-based collaborative watershed management. Unpublished Master's thesis. Columbus, OH: The Ohio State University.

Noss, R., and Cooperrider, A. (1994). *Saving nature's legacy: Protecting and restoring biodiversity*. Washington, DC: Island Press and Defenders of Wildlife.

Ohio Forestry Association. (1955). *How to develop watersheds*. Columbus, OH: Ohio Forestry Association.

O'Leary, R., Gerard, C., and Bingham, L.B. (eds.). (2006). Introduction to the symposium on collaborative public management. *Public Administration Review* 66(S1), 6–9.

Olson, E.A. (2002). Water management and the Upper Clark Fork Steering Committee. In Ronald D. Brunner, Christine H. Colburn, Christina M. Cromley, Roberta A. Klein, and Elizabeth A. Olson (eds.), *Finding common ground: Governance and natural resources in the American West* (pp. 48–87). New Haven, CT: Yale University Press.

Olsson, P., Folke, C., and Hughes, T.P. (2008). Navigating the transition to ecosystem-based management of the Great Barrier Reef, Australia. *Proceedings of the National Academy of Sciences* 105(28), 9489–9494.

Ostrom, E. (1990). *Governing the commons: The evolution of institutions for collective action*. Cambridge: Cambridge University Press.

O'Toole, Jr., L.J., Meier, K.J., and Nicholson-Crotty, S. (2005). Managing upward, downward and outward: Networks, hierarchical relationships and performance. *Public Management Review* 7(1), 45–68.

Powell, J.W. (1879). *Report on the lands of the arid region of the United States with a more detailed account of the land of Utah with maps*. U.S. Geographical and Geological Survey of the Rocky Mountain Region. Washington, DC: Government Printing Office.

Predmore, S.A., Copenheaver, C.A., and Mortimer, M.J. (2008). Ecosystem management in the US Forest Service: A persistent process but dying discourse. *Journal of Forestry* 106(6), 339–345.

Primack, R.B. (1993). *Essentials of conservation biology*. Sunderland, MA: Sinauer Associates.

Prokopy, L.S., Mullendore, N., Brasier, K., and Floress, K. (2014). A typology of catalyst events for collaborative watershed management in the United States. *Society & Natural Resources* 27(11), 1177–1191.

Raedeke, A.H., Nilon, C.H., and Rikoon, J.S. (2001). Factors affecting landowner participation in ecosystem management: a case study in south-central Missouri. *Wildlife Society Bulletin*, 195–206.

Randhir, T., and Shriver, D.M. (2009). Deliberative valuation without prices: A multiattribute prioritization for watershed ecosystem management. *Ecological Economics* 68(12), 3042–3051.

Renn, O., Webler, T., and Wiedemann, P. (eds.). (1995). *Fairness and competence in citizen participation: Evaluating models for environmental discourse*. Dordrecht, Netherlands: Kluwer Academic Publishers.

Rhodes, R.A.W. (1996). The new governance: governing without government. *Political Studies* 44(4), 652–667.

Rigg, C. (2001). Orchestrating ecosystem management: Challenges and lessons from Sequoia National Forest. *Conservation Biology* 15(1), 78–90.

Robinson, C.J., Margerum, R.D., Koontz, T.M., Moseley, C., and Lurie, S. (2011). Policy-level collaboratives for environmental management at the regional scale: Lessons and challenges from Australia and the United States. *Society & Natural Resources* 24(8), 849–859.

Sabatier, P.A., Weible, C., and Ficker, J. (2005a). Eras of water management in the United States: Implications for collaborative watershed approaches. In Paul A. Sabatier, Will Focht, Mark Lubell, Zev Trachtenberg, Arnold Vedlitz, and Marty Matlock (eds.), *Swimming upstream: collaborative approaches to watershed management* (pp. 23–52). Cambridge, MA: The MIT Press.

Sabatier, P.A., Focht, W., Lubell, M., Trachtenberg, Z., Vedlitz, A., and Matlock, M. (eds.). (2005b). *Swimming upstream: Collaborative approaches to watershed management*. Cambridge, MA: The MIT Press.

Salamon, L.M. (1981). Rethinking public management: Third-party government and the changing forms of government action. *Public Policy* 29(3), 255–275.

Samuelson, C.D., Vedlitz, A., Whitten, G.D., Matlock, M., Alston, L.T., Peterson, T.R., and Gilbertz, S.J. (2005). Citizen participation and representation in collaborative engagement processes. In Paul A. Sabatier, Will Focht, Mark Lubell, Zev Trachtenberg, Arnold Vedlitz, and Marty Matlock (eds.), *Swimming upstream: collaborative approaches to watershed management* (pp. 137–169). Cambridge, MA: The MIT Press.

Scott, T. (2015). Does collaboration make any difference? Linking collaborative governance to environmental outcomes. *Journal of Policy Analysis and Management*. DOI: 10.1002/pam.21836.

Shafer, C.L. (2001). Conservation biology trailblazers: George Wright, Ben Thompson, and Joseph Dixon. *Conservation Biology* 15(2), 332–344.

Shelford, V.E. (1933). Ecological Society of America: A nature sanctuary plan unanimously adopted by the Society. *Ecology* 14(2), 240–245.

Shindler, B., and Neburka, J. (1997). Public participation in forest planning: 8 attributes of success. *Journal of Forestry* 95(1), 17–19.

Smith, P.D., McDonough, M.H., and Mang, M.T. (1999). Ecosystem management and public participation: Lessons from the field. *Journal of Forestry* 97(10), 32–38.

Snow, D. (2001). Coming home: An introduction to collaborative conservation. In Philip Brick, Donald Snow, and Sarah Van de Wetering (eds.), *Across the great divide: Explorations in collaborative conservation and the American West* (pp. 1–11). Washington, DC: Island Press.

Stedman, R., Lee, B., Brasier, K., Weigle, J.L., and Higdon, F. (2009). Cleaning up water? Or building rural community? Community watershed organizations in Pennsylvania. *Rural Sociology* 74(2), 178–200.

Steelman, T.A., and Carmin, J. (2002). Community based watershed remediation: Connecting organizational resources to social and substantive outcomes. In Diane Rahm (ed.), *Toxic waste and environmental policy in the 21st century United States*. Jefferson, NC: McFarland Publishers.

Stoker, G. (1998). Governance as theory: Five propositions. *International Social Science Journal* 50(155), 17–28.

Thomas, C.W. (1999). Linking public agencies with community-based watershed organizations: Lessons from California. *Policy Studies Journal* 27(3), 544–564.

Ulibarri, N. (2015). Tracing process to performance of collaborative governance: A comparative case study of federal hydropower licensing. *Policy Studies Journal* 43(2), 283–308.

United States Environmental Protection Agency. (1997). *Community-based environmental protection: A resource book for protecting ecosystems and communities*. Washington, DC: U.S. Environmental Protection Agency.

Vangen, S., and Huxham, C. (2003). Nurturing collaborative relations: Building trust in interorganizational collaboration. *Journal of Applied Behavioral Science* 39(1), 5–31.

Watson, N. (2015). Adaptation through collaboration: Evaluating the emergence of institutional arrangements for collaborative catchment management and governance in England. *International Journal of Water Governance* 3(3). DOI: 10.7564/13-IJWG26.

Weber, E.P. (1998). *Pluralism by the rules: Conflict and cooperation in environmental regulation*. Washington, DC: Georgetown University Press.

Williams, P. (2002). The competent boundary spanner. *Public Administration* 80(1), 103–124.

Wondolleck, J.M., and Yaffee, S.L. (2000). *Making collaboration work: Lessons from innovation in natural resource management*. Washington, DC: Island Press.

Yaffee, S.L., Phillips, A.F., Frentz, I.C., Hardy, P.W., Maleki, S.M., and Thorpe, B.E. (1996). *Ecosystem management in the United States: An assessment of current experience*. Washington, DC: Island Press.

4. The other side of managing in networks

Robert Agranoff

Policy and administration in this dispersed power world has highlighted the importance of collaboration and multiparty implementation, particularly through organized networking and networks. Today's public programs, for example in environmental management and in programming for the disabled, require the interactive involvement of multiple levels of government plus non-profit and for-profit nongovernmental organizations (NGOs), along with increasing doses of citizen and client-based involvement. This overlapping authority and shared involvement at the operational level is an inevitable product of the multiprogram complexity of the real world in the 21st century (Agranoff and Radin 2015). At the operational level programming is increasingly external as well as internal, conductive in nature, which is an emergent field of analysis that is "celebrated" as the latest wave in management for success (e.g., Saint-Onge and Armstrong 2004; O'Leary and Bingham 2009; Vandeventer and Mandell 2007; Agranoff 2012). However, central collaborative management and networking has become the "mantra" for solving any and all program and policy problems brought on by the challenges of increased complexity; collaboration and network governance also have notable "downsides" that pose potential managerial barriers to effective joint action. These concerns are equally important for understanding and practice. In program management these issues must also be raised in this emerging shared power world, particularly in the growing number of multiorganizational process management contexts.

It is also important to bear in mind that however networks and networking are considered by many to be key to this form of collaboration in governance, they are not the "only games in town." In practice, collaboration encompasses the process of facilitating and operating in multiorganizational arrangements to solve problems that are not to be solved, or solved easily, by single organizations (Agranoff and McGuire 2003: 4). In effect this type of joined activity goes beyond consultation or cooperation to joint *activity* of some sort, either by formal or informal means

(Margerum 2011). Whereas one immediately encompasses the idea of networks or networking as the core tools of collaboration (indeed, one book on contracting bears "network" in its title but is not in the content) there are many interactive forms, ranging from practices that involve minimal management and intermittent interaction to those that maximize and regularize such interaction (Agranoff 2012: 14). Multiple practices show that in this larger scheme of collaborative activity, networks of different types represent just a small number of collaborative action practices. But they are among the most involved. Of the array of the various collaborative enterprises, networks involve highly structured interactions, and greater organizational commitment, in as much as "Networks are structures of interdependence involving multiple organizations or parts thereof, where one unit is not merely the formal subordinate of the others in some degree of hierarchical arrangements" (O'Toole 1997: 45; 2015: 361). Most other linking activities normally are not as involved as are the network structures in governance.

Concern for managing within networks and by other means of collaboration stems from the growing complexity and interdependence that has transformed public programs over the past several decades. One important contributor is the growth of intergovernmental programs. In the U.S., federal financing and regulatory programs now reach "down" deeply into state and local governments for co-design and implementation. Moreover, operations by NGOs or by joint programming brings added managerial demands. For example, one program studied by the author involves federal financing and program authorization, state program design, and extensive NGO operations by literally hundreds of programs in each state under contractual arrangements. Indeed this Medicaid Home and Community-Based Services Waiver (of federal requirements) reaches not only from federal-state to NGO but to Intellectually/Developmentally Disabled I/DD families and clients as self-advocates (Agranoff 2013). The multiplicity of programs like this are also in the environmental and other program areas, which brings on the need for collaboration and networking. As a result, the complexity-generated interactions address solutions that accelerate interdependence. To network in this chapter refers to one of the most involved aspects of interorganizational contact, beyond informal and serendipitous actions connecting agencies, programs and interests in structured, regular and usually formal ways.

Concern for real-world parameters around network management began with earlier work by the author and Michael McGuire (McGuire and Agranoff 2010, 2011). The first work involves a distinctly American context, "Networking in the Shadow of Bureaucracy," where we demonstrate that networks are influential but have not become entities that replace or fully hollow out government agencies. They can be core steering actors in policy and management in a shared power world. Networks work with governments, overlaying hierarchies, which normally retain ultimate legal authority, particularly in situations where many bureaucratic actions continue doing the routine work of organizations. There is, however, increased "boundary spanning," particularly for the few who are responsible for the growing number of extra organization linkages. Second, in "The Limitations of Public Management Networks," we take a more cross-national view, identifying from the literature that networks can often find reasonable solutions and approaches, but then run into operational, performance or legal barriers, as difficulties emerge in connecting these multiorganizational agreements into policy and programming energy, or that mission drift or simply failure to implement agreements are part of the realities of public life in a complex world.

This chapter aims to extend the direction of limits on networks as a form of collaborative management by looking deeper into their internal operational process. Hopefully, it will extend the dialogue on the more limiting aspects of networking, perhaps improving practice as a result. Early in the systematic assessment of interagency collaboration Barbara Gray (1989: 247–255) identified a number of interorganization collaborative disincentives, including networks, such as experiential and ideological preventive theories, technical shortcomings and increasing complexity, power disparities, cultural norms that emphasize individualism, differing perceptions of risk, and getting public agencies to understand and come to grips with the need for working together. These appeared to emerge as core obstacles. It is time to go deeper into some of these operational challenges, going beyond the usual heralding the importance of "shared aims" leading to "working together" to look inside network operations and how they might provide barriers (Agranoff 2007: 56).

Of particular concern the following network management issues are identified: along with mission incompatibility public agency mission versus the quest for a collaborative mission, network mission incompatibility, the pervasiveness of power or "big P" political configurations that thwart collaboration, agency and community or "small p" agency politics (e.g., without regard to political party), power differentials within network understandings, the phenomenon of process fatigue, including process barriers (e.g., incompatible data bases, planning versus doing), the realities of local operation or program implementation (operational localism) that take joint effort a long way from either policy or broad agreement, and lack of inertia or relevance to monitor and engage in related process improvements, that is continuous improvement practices. Whereas these are not the only network management barriers, they will make for a more sobering look at what happens "inside the process box."

UNDERSTANDING/MISUNDERSTANDING AGENCY MISSION

When agents of NGOs and government agencies come together to work collaboratively, a first premise is to clearly understand the mission of each organization. Process breakdown hinges or is at risk unless the parties have some clear understanding what each potential or actual organization is all about and how they might be compatible or incompatible in the network.

First and foremost in the public sphere is for parties to come to grips with the core or lead role that government agencies normally play. An excellent overview of all of the potential roles that government agencies play in environmental management, e.g., as provider of a variety of human, technical and financial resources is provided by Koontz et al. (2004: 170). Foremost is the "sweeping influence that governmental institutions do leave their mark on how issues are defined, what resources are used or are available, the structure of collaborative process, and the outcomes that these endeavors produce." Most involved actors conclude with the institutional provisions in statutes and regulations in as much as few groups rarely are given wide open "policy authority." Another study involving governance involves the California-based water quality network CALFED and demonstrates the inherent or uneasy coexistence of informal approaches in networking that are interdependent yet are often in tension. While the CALFED network's informal systems were able to move forward on several fronts, "the formal system retained the funding, the legal authority, and the perspective to intervene, provide approval, or simply allow the program to continue" (Innes et al. 2007: 170). Thus, while government actors are tied to the agencies they represent and enforce standards, regulations and guidelines, they also have the opportunity to act in ways that can foster network mission. But agencies do not always do this, resisting the advocacy of others, or at least fail to confirm problems and certain issues, thus blocking meaningful joint efforts. "The roles governmental actors played and their influence in determining group structure and decision-making processes suggest that these individuals largely determine the character of the collaboration" (ibid.: 171; see also Wondolleck and Yaffee 2000: 244).

A related note on the daunting challenges in dealing with government is failure to understand that policy and program decisions involve communities governed by decision-making bodies (e.g., city, councils, county commissions, metropolitan planning organizations, natural resources-management districts, etc.). In a study of "interactive governance" in five Dutch municipalities, Jurian Edelenbos (2005) found that such projects tend to overlook the involvement and participation of affected local decision-makers. Process overviews for council members included such summary descriptions as "mostly ritual coordination," "politicians at a distance from the interactive process," "attention to process more than policy content," "no links with the administrative system" and "politicians remained at a distance" (127). As a result, scant attention was paid to existing institutions, conflicting with the usual deliberative democracy that goes on in these venues. He concludes that in this new form of institutionalized action collaborative endeavors must be in line with existing decision points or a missing institutional link between the interactive process and the formal decision-making process arises. To not engage such links in a collaborative process like network operations becomes a high risk endeavor when core decision-makers are, in effect, out of the process.

The network process also must come to grips with important statutory-based rules that potentially impede serious attempts that go beyond mere coordination. In the arena of services for the intellectually and developmentally disabled in the U.S., the Medicaid (medical payments for low-income persons) program since the early 1980s has included a Home and Community Based Services (HCBS) waiver program to serve eligible clients who would otherwise be institutionalized. HCBS is a federal-state program that allows for purchases of a wide array of externally delivered services, most through NGOs. HCBS once proscribed payment for room and board, prohibiting other services and later adding them (e.g., day hospitalization, ventilator dependent services). Most significant was the "cold bed rule," which required states to reduce institutional beds on an equal ratio basis to those of new HCBS clients, which was ultimately eliminated. The last substantial change, adopted in 2011, was that previously prohibited family home care providers could be reimbursed under certain circumstances. Each of these rules at some point provides parameters guiding the rules of states with regard to HCBS and thus frames certain core aspects of how any network can operate.

In the environmental arena the EPA promulgated new rules in 2012 mandating that CO_2 levels fall below 2005 amounts by 2030, placing new constraints on the states. They are being challenged before federal courts by some state agencies while others are writing their own standards. Whichever route is taken, a great deal of federal-state collaboration will be necessary to meet agreed targets. In the end the process will no doubt respect the rules in some form (Kardish 2014: 48). At some point in the collaborative process rules are agreed to and the stakeholders involved must live by those rules, particularly when the regulated have been involved in any cooperative processes that led to rule adjustments (Weber 1998).

Agency building, the practice of leaders enhancing the territory for their public organization, can be regarded as either a positive or negative force in network building and operating. On the positive side, the EPA has worked in a number of areas to reduce uncertainty and build trust in its rule-making. Edward Weber (1998: 129) describes the efforts of its assistant administrator for clean air:

> During the legislative battles over clean air Rosenberg had earned a reputation as "an obsessive strategist, balancing the demands of environmentalists against the realities of a cost-conscious White House. He was . . . an entrepreneur . . . in perpetual search of clean air deals . . . In meeting after meeting . . . he looked for the sweet spot of compromise: what it would take to fix the problem" and bridge the gap among competing interests. Finally, Rosenberg's reputation as "the pit bull of clean air" earned him the respect of his EPA staff and key leaders of the national environmental lobby, while his business background and clear concern for cost effectiveness offered assurance to industry.

Such actions are not always so positive and thus can't always be counted on. Particularly because many agency managers are protective of their turf. Craig Thomas's (2003) study of interagency cooperation in biodiversity defined agency turf as protection of one's own territory or domain. Turf imperialism can be an impediment to cooperation. Often from the manager's perspective more turf is better (Bardach 1998: 177). Thomas observes that in biodiversity efforts "line managers often are convinced that they know best, and therefore, should decide on how to carry out agency tasks, develop programs, and achieve agency missions" (35). Turf protection has proved relevant as one "downside" of the collaborative coin.

Somewhere between turf protection and building the multi-stakeholder process is the "reconstitution" of government agencies for network management. This is not always an easy task, as Daniel Carpenter's (2001: 4) historical study reveals. Bureaucratic autonomy is defined as taking actions consistent with administrators' own wishes, to which politicians and organized interests defer. Carpenter maintains that autonomy prevails when agencies can establish political legitimacy, comprised of a reputation for expertise, efficiency and moral protection. Under these conditions, politicians grant administrators licenses as they defer to the wishes of the agency. Cross-case research by Thomas Koontz and associates (2004: 160–161) found that governments' leadership position can be at the core of network activity, helping participants to be innovative, providing information, securing resources or carrying forward implementation plans. On the downside, so to speak, constraining factors include agency structures designed to support more traditional approaches that lack high-level government forums or mandates to cooperate or otherwise work together, along with vague federal guidelines. Together, they serve as notable forces that can limit outcomes.

One of the cases examined by the Koontz team, the Darby Partnership in central Ohio, was also part of the author's (Agranoff 2007: 52–55) 14-network study. Darby is an example of a network that is quite limited in scope, with "a limited agenda of actions, all primarily geared to listening to partner reports at quarterly meetings" (153). It is an information and dissemination entity that is informally supported by the Nature Conservancy of Central Ohio. Under limited activity circumstances like these, collaborative management activities hardly present particular threats to bureaucratic autonomy, agency domain or agency implementation. As a result, it is important to know what a particular network undertaking is actually doing.

A related consideration is how the network process is managed. Over a decade ago Michael McGuire (2002: 600) raised the important question: "Do the actions of a manager contribute to the effectiveness of multi-organizational arrangements, and if so, how? Governing networks do not simply emerge spontaneously as self-sufficient, automated entities. There is both an operational and strategic character to networks that depends largely on the actions of managers." McGuire goes on to introduce a four-category breakdown of network managerial behavior—activation, mobilization, framing and synthesizing—encompassing the many differences in what managers do, from simple organizational goal achievement to process concerns that can be blended into analysis. The efficacy of the four-part strategic/operational sequence was later empirically tested on a network (McGuire and Agranoff 2014) and the subsequent discussion on continuous improvement also begins to introduce some preliminary answers to the McGuire questions. Finally, there is the important observation by Keith Provan and Brinton Milward (2001) that networks may be matched up to fulfill effectiveness criteria that are different: satisfying diverse community interests, multiple stakeholders with different values and goals, differing success expectations, along with differing perspectives on the anticipated "costs." Thus, it needs to be recognized that managerial actions and strategic purposes can be either positive or constraining forces.

NETWORK MISSION AND MISSION INCOMPATABILITY

Foremost among network barriers is an obvious but sometimes overlooked issue of mission incompatibility. That is, the public organizations and NGOs that set out to undertake network endeavors have different purposes that in very real terms clash in the real world of operations.

Mission incompatibility became very obvious during the 2015 western state wildfires when federal and state forest officials and private timber holders operationally clashed over wild forest preservation versus state and private concerns regarding the interests of utility companies as opposed to preservation organizations. In intellectual and development disabilities the various organizations that form service networks under HCBS include public education, for-profit counseling and job training firms, independent speech and hearing specialists, NGO development centers and state and local public agencies. They run the gamut of for-profit, non-profit and public, and, importantly, they experience different legal constraints, perform different services and operations, and are variably financed. Coming together in a network takes a great deal of activation time and effort, as they can clash with the "agendas and policies undertaken by networks [which] present perhaps the most significant barriers to collaboration results" (McGuire and Agranoff 2011: 269). It is an important step in any potential conversion to policy energy.

It is possible that many network efforts are limited or prevented from taking meaningful action by the role undertaken by network participants. Those of Darby, previously mentioned, are a case in point. Indeed, it could be that some efforts are so limited in scope or mission that they can't possibly take the kind of action that many others are able to accomplish. There have been a number of attempts to make such classifications. For example, Margerum (2011: 33–35) identifies three types of networks as social, interorganizational and political, emphasizing the important roles of social and political contacts, agency organization-based programs and budget dimensions, and the working elected officials and interest groups. Keast et al. (2004: 368) classify networks as: (1) cooperative, emphasizing participant interactions; (2) coordinative, where interactive learning and problems or solutions are clarified; and (3) collaborative, where the actors are actually doing something, to change policy or program, working toward systems change, often involved through building new collective ventures. In the 14-network study by Agranoff (2007: 10) they were classified by their core missions, which proved to range from mutual exchange, e.g. Darby, to actually making policy and program adjustments, for example federally chartered transportation networks under federal and state legal authorization. Between these two types were those that worked to enhance member capabilities and those that identified interorganizational strategies only to be carried out by respective participating organizations and public agencies. Indeed, only a few networks actually made the type of policy/program decisions as those of the transportation networks.

POLITICS: "BIG P"

A core overlooked premise is engagement of the public and political world as one essential dimension to build collaborative capacity. Engagement is set against the empirical reality of most complex decision-making premises (Weber and Khadmanian 2008: 447). It is the primacy of politics that is at the core as decisions are made in many different places. Koppenjan and Klijn (2004: 91) identify the role of elected political officeholders, who first see the need to weigh interests and confront conflicting values, whose judgments most often ultimately prevail and are ultimately accountable. As a result, tensions between political actors and those more involved in networks often surface. Despite key network deliberations political concerns are at the forefront of political decisions and cannot be overlooked. Decision-making capacity, or the lack thereof, is part of the larger stake of politics that pervades attempts to forge or hinder network success.

The historical development of the CALFED experiment, conclude Michael Hanemann and Calvin Dyckman (2009), could never really reach its potential as a water resource management network because of the fundamental political opposition of core involved interests, big water users such as water supply firms and agriculture. Regular political pressure by these interests led to water-conservation efforts and was a clear inhibiting factor. The designers thus made a calculated decision that led to voluntary solution frameworks as they would have the best chance to succeed. However, its fundamentally flawed reliance on voluntary agreements to resolve deep differences proved to be the Achilles' heel of the effort. The lack of interest, even refusal to engage, by political decision-makers to grapple with agency and jurisdictional fragmentation proved to be an overarching limiting factor: for example, state legislative unwillingness to get too deep in the process and exercise leadership along with the basic passivity of the state Water Resources Control Board, the water control risks and administrative agency. The politics of the matter, conclude the study authors, is compounded by disagreements over property rights and the perceptions by many parties that to engage in this process is to place them in zero-sum games where the risk of negative outcomes proved not worth playing (ibid.: 712). Also, to environmental policy observers collaboration in such networks must depend on political networking that is not necessarily tied to political office or administration, "A political network needs the agency to coordinate activities and allow the resources as well as provide network support functions . . ." and also to follow with implementing activities (Margerum 2011: 299–300; see also Fullerton 2009). Failure or inability to address these larger political concerns, also in the case of the aforementioned Dutch study (Edelenbos 2005), is a core limitation in building and operating successful networks.

"Big P" politics not only involves understanding and taking account of elected officials' positions and trying to address their concerns but to recognize that some positions are so hardened—another manifestation of mission incompatibility—that it becomes virtually impossible to bring some interests to the table. For example, as states now wrestle with lowering their vehicle and building emission standards, as the EPA has ruled, some coal and utility interests simply will not be willing to engage in processes that lead to a compromise that cuts deep into their basic interests. Rather, they are avoiding and will avoid formalized negotiation and problem solving and play the lobbying game to the fullest. Most prove not to be interested in coming to the collaborative table. This is "big P" politics, as opposed to "small p" politics in the network, that involves all of the working organizations and interests involved or potentially involved in any decision or position. "Big P" politics brings in a host of other actors, many of whom are the "heavy hitters," those most powerful within their respective spheres. For example, in the arena of rural development this means that political actions at high levels include much more than the familiar working interests: soil conservation districts, land grant extension services, federal and state agricultural agencies. Also, core agricultural interest groups, farm supply cooperatives, conservation district board members, and related groups plus involved community leader farmers are in the wider fray. At least potentially each of these "smaller p" forces can and do play "big P" politics and thus can be either facilitators or barriers to any network efforts, either within or usually outside non-network endeavors.

An entire volume could be written about network politics, small and large. As Gerry Stoker (2006: 47) concludes, politics is valued as a means of social coordination and it is a valued undertaking for three reasons: (1) it allows people to make choices beyond individualism and recognizes others' concerns; (2) it is based on flexibility and is a way to overcome uncertainty; and (3) politics can be used to move beyond base distribution of benefits to help establish social production processes. Concerns regarding politics are a natural by-product of trying to balance governability through joint action and external accountability (Kallis et al. 2009: 638).

POWER WITHIN NETWORKS: EXERCISE OF "SMALL P"

Related and "smaller p" network political dimensions are now discussed, as power, process and operational barriers are identified. Whereas the literature touts the virtues of networking as a leveller of power, in practice in a number of situations power is simply unequal, raising not only the concern for power as a potential or actual barrier, but also its failure to come to grips with its impact on network actions, not to mention accompanying limitations of legal authority, resource differentials and dependencies. Roderick Rhodes (1981) points out that these forces are part of the real world of power differentials. Behind the façade of trust and the rhetoric of cooperation, power is exercised by stronger partners over those who have less power (Clegg and Hardy 1996: 679). Beyond partner power, within the deliberative process Angel Saz-Carranza (2012: 100–101) found power processing within networks to include a complicated picture, a sort of three-dimensional power of decision-making, non-decision-making and meaning-making. Network building "power" to impact deliberative progress or to make joint policy as actors balances what is identified by Saz-Carranza as "the paradox of balancing unity and diversity" (101).

Overall interagency/interorganizational interaction must often face one or more power-related disincentives to work together. Barbara Gray (1989: 247–254) identifies six different types of power-related deterrents: (1) institutional disincentives, for example the concerns of environmental organizations that mediated negotiation will dilute their core missions; (2) long-standing or historical issues that hark back to bitter adversarial internal interactions; (3) concerns for loss of powerbase in a partnership, particularly those in the mix with minority or less powerful positions; (4) differing risk perceptions, such as regarding the stakes involved in eliminating certain environmental hazards; (5) technical complexity issues, for example incomplete ecosystem knowledge and/or disagreement over scientific findings; and (6) political and institutional cultures, the previously identified relevance of agencies to see negotiated agreements as feasible and desirable alternatives. If these power issues can successfully be understood and dealt with (Bryson et al. 2006) there may be more "at the table" points of convincing interests in engaging a power-related discourse to consider. They might include establishment of shared tasks, initial agreements on ground rules, self-organizing as opposed to externally imposed structures, use of high-quality research and information and continuous trust-building (Bryson et al. 2006).

More fundamentally—power dimensions that is—"small p" politics have been found to emerge within the network process itself. Four different types of operational power emerged in the author's study of 14 networks (Agranoff 2007: chapter 6). First, is the well-understood *agency power*, that is playing the power dependence game within network processes, leveraging an organization's legal charges, and mission resources. Second, is *operational power* within the network undertaking, the "games" and internal rules that define internal behaviors. Third, is *knowledge-based power* that serves as technical experts blend their specialties, experiences and investigations into insights that provide frameworks of understanding that can lead to next steps. Fourth, is *deliberative power* as technical information is infused and new possibilities emerge as a result of discussions, negotiations and multiparty engagements. The fourth or deliberative power dimension is perhaps the least understood but is central to the internal nexus of power of engagement. It emerges conceptually from urban regime theory or the social production model of Clarence Stone (1989), and Stone and associates (1999), along with a recent update to include the idea of an urban political order as a cluster of evolving relationships (Stone 2015: 109).

Each of these four types of internal power of operations can be "small p" politics facilitators or inhibitors within networks. Clearly, the absence of agency support for outcomes, supporting their rules and games, adequate technical information, tactics that are not carefully managed and breakdowns in deliberation, are process inhibitors once the actors sit down and engage. Absence of one or more "power to", in the urban regime conceptual sense—for example the inability to synergize knowledge into networks or solutions, the inability to find a feasible course of action, the inability to cope with emerging power rebalancing, or key changes in the resource dependency—can be among the notable process inhibitors (Agranoff 2012: 166).

Recent analyses of policy implementation involving network dynamics suggest that focusing on norms and policy beliefs has begun to bring out the dimension of cultural theory (CT) in such collaborative relationships as networks. It is based on the idea that the paradox of collaboration is that it is really people not organizations that are engaged in the undertaking. "Collaboration is viewed largely as an institutional phenomenon in public sector research, even though individual actors make it happen" (Gazley 2010: 275). As a guide for action CT suggests that the clash of cultures, based on traditions brought into the mix of interaction from participating agencies/organizations, can be important limiting process factors. For example, the CALFED studies cited throughout brought out the huge differences between representatives of water users and conservation interests.

In a network of disparate actors CT can be an important, "almost silent" force that can be a key process and outcome inhibitor. In Spain, a special form of government network, called mancomunidad, goes back to the early 15th century to manage forest resources across several contiguous jurisdictions. Today, there are formal networks that join local governments and also NGOs, on average about eight. In the natural resources management area they are usually governed by local government councilors, service managers (e.g., soil, water, forest) and administrators and a general manager who report to local elected officials. CT is clearly at work with regard to those formal networks, as planners, forest managers and local elected officials bring very different perspectives to the network management table (Agranoff 2010: 108). Forest preservation in these mancomunidades brings out conservation and preservation outlooks, water user concerns, forest product orientations and economic development priorities. CT suggests that the interaction and clash brings various biases to the table that need to be understood and confronted as part of the process, and sometimes will present real barriers. In much the same way as taking into account the political forces, CT also suggests that an increased degrees of cultural understanding presents a potential barrier in networks.

Christopher Weare et al. (2014) analyze CT from a collaborative perspective, concluding that divergent perspectives are manifested by the expression of actors' cultural biases or deep core beliefs that cannot be explained easily by forms of instrumental rationality (611). As the authors conclude (612):

> Cultural theory builds on a simple but powerful insight: The social relationships within which individuals are embedded generate predictable cultural biases, perspectives on how the world does and should operate, and their preferences for how to live in that world, and these biases, in turn, tend to support and sustain their extant set of social relationships.

CT has also led to understanding the possibility of fatalism, a cultural preference characterized by apathy and disengagement, a critical claim of CT (Stoker 2002). To these authors CT is an underutilized theoretical construct, and thus has potential for network process analysis. It reminds us that it is people within organizations that actually are expected to activate, mobilize, frame and synthesize (McGuire and Agranoff 2014). To facilitators, the extent that cultural differences and the clash of cultures impede the interactive process must be taken into account in network analysis as potential inhibitors in processing.

PROCESSING BARRIERS

Among the familiar barriers are, of course, the transaction costs that have been borrowed from economics and have regularly been applied to collaborative rule-making and regulation. Transaction costs refer to the costs of operating by a public organization, through contractor/grantee or other institutional arrangements, including network engagement. Edward Weber (1998: 14–15) clarifies three important transaction costs that apply to collaborative environmental rule-making that also appear to apply broadly to network processing. First, are the *process costs* or resources (time, money, disbursement of other tasks) devoted to information search, program specification, and progress in negotiations. Work across the boundaries of agencies and organizations is compounded by information asymmetries and informing others what that entity needs to know in the mix of discussion and negotiations. Second, are the *implementation costs*, including the time and effort to meet mandates, adaptions, monitoring technologies, and—most essential in network activity—the program adaptability costs. The latter refer to changing response capacity by involved organizations to others' concerns and needs, along with exogenous issues like technological advances and scientific knowledge base changes. Third, are the *costs associated with participant behavior*, which include a variety of challenges, such as accounting for non-participants, taking into account various levels of those who might react adversely, including the threat of litigation, dealing with information asymmetries, withholding by parties of critical information, delays on the part of agency or organizational executives, and the potential for "wheel spinning" brought on by heavy investments in processing by those principals who do not perceive great benefit or outcomes as a result of extensive processing.

One often misunderstood barrier that is rarely dealt with involves the clash of different network actors over coproduction of agreements that do not recognize differences in "ways of knowing among network actors." R. P. Lejano and Helen Ingram's (2009) research on CALFED indicates that construction of meaning by different parties, similar to that of CT, can lead to processing barriers unless new jointly derived constructions come out of their differences. For example, their case studies indicate that water supply engineers and executives, who see water as a commodity, look at the world very differently than do fish and wildlife officials, who look at the preservation and maintenance of ecosystems. As a result, they seldom see water issues in the same light. If new knowledge-based social or knowledge networks are not fostered, forging new relationships, the result is likely to lead to "a continuation of path dependency with only modest adjustments rather than a meaningful move toward transformation" (661). Thus an ameliorative tactic of networks is to lay these differences on the table, explore the depths of a problem, look for solid knowledge, and use the knowledge as a synthesis that can lead to new approaches that satisfy varying interests.

Rachel Fleishman (2009) has empirically surveyed these issues related to the U.S. EPA National Estuary Program. The primacy of states' agencies, that is state environmental departments, proved to be first in rank order, or the most important barrier leading to implementation delays and related "inconvenience factors." Also identified were frustration in the ability to see that goals were being met by process investment, other process costs reflected as "participation takes more time than it is worth," and concern for loss of autonomy by engaging in the process (40–42). Indeed, no matter how much the interactive game is played, these are identified as real limitations relating to the lack of prospect of a solution in the long run and by being able to overcome the transaction costs that limit management of the collaborative game (Koppenjan and Klijn 2004: 18; see also McGuire 2006).

PROCESS FATIGUE: A CORE CHALLENGE

One familiar barrier related to the process dimension is what Chris Huxham and Siv Vangen (2005: 72) call "partnership fatigue." When coupled with a lack of clarity about the one with whom one is collaborating, the challenge of managing ambiguity and complexity are identified as exhausting forces. Constant change also can lead to inertia as relationships between partners become increasingly fluid. Displaced leadership—or a shift from expected group-oriented, task-focused give-and-take to a situation where one or a few leaders do most of the work—can take the network to "move out of the control of their membership" (78). Finally, leadership activities are continually facing obstacles to success and removing them in a less than interactive fashion (e.g., by pushing partners out or isolating agencies), sort of "collaborative thuggery" as they label it, as a substitute for process facilitation. Together these issues raise real process obstacles.

Huxham and Vangen present seven valuable fatigue-related, inertia-related perspectives on collaborative management that equally apply to networks:

1. We must have common aims, but we cannot agree on them.
2. Sharing power is important, but people behave as if it is all in the purse strings.
3. Trust is necessary for successful collaboration, but we are suspicious of each other.
4. We are partnership-fatigued and tired of being pulled in all directions.
5. Everything keeps changing.
6. Leadership is not always in the hands of the members.
7. Leadership activities continually meet with dilemmas and difficulties.

As a result, these can be truly formidable processing challenges that provide risk to the network process. They need to be recognized, avoided and somehow overcome by managing the game of engagement (Kopenjan and Klijn 2004: 203).

THE POLITICAL PERILS OF OPERATIONAL LOCALISM

Most networked agreements and decisions are ultimately really potential actions, in as much as in the final analysis they are normally implemented by the organizations and government agencies that operate at the service or program level, normally local governments or locally based NGOs. This is particularly true with programs of a nation-wide scope that then filter down to local levels. No matter how a federal or central or intermediate government may settle on policies and program directives they are carried out by local governments or local NGOs that are tied not only to external policy goals but to local power structures and local regimes that inevitably are expected to balance "closer to home" demands/expectations geared to local constellations of interests within local political contexts. This localist imperative in practice operates in tandem with those higher-level goals associated with broad policies. For example, in environmental protection framework laws and regulations may operate as a local program quite differently as "it all happens locally." In the final analysis program implementation, local action or program meets activity as a product that is some form of patterned reconciliation between national/regional government objectives and local regime demands (Reed 2014). As such, operational localism is understood in general terms from the policy implementation perspective (e.g., Williams 1980). In short, "policy" can and does often change as it works its way into a program. These are networked costs or barriers that almost always lie outside of the network process. They are dealt with after the enactment or implementation stages. They are never the less potential impediments.

Focusing on the local agency level there is, first, a series of internal costs that must be balanced against the expectation of opportunity to implement network agreements. The author's (Agranoff 2007) study of 14 networks revealed over and over again six locally based pre-existing "costs" that managers and professionals in delivery organizations expressed that attenuated external, network derived expectations: (1) time and opportunity costs lost to the home agency as a result of network involvement; (2) time and energy costs resulting from the protracted decision-making process, based on non-hierarchical, multiorganizational, multicultural human relations processes; (3) agreements not reached because of the exertion of organization power or the withholding of power including local political resistance; (4) network gravitation toward consensus-based, risk-aversive decision agendas particularly to not offend powerful groups; (5) resource "hoarding," or agencies' failure or unwillingness to contribute needed resources; and (6) public policy barriers embedded in legislation, coupled with legislators' and/or key administrators' unwillingness to make needed changes, which, in turn, frustrated network decisions. All of these proved to be potential or actual barriers that in effect generate considerable operational localism, barriers that thwart progress within networks and most importantly open up opportunities for wide on-the-ground interpretation and potential displacement.

Operational localism in effect is based on on-the-ground implementation studies that "separate policy fact from policy fiction" (Brodkin 2003: 151; see also Lipsky 1980) or what Anat Gofen's (2014: 2) Israeli research highlights as "street level divergence" that leads to changes in policy by program operatives. His study of teachers, nurses and social workers indicates that such change in policy directives and guidelines is sometimes but not always self-serving by operational professionals, because they are also motivated to serving others, focusing on relationships over any policies, and it also involves collective action that encourages divergence. Moreover, such "deviation" can be through hidden or transparent actions. As a result of these heterogeneous and diverse motivations, programs at the street level need to be understood in this nuanced sense. To Gofen (17) divergence is a dimension of policy change when legitimized as practice bubbles up to the real program in operation, so to speak. At a minimum, it calls attention to the fact that, no matter what networks may agree to, operational localism is a core venue for some forms of displacement as implementers cope with their beliefs and motivations, social and work pressures and uncertainties (Maynard-Moody and Musheno 2000, 2003).

Network action at the administrative and/or the NGO board level also has to account for how such "agreements" are carried into action as the key leaders place "meaning[s]" that "shape actions" that are not just representations of people's beliefs and sentiments but fashion actions (Wagenaar 2011: 3). In administration the inherent dialogical/end interactive nature of practice is at the core. As Hendrik Wagenaar (2004: 151) concludes from his earlier studies of mental health programs:

> To be effective in practice implies that administrators must be willing to understand and be influenced by the point of view of other members of their community, be they clients or colleagues. In this way, practice theory transcends the dichotomy between individual and community. Good administrative practice is not just an individual achievement or a particular faculty of mind. The categories, norms, and standards are in everyone's possession and available for others as grounds for assessing the rightness or reasonableness

> of the administrator's actions. In fact, productive interactions with clients and colleagues are made possible through this transparency of practical judgment. Administrative judgment is not the sum of a vast series of judgments of individual administrators, who each act on the situation at hand. Instead, administrative practice expresses a community of standards, the commonality and integrity of an administrative collective.

In this process, Wagenaar concludes that administrators (and agency boards) are pressed to anchor "general descriptions into concrete objects and actions," leading to practical judgments about common situations (ibid.). Relatedly, with regard to the various CALFED studies, often interorganizational agreement can involve more than lack of authority to act, it can involve administrators acting to maintain the status quo (on water use) given diverging and conflicting interests (Hanneman and Dyekman 2009). In effect, thinking about how networks reach agreements, the "other steps" in implementation are always there, and almost always locally.

CONTINUOUS IMPROVEMENT PRACTICES

Very few networks, or dedicated collaborative operations for that matter, make the effort to engage in the kind of continuous improvement (CI) functions needed to understand the multijurisdiction, multiorganizational process undertaking they engage. CI is operationally different from the more familiar studies of network performance (Koliba, Campbell and Zia 2011; Koliba, Meek and Zia 2010, Ch. 10). CI links *process* assessment to the type of results achieved, understanding of the interworkings that lead to potential process redesign innovations that serve the self-interests of the network managers and their components because "reengineering works" in dispersed systems like networks. This has been an important theme regarding health care in the U.S. (Halvorson 2013: 217). Because network strategies involve highly complex interactive systems, CI entails a complexity perspective that includes advanced nonlinear dynamics, with continuous changing performance landscapes, systems that depend on beneficial outcomes, explanations that must go beyond outcomes to include explanations that arise from the interactions of the agents along with the patterns and feedback mechanisms, allowing for an adaptive management based on system dynamics that contribute to outcomes (Koppenjan and Klijn 2014: 159). Why is CI relevant to understanding network governance barriers? It is also the processes of networks themselves that provide understanding of obstacles and how to overcome them.

In an essay entitled "The Coming Death of Bureaucracy," Warren

Bennis (2000: 98) indicated that such revitalization is necessary to embrace the social mechanisms that stagnate and regenerate along with process cycles. Such revitalization includes abilities for learning from experience, the ability to "learn how to learn," acquiring and using feedback mechanisms on performance, and an ability to direct one's own destiny. Indeed, he foresaw that bureaucratic structures need to harness and adapt the major human problems: integration, distribution of power, adaptation and revitalization. Networks are clearly attempts to engage in such adaptive behavior.

In this regard, Julianne Mahler's analysis of organizational learning at NASA (2009: 212) suggests a multiphased sequence that might also be applied to networks: (1) emphasis on work processes along with outputs and outcomes; (2) establishing real or virtual forms for integrating information and comparing events; (3) considering competing professional standards and technologies; (4) finding ways to pass on memory of event/crises/work around/unsolved problems; (5) maintenance of professional standards; (6) dispersing new conclusions related to operating and performance; and (7) preserving that knowledge while reviewing established procedures. She concludes that, "For learning to foster reliability lessons must be widely known and reached" (211).

As an aspect of network management that has just begun to receive attention, the best way to begin to look at CI is to extend current process analysis—quantitative and qualitative—to focus more directly on operation process expectations, bottlenecks and to search for improvements. First and foremost, CI efforts need to come to grips with the interoperable demands of integrating operating involving two or more organizations. Interoperable management involves the concerted actions taken by different agencies and organizations working on the same projects. The interoperable challenge as related to CI involves the degree of connection(s) at the operating levels based on understood, negotiated and executed working processes that present the challenges to network participants. Therefore, interoperable management involves regularized programming involving two or more entities for which operating policies and processes have been interactively articulated and are executed to some considerable degree by multiple organizations. McGuire and Agranoff (2014) found in their network study that process analysis is at the heart of understanding interoperability. As a process, interoperability is not an end in itself but is a means to achieve the ability to respond when coordinated actions go the next step and reciprocal interaction is deeper, usually required. It is based on communicated and agreed-upon goals, planning, operational information, role differentiation, and an integrated operating system that supports communication.

Analysis of the CALFED process science program revealed some very important successes that have proved to be of use in overcoming its formidable obstacles. For example, one notable CI approach was the use of a Record of Decision (ROD) to decide the reasoning applied when choosing alternatives or when confronting future decision-based undertakings (Innes et al. 2007). Further, Norgaard, Kallis, and Kiparsky (2009: 649–650) reported the provision of problem explanations within the lacuna of distributed governance. This allowed for a look at problems from a broader perspective, and supported attempts to blur the lines between policy-makers and managers on the one hand and scientists on the other, bringing out different perspectives as managers call out for the "right answer," while scientists are confronted with "real-time" problems that require decisions. One involved practitioner concludes that "Science advisors cannot and should not dictate policy goals—but they can help translate those goals into clear, measurable outcomes; characterize the level of certainty and effort associated with achieving specific goals; and identify the tradeoffs between policy goals for decision makers" (Bobker 2009: 727). Process analysis indicated the importance of the science program in helping policy-makers analyze the underlying assumptions of the management choices, and has great network management potential.

Another process finding is the presence of multiple leaders in the network. As Angel Saz-Carranza and Sonia Ospina (2011) conclude, leadership should be seen as a "collective achievement rather than the property of individuals" (406). Also discovered was the fact that the network they studied did not move from one stage to the next, but that simultaneous management appeared and reappeared through concept formation, partnering, build-out and operations. This suggests that whereas CI may focus on the operating phase, it may well be a concern through the network management process. Finally, it was clear from the process analysis that each participating network component (i.e., participant) had to pay some attention to the input from the lead or core public agency or NGO, not as hierarchical replacements but due to the need to work within the boundaries adjusting structures and operations to the process nexus of networking. Recently published process analyses of network behavior (Koliba et al. 2010; Agranoff 2014; Cepiku 2014; Keast and Mandell 2014) also bear this out.

Process flows and potential process breakdowns can also contribute to assisting in CI by looking for potential bottlenecks and problem areas. Using quantitative participant questionnaires, Kolpakov (2014) examines: (1) network homophily or interactions by organizational identity; (2) degree centrality, that is numbers of ties; (3) betweenness or absence of ties; (4) density or number of existing ties; (5) reciprocity mutuality, the number of symmetric ties among actors; and (6) the transivity index, i.e., the ratio of the number of potentially transitive triads (see Wasserman and Faust 1994; Contractor et al. 2006). As applied to the Metro study, a STEM school effort, in Columbus, Ohio, Kolpakov's analysis focuses on how network structures change over time. His analysis focuses on prevailing processes as networks form and evolve, along with the structural configurations—actor, dyadic, triadic—that develop through the network stages, and the changing effect of individual characters on the network's structural makeup over time. This developmental analysis serves the CI knowledge base by looking theoretically at how networks evolve and more through various developmental and operational stages. From an instrumental or policy/program basis the study helps explain how networks respond to the type of complex problems that involve multiagency, multisector networks. In a sense, the issue of CI analysis is served by this type of robust approach to network modeling.

Future network analyses geared to CI along with outcome analysis will need to incorporate complexity and the use of open source information. For example, Koliba et al.'s (2011) "analysis of four traffic congestion management networks included real time performance data that has been adopted to both planning and operations anchored in common network and language, built from industry standards and metrics test modeling, systems planning, and economic and environmental impact assessments." In this regard, Koliba (2014) suggests that relationships between network variables may not be as linear as analysts presume. The impact of "multiplier effects" (99), bringing in *both* negative and positive feedback lags, process elements that could show critical CI results that can lead to changes. This type of analysis appears to be a fruitful avenue for examining network performance data; for example network structures and functions, performance knowledge, and complex system evolution, adaptation and performance (100; see also Innes and Booher 1999).

Joop Koppenjan and Erik-Hans Klijn (2014: 169–170) conclude from their research that four additional process-related approaches to management should be considered. First, is the need for ever-increasing adaptive management, adjusting to the content of proposals and the design of interactive processes and rules. Second, involves reducing any positive feedback that may contribute to distortion of existing equilibria as issues are worked out. Third, is negative feedback mobilizing interactions that support the existing equilibrium in order to build long-run support. Fourth, is enhancing the more constructive positive feedback particularly when there is a need to open relatively closed networks to change operational decisions. They conclude that a shift in CI analysis to incorporate complexity theory with governance networks theory may well be able to help reduce the complex array of organizations, actors and interests involved in networks. Complexity theory might also have helped to sensitize actors to the multiple concerns that stem from external feedback from turbulent fitness leads and might have suggested the need for network management strategies. In short, future research needs to delve deeper into understanding the complex practices that lead to network success and their collaborative capacity.

Along with network theory-building in general CI will be supported in future years by the type of analyses that align network performance with system dynamics, capturing network theory-building with computer simulation modeling with techniques such as system dynamics, agent-based modeling, social network analysis, and qualitative comparative analysis, as new data-mining programs allow large volumes of verbal and numerical data to be analyzed for patterns (Koliba 2014). They will no doubt enhance understanding of network performance. Other emergent techniques including augumentive mapping applied on their own or coupled with public participative or collaborative GIS programming which might promise new sets of insights into the ways in which network members cluster around spatially related problems as well as the cleavages between network members (Nielson 2012). In conclusion, examination of internal processes of network governance represents virtually untapped clues to recognizing operational barriers that network actors will potentially process in the future.

CONCLUSIONS

In the public sphere there have been three broad approaches to understanding networks: the rise and place of networks as a way to structure to face complexity; the performance advantages or results of networks at work; and analyses of networks at work/network management. The current analysis is clearly in the last category, as has been the bulk of the author's work since the 1970s' studies of human services integration (Agranoff and Pattakos 1979). This analysis examines various network process barriers as part of a "sobering" review of how operations might be improved. Based on the assumption that knowledge is a first step in such reconstruction we have identified organizational mission-related barriers, the realities of power in several dimensions, and the perils of engagement in process, and have recognized the realities of implementation that is often at a "distance" from those who forge network agreements, and the critical but normally overlooked process examination/improvement process as an obstacle that can be overcome.

Nearly two decades ago the organization guru Philip Selznik (1996: 276) concluded that in reaction to context the overall models that the move to create theoretical models of organized activity "should guard against a disposition to overlook, for the sake of the paradigm, the limited, partial, highly contingent nature of the truths discovered . . . Although we have learned a great deal about unintended effects—the so called law of unintended consequences—one does not suppose we are ready to abandon the quest for more effective and humane cooperative systems." Selznik echoes the advice of John Dewey in his *Logic: The Theory of Inquiry* (1935) that social science should be guided by life and practice rather than intellectually self-generated conceptions that grow out of social tensions, needs and troubles, the core values at stake in the social experience. It is in this spirit that the network behavior needs to be examined by a broader, more neutral diagnostic reconstruction and problem solving.

In this respect, O'Toole's (2015: 361–371) update of a 1997 groundbreaking article that attempts to define networks reminds "network followers," both academics and practitioners, that networks have great appeal but that the real variation in networks suggests that managers should be wary of "any general and precise injunctions for practice," and that "networks can also produce unattractive or even destructive outcomes," that work within networks. To network also involves varied levels of commitment and clashes of organizational cultures, public management in general involves emergent tasks and skills of interaction within the hierarchy and the network and, finally, some networks also operate, in effect for, "dark purposes," e.g., the exclusion of some interest to protect agency monopolies, or to limit the scope of action. In these areas, as well as extolling the virtues of networks, "we need to know much more about the ways in which networks and networking behavior can shape performance and affect the most salient values in our governance systems" (O'Toole 2015: 8). Aside from any dark sides, serious assessment of networks' "other side" is clearly in order, and will be for some time to come.

REFERENCES

Agranoff, Robert. 2007. *Managing within Networks: Adding Value to Public Organizations*. Washington, DC: Georgetown University Press.

Agranoff, Robert. 2010. *Local Governments and Their Intergovernmental Networks in Federalizing Spain*. Montreal and Kingston: McGill-Queen's University Press.

Agranoff, Robert. 2012. *Collaborating to Manage: A Primer for the Public Sector*. Washington, DC: Georgetown University Press.

Agranoff, Robert. 2013. "The Transformation of Public Sector Intellectual Developmental Disabilities Programming." *Public Administration Review*, 73 (Special Issue), 127–138.

Agranoff, Robert. 2014. "Reconstructing Bureaucracy for Service: Innovation in the Governance Era." In Christopher Ansell and Jacob Torfing (eds.) *Public Innovation through Collaboration and Design*. London: Routledge.
Agranoff, Robert, and Michael McGuire. 2003. *Collaborative Public Management. New Strategies for Local Governments*. Washington, DC: Georgetown University Press.
Agranoff, Robert, and Alex N. Pattakos. 1979. *Dimensions of Services Integration*. Rockville, MC: Project SHARE.
Agranoff, Robert, and Beryl A. Radin. 2015. "Deil Wright's Overlapping Model of Intergovernmental Relations: The Basis for Contemporary Intergovernmental Relationships." *PUBLIS: The Journal of Federalism*, 45(1), 139–159.
Bardach, Eugene. 1998. *Getting Agencies to Work Together: The Practice and Theory of Managerial Craftsmanship*. Washington, DC: Brookings Institution Press.
Bennis, Warren. 2000. "The Coming Death of Bureaucracy." In Warren Bennis (ed.) *Managing the Dream: Reflections on Leadership and Change*. Cambridge, MA: Perseus. Originally published in 1966.
Bobker, Gary. 2009. "The Means do not Justify the Ends: A Comment on CALFED." *Environmental Science & Policy*, 12, 631–643.
Brodkin, Evelyn. 2003. "Street-Level Research: Policy at the Front Lines." In T. Corbett and M.C. Lennon (eds.) *Policy into Action: Implementation Research and Welfare Reform*. Washington, DC: Urban Institute.
Bryson, John M., Barbara C. Crosby, and Melissa Middelton Stone. 2006. "The Design and Implementation of Cross-Sector Collaborations: Propositions from the Literature." *Public Administration Review*, 66 (December–Supplement), 44–55.
Carpenter, Daniel P. 2001. *The Forging of Bureaucratic Autonomy Reputations, Networks, and Policy Innovations in Executive Agencies, 1862–1928*. Princeton, NJ: Princeton University Press.
Cepiku, Denita. 2014. "Network Performance: Toward a Dynamic Multidimensional Model." In Robyn Keast, Myrna P. Mandell, and Robert Agranoff (eds.) *Network Theory in the Public Sector*. London: Routledge.
Clegg, Stewart R., and Cynthia Hardy. 1996. "Conclusions: Representation." In Stewart R. Clegg, Cynthia Hardy, and Walter R. Nord (eds.) *Handbook of Organizational Studies*. London: SAGE.
Contractor, N.S., Stanley Wasserman, and K. Faust. 2006. "Testing Multitheoretical, Multilevel Hypotheses about Organizational Networks: An Analytic Framework and Empirical Example." *Academy of Management Review*, 31(3), 681–703.
Dewey, John. 1938. *Logic: The Theory of Inquiry*. New York: Holt.
Edelenbos, Jurian. 2005. "Institutional Implications of Interactive Governance: Insights from Dutch Practice." *Governance: An International Journal of Policy, Administration and Institutions*, 18(1), 111–134.
Fleishman, Rachel. 2009. "To Participate or Not to Participate? Incentives and Obstacles for Collaboration." In Rosemary O'Leary and Lisa Bingham (eds.) *The Collaborative Public Manager: New Ideas for the Twenty-First Century*. Washington, DC: Georgetown University Press.
Fullerton, David. 2009. "Tinkering at the Edges." *Environmental Science and Policy*, 12(6), 733–736.
Gazley, Beth. 2010. "Improving Collaboration Research by Emphasizing the Role of the Public Manager." In Rosemary O'Leary, David M. Van Slyke, and

Soonhee Kim (eds.) *The Future of Public Administration Around the World.* Washington, DC: Georgetown University Press, pp. 275–280.

Gofen, Anat. 2014. "Mind the Gap: Dimensions and Influence of Street-Level Divergence." *Journal of Public Administration Research and Theory*, 24(2), 473–493.

Gray, Barbara. 1989. *Collaborating: Finding Common Ground for Multiparty Problems.* San Francisco, CA: Jossey-Bass.

Halvorson, George C. 2013. *Don't Let Health Care Bankrupt America.* Createspace Independent Pub.: Published by Author.

Hanemann, Michael, and Calvin Dyckman. 2009. "The San Francisco Bay-Delta: A Failure of Decision-making Capacity." *Environmental Science and Policy*, 12(6), 710–725.

Huxham, Chris, and Siv Vangen. 2005. *Managing to Collaborate: The Theory and Practice of Collaborative Advantage.* London: Routledge.

Innes, Judith E., and David Booher. 1999. "Consensus Building and Complex Adaptive Systems: A Framework for Evaluating Collaborative Planning." *Journal of the American Planning Association*, 65(4), 412–423.

Innes, Judith E., Sarah Connik, and David Booher. 2007. "Informality as a Planning Strategy: Collaborative Water Management in the CALFED Bay Delta Program." *Journal of American Planning Association*, 73(2), 145–210.

Kallis, Giorgos, Michael Kiparsky, and Richard Norgaard. 2009. "Collaborative Governance and Adaptive Management: Lessons from California's CALFED Water Program." *Environmental Science and Policy*, 12(6), 631–643.

Kardish, Chris. 2014. "The Carbon Rebellion." *Governing*, 28(1), 44–48.

Keast, Robyn, and Myrna P. Mandell. 2014. "A Composite Theory of Leadership and Management." In Robyn Keast, Myrna P. Mandell, and Robert Agranoff (eds.) *Network Theory in the Public Sector.* London: Routledge.

Keast, Robyn, Myrna P. Mandell, K. Brown, and G. W. Woolcock. 2004. "Network Structures: Working Differently and Changing Expectations." *Public Administration Review*, 64(3), 363–371.

Koliba, Christopher. 2014. "Governance Network Performance: A Complex Adaptive Systems Approach." In Robyn Keast, Myrna P. Mandelly, and Robert Agranoff (eds.) *Network Theory in the Public Sector.* New York: Routledge.

Koliba, Christopher, Jack W. Meek, and Asim Zia. 2010. *Governance Networks in Public Administration and Public Policy.* Boca Raton, FL: CRC Press/Taylor & Francis.

Koliba, Christopher, E. Campbell, and Asim Zia. 2011. "Performance Measurement Systems of Congestion Management Networks: Evidence from Four Cases." *Public Performance Management Review*, 34(4), 520–548.

Kolpakov, Aleksey. 2014. Structural Development of Public Management Networks Over Time: Where Process Meets Structure. PhD Dissertation, School of Public and Environmental Affairs, Indiana University – Bloomington.

Koontz, Thomas M., Toddi A. Steelman, JoAnn Carmin, Katrina Smith Korfmacher, Cassandra Mosely, and Craig W. Thomas. 2004. *Collaborative Environmental Management: What Roles for Government?* Washington, DC: Resources for the Future.

Koppenjan, Joop, and Erik-Hans Klijn. 2004. *Managing Uncertainties in Networks.* London: Routledge.

Koppenjan, Joop, and Erik-Hans Klijn. 2014. "What Can Governance Network Theory Learn from Complexity Theory? Mirroring Two Perspectives on

Complexity." In Robyn Karst, Myrna Mandell, and Robert Agranoff (eds.) *Network Theory in the Public Sector*. London: Routledge.

Lejano, R. P., and H. Ingram. 2009. "Collaborative Networks and New Ways of Knowing." *Environmental Science and Policy*, 12(6), 653–662.

Lipsky, Michael. 1980. *Street-level Bureaucracy: Dilemmas of the Individual in Public Services*. New York: Russell Sage Foundation.

Mahler, Julianne G. 2009. *Organizational Learning at NASA: The Challenger and Columbia Accidents*. Washington, DC: Georgetown University Press.

Margerum, Richard D. 2011. *Beyond Consensus: Improving Collaborative Planning and Management*. Cambridge, MA: The MIT Press.

Maynard-Moody, Steven, and Michael Musheno. 2000. "State Agent or Citizen Agent: Two Narratives of Discretion." *Journal of Public Administration Research and Theory*, 10: 329–358.

Maynard-Moody, Steven, and Michael Musheno. 2003. *Cops, Teachers, Counselors: Narratives of Street-Level Judgment*. Ann Arbor, MI: University of Michigan Press.

McGuire, Michael. 2002. "Managing Networks: Propositions: On What Managers Do and Why They Do It." *Public Administration Review*, 62(5), 599–609.

McGuire, Michael. 2006. "Collaborative Public Management: Assessing What We Know and How We Know It." *Public Administration Review*, 66 (Supplement), 33–43.

McGuire, Michael, and Robert Agranoff. 2010. "Networking in the Shadow of Bureaucracy." In Robert Durant (ed.) *The Oxford Handbook of American Bureaucracy*. Oxford: Oxford University Press, pp. 372–395.

McGuire, Michael, and Robert Agranoff. 2011. "The Limitations of Public Management Networks." *Public Administration*, 89(2), 265–284.

McGuire, Michael, and Robert Agranoff. 2014. "Network Management Behaviors: Closing the Theoretical Gap." In Myrna Mandell, Robyn Keast, and Robert Agranoff (eds.) *Network Theory in the Public Sector: Building New Theoretical Framework*. New York: Routledge.

Nielson, M. 2012. *Reinventing Discovery: The New Era of Networked Sciences*. Princeton, NJ: Princeton University Press.

Norgaard, R.B., G. Kallis, and M. Kiparsky, 2009. "Collectively Engaging Complex Socio-ecological Systems: Re-envisioning Science, Governance, and the California Delta." *Environmental Science and Policy*, 12(6), 644–652.

O'Leary, Rosemany, and Lisa Blomgren Bingham (eds.). 2009. *The Collaborative Public Manager*. Washington, DC: Georgetown University Press.

O'Toole, Laurence J., Jr. 1997. "Treating Networks Seriously: Practical and Research-Based Agendas in Public Administration." *Public Administration Review*, 57(1), 45–52.

O'Toole, Laurence J., Jr. 2015. "Networks and Networking: The Public Administrative Agendas." *Public Administration Review*, 75(3), 361–371.

Provan, Keith G., and H. Brinton Milward. 2001. "Do Networks Really Work? A Framework for Evaluating Public Sector Organizational Networks." *Public Administration Review*, 61(4), 414–423.

Reed, Douglas S. 2014. *Building the Federal Schoolhouse*. Oxford: Oxford University Press.

Rhodes, R. A. W. 1981. *Control and Power in Central-Local Relations*. Aldershot, UK: Gower.

Saint-Onge, Hubert, and Charles Armstrong. 2004. *The Conductive Organization*. Amsterdam: Elsevier.

Saz-Carranza, Angel. 2012. *Uniting Diverse Organizations: Managing Goal-oriented Advocacy Networks*. London: Routledge.

Saz-Carranza, Angel, and Sonia M. Ospina. 2011. "The Behavioral Dimension of Governing Inter-organizational Goal Directed Networks: Managing the Unity/Diversity Tension." *Journal of Public Administration Research and Theory*, 21(2), 327–365.

Selznik, Philip. 1996. "Institutionalism 'Old' and 'New'." *Administrative Service Quarterly*, 41(2), 270–277.

Stoker, Gerry. 2002. "Life is a Lottery: New Labor's Strategy for the Reform of Devolved Governance." *Public Administration*, 80(3), 417–434.

Stoker, Gerry. 2006. "Public Value Management: A New Narrative for Networked Governance." *American Review of Public Administration*, 36(1), 41–57.

Stone, Clarence. 1989. *Regime Politics: Governing Atlanta. 1946–1988*. Lawrence, KS: University Press of Kansas.

Stone, Clarence. N. 2015. "Reflections on Regime Politics: From Governing Coalition to Urban Political Order." *Urban Affairs Review*, 51(1), 101–137.

Stone, C. N., K. Doherty, C. Jones, and T. Ross. 1999. "Schools and Disadvantaged Neighborhoods: The Community Development Challenge." In Ronald F. Ferguson, and William T. Dickens (eds.) *Urban Problems and Community Development*. Washington, DC: Brookings Institution Press.

Thomas, Craig W. 2003. *Bureaucratic Landscapes: Interagency Cooperation and the Preservation of Biodiversity*. Cambridge, MA: The MIT Press.

Vandeventer, Paul, and Myrna P. Mandell. 2007. *Networks That Work*. Los Angeles, CA: Community Partners.

Wagenaar, Hendrik. 2004. "Knowing the Roles: Administrative Work as Practice." *Public Administration Review*, 64(6): 643–656.

Wagenaar, Hendrik. 2011. *Meaning in Action: Interpretation and Dialogue in Policy Analysis*. Armonk, NY: M. E. Sharpe.

Wasserman, S., and K. Faust. 1994. *Social Network Analysis*. New York: Cambridge University Press.

Weare, Christopher, Paul Lichterman, and Nicole Esparza. 2014. "Collaboration and Culture: Organizational Culture and the Dynamics of Collaborative Policy Networks." *Policy Studies Journal*, 42(4), 390–425.

Weber, Edward P. 1998. *Pluralism by the Rules: Conflict and Cooperation in Environmental Regulation*. Washington, DC: Georgetown University Press.

Weber, Edward P., and Anne Khadmanian. 2008. "Managing Collaborative Processes: Common Practices Uncommon Circumstances." *Administration and Society*, 40(4): 431–364.

Williams, Walter. 1980. *The Implementation Perspective: A Guide for Managing Social Services Programs*. Berkeley, CA: University of California Press.

Wondolleck, Julia, and Steven L. Yaffee. 2000. *Making Collaboration Work: Lessons from Innovation in National Resource Management*. Washington, DC: Island Press.

5. Vitality in interactive governance: conditions and challenges

Jurian Edelenbos and Ingmar van Meerkerk

1. INTRODUCTION

In this chapter we deal with the acknowledgement of the emergence of interactive governance networks in environmental governance literature and research. Interactive governance can be approached as a collaboration process between citizens, private actors and governmental actors (Kooiman, 1993; Edelenbos, 2005; see also Margerum and Robinson's introductory chapter in this book). In the European literature on networks, interactive governance is commonly seen as a necessary response to the contemporary forms of network governance. Governance networks are, according to Torfing et al. (2012: 9, 10), founded on a critique of the modus operandi of traditional forms of government. Because of an increasing fragmentation of political decision-making, caused by functional differentiation and institutional fragmentation of governing processes, a large number of public and private actors have a substantial effect on the way society is governed (Nabatchi and Amsler, 2014: 1).

Interactive governance is a specific form of governance that pays much attention to the way citizens, private actors and societal (voluntary) organizations are collaboratively involved in policy-making and implementation. Interactive governance networks have high potential for dealing with complex environmental issues, as they could bring together knowledgeable and resourceful public, private and societal actors in arenas that enjoy considerable autonomy, but remain connected to other societal and governmental institutions (Torfing et al., 2012; Van Meerkerk et al., 2015).

However, this high potential of interactive governance networks is certainly not a given. Lots of challenges have to be faced. Crucially, bringing this high potential into effect depends on the quality of the interaction between network actors. Furthermore, the way network interactions and developed solutions for wicked issues are connected to and embedded in regular institutions of policy- and decision-making contributes to the effectiveness and legitimacy of interactive governance processes. The relationship between processes of interactive governance, procedures and institutions of neoliberal and representative democracy is often coined as problematic and challenging (Edelenbos, 2005; Lawrence et al., 2002). In this chapter we go deeper into these aspects.

In discussing these topics we use the concept of vitality (Edelenbos et al., 2015). Vitality refers to energetic, adaptive and productive relationships between actors. Vitality deals with the quality of collaborative processes (energetic and adaptive) and the outcome from these processes (productive). Therefore, the concept deals with process and content quality of collaborative processes at the same time (Klijn et al., 2010). However, this vitality of interactive governance networks doesn't come about easily; in this chapter we discuss a number of conditions that are considered important to develop or sustain the vitality in interactive governance. We subsequently go deeper into the question of to what extent these conditions can be considered sufficient or necessary and how these conditions might interact with each other, discussing different mechanisms at work. Moreover, we discuss the challenges of developing and implementing these conditions in the practice of interactive governance.

The structure of the chapter is as follows. In section two we discuss the relevance of interactive governance in modern society. Section three pays attention to conceptualizing the core concept of this chapter: vitality. Various conditions are discussed that feed vitality of interactive governance networks. In this section we also discuss the problems and challenges these conditions meet in practice; establishing vitality in interactive networks is not easy to realize. In section four we propose a configurational approach to measuring vitality. We finish the chapter with concluding remarks.

2. SIGNIFICANCE OF INTERACTIVE GOVERNANCE IN MODERN SOCIETY

Nowadays it is broadly recognized and accepted that complex decision-making takes place within interdependent sets of actors (e.g. Marsh and Rhodes, 1992; Pierre, 2000; Sørensen and Torfing, 2007). This observation has led to a growing body of research on so-called governance networks. Governance networks emerge around boundary crossing policy problems that cannot be solved by one actor alone but require collective actions of a number of actors from different organizations, sectors and levels (Koppenjan and Klijn, 2004).

This development to governance networks indicates a shift from hierarchical and well-institutionalized forms of government towards less formalized, bottom-up forms of governance in which state-authority makes way for an appreciation of mutual interdependence between different stakeholders (Hajer and Wagenaar, 2003). Because stakeholders are approached as relevant, important and knowledgeable actors in the decision-making process, some authors (e.g. Kooiman, 1993; Sørensen and Torfing, 2007) explicitly stress and focus upon the *interactive* nature of governance networks. They speak of *interactive governance* to emphasize and study the actual engagement, interaction and involvement of stakeholders, like citizens, non-governmental organizations (NGOs), private companies, etc., in decision-making processes in relationship to existing institutional structures and processes (Edelenbos and Van Meerkerk, 2016).

A number of developments in society and government make interactive governance needed in order to deal with challenging societal issues and questions. Some mention individualization, value pluralism and fragmentation (Rittel and Webber, 1973; Castells, 1996). Moreover, others mention that citizens, social and private organizations, and NGOs are no longer passive objects of top-down steering activities, but are to be viewed as empowered actors who have a stake and say in decision-making processes (Kooiman, 1993). These actors have increasing resources and capacities to challenge governmental action (e.g. Dalton, 2008). In contemporary network society resources (financial means, human resources, information, knowledge, competences and support) are increasingly dispersed among various actors (Pierre and Peters, 2000; Koppenjan and Klijn, 2004).

In short, interactive governance networks could mobilize additional resources for dealing with wicked issues, improve the quality of policy- and decision-making in terms of a more integrated approach to these issues, develop more innovative solutions, and improve the coordination between interdependent actors (Koppenjan and Klijn, 2004). However, this is far from self-fulfilling. Resources and capacities need to become aligned in order to reach collective action, increased effectiveness and synergies (Rhodes, 1997; Scharpf, 1999). Reflecting on various studies on governance networks, Torfing et al. (2012: 126–127) note that the effectiveness of governance networks depends on the inclusion of relevant and affected actors, participants' willingness to exchange or pool resources, and the capacity to develop common conceptions of problems, solutions and decision-making premises. Many things can go wrong in this respect. For example, relevant stakeholders may be excluded by social or cognitive closure of key actors in the policy arena, or opportunistic behavior between actors may foster defensive and non-cooperative strategies, and give rise to damaging conflicts (ibid).

3. VITALITY OF INTERACTIVE GOVERNANCE NETWORKS: KEY CONDITIONS

Vital Interactive Governance Networks

In line with the previous mentioned developments, the emergence and call for more interactive forms of governance is touched upon in all kinds of disciplines, such as polycentric governance (e.g. Ostrom, 2010), co-management (Pomeroy and Berkes, 1997), adaptive management (Pahl-Wostl, 2007), social-ecological system thinking (Berkes and Folke, 1998; Folke et al., 2005), and network approaches (Koppenjan and Klijn, 2004; Hajer and Wagenaar, 2003). The common denominator in these studies is that the quality of interaction processes and structures are stressed as important to realize efficient, effective and legitimate governance responses to wicked issues. Vitality in this view is a concept that expresses the high quality interactions among actors (Edelenbos et al., 2015; Healey, 1995; Horlings et al., 2009). Vital actor relationships provide the trustworthy context to explore and find new alternatives and solutions to complex issues (Folke et al., 2005). But what are important conditions stimulating vitality in interactive governance? In the literature a couple of conditions and factors are mentioned such as trust, informal networks, social learning, etc. (Folke et al., 2005), but a clear framework of these factors and in-depth discussion is often lacking.

Vitality of interactive governance networks touches upon the processual and relational capacity among actors in the network, and is considered important for adaptive and flexible responses to changes in social-ecological systems (Berkes and Folke, 1998). We argue that the concept vitality is strongly related to the concept of governance capacity, and specifically relational capacity (Foster-Fishman et al., 2001; Innes and Booher, 2003). This form of capacity particularly focuses on the quality of the relations and interactions among involved actors. Vital social systems imply that actors can develop joint fact finding and mutual understanding and can generate productive interdependent relationships leading to effective, efficient and legitimate problem-solving (cf. Healey, 1995, 2006; Sullivan and Skelcher, 2002). Vitality in interactive governance leads to interaction and relational patterns which are lively, energizing and productive; it is concerned with the capacity to act (Horlings et al., 2009). Energizing means mobilizing people to become part of interaction processes, while productive means that this energy is also consolidated in output and outcome (Innes and Booher, 2003). We therefore define vitality for interactive governance as "a social system of actors with different backgrounds and from different scales and levels with lively, energetic and productive relationships that are constantly seeking to explore, develop, and consolidate common ground in dealing with complex [environmental] issues" (Edelenbos et al., 2015: 239).

Hence, vitality is a duplex concept that stresses both exploration (learning, reflexivity) and consolidation (productivity, exploitation) (Scharpf, 1999). Interactive governance processes that are exclusively characterized by exploration, learning and reflexivity are not vital as they do not consolidate efforts in specific results and in this sense waste resources. The same holds for interactive governance processes that are exclusively focused on exploitation or consolidation in decision-making and specific results. This can lead to (early) lock-in situations in which adaptive capacity is lost (Folke et al., 2005).

However, vitality in interactive governance needs to be conditioned: several requirements are needed in making governance networks vital. In the next section we pay further attention to a number of these conditions.

Vitality Increasing Conditions

In this section we pay attention to several conditions that are mostly mentioned and discussed in literature. In discussing these conditions we build upon an earlier publication in which some of these conditions are already explored (Edelenbos et al., 2015) but are further developed and discussed in this chapter. In this discussion we also pay attention to the problematic and challenging side of the conditions.

Informal settings

A first important condition is informal structures or settings in which interaction between actors takes place. Vitality requires informal networks that transcend formal organizational structures and boundaries. Informal social networks refer to settings in which interaction is less structured by formal and detailed rules. Nooteboom (2006) has described how influential informal networks (termed adaptive networks) have emerged and explicitly looked for sustainable development of a large societal system like the transport and energy system. Since in this system public and private organizations and political pressure groups are in deadlock, creative solutions are difficult to generate, but adaptive networks influenced the official leadership of these organizations to communicate in a different way with their supporter groups. By developing across borders between contrasting organizations they were able to merge their knowledge and create a joint long-term perception of sustainable transport.

Ashmos et al. (2000) argue that informal structures contributed to sharing of information between people. Furthermore, the informal character of the networks provides room for involved actors to think and behave outside their established roles and rules according to their formal position within established institutions. People are not directly pinned down to or held accountable for using certain statements. In this way informal meetings give more room for experimentation and exploration.

Informal networks in which people of different organizations and communities easily find each other seems to be an important condition for sharing information, experimenting and for innovative solutions to emerge. However, informal networks as such are certainly not a sufficient condition for vital interactive governance networks to emerge and sustain. For example, emerging and creative solutions developed in informal networks have to be connected to regular organizational processes and established institutions of policy- and decision-making to become broadly accepted, legitimatized and supported with necessary means (Edelenbos, 2005).

This aspect of institutionalization of interactive governance is often challenging and can cause problems (Lawrence et al., 2002). For one, the element of power comes in when established institutions of experts and decision-makers are activated (Edelenbos, 2005). Some emphasize the political side of collaboration: some experts and governmental institutions resist this power sharing (Warner, 2006), which causes barriers to integrating local knowledge into their plans (High et al., 2006; Tseng and Penning-Rowsell, 2012: 257). Experts for example don't accept local knowledge that easily. Moreover, decision-makers have a strong preference for expert knowledge in substantiating their decisions (High et al., 2006). Local and lay knowledge is considered too uncertain and unprofessional, lacking clear and scientific grounding (Robinson and Wallington, 2012). Furthermore, critical reflections on these informal settings related to interactive governance stress issues of accountability and transparency (e.g. Papadopoulos, 2016). An important challenge for knowledge co-production and exploration between stakeholders in these informal settings is to make explorative processes and promising outcomes legitimate. Hence, it is important to invest in the inclusion of a broader range of stakeholders and transparency of these informal processes in order to increase their throughput legitimacy.

Boundary spanning activities

In informal networks, boundary spanning activities become important in building and activating relationships among different actors in the governance network (Van Meerkerk, 2014). These boundary spanning activities activate actor relationships and in this way the exchange of information, knowledge, resources and perceptions. Competent boundary spanners are organizational members who are able to link the organization they represent with its environment (Williams, 2002).

To effectively accomplish a better fit, boundary spanners are engaged in three main (and interrelated) activities: connecting or linking different people and processes at both sides of the boundary; selecting relevant information on both sides of the boundary; and translating this information to the other side of the boundary (Van Meerkerk and Edelenbos, 2014). Boundary spanners are skilled networkers who have the ability to recognize and exploit opportunities to develop inter-organizational relationships (Williams, 2002). This means that they are able to sympathize with others and that they have a feeling for the social construction of other actors. Boundary spanners understand other actors' needs, which enables them to search for shared meanings (Levina and Vaast, 2005). In this way, sustainable relationships with actors from different organizational backgrounds are developed and maintained.

Dealing effectively with wicked issues requires a high flow of information between involved actors, coordination and mutual alignment of a diversity of stakeholders (e.g. Huntjens et al., 2011). With their role in increasing the flow of information, and translating information across organizational boundaries, connecting individuals and processes across organizational boundaries, competent boundary spanners positively affect the performance of governance networks, as is shown in the survey research of Van Meerkerk and Edelenbos (2014). Furthermore, they also found that boundary spanners have significant impact on building trustful relationships in governance networks. Trust and boundary spanning develop mutual strengths for increased cooperation and for finding integrated solutions.

The boundary spanners have a feel for the diversity of interests, for what is relevant for the different involved stakeholders, and provide opportunities for these stakeholders to engage. Besides playing an important role in creating informal and deliberative spaces between stakeholders by their connective activities, boundary spanners play a key translating and bridging role between informal networks on the one hand and formal decision-making structures and policy processes on the other hand. In other words: boundary spanning is important for developing interactions between stakeholders and due deliberation among stakeholders and for bringing over this throughput from informal networks to formal decision-making in a legitimate way (Van Meerkerk et al., 2015).

However, the work of the boundary spanners is challenging. First, boundary spanners can easily fall into a tense relationship between their home organization (which they represent) and the interactive governance network (in which they build new relationships). Very often boundary spanners can become detached from their home organization, because they develop new ideas in informal networks and "forget" to or have trouble aligning these to their home organization (Levina and Vaast, 2005). Results achieved in informal settings might easily get lost in translation. Moreover, boundary spanning can be considered as a stressful task as boundary spanners constantly work in between organizations posing different tasks and expectations (Goolsby, 1992). Meeting this diversity of expectations makes boundary work difficult and challenging to implement and demands quite a lot of different skills (Williams, 2002).

Constructive dialogue and deliberation

Regarding the vitality of interactive governance networks, it is important to consider in what ways actors approach each other. A hostile and conflict-based approach will not be favorable for the development of vitality in actor networks, as communication and interaction will become minimal and based on fixed and formalized positions (Dryzek, 2010; Foster-Fishman et al., 2001; Healey, 2006; Innes and Booher, 2003). As is shown in governance network literature, hard-nosed bargaining will not lead to vitality in social systems. Instead, due deliberation, if it is organized properly, increases exchange of information, perceptions and preferences, by which a learning process can take place and governance network performances could improve (Van Meerkerk et al., 2015). "The main reason is that arguing and reason-giving provide a mechanism to probe and challenge the normative validity of actors' interests as well as to check the empirical facts on which policy choices are based" (Risse and Kleine, 2007: 73–74).

The dialogue has to be "open" or authentic: actors have to be "able to follow a discussion where it leads rather than be artificially constrained by rules about what can be discussed or what cannot be changed in the system, practice or law" (Innes and Booher, 2003: 38). Face-to-face communication in these informal networks is considered especially crucial as it not only makes mutual alignment of strategies possible, but " . . . exchanging mutual commitment . . . creating and reinforcing norms, and developing a group identity appear to be the most important processes that make communication efficacious" (Ostrom, 1998: 7). This creates flexibility and the ability to mutually adjust to each other's points of view, interests and core values. Furthermore, it should be inclusive. In this way a variety of viewpoints, interests and values can be developed and communicated (Wagenaar, 2007). Moments of variation give individual actors the opportunity to put forward their own agenda.

However, a constructive dialogue does not emerge easily. Some people have greater abilities and capacities such as collaborative and negotiation skills (Innes and Booher, 2003, 2010; Mayer et al., 2005). Moreover, sometimes conflict and power play can easily disrupt the constructive dialogue in interactive governance processes. Some people play it hard or even don't want to reach common understanding and agreement (Warner, 2006; Mayer et al., 2005). Participation in constructive dialogue demands an open and reflexive attitude and a willingness to learn more about the ambitions, perceptions and interests of others in the collaborative process. These attitudes are not a given in interactive governance of wicked issues, which are characterized by conflicts of interests and diverging perceptions (Koppenjan and Klijn, 2004).

Trust

In the literature on interactive governance around complex environmental issues, trust is considered to be an important factor enhancing the performance of these networks (Edelenbos and Klijn, 2007; Ansell and Gash, 2008; Klijn et al., 2010). Trust is considered to be an important driver for the emergence and sustainment of collaborative efforts in interactive governance networks. It is assumed that trust positively influences relation-building and the development of social capital in networks – leading to increased interaction and knowledge exchange. Trusting another actor means that one is willing to assume an open and vulnerable position. One expects the other actor to refrain from opportunistic behavior even if the opportunity for it arises without having any guarantee that the other party will indeed act as expected (Deakin and Wilkinson, 1998). Thus, the actor believes and expects that the other actor will take both actors' interests into account in the interaction (Rousseau et al., 1998).

Klijn et al. (2010) distinguish a number of aspects that together give shape to trust in interactive governance networks, of which two are of particular importance for vitality: absence of opportunistic behavior; and reliability. Trust may be defined as confidence in the reliability of a person or organization, regarding a given set of outcomes or events (Sako, 1998). Reliability means that actors keep in mind the intentions of the other parties. The absence of opportunistic behavior is also considered a requirement for the development of trust among actors in the network. Some authors argue that trust means that actors do not exploit other actors' vulnerability (Deakin and Wilkinson, 1998; Rousseau et al., 1998).

With their large n (survey) research on Dutch water governance cases, Klijn et al. (2010) have demonstrated that trust has a significant positive impact on the outcomes of water governance networks. They have empirically shown that trust enhances integrative and sustainable performance of water governance networks. Trust stimulates and consolidates interaction between different actors from different domains and organizations in the water governance networks. It leads to more informal interaction and exploration in which actors take a receptive and reflexive (learning) attitude. Trust increases the probability that actors will invest their resources, such as money, knowledge, and so on, in collaborative and cross-domain and cross-disciplinary collaborative processes (Huntjens et al., 2011; Plummer et al., 2012). In this way, trust stimulates learning and the exchange of information and knowledge among stakeholders, which is useful to develop better tailored and integrated solutions (Edelenbos et al., 2011; Edelenbos et al., 2013; Huntjens et al., 2011). In sum, trust increases the capacity to connect different actors with different backgrounds and to develop and implement integrated and sustainable solutions.

Lewicki and Bunker (1996) propose that trust develops incrementally as partners move from one stage to the next. One level of trust in the cycle has to be attained to achieve the next and stronger level of trust. Calculus-based trust is based on the utilitarian assumption that someone can be believed to be trustworthy because there are sufficient sanctions in place to control against breach of trust, and that these outweigh the benefits of opportunistic behavior (Rousseau et al., 1998). As the relationship continues the authors argue that trust is knowledge-based (Lewicki and Bunker, 1996). At this point, partners have experienced a certain amount of interaction and know each other well enough to be able to predict behavior. Knowledge-based trust therefore presumes that you have an understanding of your partners' preferences and can predict their reactions. Such understanding only comes from repeated contact, continued communication and information exchange, in other words, greater interdependence. The more behavior (and therefore predictability) is confirmed through interaction, the more trust is developed. In addition, on the basis of the interaction, partners come to know and respect each other's capacities. Lewicki and Bunker (1996) call identification-based trust the highest order form of trust. Identification-based trust requires partners to internalize each other's preferences, see themselves as members of a group and internalize the goals of the group. Partners identify with each other's desires and intentions and mutual understanding is developed to the point that partners can act for each other.

The creation and maintenance of trust is not without problems though. Trust strongly depends on specific relationships among competent individuals (see Van Meerkerk and Edelenbos, 2014). This makes trust and its positive effects on vitality vulnerable, for example to changes in the formation of the people involved (cf. Raab et al., 2015). Carefully developed trust can easily decrease when important actors disappear from the network. These core individuals, for example boundary spanners, have invested a lot in building trustworthy relationships and much effort is required of them to maintain the (high) level of trust. When these individuals disappear, trust is no longer nurtured and can easily fall to lower levels that have impact at the level of collaboration in interactive governance processes. Trust is important but at the same time very fragile and it needs constant thought and attention (Lewicki and Bunker, 1996).

Institutionalized relational arrangements

Vitality is mostly developed in informal networks, as indicated above. However, vitality also needs consolidation, codification and formalization in institutional arrangements. This arrangement consists of a set of rules and (organization) structures (Hodge and Greve, 2005). The main purpose of institutional arrangements is that they regulate the interaction between actors involved in the interactive governance process (March and Olsen, 1989). According to Scharpf (1997: 38) these arrangements can be understood as "a system of rules that structure the courses of actions that a set of actors may choose." Institutional arrangements assure a certain stability and predictability in social behavior of and interactions between actors.

Elinor Ostrom (e.g. 1998) has paid much attention to institutional arrangement, especially regarding the management of common-pool resources. Common-pool resources are specific collective action problems that relate to the fact that the good involved is, by definition, semi-collective. Common-pool resources are supplies that are shared and used by individual (groups of) actors. But the danger is that individual members may end up using so much of the resource that other members (or potential future members – and thus future generations too) are deprived (Dietz et al., 2003). Elinor Ostrom's research focused specifically on the question of under what institutional context, rules and structures common-pool resources can be managed in a sustainable way.

Institutional arrangements can be strictly formalized in arrangements such as a steering committee or joint ventures, but can also be less formalized alliances or project group structures which function on a more ad hoc basis (Faulkner, 1995; Steijn et al., 2011). These arrangements are set in place to coordinate, supervise and control the complex interaction processes among different actors in the interactive governance network (Steijn et al., 2011). These rules and structures often are expressed in a written manner, in contracts (Bradach and Eccles, 1989).

This contract way of codifying coordination and interaction may have negative relationships with the previously discussed condition of trust (e.g. Bradach and Eccles, 1989; Gambetta, 1988; Ring and Van de Ven, 1994). They have stressed how trust and contract interact as substitutes. The idea is that the presence of trust leads to a reduction in opportunism and therefore there is less need for contracting (Gambetta, 1988). A reduction in trust would lead to an increase in opportunism and a stronger need for contracting. Moreover, contracting is thought to lead to less trust because it can be seen as a sign of distrust (see Ghoshal and Moran, 1996; Sundaramurthy and Lewis, 2003). The more an actor is able to control someone else by contract, the less he has to rely on trust. The use of control instruments may also diminish the intrinsic motivation among actors to behave in a trustworthy manner. This is called the "crowding-out effect" (Frey, 1993; 1997; Sundaramurthy and Lewis, 2003). In short, the substitutive point of view implies that trust removes the need for control and control chases away trust.

However, others argue that institutional arrangements through contracts can go together with trust, or even reinforce each other (e.g. Lane and Bachmann, 2001; Luhmann, 1988; Zand, 1972). Das and Teng (2001) for example argue that trust reduces the level of resistance, and brings harmony and interpersonal trust to the controller–controllee relationship. In other words individual and affect-based trust may assist the implementation of formal control through supervision structures and contracts. Important in this is the level of detail in the contract signing. If a contract has a lot of detailed rules and clauses it is related to a low level of trust among the partners. If a contract has less detailed rules and is more focused on general rules this opens up the possibility to develop trust (Jeffries and Reed, 2000). In this perspective the concept of a "relational contract" is used (Carson et al., 2006; Jeffries and Reed, 2000). A relational contract is a contract whose effect is based upon a relationship of trust between the parties. The explicit terms of the contract are just an outline as there are implicit terms and understandings which determine the behavior of the partners. Relational contract theory is characterized by a view of contracts as relations rather than as discrete transactions as is being done in traditional "classical" or "neo-classical contract" theory (Macneil, 1985). Macneil (1985) argues that relational contracts are agreements that are intentionally incomplete so that the contracting parties have room for maneuver. It is a logical response to bounded rationality (Jeffries and Reed, 2000: 874). The logic of relational contracting is that there are many nonlegal sanctions, like trust, reputation and the continuity of the relationship, that make it expedient for individuals to fulfill commitments (Carson et al., 2006: 1060).

However, building relational contracts can also have the same problems as with trust building and the fragile character of trust (Lewicki and Bunker, 1996). When problems and disagreements appear within areas of collaboration and trust, and the relational contract is not enough to prevent such disagreement, conflict can easily arise and take severe forms. Collaboration in turn quickly deteriorates and dissolves and can lead to judicial fighting and litigation. In relational contracts it is important that much attention and effort are paid to trust maintenance and even trust repair in situations of emerging conflict (Lewicki and Bunker, 1996).

4. INTERPLAY BETWEEN CONDITIONS: TOWARDS A CONFIGURATIONAL APPROACH

The conditions discussed above can be strongly interconnected in specific processes of interactive and collaborative governance; they can mutually reinforce each other. For example, the formation of informal spheres is often created and facilitated by boundary spanners in which trustworthy relations can be created which open up the opportunity for debate and deliberation (Van Meerkerk and Edelenbos, 2014). At the same time, a higher level of trust between actors is likely to increase their boundary spanning activities. However, if the conditions are strongly related this could also imply that a reduction in or absence of a certain condition negatively influences other conditions, leading to less collaboration in interactive governance networks. This in turn means that singular improvements or deterioration in one of the conditions is not likely to be decisive for realizing significant increases in the level of vitality. It is their mutual presence and interaction which account for the vitality of interactive governance and for the performance of these interactive governance networks. At the same time one could argue that some conditions are in some circumstances more important than others for realizing vitality. For example, in the beginning of interactive governance processes trust building can be considered as a necessary condition for developing a solid basis for collaboration.

Therefore, more empirical studies are needed to examine the interaction of these conditions and resulting outcomes. In a recent study, Edelenbos et al. (2015) found that (most of the) conditions discussed above are indeed important for the creation of vitality in interactive governance networks around wicked issues in the Netherlands. In their comparative case study they found different patterns for how factors interacted with each other. They found two distinct types of relationships among the conditions: (1) a substituting relationship, and (2) a mutually reinforcing relationship. In the former relationship, high "scores" for some conditions may compensate for or substitute lower "scores" for other conditions. This may change with the evolution of the network and the interactive governance process. For example, in one of the examined cases, very high scores on the presence of informal networks and boundary spanners compensated for lower scores on trust and institutional arrangements. Hence, a particular condition is not always as important in playing its substituting role in different phases of the network and the governance process. Each phase has its specific process-related characteristics making different conditions important for maintaining the level of vitality.

The second pattern (i.e. mutual reinforcing relations among conditions) was found in both cases. For example, in one of the cases – characterized by relatively significant changes in the level of vitality in the evolution of the case – changes started with different people (performing many boundary spanning activities) being active in constructing informal networks, which fuels constructive dialogue among actors in the social system which again further catalyzes the development of trust. How this mutually reinforcing relationship works in detail, and under which contingencies, is open for debate and future research.

Each project or case has its specific situational and contextual characteristics, leading to different patterns for developing and maintaining the level of vitality. This calls for additional studies using configurational approaches to further examine the vitality of interactive governance networks, alongside qualitative case study research and variance-based research building on surveys. A Qualitative Comparative Analysis (QCA) method is an example of such a configurational research approach (Verweij et al., 2013; Raab et al., 2015). It is interesting to examine further which conditions are related and are sufficient for developing vitality in interactive governance networks, and to what extent. Some conditions may be necessary but not sufficient and therefore may require other conditions to explain the level of vitality in interactive governance. Moreover, it can also be the case that some individual conditions are sufficient in explaining vitality. Finally, even the absence of conditions could explain vitality in interactive governance. This focus demands a specific approach in comparative case study research.

Configurational approaches are able to reveal such patterns. As noted by Raab et al. (2015: 481): "In a configurational approach, causal factors are not examined in isolation or in terms of their additive net effects, but are identified as necessary and sufficient conditions that collectively lead to a certain outcome" (see also Ragin, 1987). In configurational approaches, contextual effects are of central concern. This makes them an appropriate and interesting methodology with which to examine further the mutual relationships between the conditions of vitality and their effects. A configurational approach takes into account that the effect of an individual condition often depends on the presence or absence of other conditions.

5. CONCLUSION: FUTURE RESEARCH CHALLENGES

In this chapter we have conceptually and theoretically argued that environmental governance is in an important way *interactive* in nature. Various actors from different organizational backgrounds, different domains (public, private, societal, NGOs) and from different scales (local, regional, (trans)national) are interacting to reach a common ground for collective action in order to deal with wicked issues in an efficient, effective and legitimate way.

As argued in this chapter, the potential for securing effective and legitimate action is largely dependent on the vitality of interactive governance processes. Vitality expresses the high quality of interactions among actors (Healey, 1995; Horlings et al., 2009). Vital actor relationships provide the trustworthy context to explore and find new alternatives and solutions to complex issues (Folke et al., 2005). Vitality in interactive governance processes touches upon the processual and relational capacity among actors in the social system, and is considered important for adaptive and flexible responses to changes in ecological-environmental systems (Berkes and Folke, 1998). In our theoretical exploration and discussion we have searched for important conditions that influence the level of vitality in interactive governance networks. We have elaborated and discussed the conditions of informal spaces, boundary spanning activities, constructive dialogue and deliberation, trust, and relational arrangements as being import for developing and maintaining vitality in interactive governance networks.

However, realizing these conditions is not without challenges. Some of these conditions require specific skills and relational capacities from the participants (boundary spanning, trust building). But some of them are strongly dependent on the willingness of actors (e.g. constructive dialogue) and the institutional context in which these conditions are embedded. There is ever-existing tension between informal spaces and formal decision-making structures: it is important that power structures and processes of deliberation are nicely interfaced and connected. The throughput legitimacy of vital governance processes is served by this well-organized and functioning interface.

Moreover, these conditions may be strongly interconnected. This implies that all are cartwheels in a system that influences and mutually strengthens the others. For example, the formation of informal spheres is often created and facilitated by boundary spanners in which trustworthy relations can be created which open up the opportunity for debate and deliberation. However, this could also mean that when one cartwheel is missing the whole system is disrupted, ultimately leading to lower levels of vitality. On the other hand, from a configurational approach, one could also argue that the presence of a single condition could be sufficient for reaching vitality; moreover, one could assume that even the absence of certain conditions could be important for realizing vitality.

Hence, we still know little about the empirical mechanisms at work here. How this works empirically is for future empirical studies. In a recent study, Edelenbos et al. (2015) found that some of these conditions are indeed important for the creation of vitality in interactive governance networks. Further, this mutually reinforcing relationship among conditions was found, but how this works in detail, and under which circumstances, is open for debate and future research. For future studies we argue that configurational approaches might be promising (for example QCA), as these can study the combination of conditions, the absence of conditions and the sufficient presence of conditions regarding to collaboration and vitality in interactive governance (Raab et al., 2015). Each project or case has its specific situational and contextual characteristics, making different conditions important for developing and maintaining the level of vitality. This makes vitality an organic concept that cannot be developed or maintained mechanistically by choosing just one fixed (set of) conditions at all times. This implies that vitality should be studied in different contexts (different domains and sectors such as water, the environment, etc., and different countries, etc.) and situational settings (complexity of issue, phase of the collaboration, nature of collaboration (conflict, consensus, etc.)).

REFERENCES

Ansell, C. and Gash, A. (2008). Collaborative governance in theory and practice. *Journal of Public Administration Research and Theory*, 18(4), 543–571.

Ashmos, D.P., Duchon, D. and McDaniel, R.R. (2000). Organizational responses to complexity: The effect on organizational performance. *Journal of Organizational Change*, 13(6), 577–594.

Berkes, F. and Folke, C. (eds.) (1998). *Linking Social and Ecological Systems: Management Practices and Social Mechanisms for Building Resilience*. Cambridge, UK: Cambridge University Press.

Bradach, J.L. and Eccles, R.G. (1989). Price, authority, and trust: From ideal types to plural forms. In W. R. Scott (ed.), *Annual Review of Sociology, Volume 15*. Palo Alto, CA: Annual Reviews, pp. 97–118.

Carson, S.J., Madhok, A. and Wu, T. (2006). Uncertainty, opportunism, and governance: The effects of volatility and ambiguity on formal and relational contracting. *The Academy of Management Journal*, 49(5) (October), 1058–1077.

Castells, M. (1996). *The Rise of the Network Society*. Cambridge: Blackwell.

Dalton, R.J. (2008). Citizenship norms and the expansion of political participation. *Political Studies*, 56(1), 76–98.
Das, T.K. and Teng, B. (2001). Trust, control, and risk in strategic alliances: An integrated framework. *Organization Studies*, 22(2), 251–283.
Deakin, S. and Wilkinson, F. (1998). Contract law and the economics of inter-organizational trust. In C. Lane and R. Bachmann (eds.), *Trust Within and Between Organizations* (pp. 146–172). Oxford, UK: Oxford University Press.
Dietz, T., Ostrom, E. and Stern, P.C. (2003). The struggle to govern the commons. *Science*, 302(5652), 1907–1912.
Dryzek, J. (2010). *Foundations and Frontiers of Deliberative Governance*. Oxford, UK: Oxford University Press.
Edelenbos, J. (2005). Institutional implications of interactive governance: Insights from Dutch practice. *Governance: An International Journal of Policy, Administration, and Institutions*, 18(1), 111–134.
Edelenbos, J. and Klijn, E.H. (2007). Trust in complex decision-making networks; a theoretical and empirical exploration. *Administration and Society*, 39(1), 25–50.
Edelenbos, J., Buuren, M.W. van and Schie, N. van (2011). Co-producing knowledge: Joint knowledge production between experts, bureaucrats and stakeholders in Dutch water management projects. *Environmental Science & Policy*, 14(6), 675–684.
Edelenbos, J., Bressers, N. and Scholten, P. (2013). *Water Governance as Connective Capacity*. London: Ashgate.
Edelenbos, J., Van Meerkerk, I.F. and Van Leeuwen, C. (2015). Vitality of complex water governance systems: Condition and evolution. *Journal of Environmental Policy & Planning*, 17(2), 237–261.
Edelenbos, J. and Van Meerkerk, I. (eds.) (2016 forthcoming). *Critical Reflections on Interactive Governance*. Cheltenham, UK and Northampton, MA, USA: Edward Elgar Publishers.
Faulkner, D. (1995). *International Strategic Alliances*. Maidenhead, UK: McGraw-Hill.
Folke, C., Hahn, T., Olsson, P. and Norberg, J. (2005). Adaptive governance of social–ecological systems. *Annual Review of Environment and Resources*, 30, 441–473.
Foster-Fishman, P.G., Berkowitz, S.L., Lounsbury, D.W., Jacobson, S. and Allen, N. (2001). Building collaborative capacity in community coalitions: A review and integrative framework. *American Journal of Community Psychology*, 29(2), 241–261.
Frey, B.S. (1997). A constitution for knaves crowds out civic virtues. *The Economic Journal*, 107(443) (July), 1043–1053.
Gambetta, D. (1988). Can we trust trust? In D. Gambetta (ed.), *Trust: Making and Breaking Cooperative Relations*. New York: Basil Blackwell, pp. 213–238.
Ghoshal, S. and Moran, P. (1996). Bad for practice: A critique of the transaction cost theory. *Academy of Management Review*, 21, 13–47.
Goolsby, J.R. (1992). A theory of role stress in boundary spanning positions of marketing organizations. *Journal of the Academy of Marketing Science*, 20(2), 155–164.
Hajer, M. and Wagenaar, H. (eds.) (2003). *Deliberative Policy Analysis: Understanding Governance in the Network Society*. Cambridge: Cambridge University Press.

Healey, P. (1995). The institutional challenge for sustainable urban regeneration. *Cities*, 12(4), 221–230.
Healey, P. (2006). Transforming governance: Challenges of institutional adaptation and a new politics of space. *European Planning Studies*, 14(3), 299–320.
High, C., Slater, R. and Rengasamy, S. (2006). Are shadows dark? Governance, informal institutions and corruption in rural India. In L.V. Cheshire, V. Higgins and G. Lawrence (eds.), *Rural Governance: International Perspectives*. Abingdon: Routledge.
Hodge, G. and Greve, C. (2005). *The Challenge of Public Private Partnerships*. Cheltenham, UK and Northampton, MA, USA: Edward Elgar.
Horlings, I., Tops, P. and Ostaaijen, V. (2009). Regimes and vital coalitions in rural–urban regions in the Netherlands. In K. Andersson, M. Lehtola, E. Eklund and P. Salmi (eds.), *Beyond the Rural-urban Divide: Cross-continental Perspectives on the Differentiated Countryside and its Regulation*. Bingley: Emerald, pp. 191–220.
Huntjens, P., Pahl-Wostl, C., Flachner, Z., Neto, S., Koskova, R., Schlueter, M., NabideKiti, I. and Dickens, C. (2011). Adaptive water management and policy learning in a changing climate. A formal comparative analysis of eight water management regimes in Europe, Asia, and Africa. *Environmental Policy and Governance*, 21(3), 145–163.
Innes, J.E. and Booher, D.E. (2003). Collaborative policymaking: Governance through dialogue. In M.A. Hajer and H. Wagenaar (eds.), *Deliberative Policy Analysis: Understanding Governance in the Network Society*. Cambridge, UK: Cambridge University Press, pp. 33–59.
Innes, J.E. and Booher, D.E. (2010). *Planning with Complexity. An Introduction to Collaborative Rationality in Public Policy*. London: Routledge.
Jeffries, F.L. and Reed, R. (2000). Trust and adaptation in relational contracting. *The Academy of Management Review*, 25(4) (October), 873–882.
Klijn, E.H., Edelenbos, J. and Steijn, B. (2010). Trust in governance networks; its impact and outcomes. *Administration and Society*, 42(2), 193–221.
Kooiman, J. (ed.) (1993). *Modern Governance: New Government–Society Interactions*. London: Sage.
Koppenjan, J. and Klijn, E.H. (2004). *Managing Uncertainties in Networks*. London: Routledge.
Lane, C. and Bachmann, R. (eds.) (2001). *Trust Within and Between Organizations*. Oxford, UK: Oxford University Press.
Lawrence, T.B., Hardy, C. and Phillips, N. (2002). Institutional effects of interorganizational collaboration: The emergence of proto-institutions. *Academy of Management Journal*, 45(1), 281–290.
Levina, N. and Vaast, E. (2005). The emergence of boundary spanning competence in practice: Implications for implementation and use of information systems. *MIS Quarterly*, 29(2), 335–363.
Lewicki, R. J. and Bunker, B.B. (1996). Developing and maintaining trust in work relationships. In R.M. Kramer and T.R. Tyler (eds.), *Trust in Organizations: Frontiers of Theory and Research*. Thousand Oaks, CA: Sage, pp. 114–139.
Luhmann, N. (1988). Familiarity, confidence, trust: Problems and alternatives. In D. Gambetta (ed.), *Trust: Making and Breaking Cooperative Relations*. Oxford, UK: Oxford University Press, pp. 94–107.
Macneil, I.R. (1985). Relational contract: What we do and do not know. *Wisconsin Law Review*, 48, 483–526.

March, J.G. and Olsen, J.P. (1989). *Rediscovering Institutions. The Organizational Basis of Politics*. New York: Free Press.

Marsh, D. and Rhodes, R.A.W. (eds.) (1992). *Policy Networks in British Government*. Oxford, UK: The Clarendon Press.

Mayer, I. and Edelenbos, J. et al. (2005). Interactive policy development: Undermining or sustaining democracy? *Public Administration*, 83(1), 179–199.

Nabatchi, T. and Blomgren Amsler, L. (2014). Direct public engagement in local government. *American Review of Public Administration*, 44(4S), 63S–88S.

Nooteboom, B. (2002). *Trust: Forms, Foundations, Functions, Failures and Figures*. Cheltenham, UK and Northampton, MA, USA: Edward Elgar.

Nooteboom, S.G. (2006). *Adaptive Networks: The Governance for Sustainable Development*. Delft: Eburon.

Ostrom, E. (1998). The Institutional Analysis and Development Approach. In E.T. Loehman and D.M. Kilgour (eds.), *Designing Institutions for Environmental and Resource Management*. Cheltenham, UK and Lyme, NH, USA: Edward Elgar.

Ostrom, E. (2010). Beyond markets and states: Polycentric governance of complex economic systems. *The American Economic Review*, 100(3), 641–672.

Pahl-Wostl, C. (2007). Transitions towards adaptive management of water facing climate and global change. *Water Resources Management*, 21(1), 49.

Papadopoulos, Y. (2016 forthcoming). Interactive governance: authorisation, representation, and accountability. In J. Edelenbos and I. van Meerkerk (eds.), *Critical Reflections on Interactive Governance*. Cheltenham, UK and Northampton, MA, USA: Edward Elgar.

Pierre, J. (ed.) (2000). *Debating Governance: Authority, Democracy, and Steering*. Oxford, UK: Oxford University Press.

Pierre, J. and Peters, B Guy. (2000). *Governance, Politics and the State*. Basingstoke, UK: Macmillan.

Plummer, R., Crona, B., Armitage, D.R., Olsson, P., Tengo, M. and Yudina, O. (2012). Adaptive co-management: A systematic review and analysis. *Ecology and Society*, 17(3), 11. doi: 10.5751/ES-04952-170311

Pomeroy, R.S. and Berkes, F. (1997). Two to tango: The role of government in fisheries co-management. *Marine Policy*, 21(5), 465–480.

Raab, J., Mannak, R.S. and Cambré, B. (2015). Combining structure, governance, and context: A configurational approach to network effectiveness. *Journal of Public Administration Research and Theory*, 25(2), 479–511.

Ragin, C.C. (1987). *The Comparative Method: Moving Beyond Qualitative and Quantitative Strategies*. Berkeley and Los Angeles, CA: University of California Press.

Rhodes, R.A.W. (1997). *Understanding Governance. Policy Networks, Governance, Reflexivity, and Accountability*. Buckingham, UK: Open University Press.

Ring, P.S. and Van de Ven, A.H. (1994). Developmental processes of cooperative interorganizational relationships. *Academy of Management Review*, 19, 90–118.

Risse, T. and Kleine, M. (2007). Assessing the legitimacy of the EU's treaty revision methods. *Journal of Common Market Studies*, 45(1), 69–80.

Rittel, H.W.J. and Webber, M.M. (1973). Dilemmas in a general theory of planning. *Policy Sciences*, 4, 155–169.

Robinson, C.J. and Wallington, T.J. (2012). Boundary work: Engaging knowledge systems in co-management of feral animals on indigenous lands. *Ecology and Society*, 17(2), 16.

Rousseau, D., Sitkin, S.B., Burt, R.S. and Camerer, C. (1998). Not so different after all: A cross discipline view of trust. *The Academy of Management Review*, 23, 393–404.

Sako, M. (1998). Does trust improve business performance? In C. Lane and R. Bachmann (eds.), *Trust Within and Between Organizations: Conceptual Issues and Empirical Applications*. Oxford, UK: Oxford University Press, pp. 88–117.

Scharpf, F.W. (1997). *Games Real Actors Play, Actor-Centered Institutionalism in Policy Research*. Boulder, CO: Westview Press.

Scharpf, F. (1999). *Governing in Europe: Effective and Democratic?* New York: Oxford University Press.

Sørensen, E. and Torfing, J. (eds.) (2007). *Theories of Democratic Network Governance*. Cheltenham, UK and Northampton, MA, USA: Edward Elgar.

Steijn, A.J., Klijn, E.H. and Edelenbos, J. (2011). Public private partnerships: Added value by organisational form or management? *Public Administration*, 89(4), 1235–1252.

Sullivan, H. and Skelcher, C. (2002). *Working across Boundaries: Collaboration in Public Services*. New York: Palgrave Macmillan.

Sundaramurthy, C. and Lewis, M. (2003). Control and collaboration: Paradoxes of governance. *Academy of Management Review*, 28(3), 397–415.

Torfing, J., Peters, B.G., Pierre, J. and Sørensen, E. (2012). *Interactive Governance. Advancing the Paradigm*. Oxford, UK: Oxford University Press.

Tseng, C.-P. and Penning-Rowsell, E.C. (2012). Micro-political and related barriers to stakeholder engagement in flood risk management. *The Geographical Journal*, 178(3), 253–269.

Van Meerkerk, I. (2014). Boundary-spanning in governance networks. A study about the role of boundary spanners and their effects on democratic throughput legitimacy and performance of governance networks. Doctoral thesis. Rotterdam: Erasmus University Rotterdam.

Van Meerkerk, I. and Edelenbos, J. (2014). The effects of boundary spanners on trust and performance of urban governance networks. Findings from survey research on urban development projects in the Netherlands. *Policy Sciences*, 47(1), 3–24.

Van Meerkerk, I., Edelenbos, J. and Klijn, E.H. (2015). Connective management and governance network performance: The mediating role of throughput legitimacy. *Environment and Planning C: Government and Policy*, 33(4), 746–764.

Verweij, S., Klijn, E.H., Edelenbos, J. and Van Buuren, A. (2013). What makes governance networks work? A fuzzy set qualitative comparative analysis of 14 Dutch spatial planning projects. *Public Administration*, 91(4), 1035–1055.

Wagenaar, H. (2007). Governance, complexity, and democratic participation: How citizens and public officials harness the complexities of neighborhood decline. *American Review of Public Administration*, 37(1), 17–50.

Warner, J. (2006). More sustainable participation? Multi-stakeholder platforms for integrated catchment management. *International Journal of Water Resources Development*, 22(1), 15–35.

Williams, P. (2002). The competent boundary spanner. *Public Administration*, 80, 103–124.

Zand, D.E. (1972). Trust and managerial problem solving. *Administrative Science Quarterly*, 2, 229–239.

PART II

Problems and context

6. Where has all the salinity gone? The challenges of using science to inform local collaborative efforts to respond to large-scale environmental change

Mat Gilfedder, Cathy J. Robinson and Mike Grundy

INTRODUCTION

With unseasonal droughts and floods, and large-scale environmental degradation affecting many water-basins of the world, risk and uncertainty have become defining characteristics of watershed planning and management. In response, risk assessment has necessarily become a more sophisticated process, and has created new challenges around incorporating science to inform risk assessments and management (e.g. Rayner et al., 2005; Pollard et al., 2008; Gilfedder et al., 2014). Coupled with the unpredictability and complexity of water systems and their processes, and the ambiguity that results from diverse understandings of the problem and differing normative judgments of acceptable risk, these new challenges have prompted calls for a more relational and contextual approach to risk and uncertainty (Isendahl et al., 2010).

At the same time, water planning reforms have spurred the emergence of negotiated ecosystem management and water policy innovations that can be broadly described as collaborative (Yaffee et al., 1996; Lubell et al., 2002; Margerum and Robinson, 2015). Consensus and cooperation among multiple actors with economic, political or administrative stakes in policy outcomes are the hallmarks of such collaboration (Koontz et al., 2004; Lejano and Ingram, 2009), and collaborative partnerships have emerged between a range of government, community, corporate and non-governmental actors dissatisfied with the adversarial, command-and-control style of governance embodied by conventional environmental policies, many of which have left environmental problems unresolved (Margerum, 2011; Agranoff, 2012). Indeed, collaboration is increasingly presented as a promising means of integrating diverse knowledge and perspectives to facilitate the co-production of knowledge and action within uncertain conditions (e.g. Saravanan et al., 2009; Jacobs et al., 2010; Pahl-Wostl et al., 2010). As a result, collaborative watershed planning efforts have focused on enabling local groups to pursue and improve community-based planning agendas that are nested in basin-level goals, while maintaining the unique local values of their constituents (Curtis et al., 2014; Robinson et al., 2015a).

Insights from the sustainability science and collaborative governance literature highlight the importance of integrating a range of knowledge and perspectives into risk governance regimes and engaging a range of social actors through local and dialogue-based institutions (Hill et al., 2015; Robinson et al., 2015b). This has helped to enrich the concept of environmental risk beyond the probability of harm arising from physical, biological or social causes (accessible only to experts), and to recognize its historically, politically and culturally embedded character (Jasanoff, 1999). This development has prompted calls for "technologies of humility" that can incorporate the expectation of unforeseen consequences and acknowledge the plurality of perspectives and the need for mutual learning, and in doing so meaningfully inform collaborative policy strategies (Jasanoff, 2002).

There is now a growing body of scholarship on the nexus between the assessment and management of the "wicked problem" of broad-scale environmental risk and the design of collaborative practices, partnerships and policy instruments (Rittel and Webber, 1973; Dewulf et al., 2005; Marshall et al., 2013). This has prompted interest in the kinds of institutional arrangement that might support individual and community efforts to nest local planning goals within larger efforts (Ommer et al., 2012; Hill et al., 2015), as well as concern and uncertainty about how best to monitor and evaluate the impact of such collaboration in complex environmental management settings. Most of this concern focuses on the absence of suitable evidence that could be used to judge impact, given that environmental data take a long time to collect, and that changes in environmental conditions often occur at a rate that is incompatible with program or political timeframes and budgets (Koontz and Thomas, 2006; Robinson et al., 2009). Despite these challenges, key features of the collaborative process—including leadership (Ansell and Gash, 2008), mutual trust (McAllister et al., 2015; Stern and Coleman, 2015) and resources (Bidwell and Ryan, 2006)—continue to be linked with the delivery of outputs (such as creating plans; Mandarano, 2008) and the achievement of sustainable outcomes (e.g. Sabatier et al., 2005).

In this chapter, we build on this work by critically examining the role of science in relation to collaborative governance. Our analysis draws on the context of the Murray-Darling Basin to highlight key challenges of introducing complex and uncertain scientific information into real-world collaborative decisions and activities. We reflect on our own research conducted on regional natural resource management (NRM) and salinity issues during this period which included participation in a 2005 salinity workshop held with regional NRM staff and local Landcare coordinators in Queensland Murray-Darling Basin regions. Documentary analysis of government program guidelines was also undertaken. More specifically we examine the complexities around the science of dryland salinity in Australia and the difficulties faced by regional NRM bodies to translate this science to inform local collaborative Landcare groups' on-ground efforts. First we outline the regional NRM institutional factors that framed the way scientific information interacted and competed with local and political agendas. We then consider the characteristics of salinity and salinity science and consider the challenges of connecting this knowledge with day-to-day management agendas and needs. We draw on the challenges at the salinity science-collaborative governance interface but also note the importance of considering and debating science at the collaborative planning table, even if the information challenges fluctuating support for long-term, on-ground efforts to address broad and undesirable environmental change.

Community Participation through Landcare and Regional NRM

Australia has embarked on an ambitious experiment with voluntary community engagement in NRM. During the 1980s voluntary, self-organizing Landcare groups of farmers and community members were encouraged to apply for short-term National Heritage Trust (NHT) funding to address common problems and build a shared understanding of the broader environmental and social issues that were pertinent to sustainable NRM in the region (Curtis et al., 2014). Landcare was applauded for providing a forum for the creation of social capital which was deemed to be critical to the improvement in natural resource condition (Webb and Cary, 2005). By 1989 Landcare's success was recognized across Australia (Curtis and De Lacy, 1995, 1998) leading to a unique alliance of the National Farmers Federation and the Australian Conservation Foundation to create what was described by the then Prime Minister as a national achievement from a decade of local Landcare activities that relied on the "co-operation at all levels of government and by community groups who care for the land, who want to repair our damaged environment" (Hawke, 1989).

The NHT in 1996 and National Action Plan for Salinity and Water Quality (NAP) in 2000 together invested at least AUS$4.5 billion to help restore and conserve Australia's natural resources in collaborative

Landcare activities (Lane et al., 2009). By the 1990s a federal review of Landcare efforts funded by NHT1 in 1999 highlighted the need to concentrate planning and investment at the regional level (Australian Government Natural Resource Management Team, 2000). The Commonwealth released a national discussion paper *Managing Natural Resources in Rural Australia for a Sustainable Future* (National Natural Resource Management Task Force, 1999) that outlined the new focus on "regional empowerment and ownership through integrated regional planning." A central element to this effort was the establishment of regional NRM bodies as the focal organizational unit for investment at the regional scale. This model required a regional plan and investment strategy, which had to be accredited by the federal government in order to access resources (Lane et al., 2009). Plans had to specify a hierarchy of targets to be achieved across different temporal horizons: "aspirational" targets, which could take up to 50 years to attain; "resource condition" targets (indicators) based on biophysical attributes defined by the federal government, to be realistically achievable within a 10–20 year timeframe; and "management action" targets, which contribute to longer-term goals but are achievable within 1–5 years. Together, these targets created a framework by which to monitor and evaluate the implementation of NRM plans (Australian Government, 2003).

Under the regional NRM model, program rules stated that regional bodies had to collaborate with local Landcare groups to achieve regional targets that had to be consistent with the government's biophysical framing of national priorities (Australian Government, 2003). Scientific knowledge became critical to assess the resource condition of environmental assets such as water, soil and biodiversity. The connections in this hierarchy of targets were informed by an instrumental rationality of cause and effect relationships between program activities, outputs and ultimate resource condition outcomes (Wallington and Lawrence, 2009). The activities associated with the "management actions," delineated into categories that included resource assessment, planning, capacity building and on-ground work, were supported by government funding to the extent that they led to changes in biophysical resource condition. Local knowledge became critical to enable on-ground actions to be suited to local agendas. In this sense local and scientific knowledge were put into the mix with program rules to define the management problem and then, through some form of negotiation, consensus or advisory process, determine the "best" course of action.

Salinity and Salinity Science in Australia's Murray-Darling Basin

At the same time as Australia was embarking on the local and regional "experiment" in collaborative and coordinated approaches to NRM governance, scientists were building consensus on the nature and extent of groundwater-related salinization problems in the Murray-Darling Basin (Brown et al., 1988). This science demonstrated that salts have built up in the Australian landscape as a result of long-term natural physical processes, including rainfall carrying oceanic salts (Simpson and Herczeg, 1994)—a natural expression of salt in the landscape referred to as primary salinity. Secondary salinity, however, results from human-induced changes that mobilize salts to the land surface. This includes the increased discharge of saline water into streams and shallow groundwater systems—termed dryland salinity—caused by the removal of deep-rooted native vegetation, which increases groundwater recharge rates (Allison and Hughes, 1983; Allison et al., 1990), and by increased salt export (Peck and Hurle, 1973).

The scale of the salinity risk was highlighted by the Prime Minister's Science, Engineering and Innovation Council (PMSEIC, 1999) and in the National Land and Water Resources Audit (NLWRA, 2001), both of which emphasized the complexity of the relationship between management actions and environmental outcomes:

> [T]he time scales over which salinity establishes itself, spreads and has its effects can be long, but once established it can be very difficult or impossible to contain or reverse. As a consequence, salinity must inevitably continue to get worse in Australia as a result of land use decisions already made. (PMSEIC, 1999, p. 8)

It was found that the intensification of agriculture and clearing of native vegetation in the Murray-Darling Basin had led to rising water tables and soil salinization, prompting concerns among farmers and environmental groups about the significant risks of salinity to agricultural production and the natural environment (Walker et al., 1999).

The physical processes underlying salinity are well understood in general terms (Grundy et al., 2007) but there is great variability in how salinity changes over time. The rainfall input to the system is also highly variable, and catchment properties such as topography, aquifer parameters, and the scale of the groundwater system result in different groundwater response times (Gilfedder et al., 2009; Walker et al., 2015). This variability makes it difficult to predict with certainty the expression of dryland salinity in the landscape. This body of science has also shown that there are large areas in Australia, including regions in the Murray-Darling Basin, that are partly or wholly dependent on groundwater systems to support agricultural production and environmental systems (Murray-Darling Basin Commission, 1999).

In response, the newly established Murray-Darling Basin Commission initiated a basin-scale salinity management effort. Management attention

Figure 6.1 Map showing the Murray-Darling Basin in southeastern Australia

and resources focused on addressing the impact in irrigation areas and implementing large-scale engineering works to reduce stream salinity, including salt interception schemes and drainage diversion schemes. The key metric used to determine the efficacy of these efforts was the stream salinity recorded at Morgan, in the lower River Murray (and the location of one of the major water off-take pipelines for South Australia) (Figure 6.1).

More sophisticated scientific assessments of the basin continued and showed the growing risk caused by dryland salinity to both streams and land. Summarizing historical stream salinity trends and catchment salt balances across the Murray-Darling Basin (Jolly et al., 2001), these studies predicted increased dryland salinity, resulting in stream salinity (e.g. Earl, 1988; Evans, 1994). To address this, basin planners increased the scope of salinity management to include dryland areas (Murray-Darling Basin Ministerial Council, 1999), and targets for "end-of-valley" stream salinity, salt load and flow for each tributary valley were established to provide locally relevant targets for salinity management actions (Murray-Darling Basin Ministerial Council, 2001).

We now turn to examine the institutional factors affecting the salinity science-collaborative interface which was framed by a national effort to tackle these large complex environmental issues through collaborative arrangements and processes working between local and regional scales. National objectives had to be re-framed into regional priorities that were highly reliant on voluntary activities of rural landholders. This demanded significant efforts by regional NRM bodies to create the knowledge base used to guide local on-ground activities and support.

Challenges at the Salinity Science-collaborative Governance Interface

Landcare efforts to plant trees that were coordinated through regional NRM planning efforts became a key response to the salinity crisis. The first major program of investment under the regional NHT2 program was the announcement of the National Action Plan for Salinity and Water Quality (NAP) in 2000. This program was designed with the specific intention to target investment to 21 priority regions that would receive a total of AUS$700 million of funding over eight years. Many of these lay in the Murray-Darling Basin (Figure 6.2). A key goal of the NAP was to "motivate and enable regional communities to use coordinated and targeted action" to prevent, stabilize and reverse trends in dryland salinity, which were affecting the sustainability of production, the conservation of biological diversity and the viability of infrastructure (Australian Government Natural Resource Management Team, 2000). By 2006, the Federal Department of Environment was noting in its annual report that tree planting and other salinity and soil erosion management measures now covered over 600,000 hectares of land across the 21 regions and involved 800,000 volunteers (Australian Government, 2007).

Workshop participants who reflected on salinity partnerships and activities in Queensland's part of the Murray-Darling Basin noted that regional targets set to direct on-ground tree-planting programs were based on interpretations of a confusing range of government guidelines and frameworks, incomplete science and diverse contributions from "local" knowledge. As one workshop participant put it, salinity had to "make sense" within the social, biophysical and political context of the region. This meant that available knowledge had to be embedded in local landscapes and social networks:

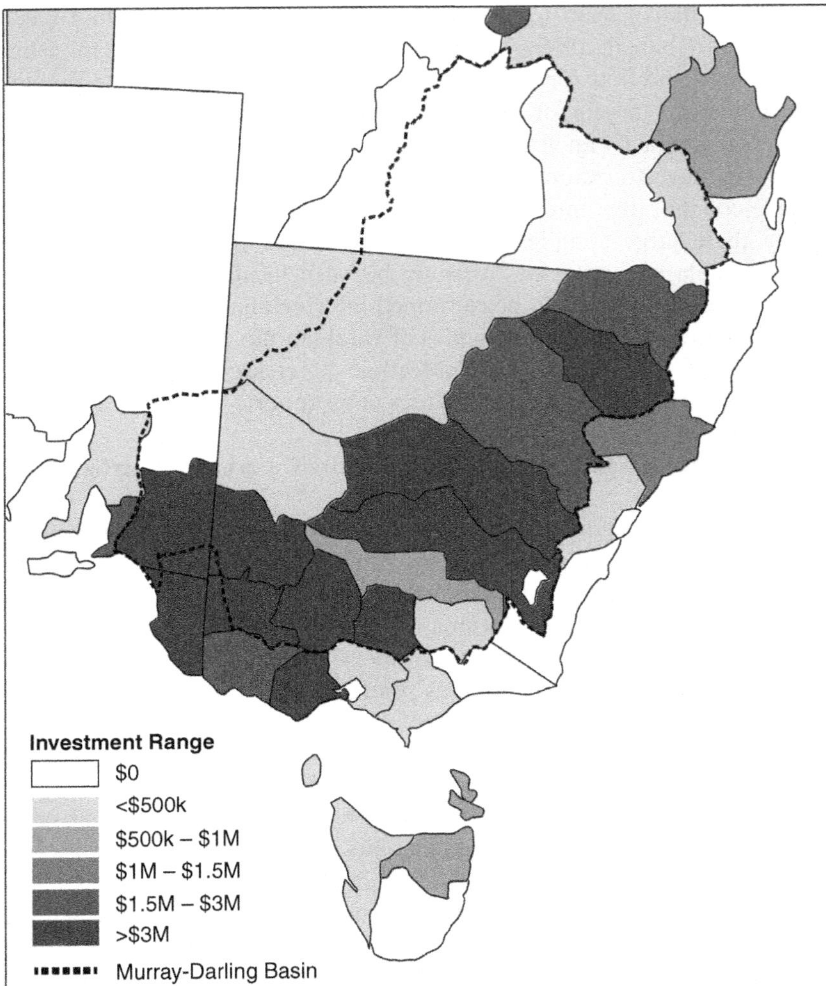

Source: Data from Figure 3.1 in National Action Plan for Salinity and Water Quality Natural Heritage Trust, 2005.

Figure 6.2 Regions addressing land salinity through investments funded through the NAP in the Murray-Darling Basin in 2004–2005

> We had to ensure that the benefits of tackling salinity matched the motivations of landholder to voluntarily engage in these activities. Planting trees was a great solution as it was a tangible activity that was valued by locals . . . it was also a solution for salinity that was backed up by science. (Queensland Salinity Workshop, 2005)

Although local land-use and management options to address salinity risk were identified (Stirzaker et al., 2000), scientific understandings of the underlying groundwater system were still limited. Modeling tools were developed to investigate the balance between land-use change, recharge change, groundwater response and salt discharge to streams. These included simple catchment models such as BC2C (Gilfedder et al., 2009) and 2CSalt (Stenson et al., 2011), which helped estimate the impacts of land-use change on groundwater recharge at a catchment scale. Yet despite these advances in understanding the nature and impact of salinity there remained a challenge of enabling local collaborative institutions to use this information to guide planning and on-ground activities.

Some of the challenges facing the salinity science-collaborative interface were related to the difficulties faced by regional NRM bodies to account for their progress towards the achievement of resource condition targets, and ultimately national priorities. A key uncertainty in the process was the time lag between taking an action (such as re-vegetation) and observation of the expected result (such as reduction in dryland salinity). Independent evaluations of regional NRM arrangements also found that the processes to administer and demonstrate performance were cumbersome and inefficient, and this led to a focus on activities and outputs at the expense of delivering outcomes (see Robinson et al., 2009).

Regional NRM bodies responded to this challenge by negotiating data sharing agreements and partnerships to build scientific expertise in the regions. Technical, operational and Indigenous advisory structures were also created to secure community credibility and legitimacy in regional NRM priorities and activities. A plethora of scientific summaries, tool kits and community-based information sheets about salinity issues were created and passed on to regional NRM bodies and Landcare groups. Despite these efforts, surveys of local Landcare groups and regional NRM body members showed that local and regional NRM institutions struggled to translate this information to inform and manage stakeholder efforts and expectations (see Davis et al., 2001). Landcare facilitators reportedly lacked sufficient technical and agricultural knowledge to function as useful knowledge brokers (Pannell, 2001), and local communities reported that they had little confidence in the information systems in place, and that it was difficult to obtain and translate available scientific information to inform local and regional planning efforts (e.g. ANAO, 2004, 38–40).

High transaction costs involved in managing the science to ensure alignment of available research to local and regional priorities was reported as a key issue in many regions. Scientific contributions that could support livelihood agendas, bolster the power behind community-driven regional targets, or accept the uncertainty of information available in this region were highlighted as "appropriate forms of best-science practice" (cf. McDonald et al., 2005). When classical notions of expertise were considered inappropriate, regional body members who attended the Queensland salinity workshop described how they began to develop and legitimate their own evidence base to inform local efforts. This involved balancing scientific rigor against utility, adopting a critical and flexible approach in using and ignoring science, and drawing on a diversity of knowledge suppliers.

Meanwhile increased investment in salinity science continued to highlight the challenges of managing this large-scale and complex environmental issue. Studies in the Murray-Darling Basin demonstrated the magnitude of water leakage into groundwater systems caused by different land-use systems (compared to native vegetation; Walker et al., 2003), reaching the challenging conclusion that some groundwater systems may take hundreds of years to respond to land-use changes. As this increased recharge drives' changes in groundwater storage (rising water tables) and increased discharge of saline groundwater to the land surface and to streams, it highlights that there could be limitations to the impact on salinity causing processes due to local Landcare re-vegetation efforts (Figure 6.3). In light of this finding, scientists expressed growing concerns about managing stakeholder and government expectations about the speed with which salt-affected landscapes would respond to tree planting and other community-based land management activities.

Studies also showed that adoption of best management practices for salinity among farmers was modest, and that most farmers were not overly concerned about the impacts caused by rising groundwater tables (Pannell, 2001). Some critics even argued that the NAP program was fatally flawed because it was premised on the government's assumption that local ownership of problems would motivate sufficient voluntary community action to ensure that large-scale NRM problems, such as salinity, could be managed affordably (Marshall, 2011; Curtis et al., 2014).

These concerns led to the Australian National Audit Office Report (2004–2005) into the National Action Plan for Salinity and Water Quality which noted the complexity of the risks associated with salinity and its management (ANAO, 2004). In particular, it was becoming clear that a low-cost solution—such as planting a relatively small proportion of the landscape with trees—did not exist, and that there were limits to the impact of funding collaborative and capacity building efforts to encourage landscape change. The ANAO (2008) concluded it was "not possible to report meaningfully on the extent to which . . .

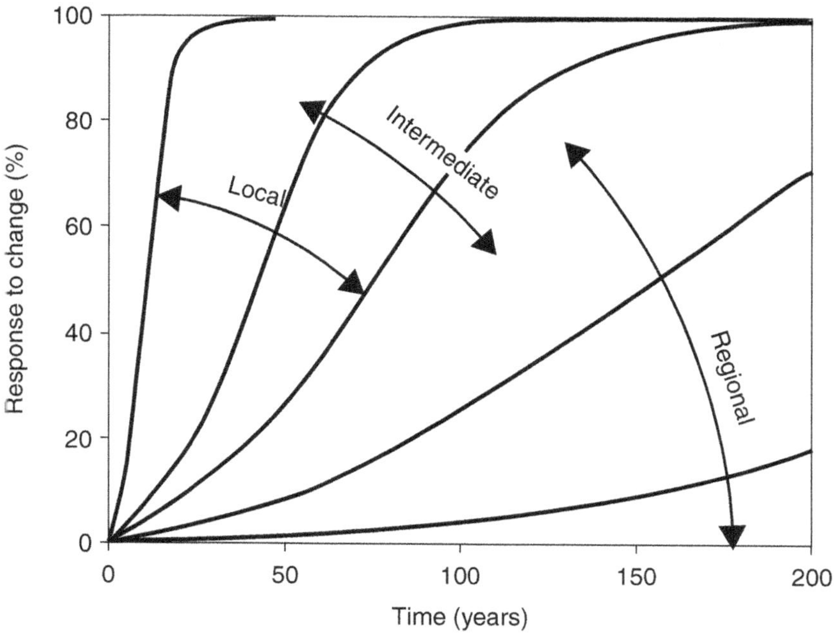

Source: From Walker et al., 2003.

Figure 6.3 Groundwater response to changes is variable, and can take centuries to respond

outputs (delivered by on-ground activities) contribute to the outcomes sought by the government." In part, this was due to "the absence of consistently validated data" and "the lack of agreement on performance indicators" (ANAO, 2008, 6). As a result, the challenges such as dryland salinity required "strong collaborative efforts at all levels (national, regional and local) if resources are to be well targeted and used effectively under [planned government funding] investment" (ANAO, 2008, 19).

When the NAP ceased on 30 June 2008, the Australian Government commenced with a "Caring for our Country" initiative, which consolidated previous measures including the NHT and the National Landcare Program. When the Australian Government rationalized its reduced support for on-ground salinity management measures, the politics at the science-policy interface were apparent. The difficulty of implementing key research findings in salinity programs was highlighted as a key and enduring issue, and the Australian Government argued that short-term and long-term climate change caused by a prolonged drought had reduced the risk of salinity:

> . . . recent research on the extent of salinity . . . conducted by the Australian Bureau of Agricultural and Resource Economics and Sciences . . . demonstrated that ground water levels across eastern Australia had fallen since 2000 as a result of reduced rainfall. Climate change predictions suggest that there will be ongoing reductions in average annual rainfall, further reducing the area considered to be at risk from salinity. (Australian Government, 2006)

The salinity workshop held between the Murray-Darling Basin's Queensland regional NRM staff and Landcare representatives was at the end of salinity program funding effort and prompted collaborators to reflect on this experience for future partnerships and activities. A participating farmer noted that it didn't matter if landholders were no longer being asked to plant trees for salinity because he had always planted trees to deliver locally determined social and environmental goals. Workshop participants agreed that the challenge of keeping local-regional NRM body partnerships strong was to embed these local values into the next program logic because, as one workshop participant put it:

> Planting trees is good . . . maybe for salinity, maybe for things we value . . . We do need to be clear that this [salinity] experience tells us what we can't be expected to do . . . to rely on the efforts of locals to solve a difficult environmental issue . . . It needs a long-term partnership with government which brings us all in to tackle this for the long haul. (Queensland Salinity Workshop, 2005)

DISCUSSION AND CONCLUSION

The long-term effort to manage Australia's dryland salinity was fuelled by the hope that a large investment of science, enduring local on-ground effort and multi-scalar collaboration would reduce or eliminate the salinity crisis. In reality, however, locals were tasked with an impossible job and the limits of local and collaborative efforts, coupled with unrealistic expectations, resulted in salinity being taken off the NHT/NAP resource table. Today, salinity is a very small part of current on-ground tree planting programs, including the AUS$50 million 20 Million Trees Program (focused on creating green corridors), the AUS$525 million Green Army Program (focused on providing training and employment opportunities for young Australians; Commonwealth of Australia, 2015), and the Carbon Farming

Initiative biodiversity fund, created as part of Australia's legislative response to climate change.

The legacy of Australia's efforts to tackle dryland salinity reflects the importance of building the institutional capacity to integrate different actors and different types of knowledge—a capacity that is critical to help understand resource governance problems and to identify innovative solutions (Berkes and Folke, 2002; Jacobs et al., 2010). With salinity low on Australia's NRM program priority list, planners, local farmers and rural communities in the Murray-Darling Basin are now engaging with different scientists (who have expertise in forecasting seasonal and inter-annual variation in climate conditions) and are applying to initiate on-farm revegetation activities under climate adaptation and training programs. It is still difficult to maintain scientific and technical fidelity in environmental management when significant activities are devolved to collaborative processes and on-ground work is controlled by voluntary landholder efforts (e.g. Renwick et al., 2014; Robinson et al., 2016).

Empirical studies show that managers are often receptive toward the use of scientific information in decision making, but they also reveal that such information is rarely acted upon directly (Rayner et al., 2005). More generally, the assumption that good information will automatically influence strategic collaborative management decisions has been discredited by a growing stock of evidence (e.g. Cash et al., 2002; Roux et al., 2006). When scientific evidence suggests management responses that are disconnected from the local temporal and spatial scales driving on-ground collaborative efforts it can be difficult to ensure science contributions remain on the collaborative decision-making table (Gilfedder et al., 2014; Wyborn and Bixler, 2013).

Other challenges facing the science-collaborative governance interface are associated with the conflict faced by hybrid organizations charged with brokering local collective efforts while meeting program goals and priorities (Lubell et al., 2002; Robinson et al., 2014). Some of these science-management tensions reflect the nature of complex environmental issues and solutions that do not present win-win scenarios for all stakeholders involved (Sullivan and Skelcher, 2002). This can create high transaction costs as partners struggle to commit to long-term and difficult actions that are often required (Lubell et al., 2002) and this commitment can be further tested when the scientific knowledge underpinning these solutions is not trusted, remains uncertain or becomes unstable (Cash et al., 2002; Sabatier et al., 2005). The example of how salinity science was worked and reworked by regional NRM bodies in Australia also highlights the challenges faced by hybrid entities to account for multiple relationships because they rely on government *and* community resources and support. As a result, watershed groups, NRM bodies and other hybrid organizations can be involved in challenging knowledge brokering and blocking activities in their efforts to try to navigate the multiple and contradictory accountability regimes that seek to respond to the needs of local stakeholders and also to central government who require them to ensure that national goals are met (Wallington and Lawrence, 2009).

Scientists also need to step up to the collaborative governance challenge. Communication and knowledge transfer are vital to collaborative efforts if advances in scientific and other forms of knowledge are to be translated and integrated into organizational decision making (Owens et al., 2006), and selecting an effective knowledge transfer model is therefore of critical importance. Recognition that complex issues are affected by dynamic social-ecological system interactions has stimulated growth in trans-disciplinary approaches that consider and create pathways that bring science and management together in more productive ways (Goldstein, 2010; Jacobs et al., 2010). This body of work highlights the need for more pragmatic ways to translate science to inform local collaborative efforts—a process that requires knowledge-making practices that interpret and reinterpret scientific evidence and enables collaboration between multiple social actors and sources of knowledge (Ommer et al., 2012; Hill et al., 2015).

Science-action system linking practices such as the conduct of brokers, the co-production of planning maps, models and the role of leading influencers from policy, management and science have become the focus of recent scholarly attention (Jasanoff, 2002; Roux et al., 2006; Lynch et al., 2015). Even so, there is still much to learn about the collaborative institutional conditions that support science-knowledge partnerships and lead to sustainable outcomes (Hill et al., 2015). What is clear is that the issue of power and agency that permeates processes of knowledge production and quality control affect scientific knowledge (e.g. Rayner et al., 2005) and the way scientific evidence is handled within collaborative decision-making structures and processes (Muñoz-Erickson et al., 2010). Scientists are a part of rather than separate to this collaborative effort and this demands an approach that views science as one part of the collaborative network.

Scientific analyses indicate that effective collaboration is urgent as large-scale environmental degradation and human activities exceed many biophysical parameters of our planet (e.g. Costanza et al., 2014). Science can help ensure collaboration handles the notoriously difficult task of mediating and translating connections between different types of knowledge and action for sustainable management outcomes. This can be challenging—particularly in contexts where the credibility of scientific knowledge is contested and the process through which knowledge is legitimized requires careful negotiation. Different values, expectations, knowledge systems and motivations may have led to a tension between democracy and technocracy which resulted in salinity being taken off the regional NRM planning table (Lane et al., 2009). Yet salinity remains a key risk facing Australia's rural industries, communities and landscapes. Technical and scientific information needs to remain part of the collaborative decision-making effort to provide balanced interpretations of multiple time lags between management interventions and responses, different and interacting drivers of landscape change, and to account for less tangible or socially rewarding environmental management outcomes.

REFERENCES

Agranoff, R. (2012). *Collaborating to Manage: A Primer for the Public Sector*. Washington, DC: Georgetown University Press.

Allison, G. B., and Hughes, M. W. (1983). The use of natural tracers as indicators of soil-water movement in a temperate semi-arid region. *Journal of Hydrology*, 60, 157–173. doi:10.1016/0022-1694(83)90019-7

Allison, G. B., Cook, P. G., Barnett, S. R., Walker, G. R., Jolly, I. D., and Hughes, M. W. (1990). Land clearance and river salinisation in the western Murray Basin, Australia. *Journal of Hydrology*, 119(1–4), 1–20. doi:10.1016/0022-1694(90)90030-2

ANAO (2004). The Administration of the National Action Plan for Salinity and Water Quality. ANAO Audit Report No.17 2004–05. Canberra: Commonwealth of Australia. Retrieved from http://www.anao.gov.au/~/media/Uploads/Documents/2004%2005_audit_report_17.pdf

ANAO (2008). Regional Delivery Model for the Natural Heritage Trust and the National Action Plan for Salinity and Water Quality. ANAO Audit Report No.21 2006–07. Canberra: Commonwealth of Australia. Retrieved from http://www.anao.gov.au/~/media/Uploads/Documents/2007%2008_audit_report_21.pdf

Ansell, C., and Gash, A. (2008). Collaborative governance in theory and practice. *Journal of Public Administration Research and Theory*, 18(4), 543–571. doi:10.1093/jopart/mum032

Australian Government (2003). National Framework for Natural Resource Management Standards and Targets. Natural Resource Management Ministerial Council, Canberra.

Australian Government (2006). Living with Salinity. Retrieved from http://www.agriculture.gov.au/ag-farm-food/natural-resources/salinity/australian-government-response-living-with-salinity (accessed 11 September 2015).

Australian Government (2007). Annual Report 2006–2007. Canberra: Department of the Environment and Water Resources. Retrieved from http://www.environment.gov.au/archive/about/publications/annual-report/06-07/pubs/vol1-full.pdf

Australian Government Natural Resource Management Team (2000). A National Action Plan for Salinity and Water Quality. Canberra: Department of

Agriculture, Fisheries and Forestry. Retrieved from http://nrmonline.nrm.gov.au/catalog/mql:2573

Berkes, F., and Folke, C. (2002). Back to the future: ecosystem dynamics and local knowledge. In L. H. Gunderson, and C. S. Holling (eds.), *Panarchy: Understanding Transformations in Human and Natural Systems* (pp. 121–146). Washington, DC: Island Press.

Bidwell, R. D., and Ryan, C. M. (2006). Collaborative partnership design: the implications of organizational affiliation for watershed partnerships. *Society & Natural Resources*, 19(9), 827–843. doi:10.1080/08941920600835585

Brown, C. M., Kellett, J. R., and Evans, W. R. (1988). Conference Summary Report – Murray 88 Conference – Geology, Groundwater and Salinity Management. Record 1988/43. Canberra: Bureau of Mineral Resources, Geology and Geophysics.

Cash, D., Clark, W. C., Alcock, F., Dickson, N., Eckley, N., and Jäger, J. S. (2002). Credibility, Legitimacy and Boundaries: Linking Research, Assessment and Decision Making. KSG Working Papers Series RWP02-046. Retrieved from http://ssrn.com/abstract=372280

Commonwealth of Australia (2015). About the Green Army Programme. Retrieved from http://www.environment.gov.au/land/green-army/about

Costanza, R., de Groot, R., Sutton, P., van der Ploeg, S., Anderson, S. J., Kubiszewski, I., Farber, S., and Turner, R. K. (2014). Changes in the global value of ecosystem services. *Global Environmental Change*, 26, 152–158. doi:10.1016/j.gloenvcha.2014.04.002

Curtis, A., and De Lacy, T. (1995). Examining the assumptions underlying Landcare. *Rural Society*, 5(2–3), 44–55. doi:10.5172/rsj.5.2-3.44

Curtis, A., and De Lacy, T. (1998). Landcare, Stewardship and Sustainable Agriculture in Australia. *Environmental Values*, 7(1), 59–78. doi:10.3197/096327198129341474

Curtis, A., Ross, H., Marshall, G. R., Baldwin, C., Cavaye, J., Freeman, C., Carr, A., and Syme, G. J. (2014). The great experiment with devolved NRM governance: lessons from community engagement in Australia and New Zealand since the 1980s. *Australasian Journal of Environmental Management*, 21(2), 175–199. doi:10.1080/14486563.2014.935747

Davis, J. A., Finlayson, B. L., and Hart, B. T. (2001). Barriers to science informing community-based land and water management. *Australasian Journal of Environmental Management*, 8(2), 99–104. doi:10.1080/14486563.2001.10648518

Dewulf, A., Craps, M., Bouwen, R., Taillieu, T., and Pahl-Wostl, C. (2005). Integrated management of natural resources: dealing with ambiguous issues, multiple actors and diverging frames. *Water Science & Technology*, 52(6), 115–124.

Earl, G. C. (1988). Stream Salinities and Saltloads in the Goulburn and Broken River Catchments. Investigation Branch Report 1988/4, Melbourne: Rural Water Commission.

Evans, W. R. (1994). Regional salt balances and implications for dryland salinity management. In *Proceedings of XXV Congress of the IAHR and IAHS – Water Down Under*, 2, 349–353. Adelaide: Institution of Engineers, Australia.

Gilfedder, M., Walker, G. R., Dawes, W. R., and Stenson, M. P. (2009). Prioritisation approach for estimating the biophysical impacts of land-use change on stream flow and salt export at a catchment scale. *Environmental Modelling and Software*, 24, 262–269. doi:10.1016/j.envsoft.2008.06.009

Gilfedder, M., Podger, G., Rassam, D., Pagendam, D., and Robinson, C. J. (2014). Trajectory river modelling – A decision-support tool to help manage multiple risks associated with planning around variable water resources. *Marine & Freshwater Research*, 65(12), 1072–1081. doi:10.1071/MF14002

Goldstein, B. E. (2010). The weakness of tight ties: why scientists almost destroyed the Coachella valley multispecies habitat conservation plan in order to save it. *Environmental Management*, 46(2), 268–284.

Grundy, M. J., Silburn, D. M., and Chamberlain, T. (2007). A risk framework for preventing salinity. *Environmental Hazards*, 7, 97–105. doi:10.1016/j.envhaz.2007.07.004

Hawke, R. J. (1989). The Hon Bob Hawke, Prime Minister, Launch of statement on the environment, 20 July 1989. Retrieved from http://www.bobhawkelandcareaward.com.au/bob-hawke-speech.pdf (accessed 22 September 2014).

Hill, R., Davies, J., Bohnet, I., Robinson, C. J., Maclean, K., and Pert, P. L. (2015). Collaboration mobilises institutions with scale-dependent comparative advantage in landscape-scale biodiversity conservation. *Environmental Science & Policy*, 51, 267–277. doi:10.1016/j.envsci.2015.04.014

Isendahl, N., Pahl-Wostl, C., and Dewulf, A. (2010). Using framing parameters to improve handling of uncertainties in water management practice. *Environmental Policy and Governance*, 20(2), 107–122. doi:10.1002/eet.533

Jacobs, K., Lebel, L., Buizer, J., Addams, L., Matson, P., McCullough, E., Garden, P., Saliba, G., and Finan, T. (2010). Linking knowledge with action in the pursuit of sustainable water-resources management. *Proceedings of the National Academy of Sciences*. doi:10.1073/pnas.0813125107

Jasanoff, S. (1999). The songlines of risk. *Environmental Values*, 8(2), 135–152. http://www.jstor.org/stable/30301700

Jasanoff, S. (2002). Citizens at risk: cultures of modernity in the US and EU. *Science as Culture*, 11(3), 363–380. doi:10.1080/0950543022000005087

Jolly, I. D., Williamson, D. R., Gilfedder, M., Walker, G. R., Morton, R., Robinson, G., Jones, H., Zhang, L., Dowling, T. I., Dyce, P., Nathan, R. J., Nandakumar, N., Clarke, R., and McNeill, V. (2001). Historical stream salinity trends and catchment salt balances in the Murray-Darling Basin, Australia. *Marine & Freshwater Resources*, 52(1), 53–63. doi:10.1071/MF00018

Koontz, T. M., and Thomas, C. W. (2006). What do we know and need to know about the environmental outcomes of collaborative management? *Public Administration Review*, 66, 111–121. http://www.jstor.org/stable/4096575

Koontz, T. M., Steelman, T. A., Carmin, J., Smith Korfmacher, K., Mosely, C., and Thomas, C. W. (2004). *Collaborative Environmental Management: What Roles for Government?* Washington, DC: Resources for the Future.

Lane, M., Robinson, C. J., and Taylor, B. (eds.) (2009). *Contested Country*. Melbourne: CSIRO Publishing.

Lejano, R. P., and Ingram, H. (2009). Collaborative networks and new ways of knowing. *Environmental Science & Policy*, 12(6), 653–662. doi:10.1016/j.envsci.2008.09.005

Lubell, M., Schneider, N., Scholz, J. T., and Mete, M. (2002). Watershed partnerships and the emergence of collective action institutions. *American Journal of Political Science*, 46(1), 148–163. http://www.jstor.org/stable/3088419

Lynch, A. J. J., Thackway, R., Specht, A., Beggs, P. J., Brisbane, S., Burns, E. L., Byrne, M., Capon, S. J., Casanova, M. T., Clarke, P. A., Davies, J. M., Dovers, S., Dwyer, R. G., Ens, E., Fisher, D. O., Flanigan, M., Garnier, E., Guru,

S. M., Kilminster, K., Locke, J., Mac Nally, R., McMahon, K. M., Mitchell, P. J., Pierson, J. C., Rodgers, E. M., Russell-Smith, J., Udy, J., and Waycott, M. (2015). Transdisciplinary synthesis for ecosystem science, policy and management: the Australian experience. *Science of the Total Environment*, 534, 173–184. doi:10.1016/j.scitotenv.2015.04.100

Mandarano, L. A. (2008). Evaluating collaborative environmental planning outputs and outcomes: restoring and protecting habitat and the New York–New Jersey harbor estuary program. *Journal of Planning Education and Research*, 27(4), 456–468. doi:10.1177/0739456X08315888

Margerum, R. D. (2011). *Beyond Consensus: Improving Collaborative Planning and Management*. Cambridge, MA: The MIT Press.

Margerum, R. D., and Robinson, C. J. (2015). Collaborative partnerships and the challenges for sustainable water management. *Current Opinion in Environmental Sustainability*, 12, 53–58. doi:10.1016/j.cosust.2014.09.003

Marshall, G. R. (2011). What 'community' means for farmer adoption of conservation practices. In D. J. Pannell, and F. M. Vanclay (eds.), *Changing Land Management: Adoption of New Practices by Rural Landholders* (pp. 107–126). Melbourne: CSIRO Publishing.

Marshall, G. R., Connell, D., and Taylor, B. M. (2013). Australia's Murray-Darling Basin: a century of polycentric experiments in cross-border integration of water resources management. *International Journal of Water Governance*, 1, 197–218. doi:10.7564/13-IJWG17

McAllister, R., Robinson, C. J., Maclean, K., Guerrero, A., Collins, K., Taylor, B., and De Barro, P. (2015). From local to central: a network analysis of who manages plant pest and disease outbreaks across scales. *Ecology and Society*, 20(1), 67. doi:10.5751/ES-07469-200167

McDonald, G., Taylor, B., Bellamy, J., Robinson, C.J., Walker, M., Smith, T., Hoverman, S., McAlpine, C. and Dawson, S. (2005). Benchmarking Regional Planning Arrangements for Natural Resource Management 2004–5: Progress, Constraints and Future Directions for Regions. Healthy Savanna Planning Systems Project. Tropical Savannas Management CRC.

Muñoz-Erickson, T. A., Cutts, B. B., Larson, E. K., Darby, K. J., Neff, M., Wutich, A., and Bolin, B. (2010). Spanning boundaries in an Arizona watershed partnership: information networks as tools for entrenchment or ties for collaboration? *Ecology and Society*, 15(3), 22. http://www.ecologyandsociety.org/vol15/iss3/art22/

Murray-Darling Basin Commission (1999). Groundwater: A Resource for the Future. Canberra: Murray-Darling Basin Commission. Retrieved from http://www.mdba.gov.au/sites/default/files/archived/mdbc-GW-reports/2173_GW_a_resource_for_the_future.pdf

Murray-Darling Basin Ministerial Council (1999). The Salinity Audit of the Murray-Darling Basin: A 100-year Perspective, 1999. Canberra: Murray-Darling Basin Commission. Retrieved from http://www.mdba.gov.au/sites/default/files/archived/mdbc-salinity-reports/439_Salinity_audit_of_MDB_100_year_perspective.pdf

Murray-Darling Basin Ministerial Council (2001). Basin Salinity Management Strategy 2001–2015. Canberra: Murray-Darling Basin Commission. Retrieved from http://www.mdba.gov.au/sites/default/files/pubs/BSMS-full.pdf

National Action Plan for Salinity and Water Quality Natural Heritage Trust (2005). Regional Programs Report 2004–2005. Canberra: Departments of the

Environment and Heritage and Agriculture, Fisheries and Forestry. Retrieved from http://nrmonline.nrm.gov.au/downloads/mql:2712/content

National Natural Resource Management Task Force (1999). *Managing Natural Resources in Australia for a Sustainable Future*. Canberra: Agriculture, Fisheries and Forestry, Australia.

NLWRA (2001). Australian Dryland Salinity Assessment 2000. Canberra: National Land & Water Resources Audit. Retrieved from http://nrmonline.nrm.gov.au/downloads/mql:1798/content

Ommer, R. E., Perry, R. I., Murray, G., and Neis, B. (2012). Social-ecological dynamism, knowledge, and sustainable coastal marine fisheries. *Current Opinion in Environmental Sustainability*, 4(3), 316–332. doi:10.1016/j.cosust.2012.05.010

Owens, S., Petts, J., and Bulkeley, H. (2006). Boundary work: knowledge, policy and the urban environment. *Environment and Planning C: Government and Policy*, 24(5), 633–643. doi:10.1068/c0606j

Pahl-Wostl, C., Holtz, G., Kastens, B., and Knieper, C. (2010). Analyzing complex water governance regimes: the management and transition framework. *Environmental Science and Policy*, 13(7), 571–581. doi:10.1016/j.envsci.2010.08.006

Pannell, D. J. (2001). Dryland salinity: economic, scientific, social and policy dimensions. *The Australian Journal of Agricultural and Resource Economics*, 45(4), 517–546. doi:10.1111/1467-8489.00156

Peck, A. J., and Hurle, D. H. (1973). Chloride balance of some farmed and forested catchments in southwestern Australia. *Water Resources Research*, 9(3), 648–657. doi:10.1029/WR009i003p00648

PMSEIC (1999). Dryland Salinity and its Impact on Rural Industries and the Landscape. Occasional Paper Number 1, Prime Minister's Science, Engineering and Innovation Council. Canberra: Commonwealth of Australia.

Pollard, S. J. T., Davies, G. J., Coley, F., and Lemon, M. (2008). Better environmental decision-making – recent progress and future trends. *Science of the Total Environment*, 400(1–3), 20–31. doi:10.1016/j.scitotenv.2008.07.022

Queensland Salinity Workshop (2005). Meeting of NRM planners and Landcare coordinators. Toowoomba, Queensland.

Rayner, S., Lach, D., and Ingram, H. (2005). Weather forecasts are for wimps: why water resource managers do not use climate forecasts. *Climatic Change*, 69(2–3), 197–227. doi:10.1007/s10584-005-3148-z

Renwick, A., Robinson, C. J., Martin, T., May, T., Polglase, P., Possingham, H. P., and Carwardine, J. (2014). Biodiverse planting for carbon and biodiversity on Indigenous land. *PLOS ONE*, 9(3), e91281. doi:10.1371/journal.pone.0091281

Rittel, H. W. J., and Webber, M. M. (1973). Dilemmas in a general theory of planning. *Policy Sciences*, 4(2), 155–169. doi:10.1007/BF01405730

Robinson, C. J., Taylor, B., and Margerum, R. D. (2009). On a learning journey to nowhere? The practice and politics of evaluating outcomes of natural resource management in northern Queensland regions. In M. Lane, C. Robinson, and B. Taylor (eds.), *Contested Country* (pp. 201–214). Melbourne: CSIRO Publishing.

Robinson, C. J., Taylor, B., Vella, K., and Wallington, T. (2014). Working knowledge for collaborative water planning in Australia's Wet Tropics region. *International Journal of Water Governance*, 2, 43–60. doi:10.7564/7513-IJWG7564

Robinson, C. J., Bark, R. H., Garrick, D., and Pollino, C. A. (2015a). Sustaining local values through river basin governance: community-based initiatives in

Australia's Murray-Darling Basin. *Journal of Environmental Planning and Management*, 58(12), 2212–2227. doi:10.1080/09640568.2014.976699
Robinson, C. J., Maclean, K., Hill, R., Bock, E., and Rist, P. (2015b). Participatory mapping to negotiate indigenous knowledge used to assess environmental risk. *Sustainability Science*, 11, 115–126. doi:10.1007/s11625-015-0292-x
Robinson, C. J., Renwick, A. R., May, T., Gerrard, E., Foley, R., Battaglia, M., Possingham, H. P., Griggs, D., and Walker, D. (2016). Indigenous benefits and carbon offset schemes: an Australian case-study. *Environmental Science and Policy*, 56, 129–134. doi:10.1016/j.envsci.2015.11.07
Roux, D. J., Rogers, K. H., Biggs, H. C., Ashton, P. J., and Sergeant, A. (2006). Bridging the science-management divide: moving from unidirectional knowledge transfer to knowledge interfacing and sharing. *Ecology and Society*, 11(1), 4. http://hdl.handle.net/10204/953
Sabatier, P. A., Focht, W., Lubell, M., Trachtenberg, Z., Vedlitz, A., and Matlock, M. (eds.) (2005). *Swimming Upstream: Collaborative Approaches to Watershed Management*. Cambridge, MA: The MIT Press.
Saravanan, V. S., McDonald, G. T., and Mollinga, P. P. (2009). Critical review of Integrated Water Resources Management: moving beyond polarised discourse. *Natural Resources Forum*, 33(1), 76–86. doi:10.1111/j.1477-8947.2009.01210.x
Simpson, H. J., and Herczeg, A. L. (1994). Delivery of marine chloride in precipitation and removal by rivers in the Murray-Darling Basin, Australia. *Journal of Hydrology*, 154(1–4), 323–350. doi:10.1016/0022-1694(94)90224-0
Stenson, M. P., Littleboy, M., and Gilfedder, M. (2011). Estimation of water and salt generation from unregulated upland catchments. *Environmental Modelling and Software*, 26(11), 1268–1278. doi:10.1016/j.envsoft.2011.05.013
Stern, M. J., and Coleman, K. J. (2015). The Multidimensionality of trust: applications in collaborative natural resource management. *Society and Natural Resources*, 28(2), 117–132. doi:10.1080/08941920.2014.945062
Stirzaker, R., Lefroy, T., Keating, B., and Williams, J. (2000). A Revolution in Land Use: Emerging Land Use Systems for Managing Dryland Salinity. Canberra: CSIRO. Retrieved from http://www.mdba.gov.au/sites/default/files/archived/mdbc-NRM-reports/2224_Revolution_in_landuse_CSIRO.pdf
Sullivan, H., and Skelcher, C. (2002). *Working Across Boundaries: Collaboration in Public Services*. Basingstoke, UK: Palgrave Macmillan.
Walker, G., Gilfedder, M., and Williams, J. (1999). Effectiveness of Current Farming Systems in the Control of Dryland Salinity. Canberra: CSIRO. Retrieved from http://www.clw.csiro.au/publications/Dryland.pdf
Walker, G., Gilfedder, M., Evans, W. R., Dyson, P., and Stauffacher, M. (2003). Groundwater Flow Systems Framework: Essential Tools for Planning Salinity Management. MDBC Publication 14/03. Canberra: Murray-Darling Basin Commission. Retrieved from http://www.clw.csiro.au/publications/general2003/Groundwater_Flow_Systems_Full_Report.pdf
Walker, G. R., Gilfedder, M., Dawes, W. R., and Rassam, D. W. (2015). Predicting aquifer response time for application in catchment modelling. *Groundwater*, 53(3), 474–484. doi:10.1111/gwat.12219
Wallington, T., and Lawrence, G. (2009). Accounting for performance: public environmental governance in the shadow of the future. In M. Lane, C. Robinson, and B. Taylor (eds.), *Contested Country* (pp. 91–107). Melbourne: CSIRO Publishing.
Webb, T., and Cary, J. (2005). Social capital and natural resource management:

an application to Landcare. *Rural Society*, 15(2), 119–131. doi:10.5172/rsj.351.15.2.119

Wyborn, C., and Bixler, R. P. (2013). Collaboration and nested environmental governance: scale dependency, scale framing, and cross-scale interactions in collaborative conservation. *Journal of Environmental Management*, 123, 58–67. doi:10.1016/j.jenvman.2013.03.014

Yaffee, S. L., Phillips, A. F., Frentz, I. C., Hardy, P. W., Maleki, S. M., and Thorpe, B. E. (1996). *Ecosystem Management in the United States: An Assessment of Current Experience*. Washington, DC: University of Michigan and The Wilderness Society, Island Press.

7. Collaborative governance – does it work for climate change adaptation? Insights from the Dutch Delta Programme

Arwin van Buuren and
Jitske van Popering-Verkerk

1. INTRODUCTION

Climate change is often defined as a "super-wicked problem" (Levin et al. 2012). It is surrounded by many deep uncertainties and normative controversies. The urgency to anticipate unknown future consequences is often low. Furthermore, it is a multifaceted issue with many different (and often contradictory) impacts. Finally this issue is interrelated with many different functional domains, which makes it difficult to design strategies that address its impacts (Van Buuren et al. 2014).

Although the issue of climate change remains controversial, many governments on different scales are developing action plans for adaptation. This is quite a difficult job, as the urgency felt is rather low and the complexity of the issue is high. Designing both effective and legitimate governance arrangements that enable the adaptation challenge is far from easy, especially because of the fragmented governance context in which this has to be done (Termeer et al. 2011).

Oftentimes a collaborative governance approach is presented as a suitable way to deal with the issue of climate change adaptation (Emerson and Murchie 2010; Hedensted Lund et al. 2012). There are indeed very good reasons to opt for such an approach, especially given the controversial character of the issue of climate change (adaptation), the various conflicting frames surrounding this issue, and the fragmented, polycentric multi-actor context in which resources are widely dispersed among many different actors. In such a context, collaborative governance can help generate effective and legitimate policies (Termeer et al. 2011).

However, in this chapter we will study and critically reflect upon the question: *to what extent does a collaborative governance approach suit the issue of climate change adaptation?* We answer this question by focusing upon the Dutch context and in this chapter we analyze the Dutch Delta Programme, a national programme for drafting new policies and measures to cope with the consequences of climate change in the water domain. The programme design was based upon the principles of collaborative governance. In a period of five years, the Dutch Delta Programme has to analyze the consequences of climate change on water management and prepare for decisions (the so-called Dutch Delta Decisions) about future flood risk management, safeguarding fresh-water supply and adaptive spatial planning. In this programme, both national and regional authorities worked together in order to come to a set of overarching decisions with regard to – for example – new flood risk norms and criteria for climate-robust planning. Furthermore, they developed regional strategies for how to implement these decisions in such a way that regional agendas (with regard to recreation, nature, spatial development) were incorporated. In the Dutch context – with a strong, autonomous position of water authorities and a strong sectoral focus in the water domain on flood protection – this programme was a major step towards more integrated water management (Verkerk and Van Buuren 2013).

After five years of preparation, the Dutch Delta Decisions and the underlying studies were presented to the Dutch Parliament. They were broadly supported among the key stakeholders involved at national and regional level. Also, the integrated way of dealing with water issues and the way in which joint fact-finding helped to come to agreed-upon knowledge as a basis for the decisions in the Delta Programme was commended (Van Buuren et al. 2014). However, a couple of touchy issues were either postponed or downplayed, such as, for example, the debate about more formal obligations to come to a more water-robust spatial planning at the regional level, and the debate about application of the "user-pays principle" with regard to fresh-water supply. Furthermore, when it comes to implementing the Dutch Delta Decisions, it proves to be very difficult to sustain the collaborative approach, because the involved organizations are tempted to return to their old habits.

This raises the question of whether the collaborative approach of the Delta Programme indeed contributes to effective and legitimate climate change adaptation. And this makes the five-year experience of collaborative governance in the Dutch Delta Programme a very interesting case for studying the suitability of this governance approach in the field of climate change adaptation.

This chapter first deals with the question of what makes climate change adaptation a complex governance issue (section 2) and then goes on to describe the principles of collaborative governance (section 3). In section

4 we confront the characteristics of climate change adaptation with these principles to make a theoretical assessment as to the extent that the collaborative governance approach fits this issue. In section 5 we describe the methodological approach we used in this chapter. Section 6 presents the Dutch Delta Programme and its outcomes. After that we analyze the effectiveness of the collaborative approach used and answer our main question and give some reflections.

From our analysis we can conclude on the one hand that using a collaborative governance approach works well in the context of climate change adaptation (to come to consensus in a context of deep uncertainties and strong value controversies). At the same time, our analysis underlines the thesis of Giddens (2009) that climate change adaptation (especially when it comes to the really contentious issues and when the urgency for action is not broadly felt) asks for more powerful political leadership because of the difficulties of realizing enough decisiveness by consensus-oriented dialogue. In our conclusion we reflect upon the question of whether the principles of collaborative governance can go hand-in-hand with a plea for more political firmness.

2. CLIMATE CHANGE – A "SUPER-WICKED" ISSUE

2.1 Characteristics of Climate Change Adaptation

For a long time, climate change was hardly on the agenda in the Netherlands. Although there were some cautious attempts to come to a national climate change adaptation agenda, the impact of climate change was not a policy issue. This changed the moment that the Dutch Cabinet decided to install a second Delta Committee. This committee had to study the impact of climate change on water management in the aftermath of Hurricane Katrina that hit New Orleans. The committee concluded in 2008 that climate change will have a major impact upon flood safety and fresh-water supply in the Netherlands (Veerman 2008):

> Given the state of a number of diked areas, the safety issue is urgent right now and, with rising sea levels, greater variation in river discharge, and a further growth of interests that need protecting, it will only become more so. A disastrous breach in a dike anywhere in the country would disrupt the entire country. . .Water intake and with it the country's fresh-water supply come under pressure when the sea level rises and salt water penetrates further inland via the rivers and ground water.

It is thus especially the combination of sea-level rises and greater extremes of river discharges that make the Netherlands vulnerable to climate change. These conclusions bring climate change onto the political agenda. However, the main focus is on water management, with less attention given to other adaptation issues.

One of the main recommendations is to start a so-called Delta Programme. Because of the uncertainty about the facts, but also the normative ambiguity of the climate change adaptation issue, the Delta Committee recommends starting a programme in which the impact of climate change is studied further, and in which an investment programme for water management is developed to make the Netherlands "climate proof". Based upon broad political support, the Cabinet decided to follow the main recommendation and to start a Delta Programme.

The issue of climate change in the Netherlands, but also in other countries, is often labelled as a super wicked issue (Levin et al. 2012). It is not only surrounded by uncertainty about the facts (the causes and consequences of climate change) but there is also huge normative ambiguity about questions such as who has to take responsibility for adaptation and at what level. There are at least four characteristics of climate change adaptation which make it an intricate issue for governance and which pose high demands on the governance arrangements dealing with it (Van Buuren et al. 2014).

Firstly, the issue of climate change is surrounded by many uncertainties (Pahl-Wostl 2007; Levin et al. 2009), both about its causes and its future impacts. Many contest the necessity of adaptation and there is much debate about how much adaptation is needed now, and what can be postponed for later. This uncertainty makes it very difficult to decide what to do and when. It necessitates the use of different scenarios and a need to assess whether policy strategies are robust in the light of different scenarios, in order to be able to choose no-regret strategies.

Secondly, the issue of climate change is highly controversial. People frame the issue of climate change in very different ways (whether it is a consequence of human action, how severe its impacts are) and thus disagree on fundamental questions such as whether it is necessary to take action and who is responsible for taking action: is it a public responsibility or is it a private responsibility? And, especially when adaptation means that existing rights are challenged, people are not ready to accept changes, especially when the urgency is not proven.

Thirdly, climate change is a highly multifaceted issue (Adger et al. 2005; Dewulf et al. 2015). For example, it both implies more extreme rainfall and longer periods of drought. Some consequences are beneficial for regional economies (such as an increase in tourism due to warmer weather conditions), but others are highly detrimental when it comes to salt-water intrusion or fresh-water shortage. Some climate effects reinforce each other, such as higher river water discharges and sea level rises. This multifacetedness requires the involvement of many different actors in order to do justice to the many values climate change touches upon. As Levin et al. (2009) stress: impacts of climate change are often cumulative. Thus, addressing these problems may require significant interventions long before the most severe consequences of the problem become manifest.

Finally, climate change is a complex issue. Its consequences can be non-linear and erratic, stemming from multiple activities and interactions across social and natural systems. These consequences interfere with developments in other subdomains, such as economic or spatial developments, demographic or transport trends etc. The complexity of climate change also has a temporal and a spatial dimension (Levin et al. 2009; Termeer et al. 2011). In addition, proposed solutions may produce unintended and perverse consequences.

Besides these substantial characteristics, we want to highlight one other characteristic of the issue of climate change adaptation: its relative immaturity. The issue of climate change is relatively new, which has two contradictory consequences. On the one hand adaptation policies have to be developed within an institutional vacuum: new institutional arrangements, policy instruments, norms and routines have to be developed. As Termeer et al. (2011: 164) state: "The emergence of adaptation as a new domain of policy and practice is in itself an important challenge. Within this institutional void, adaptation is, for the moment at least, characterized by weakly defined ambitions, responsibilities, procedures, routines, and solutions." On the other hand, adaptation policies have to be developed within highly complex, institutionally overcrowded arenas in which many competing rules and principles are already present. Climate change adaptation thus has to fight for its own domain in order to organize attention, but also it has to develop meaningful connections with other domains in order to realize policy integration or mainstreaming, which is essential for its success (Uittenbroek 2016).

2.2 From Characteristics to Challenges for Governance

These various characteristics of climate change adaptation can be translated into challenges or demands for the governance of climate change adaptation (cf. Termeer et al. 2011). Firstly, in order to deal with the issue of uncertainty, climate change adaptation has to be based upon scientific evidence which is also agreed-upon by stakeholders and the general public because of the controversial character of the issue. We call this *informed decision-making*.

Secondly, due to their inherent controversial character, adaptation measures need to be embedded in a convincing, shared agenda based upon a deliberately mutually shared and legitimate frame (Dewulf 2013). This criteria can be called *consensual decision-making*.

Thirdly, climate change adaptation measures have to be comprehensive or integrative because of the multiplicity and interconnectedness of climate change consequences. Measures within one domain do have consequences for other domains. The same holds true for scale-interferences. So it is important that adaptation strategies encompass all relevant aspects to prevent unexpected interferences and feedback loops. This aspect we can label as *coherent decision-making*.

Fourthly, because of the long-term and cumulative character of climate change, measures have to be adaptive or flexible: it has to be possible to adjust them when circumstances change and they have to anticipate the long-term picture. Realizing *adaptive decision-making* is thus the fourth challenge.

And, finally, due to its relative newness, the governance of climate change adaptation has to have the capability to settle itself in an existing institutional context. This not only calls for finding creative ways to pave the way for mainstreaming new policies, but it also asks for a certain degree of powerfulness to influence the agenda. We call this *impactful decision-making*, which means that adaptation has to make a lasting impact upon existing policies in order to become mainstream.

In summary, there are five challenges for the governance of climate change adaptation. These are represented in Table 7.1.

Table 7.1 Challenges for the governance of climate change adaptation

Challenges	Description
Informed decision-making	Due to uncertainty, decisions have to be based upon the best available knowledge
Consensual decision-making	Due to ambiguity (frame controversies), decisions have to be accomplished by extensive frame reflection
Coherent decision-making	Due to its multi-scale and multi-domain character, decision-making has to integrate multiple issues and interests
Adaptive decision-making	Non-linear feedback relations, unclear interferences with multiple systems
Impactful decision-making	New policies have to compete with other issues and have to be embedded in already existing institutional structures and arenas

3. THE CHARACTERISTICS OF COLLABORATIVE GOVERNANCE

The literature on collaborative governance reflects a variety of strands and specific interpretations (see Chapter 2 of this volume). We conceptualize collaborative governance by focusing on the following four characteristics:

1. Collaborative governance is a way to come to cooperation and mutual adjustment between different agencies which operate in a fragmented institutional context (Healey 2003; Ansell and Gash 2008). Within such a context both responsibilities and resources are widely dispersed among different actors. Actors with different ambitions and problem perceptions have to collaborate – in order to mobilize the means necessary to solve their joint problems.
2. Collaborative governance is based upon the principles of dialogue and mutual learning and is aimed at realizing consensus based upon a transparent, democratic and participatory process (Foster-Fishman et al. 2001; Innes and Booher 2003). Collaboration is thus based upon the principle of equality and mutual dependency.
3. Collaborative governance is about collaboration of organizations as well as collaboration of individuals. Successful collaboration depends on the engagement of organizations as well as the motivation of individuals, it depends on the resources of organizations as well as the skills and the commitment (shared motivation) of the individuals representing this organization (Huxham et al. 2000; Foster-Fishman et al. 2001; Emerson et al. 2012).
4. Collaborative governance ultimately results not only in consensus about what to do, but also in joint actions which could not be realized by the single organizations (Huxham et al. 2000; Emerson et al. 2012). Collaborative governance could thus generate "a new capacity for joint action that did not exist before and sustain or grow that capacity for the duration of the shared purpose" (Emerson et al. 2012: 14).

Collaborative governance has a relatively long history of applications in the field of planning and infrastructure projects, environmental management and natural resource issues (Healey 2003; Emerson et al. 2012). But as we said in the introduction it is also seen as a valuable way of dealing with the issue of climate change, when it comes both to mitigation and adaptation.

4. COLLABORATIVE GOVERNANCE AND CLIMATE CHANGE ADAPTATION – SOME EXPECTATIONS

At first sight, the paradigm of collaborative governance seems to fit nicely into the characteristics of climate change. Authors studying the issue of climate change emphasize the importance of stakeholders' involvement in order to realize consensus and legitimacy. Especially given the multifaceted character of climate change, involving a wide range of actors can help to address the various consequences of climate change (Lebel et al. 2006; Van Buuren et al. 2014). Collaborative governance is also seen as suitable to climate change adaptation, because it is helpful in a fragmented institutional context in which many interdependent actors have to come to an agreement about a common purpose and accompanying strategy (Adger et al. 2005; Lebel et al. 2006; Dewulf et al. 2015). It thus helps to realize integrative results. Further, a collaborative approach can also help to come to solutions that are broadly shared, and it can fuel learning processes which are necessary to create shared urgency. In this way, joint fact-finding ideally can contribute to reducing uncertainty and ignorance (Folke et al. 2005; Pahl-Wostl 2007). Furthermore, collaborative governance seems to be especially helpful as a device to initiate new policies and design policy strategies in a situation in which there are no predecessor policies.

Thus, there seems to be a very good argument to plea for a collaborative approach to deal with climate change adaptation. We could expect a collaborative governance approach to fit well into the various demands that the issue of climate change adaptation poses on its governance.

At the same time, it is questionable to what extent collaborative governance is able to deliver effective adaptation policies. It is often argued that consensual decision-making results in compromises that do not enable the decisive action necessary for urgent problems. Collaborative governance seems to be less applicable when hard choices have to be made, because it focuses more upon agreeable proposals instead of effective ones (Coglianese 1999). Furthermore, collaborative dialogues often tend to neglect (long-term) future dilemmas and tend to stick to urgent issues – the here and now (Lazarus 2009). Besides, it is questionable whether collaborative governance is successful when it comes to issues that are quite knowledge-intensive. Finally, it is rather doubtful as to whether collaborative governance leads to the implementation of adaptation measures. Collaborative approaches seem to be especially helpful to draft policy strategies, but when they hit the ground it is much more difficult to sustain collaboration, especially because in that phase standard (bureaucratic) operating procedures come again into play and top-down performance-based management becomes dominant (Newman et al. 2004; Van Popering-Verkerk and Van Buuren 2016).

Although there are many arguments that plea for collaborative governance to deal with climate change adaptation, there are also authors who criticize this position and argue that a collaborative governance approach will slow down or even hinder effective and legitimate climate change adaptation.

Departing from these two different expectations of the suitability of collaborative governance for this super wicked issue of climate change adaptation, we will present an analysis of a large-scale adaptation programme in the Netherlands that was to a large extent organized along the principles of collaborative governance. By assessing how and to what extent the collaborative approach was helpful in arriving at effective and legitimate adaptation strategies, we could reflect upon the idea of collaborative climate change adaptation.

5. RESEARCH METHODS

This chapter is based upon a secondary analysis of an in-depth evaluation study of the Dutch Delta Programme, conducted by the authors (2014). For this evaluation the authors carried out 30 in-depth interviews with key players in this Delta Programme (top officials, governors, mayors and other people participating in various arenas in the context of the Delta Programme). The authors investigated how interviewees evaluated the methods and outcomes of the Delta Programme and their views about the phase that followed from the key decisions. This evaluation was used to advise the Dutch Government on how to organize the next phase of the Dutch Delta Programme (Van Buuren and Teisman 2014). We evaluated the approach of the Delta Programme and the outcomes it generated. The interviews were supplemented by focus groups with people directly involved (sub-programme managers, representatives of interest groups).

Furthermore we conducted another survey (Van Buuren and Teisman 2014) aimed at reconstructing how the people involved assessed the outcomes of the Delta Programme. One part of the survey focused on the quality and added value of the collaborative approach. The results of this part of the survey are used in this chapter to study the challenges of collaborative governance in relation to the issue of climate change adaptation. The survey was sent to 1,481 people, all visitors of the yearly Delta Programme Congress, a congress for people involved in the Delta Programme (coming from various public and private organizations, knowledge institutes and interest groups). We received responses from 645 visitors (43.6%).

For this chapter we made a secondary analysis of this extensive material. We reanalyzed the transcripts and survey results related to the collaborative approach based on the five challenges as described in section 2. In the empirical analysis we present the survey results and provide some observations based upon the interviews, in order to give more relief to the quantitative findings.

6. THE DUTCH DELTA PROGRAMME: A COLLABORATIVE APPROACH

6.1 Description of the Dutch Delta Programme

At the end of 2009, the Delta Programme was established as a follow-up to the Delta Committee (see section 2). The main goal of the Delta Programme was to design a set of measures that would make the Dutch water system fit for the future. It had to develop the necessary policy proposals for investments and policy instruments that could make the water system not only more robust against flooding but also more resilient in the face of other water issues like water nuisance and drought.

The Delta Programme was organized as a collaborative initiative with the national government, the provinces, water boards, and municipalities. It was headed by a newly created governmental commissioner, the so-called Delta Commissioner. This top official was positioned outside the administrative hierarchy, with direct access to the Dutch Government. A Delta Fund was established to safeguard the means necessary for implementing the measures that arose from the Delta Programme. The Delta Law formed the legal basis for this new structure.

6.2 The Collaborative Approach of the Delta Programme

The Delta Programme developed its own approach that could be characterized as collaborative. Firstly, the Delta Programme is based upon the principles of cooperation and mutual adjustment. The Delta Programme is designed as a multilevel programme: one national programme with three thematic sub-programmes and six regional sub-programmes. In this programme, and in these sub-programmes, people from different domains are involved. In this multilevel structure, the joint responsibility of governments at all levels is reflected. Further, coherence is one of the key values of the Delta Programme: coherence between various geographical areas,

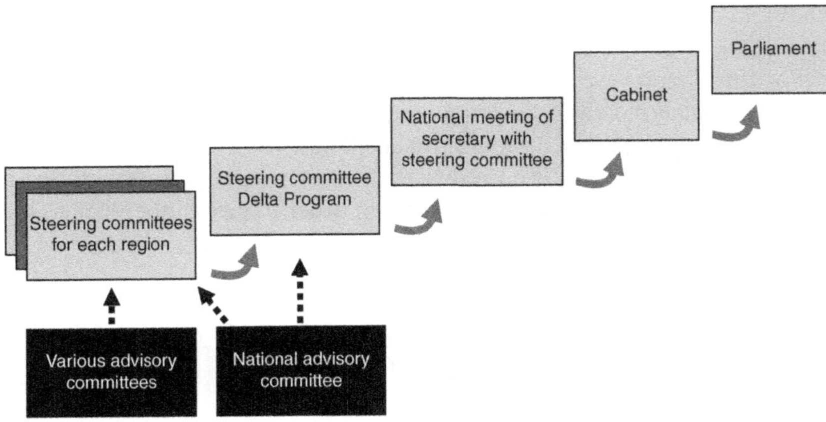

Figure 7.1 The multilevel governing structure of the Delta Programme

coherence between different domains, coherence between long term and short term, and coherence between different financial sources.

Secondly, the process of the Delta Programme is dominated by a process of dialogue and joint fact-finding. The Delta Programme follows a stepwise process: (1) problem analysis, (2) collection of all possible water management strategies, (3) assessment of these water management strategies, and (4) selection of the preferred water management strategies. Each step is taken by a combination of knowledge development and deliberation.

Thirdly, the Delta Programme is organized in such a way that people from different hierarchical levels in their organizations are represented in the programme (see Figure 7.1). In addition, each step in the decision-making process included the participation of governors and civil servants – as well as (representatives from) NGOs, interest groups and companies.

Finally, the aim of the Delta Programme is to arrive at a joint vision on future water management and an accompanying investment programme. To arrive at these results, decision-making procedures are designed in the programme. The procedures are designed in such a way that each level may discuss the proposed decision and that decision can only be taken by consensual decision-making.

Thus, we see that the Delta Programme is designed following the principles of collaborative governance and that this collaborative approach is strengthened during the process.

6.3 The Results of the Delta Programme

The Delta Programme ultimately resulted in five so-called Delta Decisions in 2015, and in a couple of regional preferential strategies. The most important decision concerns new norms for flood risk management, which imply new standards on the height of dikes, based upon the estimated probability of flooding and impact severity. The second Delta Decision concerns a fresh-water strategy. This decision proposes to determine what the government's role would be in safeguarding enough fresh-water, and advocates making agreements on fresh-water supply levels. The third Delta Decision concerns spatial adaptation, determining that greater effort should be made at the planning stage to consider the potential impact of flooding and keeping cities cool during hot summers. It is important to note that this Decision emphasizes the voluntary cooperation of all public agencies to implement climate-proof planning. No formal obligations are introduced.

The two other Delta Decisions revolve around the organization of the water system in two regions of the Netherlands (the Lake Ijssel and the Rhine Meuse river basins) – important from a water systems perspective. These Delta Decisions can be seen as relatively incremental, compared to the initial thoughts about what would be necessary for these regions.

The five Delta Decisions are accompanied by regional water management strategies in which the implementation of the five decisions is entwined with proposals for regional development. This means, for example, that along the main rivers the regional authorities have drafted a long-term strategy of combining river widening (and thus stimulating new nature, recreational opportunities etc.) and dike enforcements to meet the new flood risk norms. For the coastal zone the regional authorities developed an ambitious long-term vision of how to combine recreational development with nature development and sand nourishment.

Overall, the actors involved were satisfied with the chosen approach. On a number of important characteristics they gave the Delta Programme a good evaluation. Firstly, they were satisfied with the fact that within the Delta Programme a valuable collaboration was organized between the national government and the regional authorities. Respondents perceived the collaboration as equal and were satisfied that the agenda was about strategic policy formulation rather than the implementation of policies made up by the national government.

Furthermore the actors involved were satisfied with the improved relationship between the water-oriented authorities on the one hand and the local and regional authorities on the other. Due to the Delta Programme, a mutual understanding grew among the actors, who became better informed about each other's agendas and possibilities for synergy. The collaboration between actors from water management and from spatial planning had been rather problematic for decades (because both domains acted from their own logic and were not very willing to invest much in mutual adjustment), but the Delta Programme seems to have made a good step in establishing a fruitful relation between them. In addition, the approach chosen was also helpful in coming to a more integrated way of dealing with water issues, previously dealt with mainly in a self-contained policy subdomain. By organizing five Delta Decisions entwined with regional strategies, this integration could emerge.

7. THE DUTCH WAY OF CLIMATE CHANGE ADAPTATION: ANALYZING THE DUTCH DELTA PROGRAMME

In the previous section, we showed how the Delta Programme developed an approach that could be characterized as collaborative. The following question is to what extent the collaborative approach of the Delta Programme suits the challenges of climate change adaptation? To answer this question, in the following sections we will look at how the collaborative approach helps to deal with the challenges related to climate change adaptation: informed decision-making, consensual decision-making, coherent decision-making, adaptive decision-making and impactful decision-making. In these sections we use the results of the interviews and of the survey. The survey results are summarized in Tables 7.2 to 7.6, highlighting the extent to which respondents agree on the value of various elements of the collaborative approach to decision-making in the Delta Programme and the mean evaluation (ranging from 1= strongly disagree to 5= strongly agree).

In the survey as well as in the interviews, the various actors stated that the Delta Programme was successful in organizing joint fact-finding. They were enthusiastic about the mobilization of expertise in order to prepare for well-informed decision-making. The approach of the Delta Programme – starting with a broad exploration of options in order to funnel this in a couple of stages towards a small set of preferred strategies – was widely acknowledged as very helpful.

At the same time, however, the vigorous involvement of stakeholders such as regional authorities also necessitates the simplification of the various substantial dilemmas into more simplified policy options and the translation of the scientific findings into relatively undifferentiated and straightforward information. In particular, the more technically oriented

Table 7.2 Collaborative and informed decision-making in the Delta Programme

	Mean	Strongly disagree (%)	Disagree (%)	Un-decided (%)	Agree (%)	Strongly agree (%)	Un-known (%)
Cooperation and adjustment							
DP leads to joint exploration of informed options	4.04 *n = 554*	0.5	3.6	10.6	58.5	23.3	*3.4*
Dialogue and learning							
DP is based upon best available knowledge	3.76 *n = 541*	1.3	7.2	15.3	59.1	11.3	*5.7*
The scenario tool was helpful	3.76 *n = 534*	0.4	3.7	23.6	55.4	9.7	*7.1*
The assessment tool was helpful	3.30 *n = 536*	2.8	8	31.7	32.6	2.2	*22.6*
DP connects knowledge of different resources	3.84 *n = 541*	1.1	5.4	16.8	60.4	14.8	*1.5*
Organization and participation							
Knowledge from abroad is used	3.05 *n = 534*	0.7	12.7	40.8	14.8	1.3	*29.6*

actors from the water domain were somewhat disappointed with the quality of the analysis and the hegemony of the stakeholder process over the analytical process, in which substantial uncertainties were neglected and politically driven simplifications restricted scientific analysis.

Despite these doubts, the process itself is seen as very valuable. Thus, the collaborative approach led to well-informed actions regarding the uncertainties of climate change adaptation in which the uncertainties are incorporated.

The contribution of collaborative governance to the controversies around the issue of climate change adaptation is less undisputed. The survey results show that the collaborative approach helps to foster decision-making about water management measures and investments. However, the interviewees emphasize that although some decisions were made, some touchy issues were either postponed or downplayed; for example the debate about more formal obligations to come to a more water-robust spatial planning at the regional level and the debate about application of the "user-pays principle" with regard to fresh-water supply.

In addition, the way in which deliberation and participation helps to deal with controversies is questioned. On the one side, people agree that dialogue helps parties to arrive at a mutual understanding, but participation is

Table 7.3 *Collaborative and consensual decision-making in the Delta Programme*

	Mean	Strongly disagree (%)	Disagree (%)	Un-decided (%)	Agree (%)	Strongly agree (%)	Un-known (%)
Cooperation and adjustment							
DP contributes to mutual understanding	3.85 *n = 508*	0.2	3.1	16.3	64.2	8.9	*7.3*
DP contributes to mutual trust	3.66 *n = 508*	0.6	3.5	27.2	53.1	5.5	*10*
Dialogue and learning							
DP fosters deliberation	3.53 *n = 556*	1.4	9.4	27.9	50.7	5.9	*4.7*
The DP process was transparent	3.61 *n = 537*	1.3	7.1	25	53.4	6.9	*6.3*
The DP organized dialogues effectively	3.62 *n = 506*	0.6	4.7	26.9	49.4	5.1	*13.2*
Organization and participation							
Involvement of NGOs	3.13 *n = 557*	1.4	21.7	33.9	32.1	2.3	*8.4*
Involvement of companies	2.86 *n = 554*	3.6	30.5	33.2	20.8	2	*9.9*

focused on the "usual suspects" (the formal representatives of the various governmental layers) and less on NGOs and companies, and the dialogues are seen as not decisive enough.

In the Delta Programme, there is appreciation for the way in which the collaborative approach leads to integrated decisions in the domains of flood management and fresh-water supply. The survey results show that the collaborative governance system facilitated connections within the fragmented Dutch governmental system, between different levels and different domains. Although the multilevel programme structure was seen as time-consuming, it was also acknowledged that it helps to arrive at a coherent and national long-term programme.

However, the level of policy integration is not as significant as was desired by many at the start of the programme. It proved to be difficult to arrive at integrated plans and visions in which measures for flood risk reduction (dike enforcements for example) or fresh-water supply (such as new water channels) are integrated with the needs of other domains, such as nature development, water-related business and spatial planning. At the level of visions, some integration was realized, but many of the actors were cautious about what will be realized when decisions have to

Table 7.4 Collaborative and coherent decision-making in the Delta Programme

	Mean	Strongly disagree (%)	Disagree (%)	Un-decided (%)	Agree (%)	Strongly agree (%)	Un-known (%)
Cooperation and adjustment							
DP functions as multilevel network	3.89 *n = 507*	0.6	3.7	16.2	58	15	*6.5*
DP fosters understanding between different domains	3.84 *n = 512*	0	3.7	16.6	65.4	8.6	*5.7*
DP helps to deal with dependencies	3.61 *n = 506*	0.6	4	29.2	42.7	6.5	*17*
Dialogue and learning							
DP delivers an integrated vision	3.53 *n = 606*	1.5	14	26.2	40.8	13.4	*4.1*
The DP plans integrate multiple issues	3.6 *n = 555*	1.1	8.3	26.3	52.8	7.9	*3.6*
Organization and participation							
The DP Commissioner connects the national departments	4.05 *n = 517*	0.4	2.9	12	48.9	23.6	*12.2*
The multilevel programme structure functions effectively	3.74 *n = 507*	1.4	5.9	21.3	49.3	13.4	*8.4*
Consensus and action							
DP connects national problems and regional ambitions	3.73 *n = 554*	0.5	5.6	25.1	55.6	11.2	*2*

be implemented. For example, the funding of the Delta Programme (the so-called Delta Fund) is strictly designated for investments in water-related measures. Although a deliberate attempt to come to a more integrated approach, the Delta Decisions have a relatively significant emphasis upon flood risk, and less of an emphasis on integrated (climate-robust) spatial development.

The Dutch Delta Programme made extensive use of adaptive delta management as a method to arrive at adaptive pathways that enable the connection of long-term challenges to short-term urgencies and the switch to alternative implementation paths when tipping points occur. This approach was valued highly by the respondents. They saw it as a way to start dealing with long-term challenges, while recognizing the many uncertainties about climate change and enabling the rise of new insights and demands. Both

Table 7.5 Collaborative and adaptive decision-making in the Delta Programme

	Mean	Strongly disagree (%)	Disagree (%)	Un-decided (%)	Agree (%)	Strongly agree (%)	Un-known (%)
Cooperation and adjustment							
DP delivers a joint vision on long-term water management	3.94 *n = 558*	1.1	6.1	10.8	61.6	19.7	*0.7*
Consensus and action							
DP connects long-term vision and short-term action	3.79 *n = 556*	1.4	5.4	18.7	57.9	13.8	*2.7*
DP delivers climate adaptive policy for flood management	4.24 *n = 608*	0.8	2.3	6.1	52.2	36.7	*1.6*
DP delivers climate adaptive freshwater policy	3.94 *n = 607*	1.2	3.1	16.3	53	20.6	*5.8*
DP delivers climate adaptive regional policy	3.65 *n = 605*	0.3	6.3	30.9	43.8	11.6	*7.1*

the survey respondents and the interviewees were quite positive about this approach and saw the Delta Programme as very successful in using a long-term horizon for developing short-term investment programmes.

However, in the Delta Programme adaptive decision-making was only perceived as a matter of planning water management measures in conjunction with other agendas. It was seen less as a way to organize reflexive processes of decision-making and flexible implementation pathways. For this reason, and despite their enthusiasm, the respondents were less positive about the possibility of sustaining this adaptive approach, as it requires greater institutional adjustment, flexible policies and other implementation routines. It is easier to draft adaptive plans than to implement them in an adaptive way.

The collaborative approach of the Delta Programme contributes to the agenda setting of climate adaptation. Working with an independent organization in-between existing institutions – including an independent and high-stature commissioner – means that it was possible to set the topic of climate adaptation quite high on the agenda of regional and national governments. However, many of the ultimate outcomes relate strongly to the daily business of the Dutch water authorities and thus are not very innovative, contributing mainly to an increased awareness

Table 7.6 Collaborative and impactful decision-making in the Delta Programme

	Mean	Strongly disagree (%)	Disagree (%)	Undecided (%)	Agree (%)	Strongly agree (%)	Unknown (%)
Cooperation and adjustment							
DP leads to cooperation which was not possible before	3.65 *n = 510*	0.6	5.5	26.1	50.4	7.5	*10*
Dialogue and learning							
DP fosters governance innovations	3.35 *n = 533*	1.7	10.3	34.5	36.2	3.9	*13.3*
Organization and participation							
The DP approach is complementary to existing approaches	3.91 *n = 509*	0.8	5.1	16.3	51.1	19.1	*8.4*
The DP Commissioner is an effective front man	4.23 *n = 518*	0.8	1.2	11.8	49.6	37.3	*1.4*
The support of an independent DP staff is helpful	4.02 *n = 512*	1.2	4.9	13.5	46.3	28.5	*5.7*
Consensus and action							
DP helps agenda setting of climate change adaptation	3.92 *n = 556*	0.7	3.2	18	56.3	18.9	*2.9*
DP delivers activating goals	3.54 *n = 509*	2.2	8.3	24	55.6	4.1	*5.9*
DP delivers clear investment programmes	3.72 *n = 558*	1.5	5.6	25.1	50.4	13.9	*3.5*
The DP key decisions help to bring results	3.95 *n = 512*	0.4	1.4	14.5	64.5	13.9	*5.5*

of the consequences of climate change in the water domain. At the same time, the outcomes – in terms of putting new issues upon the agenda – are more nuanced. It is questionable for example whether the issue of climate-robust spatial planning will be mainstreamed in Dutch planning processes. In addition, it is quite difficult to assess whether the various policy innovations in flood risk as suggested by the Delta Commissioner (such as adaptive delta management) will survive when the Delta Decisions are implemented.

8. WHAT COLLABORATIVE GOVERNANCE (HAS NOT) CONTRIBUTED TO CLIMATE CHANGE ADAPTATION

In section 2 we presented a couple of characteristics of climate change adaptation that make it a wicked governance issue. The question that is central to this chapter is the extent to which a collaborative approach is helpful for effective and legitimate climate change adaptation. In Table 7.7 we summarize our findings with regard to the five characteristics as mentioned in Table 7.1.

With regard to the issue of informed decision-making, the case of the Delta Programme reveals that applying collaborative governance also brings about a trade-off between scientific depth, which is necessary to understand what the impacts of climate change really are, and negotiated knowledge, which is understood by stakeholders and provides them with a basis for action.

When it comes to consensual decision-making, the Delta Programme provides a powerful illustration that it is possible to develop adaptation measures based upon a broad consensus. At the same time, once more we can see a trade-off around this issue; a trade-off between consensus and decisiveness – realizing consensus was only possible within the comfort zone of involved actors and by postponing or excluding from the agenda the more intricate issues.

The Delta Programme was quite successful in realizing coherent decision-making by taking a system-wide perspective. It dealt with the water system with its different scales and functionalities. Despite this system-wide perspective, the scope remained quite domain-specific and very water-oriented. Other climate-related issues like heat stress and public health, and the relationship with the spatial system, were not dealt with. On the one hand, this was a deliberate choice, to focus upon an issue that is very urgent for the flood-prone Netherlands. On the other hand, we can explain this as a strategy to reduce complexity and to keep things as simple as possible in order to make progress.

The attempt to apply an adaptive logic can be seen as very successful. The actors appear very satisfied with the focus on the long term and the connections that were established between long-term challenges and short-term agendas.

Finally, with regard to impactful decision-making, it is difficult to come to a conclusion. On the one hand, the Delta Programme was reasonably successful in introducing a new way of working and to get the issue of climate adaptation higher up the agenda. On the other hand, it remained very difficult to adjust the standard routines within the water domain.

Currently, it is difficult to say whether the Delta Programme succeeded in making a lasting impact.

Table 7.7 The contribution of collaborative governance

Challenge	Positive	Negative
Informed decision-making	Much emphasis on joint fact-finding. Much time devoted to problem analysis and exploration of possible strategies. Transparent method to arrive at decisions	Emphasis upon collaboration also diminishes room for in-depth analyses and more fundamental questions
Consensual decision-making	The collaborative approach was very successful in realizing a shared (national) agenda for implementation	Some more far-reaching proposals were not adopted because of the significant focus on support and consensus. Proposals have to fit within the existing distribution of rights and responsibilities
Coherent decision-making	By taking a system-wide perspective the DP tried to do justice to the multiplicity of the issue of adaptation	The focus remained rather one-sided upon water issues and flood risk in particular
Adaptive decision-making	Very successful collaborative dialogue about adaptation pathways and connecting long-term challenges to short-term goals	Questionable whether it is possible to transfer the adaptive logic to the next phase
Impactful decision-making	Climate change adaptation higher on the public agenda of water and planning	Changing existing routines in water domain requires more than a collaborative process

9. CONCLUSIONS AND DISCUSSION

To what extent can a collaborative approach help us to come to effective and legitimate collective action in the face of climate change? The Dutch Delta Programme taught us that a collaborative approach is certainly promising and fits nicely into the various characteristics of climate change adaptation, especially when it comes to its uncertain and controversial character. In this final section we will summarize what we can learn from our case study and will present some more generic insights on how collaborative governance can help to come to effective and legitimate climate change adaptation.

Firstly, from our case study we can learn that a collaborative approach can be quite successful in realizing a shared agenda for climate change adaptation. The Delta Programme was very successful in drafting a limited number of far-reaching decisions with broad support and accompanied by a rather large programme of concrete measures to realize the decisions.

Such a collaborative approach was especially helpful as it brought the focus from the short term to the long term. Only by taking such a long-term perspective did the problems to be expected with regard to river dischargers and sea-level rises become clearer. But the long-term horizon also enabled actors to think about stepwise pathways to implement the necessary measures and to make them more manageable. This also made it easier for them to accept the various policy proposals.

When dealing with a very controversial issue like climate change such a collaborative approach is not simple. Significant efforts must be taken to realize agreed-on knowledge and to organize a deliberative process of frame reflection. Such a process costs money and takes time (in the case of the Delta Programme it took five years to develop the Delta Decisions). However, it is a necessary investment for decision-making.

At the same time, the Delta Programme shows that a consensus-oriented dialogue alone will not suffice. The case study highlights that a collaborative approach often results in proposals that fit within the comfort zone of the actors involved. A more fundamental debate about changing the existing set of principles is then postponed. Furthermore, the adaptive approach also made it possible to give preference to so-called no-regret measures where the more fundamental measures have to be taken later on. It is thus questionable whether a collaborative approach facilitates actors enough to bring about more path-breaking, radical change.

Finally, collaborative governance calls for an auxiliary process arrangement that facilitates inter-organizational and multilevel dialogue. However, such an additional arrangement also leaves intact the routines within the existing institutional domain. A collaborative approach that is to make a lasting impact has to be accompanied by a more enforcing set of measures that provoke the necessary institutional adjustments.

This issue also relates to the question of whether climate change adaptation can succeed without political steering and enforcement. In our case, the independent position of the Delta Commissioner was a very important factor for the success of the Delta Programme. However, as we saw, it remains questionable as to whether more controversial decisions could be taken in the same consensus-oriented context.

REFERENCES

Adger, W.N., N.W. Arnell and E.L. Tompkins (2005) Successful adaptation to climate change across scales, *Global Environmental Change*, 15: 77–86.

Ansell, C. and A. Gash (2008) Collaborative governance in theory and practice, *Journal of Public Administration Research and Theory*, 18(4): 543–571.

Coglianese, C. (1999) The limits of consensus: the environmental protection system in transition: toward a more desirable future, *Environment: Science and Policy for Sustainable Development*, 41(3): 28–33.

Dewulf, A. (2013) Contrasting frames in policy debates on climate change adaptation, *Wiley Interdisciplinary Reviews: Climate Change*, 4(4): 321–330.

Dewulf, A., S. Meijerink and H. Runhaar (2015) The governance of adaptation to climate change as a multi-level, multi-sector and multi-actor challenge: a European comparative perspective, *Journal of Water and Climate Change*, 6(1): 1–7.

Emerson, K. and P. Murchie (2010) Collaborative governance and climate change: opportunities for public administration. In R. O'Leary, D.M. van Slyke and S. Kim (eds), *The future of public administration around the world: the Minnowbrook perspective*. Washington, DC: Georgetown University Press (pp. 141–153).

Emerson, K., T. Nabatchi and S. Balogh (2012) An integrative framework for collaborative governance, *Journal of Public Administration Research and Theory*, 22(1): 1–29.

Folke, C., T. Hahn, P. Olsson and J. Norberg (2005) Adaptive governance of social-ecological systems, *Annual Review of Environment and Resources*, 30: 441–473.

Foster-Fishman, P.G., S.L. Berkowitz, D.W. Lounsbury, S. Jacobson and N.A. Allen (2001) Building collaborative capacity in community coalitions: a review and integrative framework, *American Journal of Community Psychology*, 29(2): 241–261.

Giddens, A. (2009) *The politics of climate change*, Cambridge: Cambridge University Press.

Healey, P. (2003) Collaborative planning in perspective, *Planning Theory*, 2(2): 101–123.

Hedensted Lund, D., K. Sehested, T. Hellesen and V. Nellemann (2012) Climate change adaptation in Denmark: enhancement through collaboration and meta-governance? *Local Environment*, 17(6–7): 613–628.

Huxham, C., S. Vangen, C. Huxham and C. Eden (2000) The challenge of collaborative governance, *Public Management*, 2(3): 337–358.

Innes, J.E. and J.E. Booher (2003) *The impact of collaborative planning on governance capacity*, Institute of Urban and Regional Development, Working Paper 2003–03.

Lazarus, R.J. (2009) Super wicked problems and climate change: restraining the present to liberate the future, *Cornell Law Review*, 94(5): 1153–1233.

Lebel, L., J.M. Anderies, B. Campbell, C. Folke, S. Hatfield-Dodds, T.P. Hughes and J. Wilson (2006) Governance and the capacity to manage resilience in regional social-ecological systems, *Ecology and Society*, 11(1): 19.

Levin, K., S. Bernstein, B. Cashore and G. Auld (2009) Playing it Forward: Path Dependency, Progressive Incrementalism, and the "Super Wicked" Problem of Climate Change, Paper prepared for presentation to the Climate Change: Global Risks, Challenges and Decisions Congress, 10–12 March 2009, Copenhagen, Denmark.

Levin, K., B. Cashore, S. Bernstein and G. Auld (2012) Overcoming the tragedy of super wicked problems: constraining our future selves to ameliorate global climate change, *Policy Sciences*, 45(2): 123–152.
Newman, J., M. Barnes, H. Sullivan and A. Knops (2004) Public participation and collaborative governance, *Journal of Social Policy*, 33(2): 203–223.
Pahl-Wostl, C. (2007) Transitions towards adaptive management of water facing climate and global change, *Water Resources Management*, 21(1): 49–62.
Termeer, C., A. Dewulf, H. van Rijswick, A. van Buuren, D. Huitema, S. Meijerink and M. Wiering (2011) The regional governance of climate adaptation: a framework for developing legitimate, effective, and resilient governance arrangements, *Climate Law*, 2(2), 159–179.
Uittenbroek, C.J. (2016) From policy document to implementation: organizational routines as possible barriers to mainstreaming climate adaptation, *Journal of Environmental Policy & Planning*, 18(2): 161–176.
Van Buuren, A. and G.R. Teisman (2014) *Samen verder werken aan de Delta: de governance van het Nationaal Deltaprogramma na 2014*. Rotterdam: Erasmus Universiteit Rotterdam.
Van Buuren, A., P. Driessen, G. Teisman and M. van Rijswick (2014) Toward legitimate governance strategies for climate adaptation in the Netherlands: combining insights from a legal, planning, and network perspective, *Regional Environmental Change*, 14(3): 1021–1033.
Van Popering-Verkerk, J. and M.W. van Buuren (2016) Decision making patterns in multilevel governance: the contribution of informal and procedural interactions to significant multilevel decisions, *Public Management Review*, 18(7): 951–971.
Veerman, C. (2008) *Working together with water. A living land builds for its future*. The Hague: Secretariat Delta Committee.
Verkerk, J. and M.W. van Buuren (2013) Integrated water resources management in the Netherlands. Historical trends and current practices in the governance of integration, *International Journal of Water Governance*, 1(3/4), 427–452.

8. Collaboration challenges in addressing natural resource management problems: Australian regional case studies

Helen Ross, Jennifer Bellamy and Brian Head

INTRODUCTION

Wicked natural resource management (NRM) problems are often addressed through collaborative approaches, owing to the complexity of wicked problems and their tendency to cut across the responsibilities and influences of multiple stakeholders (Bellamy 2007; Head and Alford 2015). This chapter focuses on the challenges of collaboration as a strategy for managing wicked problems in NRM. We adopt a regional[1] focus for analyzing both the wicked problems, and the collaborative attempts to solve or manage them. We take the perspective of valuing collaboration as an important approach in NRM, particularly where no single party has responsibility for and effective influence over a problem. Nevertheless, any approach or instrument has limitations or faces challenges, and addressing wicked NRM problems represents an 'extreme case' for exploring the limitations and challenges for collaboration. These challenges range from those intrinsic to all cooperative endeavours, such as the well-recognized requirements of building relationships and trust (Holley 2009), through to institutional 'multi-level' challenges (Bellamy 2007; Head and Alford 2015), including the influence of public policy changes on the collaborators' management environment (Bouwen and Taillieu 2004; Innes and Booher 2010; Head and Alford 2015).

We recognize wicked problems as complex, uncertain, conflictual and intractable (Head 2008). They typically involve complex inter-linked issues, conflicting values and perceptions, and uncertainty about the impact of options. They are thus difficult to manage or resolve, especially as no single party has the authority to manage or capacity to influence all the issues involved. They thus defy rational planning (Rittel and Webber 1973; Head and Alford 2015).

'Collaboration' in wicked problem situations is understood in a variety of ways. One of the most popular, and flexible, definitions is that of Gray (1989) who broadly defines it as 'a process through which parties who see different aspects of a problem can constructively explore their differences and search for solutions that go beyond their own limited vision of what is possible' (p. 5), and as 'a process of joint decision-making among key stakeholders of a problem domain about the future of that domain' (p. 11). This can encompass short- or longer-term efforts, for instance a finite planning task, versus a long-term commitment to solve a wicked problem in an organized, multi-party way (e.g. Bouwen and Taillieu 2004; Innes and Booher 2010; Margerum 2011).

Collaboration is favoured in issues of intense conflict, or jurisdictional complexity, which no other approach can handle adequately (Rittel and Webber 1973; Gray 1989; Innes and Booher 2010; Head and Alford 2015). Proponents of 'collaboration' generally claim that inclusive processes may increase information, reduce adversarial behaviour, broaden responsibility for identifying and solving difficult problems, and channel conflict into considering effective and affordable strategies for achieving agreed long-term goals (Gray 1989; Wondolleck and Yaffee 2000; Head 2008; Innes and Booher 2010). In reality a regional collaboration to solve a wicked problem is not simply a matter of relevant parties deciding to work together, as Gray's definition implies. Such a collaboration develops within a web of organizations, obligations and policy instruments, with its members combining their mandates and the capacities available to them through the collaboration, while each also continues to act upon (and may prioritize) their responsibilities as separate entitles. Critics of state-sponsored collaboration also note that the rhetoric of collaboration often obscures the power relations, contexts and goals of joint activities (Moore 2005).

We need to accept that Australia, like other parts of the world, is now trying to use a relatively new and not always familiar policy 'instrument', collaboration, on problems that originated under other governance regimes. Collaborations must work across members with varying degrees of experience in collaboration and willingness to bend their organizational mandates to a collective endeavour, as well as constituencies with willingness or reluctance to downplay diverse sectional interests in order to pursue collective goals. Meanwhile each collaboration must connect, and coexist with, the standard organizational and policy structures of governance. Some collaborations may be restricted to this connecting role and must rely on the member or other organizations for the implementation of proposed strategies. Others may have implementation resources of their own, but may need to combine them with those of their members. All of these factors may disempower a collaboration relative to single organizations such as government departments.

In examining collaboration as a strategy for resolving wicked problems at regional scales, we take an inter-disciplinary social science perspective, with particular attention to the social and institutional aspects of NRM and policy issues. While it has some limitations for political and social analysis (Berkes and Ross 2013; Brown 2014), the social-ecological systems way of thinking is helpful for considering wicked problems in NRM because of the complex ecological change patterns involved, and the multifaceted human interactions with local environments. Social-ecological systems, i.e. coupled natural and social systems, are posited as self-organizing complex adaptive systems (Gunderson and Holling 2002; Berkes et al. 2003). They are multi-level systems, in which influences on a region may come from higher and lower levels within the spatial or political decision-making system such as national policy or local land use change (Folke et al. 2005; Bellamy 2007). Thus we need to view a 'regional' collaboration as linked both to higher levels of governance (e.g. state, federal) and to lower levels (different catchments and communities within the region), as well as laterally to other regional endeavours such as regional collaborations for economic development. The literature on social-ecological systems also emphasizes adaptive governance approaches, which incorporate collaboration as an appropriate strategy for addressing wicked problems of these systems (e.g. Folke et al. 2005; Bellamy 2007), albeit with significant challenges.

This chapter explores the challenges of collaboration as a strategy to address wicked natural resource problems through four regional Australian case studies, outlined below. Following some background on Australia's forms of regional collaboration in NRM, we explore some of the key challenges and limitations met by our case studies in developing and maintaining effective approaches for addressing their respective wicked problems.

BACKGROUND

Australia's forms of collaboration to address NRM issues have developed somewhat differently to those in other western countries. In the USA and Canada, collaborations, sometimes with supporting organizations have tended to develop as specific local or regional initiatives, usually as negotiated responses to environmental conflicts (Allan et al. 2008; Innes and Booher 2010). While some collaborations in North America cover large regions, there is no national system of regional responses. European countries also have had localized initiatives rather than national systems, though more systematic approaches to water issues are emerging as a result of EU Directives. New Zealand has a national system of regional councils and nested local arrangements, originally driven by legislative reform, that is required to engage key stakeholders, Maori, and the wider public in developing regional priorities and investments (Curtis et al. 2014), and is characterized as collaboration (Memon et al. 2010).

Australia has both independently-auspiced collaborations which have formed for unique reasons, and nationally mandated collaborations for NRM (Bellamy et al. 2012). It also has relatively long experience in collaboration, growing from local to regional scales, where the precursors to local Landcare groups and integrated catchment management grew originally in the early 1980s from agricultural extension practices in land and water management (DAFF 1999; Curtis et al. 2014). It grew from patchworks of independent collaborations, each formed to address particular issues, to increasing institutionalization in certain states, then nationally, as the successes of Landcare and integrated catchment management attracted state and national government support (Curtis et al. 2014). Landcare groups became nationally supported in the 1990s, and integrated catchment management was made statutory in several states. Regional collaborations, many based on catchment boundaries, became nationally mandated in the early 2000s following concerns that local collaborations were unable to deal well with the most significant environmental issues (DAFF 1999; Head et al. 2016). These regional collaborations were formed and supported financially under Commonwealth-state agreements for each state. Each comprised multiple collaborating parties, precluding the direct participation of state and federal governments, which had oversight, and were deemed 'community based' (see Curtis et al. 2014). Those states with pre-existing statutory integrated catchment management merged those organizations into the new national scheme.

CASE STUDIES AND METHODS

The chapter draws from a comparative study of four Australian cases where regional collaborations are engaged long term in trying to solve challenging NRM problems (see Figure 8.1). In their selection we sought geographical diversity (three Australian states and a cross-jurisdictional example), a diversity of wicked NRM problems with a regional focus, a history of engagement in NRM planning and action, a combination of mandated and self-organized regional arrangements and a willingness to participate. All involve issues of land and water management.

Two of the cases, both dealing with salinity, are 'mandated' collaborations

Figure 8.1 Case study locations

originally auspiced under inter-governmental agreements between individual states and the federal government from 2002 (Bellamy 2007; Curtis et al. 2014; Head et al. 2016). Of these, the Goulburn-Broken Catchment Management Authority (northern Victoria) is statutory, while Wheatbelt Natural Resource Management (southwest Western Australia) is non-statutory. The other two cases, Lake Eyre Basin (LEB) in Central Australia and Healthy Waterways in South East Queensland, became established and continued to evolve as unique self-organized arrangements; although both were significantly influenced in particular and challenging ways by the 'mandated' arrangements for regional NRM established throughout Australia from 2002. LEB's wicked problem concerns the avoidance of the adverse impacts of water and related NRM across borders, in a complex and vulnerable arid environment faced with growing regional development pressures (Bellamy et al. 2012, forthcoming). Healthy Waterways addresses the risks to water quality in South East Queensland, a region dominated by urban expansion around the state capital of Brisbane, affecting the major rivers and ecologically sensitive Moreton Bay (Bunn et al. 2007).

Each case study involved secondary data analysis focused on official documentation, and semi-structured interviews, exploring the antecedents to, development and evolution of the regional collaborative processes in their contexts of dealing with a wicked problem, with exploration of the access to knowledge and the effects of federal government programmes from 1997 (Head et al. 2016). Overall, 60 interviews were conducted across the four cases, with key informants who were directly involved in the collaborations, or in partner or observer organizations. Participants were asked about their roles with respect to the wicked problem, the collaboration and NRM more generally, and then to identify and elaborate on the key changes they had experienced over their history of involvement. Analysis was based on a set of core questions that focused on how collaborative approaches emerged in response to the wicked problems; the processes for initiating and enabling these collaborative arrangements to evolve; challenges faced in addressing NRM problems; and the strengths and limitations of collaboration as a method for addressing wicked problems. In doing so it conceptualized wicked problems in NRM as coupling social and ecological systems at multiple levels of governance and geographical interest. In line with the complexity theory underpinnings of the social-ecological systems literature, it took a long-term view that could identify adaptations in the collaborations.

CHALLENGES AND LIMITATIONS

The case studies show several key challenges related specifically to the use of collaboration as a strategy for addressing wicked problems. We begin with the extent of the challenge of addressing major wicked problems through a relatively new and to some unfamiliar process, collaboration. We then explore a set of issues that contribute to this overall challenge: the entrenchment of the wicked problems, building and maintaining collaboration, knowledge for learning and adapting, persistence in the face of mismatched ecological and political timeframes, and managing adaptively in a multi-level governance context.

Challenge 1: Entrenched Wicked Problems

Wicked problems, by their very nature, are not 'solved' but can be better managed through collaborative processes. They are also insidious by nature and the severity and extent of the problems not necessarily easily recognized as such. Even where a problem is recognized early, it may need to reach a major crisis point before enough political momentum builds to give it priority. By then the problem has grown substantially, and the effort required to arrest, let alone improve it, can be immense. All of our cases suffered from such past challenges. In Western Australia, the problems of soil salinization were first noted early in the 20th century in areas not far from our current case, and the underlying cause – land clearing – was recognized soon after. However Western Australia was rapidly developing its agriculture and seeking to populate rural areas, and constraining land clearing would have been unpopular. The problem continued growing despite concern mounting in the 1960s, and a succession of government enquiries investigating options particularly in the 1990s. Similarly in South East Queensland, water quality deteriorated over decades under the dual influences of rural land clearing and urban expansion (Bunn et al. 2007), and by the time political and public concern mounted to the point of action, the extent of intervention necessary was much magnified. Similarly soil salinization was recognized as a potential problem in the Goulburn-Broken catchment soon after colonization in the 1830s (Walker et al. 2009). In the LEB, awareness of the salience of cross-border issues emerged progressively. Proposals for RAMSAR listing of the extensive Lake Eyre wetlands in South Australian portion commenced in the 1980s. Significant tensions among diverse stakeholders did not emerge until the early 1990s when growing developmental pressures (irrigated agriculture, mining) in the broader LEB combined with a new World Heritage listing proposal led to open social and political conflict across the LEB. This catalyzed a self-organized approach at a whole-of-basin scale (Bellamy et al. 2012, forthcoming).

Challenge 2: Building and Maintaining Collaboration

Many generic challenges of building and maintaining any multi-party collaboration, regardless of its purpose and the sector it occurs in, are known (e.g. Folke et al. 2005 and Holley 2009 emphasize the role of trust and mutual adjustment in sustaining policy and delivery networks with multiple stakeholders including non-government actors). Collaboration involves building, and maintaining, cooperation across diverse interests; no easy matter where an issue is perceived as highly salient to many parties and their roles offer different standpoints for viewing the problem. Different knowledge and capacities for action may affect beliefs and prescriptions about what should be done. When dealing with wicked problems in NRM, the collaborations must also be sustained, and reinvigorated, over decades.

Our case studies show that collaborations can begin in very different ways. One driver is crises. The roots of collaboration in the LEB case can be traced to two 'crises' for those living in the region, federal proposals to achieve World Heritage listing of the South Australian portion of Lake Eyre and its related wetlands (1983–1998), and the proposal for a major irrigated cotton development in the headwaters of Cooper Creek catchment in Queensland in 1995. In SEQ (Healthy Waterways) a science and local-government coalition formed in resistance to state government proposals to regulate water quality, under which imported standards were about to be applied in the absence of Queensland standards. In the other two cases, collaborations were 'mandated' under state (Victorian adoption of statutory integrated catchment management in the 1990s) and federal-state (the national system of regional collaborations for NRM) arrangements, though these responded to perceived crisis issues in salinity and water quality. Both regions – Goulburn-Broken and Wheatbelt – had long-standing documented concerns about salinity, and parties formed readily around the problem (and available resources).

Maintaining collaboration is difficult enough over extended periods, for a wide range of reasons including sustaining collective motivation and vision, keeping the benefits of collaboration stronger than the costs, seeing successes without demotivating continued collaboration, coping with member, staff and volunteer turnover, and having sufficient and long-term resourcing (Holley 2009). Bonnell and Koontz (2007) point out that logistical issues in collaborating can overshadow work on the target problem. Each of the collaboration arrangements in our cases has been modified, some drastically, in adapting to combinations of internal and external pressures, as policy, resourcing and other changes, sometimes extraneous to the collaboration itself or its focal issue, have repositioned the partners and their responsibilities and priorities (Head et al. 2016). In each case, the official introduction of the national system of regional NRM around 2002, then significant changes to it in 2008, created disturbances requiring major adjustment, even in the independently auspiced arrangements (Moore 2005; Pannell and Roberts 2010; Robins and Kanowski 2011; Head et al. 2016). For the two cases that are part of the national system these changes included reduced resourcing for the regional bodies, and dropping salinity as an overt priority for attention while changing the funding basis towards a more nationally competitive one around different named priorities. Wheatbelt NRM adapted to this in a variety of ways, including taking advantage of the forced change in policies and resourcing to address some challenges in the regional acceptance of the still-new organization (making Board and Chair changes, for example), while maintaining and financing its landscape strategies for salinity and multiple environmental benefits under a new rationale of 'dust control'. This rebadging of activity provided an opportunity to sidestep the fear of the region being stigmatized for suffering salinity. Meanwhile the independently auspiced arrangements had to find ways to coexist with the newly created regional bodies for NRM. The new provisions divided the hitherto integrated LEB arrangements into four separate state/territory regions and led to the demise of the self-organized cross-border integrated catchment management processes (see Bellamy et al. 2012, forthcoming). For Healthy Waterways, it required a role rationalization, a crisis in resourcing and tensions with the new emerging regional processes.

Part of the challenge in maintaining a vibrant, active collaboration particularly at the regional scale is maintaining stability without becoming rigid in the face of changing circumstances. Collaborations can be faced with choices about incorporating relevant new parties, which can bring new ideas and vigour, but requires forming new relationships and inducting the new parties into a long-standing culture of collaboration. Both options – including or avoiding new membership – can entail loss of momentum in the collaboration. Healthy Waterways faced this challenge twice, first in expanding its scope and membership to the upper catchments of its region, and later in needing to lean more strongly towards corporate members after local government roles in water management were reduced and water supply and water quality issues were joined under state policies. On both occasions the business model was affected, and developing new relationships was testing for the partnership.

Challenge 3: Knowledge for Learning and Adapting

Knowledge issues permeate the recognition of a wicked problem, and the selection and adaptation of strategies to solve it. Both the wicked problem, and collaboration, can require different forms of knowledge, among different sets of people (e.g. Van Buuren 2009). Scientific knowledge is highly important, but recognition of a problem may also rely on political and local knowledge (Brown et al. 2005). All of our cases were fortunate in their access to science, overtly arranged or attracted incrementally.

Science has been most central perhaps to Healthy Waterways, given its origins in a large scientific study. Healthy Waterways formed and maintained a scientific experts' panel (initially biophysical then including the social sciences from 2003), and undertook planned series of studies and modelling to expand knowledge of the system, inform and motivate action. Science communication played an important role, particularly in the early years, and a well-resourced annual water quality monitoring system with highly publicized report cards is internationally envied (Bunn et al. 2007; Abal et al. 2001). This knowledge has been developed in a highly adaptive way. After an initial focus on point source pollution in Moreton Bay and the lower rivers, leading to upgrade to all major sewerage treatment plants, attention turned to other major sources of pollution, particularly diffuse sources from the rural upper catchments (Bunn et al. 2007; Delfau and Cottingham 2012; Patterson et al. 2015). This required research into the sources, research to prioritize where action would be most fruitful, and research into the influences of potential management actions. The increasing knowledge prompted adaptations in the collaboration arrangement, principally through the recognition that the diffuse source pollution challenge lay beyond the territory of the original members, so the focal area and membership were expanded. It proved more difficult to manage across the larger set of members, and in some cases to incorporate the less well-resourced small local governments of the upper catchments fully into the collaborative culture that had built up among the first partners, and this was one of several contributors to a regime shift about 2011.

The other three cases all had legacies of and continuing access to research on the wicked problem in their regions. For example, CSIRO (the national science organization) had a long-standing research programme into ecosystem services and landscape processes in the Goulburn-Broken which provided a sound basis of understanding for managers and has also been internationally seminal in the development of theory on ecosystem services and on social-ecological systems (Walker et al. 2009). Thanks to this research the problem of salinity was seen as occurring within a complex adaptive system rather than one that could respond in a linear and predictable way to interventions, and alternative landscape approaches using tree planting to mitigate the rising water table have been influential. The Wheatbelt in Western Australia has to a lesser extent gained from the interest of Perth-based scientists and CSIRO, including economic (e.g. Pannell and Roberts 2010) and social inputs (Measham 2009) into the system understanding. Having a scientist on staff, experienced in salinity, has assisted this process. The LEB also has access to relevant science, and when the collaborative approach there shifted from its community-based and integrated catchment management basis (focused on its cross-border catchments) into a more government-coordinated arrangement based on an inter-governmental agreement (Bellamy et al. 2012), scientists and the LEB community were involved through three bodies (a Scientific Advisory Panel of six appointed members; a Community Advisory Committee with 17 appointed Indigenous and non-Indigenous members; and more recently a Senior Officer's Group for coordinating implementation across state borders). Each of these cases indicates the important role of generating and integrating diverse sources of knowledge, as well as the roles of scientists as participants in the collaborations (e.g. through both formal and informal collaborative arrangements).

In commenting on scientific knowledge, we recognize that government enquiries (e.g. on salinity in Western Australia) and national reports into salinity (MDBMC 1999; SCARM 2000) have consolidated knowledge and influenced policy and action (e.g. COAG 2000).

The message from our case studies is that knowledge is highly important, to recognition and framing (sometimes reframing, e.g. in the case of the LEB, Bellamy et al. 2012; Head et al. 2016) of the wicked problem as important, for example, understanding its behaviour within a complex system, and experimenting and learning about context-appropriate collective action (e.g. Patterson et al. 2015). This is a long-standing and somewhat cyclical process in which mutual adjustments between the nature of the knowledge, and the nature of the collaboration, can occur. There are issues of confidence in the strategies proposed, both due to scientific uncertainty within a complex system, and the collaborating parties' degrees of confidence in the science.

While all of these case studies have significant strengths in access to knowledge and sophisticated use of that knowledge in a range of ways from problem understanding, identifying solutions, monitoring, and building public and political support, access to and acceptance of knowledge presents its own challenges for collaborative approaches for addressing wicked problems at a regional scale. These include resourcing or attracting the level of research needed, expanding the knowledge base, as needs for information evolve, and linking scientific knowledge to viable management strategies.

Challenge 4: Persistence in the Face of Mismatched Ecological and Political Timeframes

Wicked problems by their nature require long-term engagement and action. Meanwhile time is needed both for a new collaboration to mature, and to proceed from deliberation to collective action. Nevertheless the members of a collaboration, their funders and their constituents, are understandably eager to see early outcomes and return on investment, in an era of much emphasis on accountability. Thus there is a fundamental mismatch between wicked problems developing and requiring resolution on decadal timescales, and decision-making and resource allocation tied to political timeframes of very few years (Head et al. 2016). For instance Australia's National Action Plan for Salinity and Water Quality was planned for an initial five-year investment, despite the long-term nature of the challenge, then significantly downplayed within replacement programme arrangements.

Monitoring, when set up at all, can be very slow to show results on wicked NRM problems. Wheatbelt NRM, like the other non-statutory regional bodies for NRM, was established with a short or uncertain time horizon. This gave it little incentive to establish a monitoring scheme, and no time for one to demonstrate results. An interviewee pointed out that even if monitoring had been built into its programme, the collaboration and its staff had no confidence in being present five years later to read the measurements.

Healthy Waterways was fortunate in being able to model, then demonstrate, positive results in its early years (Bunn et al. 2007), having picked the 'low hanging fruit' of sewerage treatment upgrades as its first goal. These were under the direct control of some of the collaborators (local governments). Later, as subsequent priorities shifted to more diffuse sources of pollution (Delfau and Cottingham 2012), scientific staff grappled with communication issues in explaining to members of the collaboration that rapid progress on water quality is difficult to demonstrate, and in many areas the collaboration is doing well to retard rapid worsening of water quality which would be expected given rapid rates of urban development (and insufficient action to stay abreast of the increased population pressures).

This tension between ecological and political timeframes places great pressure on a collaboration. It can lead to reframing of the issues, sometimes a healthy process that can assist the sustainability of collaborative arrangements (Gray 2004). For instance in the LEB, the wicked problem was reframed from environmental rehabilitation in the early–mid-1990s, to building a self-sustaining process for change focused on keeping the LEB in good condition from the late 1990s (Bellamy et al. 2012). However, given the inherent nature of wicked problems including the common scenario of short-term results being highly difficult to demonstrate, collaborative arrangements may be abandoned, replaced, or undergo major institutional changes. At state and federal level, political pressures to invest wisely and secure results can and do prompt major changes in policy and funding, creating administrative contextual change. Our case studies suggest that the challenges these timeframe issues pose go beyond the problem of maintaining political will, and sufficient investment, to those of continually addressing the problem in practice (Dovers and Wild River 2003; Bellamy et al. 2012).

Challenge 5: Managing in a Multi-level Context

The public policy, planning and social-ecological systems literatures emphasize multiple interacting levels within a system (e.g. Folke et al. 2005; Bellamy 2007; Innes and Booher 2010). A regional collaboration cannot be an independent entity. In reality it depends on and must respond to policy and programme changes coming from governments (state and federal, in Australia's case), while also needing to manage its constituency relationships at local levels within its region. Meanwhile it contends with ecological or environmental change at various scales.

(a) Adapting to change

Our cases have all shown a need for local and regional collaborations to adapt to changing political and administrative conditions that are beyond their control. We described earlier how the two-tiered collaborative arrangements of the LEB from the late 1990s, in which self-organized, community-based, cross-border catchment management groups were nested within more formal Commonwealth-state arrangements under an inter-governmental agreement, were disrupted by the introduction of the national arrangements for NRM in the early 2000s (Bellamy et al. 2012, forthcoming). Four new regional bodies for NRM were established as state-based (rather than cross-border) entities, undermining the fundamental focus of the recently established LEB multi-tiered arrangements on managing cross-boundary issues (Bellamy et al. 2012). This threatened local ownership and participation opportunities, which continued with reduced focus, while major changes to institutional arrangements including Indigenous engagement gradually evolved over the next decade (Bellamy et al. forthcoming).

Healthy Waterways was forced to adapt to a series of state-government-led organizational changes in the water sector for SEQ from 2006 to 2009 (Head 2014) that reduced the role of local government (and hence their incentive to contribute funds and staff time to sustain the collaboration and secretariat). Meanwhile the local governments were also being forced to merge to achieve economies of scale. By this time, the regional body for NRM for the region (SEQ Catchments) had become well established, involving many of the same collaborators as Healthy Waterways. Questions were raised concerning the need for separate collaborative bodies in SEQ. This created a perceived crisis in relevance for Healthy Waterways, which was eventually resolved with agreement that Healthy Waterways was worth retaining as a separate collaboration, especially given its science and monitoring strengths, but roles should be shared to focus Healthy Waterways at a more strategic level, with the regional body to concentrate on coordinating on ground implementation including direct relationships with landholders and local voluntary groups.

Wheatbelt NRM, as one of the regional bodies for NRM, had to adapt to major amendments to the national programme under which it had been initially created. From being one of 23 priority regions under the National Action Plan for Salinity and Water Quality in 2003, as well as a regional body for NRM from 2002, it needed to survive significantly changed programme rules and system of funding allocation under the Caring for our Country Program from 2008 (Robins and Kanowski 2011). These included removal of salinity as a designated national priority, reduced core funding to sustain the collaboration's staff and activities, and reliance on competitive funding towards completely different national priorities. It was proactive in this process. It had prepared itself from the beginning by avoiding building a large staff of its own. It took advantage of a 'window of opportunity' in the transition time between programmes to make board and CEO changes to address issues with community engagement and acceptance that had built under its period of strong focus on accountability to government, and to make some new investments.

Environmental conditions will also vary over time, and affect the wicked problem or its presentation. Much of Australia suffered a 'millennial drought' in the 2000s, which was broken by major flooding across much of the country in 2011. Paradoxically, the rising water table that follows from floods can intensify salinity problems, as in the Goulburn-Broken irrigation areas in Victoria. But salinity had ceased to be a federal government funding priority in the Caring for our Country programme in 2008, and the catchments within the Murray-Darling Basin had by then become preoccupied with debates about new arrangements to balance the water needs of primary industries and the 'environmental flows' needed for ecosystem health, as well as participating in a new programme to fund irrigation efficiencies.

The cases suggest that maintaining an energetic and effective collaboration is a periodic, if not persistent, struggle. The collaboration needs refreshing at times to deal with externally generated challenges, internal ones, and the ongoing challenge of attaining traction and results on the wicked problem. Members may need to change, especially if their organizational roles with respect to the problem change, as happened to the local governments in Healthy Waterways. Invariably the staff and champions among the member organizations experience turnover, which also affects the collaboration dynamics.

(b) Incorporating community engagement and local participation

In a multi-level context, regional collaborations tackling wicked problems also need to engage with local participants effectively. Firstly, wicked natural resource problems in Australia tend to occur on rural land which is largely under private ownership or long-term leasehold, so landholder action in addressing the problems is imperative. This is not purely a matter of dealing with individuals; they can be reached collectively through their diverse organizational linkages. For example, Wheatbelt NRM was very strategic in partnering with large-scale farmer organizations such as no-till farmers, and a farmer organization promoting tree planting for biofuels, in order to change land cover in ways that helped to reduce salinity. One of the Landcare groups in its region was strategic in coupling the desires of upland farmers to enhance biodiversity, with those of lowland farmers in arresting salinity, through planting of tree belts that supported both needs.

Our cases are inconsistent, however, in the extent to which working at or connecting with local levels is seen as an important part of the collaboration effort, the interpretation of local roles in tackling the wicked problem, and how this is structured into the collaboration and its activities. In Wheatbelt NRM, landholder understanding and support for landscape-scale efforts to reduce salinity, and change in management practices, were recognized as critical. Wider community support was also sought, including engagement with Aboriginal people. The collaboration had two key strategies, incorporation of leading individuals initially representing local environment and farming interests on its board (and retaining these interests after transition to an expert board), and partnering with delivery organizations (see above). As mentioned above, it also adapted its board and community engagement strategies to improve its orientation towards community engagement. Wheatbelt NRM has also benefited from legacies of experience in collaboration, with individuals inculcated in Landcare and catchment management in the 1990s emerging to join and bring a collaborative culture to the new regional body in the 2000s. Meanwhile some state government departments shared this culture of collaboration, but were unable to bring all their experience to the regional body as state bodies were structured to remain outside the collaborations themselves.

In the LEB (Bellamy et al. 2012), the regional collaboration has strong local roots given its emergence in response to significant conflict among diverse basin stakeholders (Bellamy et al. forthcoming). The collaborative processes that emerged led to the creation of an LEB identity that had not existed, and a willingness to build collective understanding of diverse perspectives (without necessarily reaching agreement on a single perspective). This in turn led to cooperation across political jurisdictions in water management planning processes and common assessment basis for state-based monitoring systems. The self-organizing in the LEB tends to be given impetus by key individuals, and sometimes advocacy groups, who have been seminal in raising the problem to prominence (e.g. campaigns against the threat of cotton farming in the 1990s), then in framing and reframing the issues, creating opportunities for change, and keeping strategic focus (Bellamy et al. 2012). In doing so, social entrepreneurs worked across administrative levels, through formal arrangements and informal alliances or advocacy groups (Bellamy et al. forthcoming).

Healthy Waterways has been inconsistent in the degree of priority it has given to local engagement and rationale for its necessity across different phases of the collaboration. In the early years, communication with the general public was a priority, with a sense that public awareness was important towards solving water quality at that stage. Local organizations such as Landcare and catchment management groups were also counted directly among members, and continue to be celebrated in annual awards although they are no longer structured formally into the collaboration (and perhaps were never central in reality).

Some interesting motivators and demotivators for local people to contribute to, or support, the collaboration in addressing the wicked problem emerged through the cases. These contributed to challenges and opportunities in addressing the wicked problems. In the Wheatbelt there was an underlying concern about the region being stigmatized by salinity. This made it somewhat difficult to discuss collaboration and engage cooperation. When funding for salinity was dropped as a national priority in 2008, and the collaboration adapted by pursuing its strategies under other public rationales, the opportunity to avoid this stigmatization was seen as some advantage.

CONCLUSIONS

The challenges related to a collaboration addressing a wicked problem have parallels with those identified by Westley (2002) for a highly influential and well-connected individual manager of a complex region. Here Westley's four components of managing 'in' (managing oneself and one's organization's bureaucratic process), managing 'up' (managing the political process that governs one's organization), managing 'through' (adaptive science-based process), and managing 'out' (a community outreach process) approximate a collaboration's challenges in:

- managing its own changing dynamics, among its members, over time and contextual changes;
- managing vertical influences, contextual changes coming from higher levels of governance;
- having the knowledge available to manage the wicked problem adaptively; and
- incorporating local relationships constructively, particularly where these have significant roles in the ability to act on the wicked problem.

These represent a combined challenge for collaborations; they cannot be treated separately. Overall, regional collaborations dealing with wicked NRM problems can be seen as adapting themselves to a changing (or reframed) problem, within changing contexts. While doing so is highly challenging, this ability to adapt is a strength, not a limitation.

Collaboration seems to be the main option to address wicked problems at regional scales, but it is not a panacea. Our cases confirm that collaboration is difficult to build and sustain, and to keep energized and focused (Bellamy et al. 2012; Head et al. 2016). Collaborations need to deal with the reality that most member organizations and individuals lack experience or an organizational culture favouring collaboration, and that collaboration tends to conflict with the top-down managerial logic that is well institutionalized in legislation and professional training.

In considering ways to reduce some of these challenges, and enable collaboration to be a more effective instrument in addressing wicked NRM problems, we have found that an overarching requirement is recognition at the regional scale of the need for long timeframes to address wicked NRM problems. While the collaborations need persistence and at times refreshing, they would be helped in their task if all parties, internal and external to the collaborative processes, were to recognize that continuity is necessary beyond the short-term timeframes of electoral democracy. Easily demonstrable progress, in terms of measurable NRM outcomes, is unlikely in the short term, owing to the very nature of the wicked problems (Head 2008; Innes and Booher 2010), but slow progress does not necessarily represent failure.

We suggest a need for greater attention, at national and international levels, to the culture and mechanisms of collaborating, including the development of new organizational skills. While important for the internal processes of each collaboration, it is also vital in supporting collaboration as a cross-cutting component within a horizontally and vertically aligned mix of governance arrangements. Our cases show that for a regional collaboration to have sufficient opportunity to address its key problems, it needs a supportive environment. Improving this environment is a long-term endeavour. The arts and ethos of collaboration need to permeate education systems and organizational behaviour. This sounds difficult, but may be no more challenging than other cultural and strategic adaptations the business sector has made in recent decades. Meanwhile there is a continuing need for good mechanisms for continual improvement of knowledge and its dissemination, combining research, local knowledge, and monitoring, each evolving as needs and the framing of the problem alter.

ACKNOWLEDGEMENTS

The authors acknowledge assistance from ARC research grants DP0987727 and DP140101532, and the organizations and individual participants involved in the four case studies.

NOTE

1. Here we refer to a large area within a nation, in contrast to a multi-national region within a global context.

REFERENCES

Abal, E.G., Dennison, W.C. and Greenfield, P.F. (2001). Managing the Brisbane River and Moreton Bay: An integrated research/management program to reduce impacts on an Australian estuary. *Water Science & Technology*, 43(9): 57–70.

Allan, C., Curtis, A., Stankey, G. and Shindler, B. (2008). Adaptive management and watersheds: A social science perspective. *Journal of the American Water Resources Association*, 44(1): 166–174.

Bellamy, J. (2007). Adaptive governance: The challenge for natural resource

management. In A.J. Brown and J.A. Bellamy (eds), *Federalism and regionalism: New approaches, new institutions?* (pp. 97–120). Canberra: ANU E-Press.
Bellamy, J., Head, B.W. and Ross, H. (2012). Blurring boundaries and building bridges: Challenges of managing across borders in the Lake Eyre Basin. In J.R. Grove and I. Rutherford (eds), *Proceedings of the 6th Australian Stream Management Conference – Managing for Extremes*, Canberra, ACT, Australia, 6–8 February 2012 (pp. 151–158). River Basin Management Authority. http://www.asm6.org.au/assets/6ASM/Abstracts/022.pdf
Bellamy, J., Head, B.W. and Ross, H. (forthcoming). Crises and institutional change: Cross-border water governance in Lake Eyre Basin, Australia. *Society and Natural Resources*.
Berkes, F., Colding, F. and Folke, C. (eds) (2003). *Navigating social-ecological systems: Building resilience for complexity and change*. Cambridge, UK: Cambridge University Press.
Berkes, F. and Ross, H. (2013). Community resilience: Toward an integrated approach. *Society and Natural Resources*, 26(1): 5–20.
Bonnell, J.E. and Koontz, T.Z. (2007). Stumbling forward: The organizational challenges of building and sustaining collaborative watershed management. *Society and Natural Resources*, 20(2): 153–167.
Bouwen, R. and Taillieu, T. (2004). Multi-party collaboration as social learning for interdependence: Developing relational knowing for sustainable natural resource management. *Journal of Community & Applied Social Psychology*, 14(3): 137–153.
Brown, K. (2014). Global environmental change I: A social turn for resilience? *Progress in Human Geography*, 38, 107–117.
Brown, V., Grootjans, J., Ritchie, J., Townsend, M. and Verinder, G. (2005). *Sustainability and health*. Crows Nest, NSW: Allen and Unwin.
Bunn, S.E., Abal, E.G., Greenfield, P.E. and Tarte, D.M. (2007). Making the connection between healthy waterways and healthy catchments: South East Queensland Water Australia. *Science & Technology: Water Supply*, 7(2), 93–100.
Buuren, A. van (2009). Knowledge for governance, governance of knowledge: Inclusive knowledge management in collaborative governance processes. *International Public Management Journal*, 12(2): 208–235.
COAG (Council of Australian Governments) (2000). A National Action Plan for Salinity and Water Quality. Canberra: Commonwealth Government.
Curtis, A., Ross, H., Marshall, G.R., Baldwin, C., Cavaye, J., Freeman, C., Carr, A. and Syme, G. (2014). The great experiment with devolved NRM governance: Lessons from community engagement in Australia and New Zealand since the 1980s. *Australasian Journal of Environmental Management*, 21(2): 175–199.
Delfau, K. and Cottingham, R. (2012). Addressing complexities in integrated water resource management using systems thinking: South East Queensland diffuse pollution case study. *Australasian Journal of Natural Resources Law and Policy*, 15(1): 42–76.
Department of Agriculture, Fisheries and Forestry (DAFF) (1999). *Managing natural resources in rural Australia for a sustainable future*. Canberra: DAFF.
Dovers, S. and Wild River, S. (eds) (2003). *Managing Australia's environment*. NSW: Federation Press.
Folke, C., Hahn, T., Olsson, P. and Norberg, J. (2005). Adaptive governance of social-ecological systems. *Annual Review of Environmental Resources*, 30, 441–473.

Gray, B. (1989). *Collaborating: Finding common ground for multiparty problems*. San Francisco, CA: Jossey-Bass.

Gray, B. (2004). Strong opposition: Frame-based resistance to collaboration. *Journal of Community and Applied Social Psychology*, 14, 166–176.

Gunderson, L.H. and Holling, C.S. (eds) (2002). *Panarchy. Understanding transformations in human and natural systems*. Washington, DC: Island Press.

Head, B.W. (2008). Wicked problems in public policy. *Public Policy*, 3(2): 101–118.

Head, B.W. (2014). The collaboration solution? Factors for collaborative success. In J. O'Flynn, D. Blackman and J. Halligan (eds), *Crossing boundaries in public management and policy* (pp. 142–157). London: Routledge.

Head, B.W. and Alford, J. (2015). Wicked problems: Implications for public policy and management. *Administration and Society*, 47(6): 711–739.

Head, B.W., Ross, H. and Bellamy, J. (2016). Managing wicked natural resource problems: The collaborative challenge at regional scales in Australia. *Landscape & Urban Planning*, 154. [Online first]: http://www.sciencedirect.com/science/article/pii/S0169204616300299

Holley, C. (2009). Aging gracefully? Examining the conditions for sustaining successful collaboration in environmental law and governance. *Environment and Planning Law Journal*, 26: 457–485.

Innes, J.E. and Booher, D.E. (2010). *Planning with complexity: An introduction to collaborative rationality for public policy*. London: Routledge.

Margerum, R.D. (2011). *Beyond consensus: Improving collaborative planning and management*. Cambridge, MA: The MIT Press.

MDBMC (Murray-Darling Basin Ministerial Council) (1999). *The salinity audit of the Murray-Darling Basin: A hundred year perspective*. Canberra: MDBMC.

Measham, T.G. (2009). Social learning through evaluation: A case study of overcoming constraints for management of dryland salinity. *Environmental Management*, 43(6): 1096–1107.

Memon, A., Painter, B. and Weber, E. (2010). Enhancing potential for integrated catchment management in New Zealand: A multi-scalar, strategic perspective. *Australasian Journal of Environmental Management*, 17(1): 35–44.

Moore, S.A. (2005). Regional delivery of NRM in Australia: Is it democratic and does it matter? In R. Eversole and J. Martin (eds), *Participation and governance in regional development* (pp. 121–136). Aldershot: Ashgate.

Pannell, D.J. and Roberts, A.M. (2010). Australia's National Action Plan for Salinity and Water Quality: A retrospective assessment. *Australian Journal of Agricultural and Resource Economics*, 54(4): 437–456.

Patterson, J.J., Smith, C. and Bellamy, J. (2015). Enabling and enacting 'practical action' in catchments: Responding to the 'wicked problem' of nonpoint source pollution in coastal subtropical Australia. *Environmental Management*, 55(2): 479–495.

Rittel, H.W.J. and Webber, M.M. (1973). Dilemmas in a general theory of planning. *Policy Sciences*, 4(2): 155–169.

Robins, L. and Kanowski, P. (2011). Crying for our Country: Eight ways in which 'Caring for our Country' has undermined Australia's regional model for natural resource management. *Australasian Journal of Environmental Management*, 18(2): 88–108.

SCARM (Standing Committee on Agriculture & Resource Management) (2000). Management of dryland salinity: Future strategic directions. Report No. 78. Canberra: SCARM.

Walker, B.H., Abel, N., Anderies, J.M. and Ryan, P. (2009). Resilience, adaptability, and transformability in the Goulburn-Broken Catchment, Australia. *Ecology and Society*, 14(1): 12. [Online]: http://www.ecologyandsociety.org/vol14/iss11/art12/

Westley, F. (2002). The devil in the dynamics: Adaptive managment on the front lines. In L.H. Gunderson and C.S. Holling (eds), *Panarchy: Understanding transformations in human and natural systems* (pp. 333–360). Washington, DC: Island Press.

Wondolleck, J. and Yaffee, S. (2000). *Making collaboration work: Lessons from innovation in natural resource management*. Washington, DC: Island Press.

PART III

Policy, politics and power

9. When voluntary is prescribed but mandated is necessary: the challenges of compulsory collaboration on complex public issues

Julia M. Wondolleck and Susan D. Lurie

Collaboration in public management is widespread and its central role in facilitating progress on today's complex public issues is well recognized (McGuire, 2006). Collaborative public management processes engage diverse stakeholders and agencies in addressing public problems that "do not fit jurisdictional boundaries and agency silos," (Fredrickson, 2007, p. 11). They are increasing in their frequency and breadth of application (Agranoff, 2007; Heikkila and Gerlak, 2005; Margerum, 2011; Weber, 2003; Wondolleck and Yaffee, 2000), and are most often characterized by voluntary, purposive relationships among organizations and levels of government to facilitate joint problem-solving (Agranoff, 2006; Agranoff and McGuire, 2003).

Multiple factors over the past few decades have set the stage for collaborative public management. Predominant among these factors is the recognition that many contemporary policy problems are "wicked" (Rittel and Webber, 1973; Weber and Khademian, 2008a) or "messes" (Ackoff, 1974), possessing interdependencies that defy isolated solutions. Of particular interest to this chapter are the challenges associated with compulsory participation in collaborative processes involving complex environmental management issues that exhibit the central characteristics of wicked problems (Weber and Khademian, 2008a). Traditional administrative rationality—neutral professionals carrying out cost-benefit decisions within hierarchically structured bureaucracies constrained by rigid boundaries—is mismatched to the policy and governance complexity of these problems (Durant, 2004; Kettl, 2006).

Much of the theory and practice of collaborative governance processes has been drawn from the Alternative Dispute Resolution (ADR) field (Bacow and Wheeler, 1984; Bingham, 1986; Daniels and Walker, 2001; Gray, 1989; O'Leary and Raines, 2001; Susskind et al., 1999) which emphasizes the centrality of voluntary engagement (Wondolleck, 2010). However, many collaborative governance processes today entail compulsory participation and hence defy this voluntary prescription. These are situations in which a wicked problem necessitates a more integrative approach yet where organizational or political resistance suggests that collaboration is not likely to emerge without an external compelling force. Wondolleck and Yaffee (2000) examined the challenges associated with collaboration when public managers desire to work in a collaborative manner but agency policy, procedures and norms impede their ability to do so. In contrast, this chapter looks at the inverse situation and asks what are the implications for theory and practice when collaboration is compulsory but parties are reluctant. It attempts to begin bridging the fields of Alternative Dispute Resolution and Public Administration, as called for by Bingham and O'Leary (2006), and draws broadly from the dispersed literature on collaboration. In so doing, it seeks to expand understanding of this unexamined dimension of collaborative governance and encourage greater research attention to this topic. Public managers finding themselves in mandated collaborative processes but following prescriptions based in theories of voluntary engagement may rapidly find themselves in uncharted terrain facing unanticipated challenges. The purpose here is to start mapping this terrain.

This chapter examines the mandated participation dimension of the CALFED Bay-Delta Program (CALFED), a multi-party collaborative process at the interface of California's contentious environmental and water resource issues. The key attributes of the CALFED process that appear to have played a role in encouraging the emergence of a constructive collaborative dynamic despite imposition of a largely unwelcome mandate to participate are identified. Specifically, the chapter examines the challenges associated with mandating engagement of parties who had varying perceptions of the urgency of the problem, the degree to which they were interdependent and needed to work together, what other alternatives were available for managing the problem, and the fairness of the process that was imposed. The chapter explores the ways in which these challenges were addressed and assesses the potential for instilling within a mandated process the essential qualities associated with voluntary engagement. Finally, the chapter concludes with a discussion of two unique characteristics and challenges associated with mandated collaboration in public management that warrant further research.

VOLUNTARY PRESCRIPTIONS BUT MANDATED REALITIES

Long-standing theory and practice of collaborative public management prescribes *voluntary* engagement as a necessary precondition (Wondolleck, 2010). This fundamental tenet dictates that parties can choose whether or not to participate and whether to remain engaged in a process once underway. Two of the five "principle elements of ADR" cited by O'Leary and Raines (2001, p. 683) are that "parties agree to participate in the process," and "any participant may withdraw and seek a resolution elsewhere." As Daniels and Walker (2001, p. 57) emphasize, "whether collaborative behaviors emerge depends first and foremost on the participants, and there is no practical way or ethical reason to force them to interact collaboratively. Collaboration cannot be forced, scheduled, or required; it must be nurtured, permitted, and promoted." Huxham (1996, p. 15) observed that because "collaboration is voluntary, partners generally need to justify their involvement in it in terms of its contribution to their own aims." Thomson and Perry (2006, p. 29) warn: "*Don't collaborate unless you are willing to thoughtfully consider and educate yourself about the nature of the process involved*" (emphasis in original).

This premise of voluntary engagement was reaffirmed in policy prescription when the Directors of the Office of Management and Budget (OMB) and Council on Environmental Quality (CEQ) issued a joint "Memorandum on Environmental Conflict Resolution" in November 2005, directing federal agencies "to increase the effective use of environmental conflict resolution and build institutional capacity for collaborative problem-solving" (Bolton and Connaughton, 2005). The memo summarized 25 years of scholarship and professional practice in a set of eight core principles, one of which is to "Ensure balanced, voluntary inclusion of affected/concerned interests; all parties should be willing and able to participate and select their own representative."

There are many reasons why voluntary engagement is both embedded in theory and preferred in practice. Voluntary engagement enables participants to make their own determination about the potential value of a process. The ability to make a choice encourages thoughtful assessments of the purpose and functioning of the proposed process and how it might compare with alternatives for dealing with the issues at hand (Bacow and Wheeler, 1984; Daniels and Walker, 2001; Fisher et al., 1991; Gray, 1989). Such assessments enable parties to make informed judgments about their participation and, moreover, instill a sense of commitment to good faith participation should the choice be made to participate (Bean et al., 2007; Carlson, 1999). As O'Leary and Raines (2001, p. 688) found, "the most successful use of ADR in EPA regional offices stems from the commitment of enthusiastic and skillful key staff persons." Thomson and Perry (2006, p.28) suggest that "public managers, if they enter collaborations with their eyes open, will be more likely to appreciate, reflect on, and support the relationships that are so critical to collaborative efforts." In contrast, research has shown that parties who enter a collaborative process by directive are more likely to be resistant and uncommitted to it, maintaining their adversarial stance rather than adopting the collaborative perspective necessary for the process to succeed (Cohen, 1991; Daniels and Walker, 2001; Katz, 1993; Leahy, 2006).

Others have discovered unanticipated consequences associated with mandated participation in public sector collaboratives. Just because organizations are directed to work together does not mean that they will do so in the intended manner (Brummel et al., 2012; Kumar et al., 2007; Lewis et al., 2009; Rodriguez et al., 2007; Schneider, 2009). Sandfort (1999) describes the effect of a mandate in a social services program where collaboration between public agencies was actually impeded rather than facilitated by the mandate. Latent identities and characterizations introduced unexpected barriers to interaction and the agencies involved collaborated less following the mandate than they had before it was imposed.

INCENTIVES THAT PROMPT VOLUNTARY ENGAGEMENT

The centrality of incentives to participate to the successful functioning of collaborative processes is well established (US Institute for Environmental Conflict Resolution, 2006) and these incentives determine whether or not engagement will occur voluntarily. Foundational theory that gave rise to the prominence of collaborative approaches in public management today was developed acknowledging essential factors that motivate engagement. Incentives for participation are rooted in a sense of urgency to resolve a dispute or solve a problem (Cormick, 1980; Moore, 1996), acknowledgement of interdependence and compelling need for parties to work together (Cormick, 1980; Gray, 1989; Susskind and Cruikshank, 1987), recognition that alternatives to collaboration are not preferred (Bacow and Wheeler, 1984; Fisher et al., 1991), and a belief that the proposed process will be fair (Fisher et al., 1991; Lawrence et al., 1997; O'Leary and Bingham, 2003; Smith and McDonough, 2001).

When the above conditions are not satisfied, parties will perceive little incentive to collaborate and voluntary engagement is unlikely. If parties do not perceive urgency to resolve an issue, recognize their interdependence and the need to work together, nor acknowledge that collaboration is a more promising and hence preferred alternative for addressing their interests, they will not likely enter a process with commitment and in a good faith manner. Yet, commitment and the presence of a collaborative mindset have been shown to be "a critical component of effective collaborative problem-solving capacity when the context involves a wicked problem" (Weber and Khademian, 2008a, p. 338). Furthermore, if parties enter a collaborative process under duress they will be less likely to trust the process and perceive that they will be treated fairly in it. Constructive communication, knowledge-building and creative problem-solving will be constrained. In all of these ways a mandate to participate challenges the very essence of what makes collaboration work (Wondolleck and Yaffee, 2000).

MANDATES INCREASINGLY CHALLENGE THE VOLUNTARY TENET

While voluntary participation, for the above good reasons, is a central tenet embedded in theories of collaboration and dispute resolution, not all collaborative governance processes are voluntary. Weber and Khademian (2008a, p. 334) note that collaborative networks struggling with wicked public problems are not only the product of entrepreneurial managers and collaborative capacity builders but at times are initiated "by mandate or regulatory requirement." No fewer than four mandated collaborative processes exist for the USDA Forest Service alone (Cheng, 2006). The Secure Rural Schools and Community Self Determination Act of 2000 mandates that the Forest Service collaborate with local communities in Resource Advisory Councils "whether they want to or not, or know how to or not" (Leahy, 2006, pp. 5–6). The Clean Air Act statutorily mandates the US Environmental Protection Agency (EPA) to resolve selected disputes involving tribes and the states through collaborative negotiation processes (Van de Wetering and McKinney, 2006). The National Oceanic and Atmospheric Administration (NOAA) and other federal agencies have been mandated by Executive Order to collaborate in restoration of the Great Lakes (US Department of Commerce, 2007). The Congressional Accountability Act of 1995 mandates ADR for employment disputes in legislative agencies (Nabatchi, 2007, p. 646). Mandated collaborative management arrangements are increasingly prevalent in social services delivery (Graddy and Chen, 2006; Sandfort, 1999) and health care provision (Lurie, 2004a; Rodriguez et al., 2007). Other examples of mandated legal-political inter-organizational partnerships include those required for inter-governmental revenue sharing and regulatory control (Alexander, 1995; Raelin, 1980).

Mandating collaboration is necessary in some situations for both organizational and logistical reasons (Brock, 1991). While the antecedent conditions (Gray, 1989; Thomson and Perry, 2006) indicating an issue is amenable to collaborative resolution may exist, or the issue may exhibit those characteristics necessitating collaborative management (Weber and Khademian, 2008b), the opportunity or incentive to collaborate may not be present. The disinclination of public agencies to either cooperate with one another or to invite public groups into their decision-making domain has been well established (Bardach, 1998; Kumar et al., 2007; Nabatchi, 2007). Furthermore, the reach and magnitude of some public issues extends beyond existing opportunities that might accommodate voluntary engagement even if parties might be willing. Without a ready forum and with many parties to involve, collaboration can be logistically precluded. This disconnect between long-standing theory, undercurrent resistance, issue imperative, emerging executive directives, legislative prescriptions and administrative programs, presents a seeming paradox for public administrators: at times engagement in collaborative public management will only occur if mandated, yet theory suggests that for it to succeed engagement must be voluntary. Can these conflicting realities be reconciled?

HOW MIGHT MANDATED PARTICIPATION INFLUENCE COLLABORATIVE DYNAMICS?

While mandated collaboration in the management of public issues is becoming more prevalent, research into its unique attributes, dynamics and challenges is largely non-existent (Wondolleck, 2010). The purpose of this analysis is to take some initial steps down this path of inquiry by probing the dynamics of a single, large-scale collaborative public management process in which participation was compelled by a mandate, not by individual or organizational choice. This analysis identifies the factors that appear to have enabled a collaborative dynamic to emerge despite the mandate as well as what challenges and cautions appear particular to a collaborative governance process in which participation is mandated.

The CALFED Bay-Delta Program (CALFED), a multi-party collaborative process at the interface of California's contentious environmental and water resource issues, provides a unique case situation for this analysis. The challenges and accomplishments of CALFED have been examined by many researchers (e.g. Dutterer and Margerum, 2015; Heikkila and Gerlak, 2005; Ingram and Fraser, 2006; Innes et al., 2006; Lund et al.,

2007). In 2009, a special issue of *Environmental Science and Policy*, 12(6), focused on CALFED. What makes this chapter's case analysis unique is its focus on the compulsory aspect of the collaboration: how did the fact that engagement was mandated alter the collaborative dynamic and challenge process management? Despite a series of top-down initiatives that mandated collaboration (Babbitt, 2005; Ingram and Fraser, 2006), and despite an organizational and political context that often challenged serious collaboration among the diverse stakeholders and agencies (Innes et al., 2006; Lurie, 2011), CALFED was nonetheless able to make some important headway. CALFED is an instructive case because it was, in essence, an experiment in mandated collaboration. Prior to the mandate few organizations had incentive or inclination to collaborate; after the mandate they were forced to work together and, while the process was challenging, they devised ways to make progress.

This analysis draws from primary and secondary sources. Open-ended interviews were conducted in 2002 with 42 individuals directly involved with CALFED either as staff, stakeholders or outside observers, and who were asked about their perceptions of the enabling factors and challenges associated with the collaborative process. It became apparent during these interviews that there were dynamics at play that distinguished this collaborative process from those predominately discussed in the literature. In particular, while most collaborative processes inevitably experience the tensions between cooperative and competitive behaviors among participants that are inherent in any negotiation process (Lax and Sebenius, 1986), the undercurrent resistance to cooperation in CALFED was at times palpable. The reality that the process had been mandated and participation was required was referenced by some interviewees and appeared to be influencing collaborative behaviors and process dynamics in unique ways. Other published accounts of the CALFED process were subsequently reviewed to determine if these same undercurrent tensions were observable in those accounts. In particular, the reflections of CALFED participants reported in Innes et al.'s (2006) work are quoted here when reflecting the compulsory dimension of the process.

INSIGHTS FROM A MANDATED COLLABORATIVE: THE CALFED EXPERIENCE

The Sacramento–San Joaquin Delta (the Delta) in northern California is the heart of the state's water supply system, providing drinking water to two-thirds of the state's population. It is where two of California's major rivers come together, eventually flowing out through San Francisco Bay;

hence, the reference to California's Bay-Delta. It is ecologically important because it provides habitat to a variety of terrestrial and aquatic species, some of which are listed as either threatened or endangered under the federal Endangered Species Act. The Delta houses two of the world's largest water diversion projects that deliver water to urban and agricultural users: the federal Central Valley Project and the State Water Project. The State Water Project involves an inter-basin transfer system, pumping water over the Tehachapi Mountains and into the Los Angeles Basin. Although approximately 75 percent of the state's available water comes from the northern one-third of the state, nearly 80 percent of the water demand comes from the southern two-thirds, which includes Los Angeles. California's population, estimated at 36 million at the turn of the 21st century, is projected to nearly double to over 63 million by the year 2040 (Hundley, 2001; McClurg, 1997a; McClurg and Newcom, 1998).

A Wicked Problem Defying Resolution

Disjointed state and federal water development institutions, a rapidly growing population, and increasing Delta environmental problems including water quality and species decline created intractable conflicts in multiple arenas. These lingering tensions have been exacerbated by the prolonged drought of 2011–2015. As remains true today, northern Californians at the time viewed any project that included water diversions to southern California as attempts to "steal" water from the north. There was an expanding reservoir of public resentment regarding perceived water grabs by agribusiness at the expense of urban and environmental water needs. Agricultural interests, a powerful political force, compounded the conflict with its own infighting (Gottlieb, 1988; Hundley, 2001). Numerous groups and coalitions increasingly caused policy impasses and filed court actions. There were also conflicts, including lawsuits in some instances, among different configurations of agencies: between state agencies, between federal agencies, and between state and federal agencies (Hundley, 2001; Littleworth and Garner, 1995; Reisner, 1993).

Despite different efforts at consensus among various sets of stakeholders in the early 1990s, impasses over water quality, water supplies and environmental issues continued (Lurie, 2011). In 1994, Standard & Poor's issued a warning to bond investors that "political gridlock surrounding unresolved environmental issues in the Bay-Delta threatened to downgrade the credit ratings of public utilities throughout the state" (Innes et al., 2006, p. 10). In a water policy speech, then-California Governor Pete Wilson pronounced the Delta "broken." A coalition of environmental groups sued the federal government over failure to enforce Clean Water Act standards

(Hundley, 2001; McClurg, 1997b). The US EPA subsequently announced its intention to implement a water quality plan that would include federal control over water allocations, historically an area of state primacy.

The state of California had already made it clear that it could not produce a Delta water quality plan fully consistent with federal Clean Water Act requirements within the time frame set by the EPA. The federal government, despite its announcement, concluded that it likely could not override the state's authority despite the regulatory hammers of the Clean Water Act.

Prolonged Impasse Prompts a Mandate to Collaborate

Escalating issues yet prolonged impasse over acceptable solutions eventually prompted a high-level directive mandating the parties to begin collaborating. It was clear that something had to be done as state and federal agencies acting independently would only sustain conflict while problems worsened. Governor Wilson, Secretary of the Interior Bruce Babbitt, and EPA Administrator Carol Browner directed the state and federal agencies under their respective authorities to form a collaborative planning and management process (Rieke, 1996). Following a series of intense negotiations, federal and state agency representatives, along with representatives from various water user groups, signed what became known as the "Delta Accord" on December 15, 1994. The CALFED Bay-Delta Program was created in 1995 to implement this Accord and ostensibly to put an end to the decades-old "water wars."

CALFED had three general goals: adopting water quality standards acceptable to both the state and federal governments; coordinating federal and state water project operations in the Delta to protect endangered species and implement water quality standards; and developing a long-term plan covering four common program areas: levee system stability, ecosystem restoration, water quality, and water supply (McClurg, 1997a). It eventually delivered its Record of Decision (ROD), which exceeded 7,000 pages, in August 2001. The plan had a time line of over 30 years and covered nearly the entire length of the nation's third largest state. Over two dozen state and federal agencies and numerous stakeholder groups spanning agricultural, environmental and municipal interests throughout the state were involved in the plan's development. The six-year process included hundreds of public meetings. In addition, there were round tables, symposia, and standing and ad hoc technical and other committees reporting to a core group of stakeholder representatives comprising the Federal Advisory Committee Act-chartered CALFED Bay-Delta Advisory Committee. Following issuance of the ROD, CALFED moved into its plan implementation phase.

The CALFED planning process transformed a seemingly intractable conflict. While the scientific and technical complexity of the issues remains, as do the divergent interests of many parties, the nature and extent of the interaction among those possessing the knowledge, capabilities and authority to deal with the issues in new ways was fundamentally altered. Innes et al. (2006, p. 5) summarize the magnitude of the change instituted by CALFED at the time:

> Collaborative processes have replaced gridlock and litigation; a comprehensive framework with linkages and balance among activities replaced project-by-project decisions; multipurpose interagency projects increasingly became the norm rather than single agency projects; local and regional solutions were used instead of just centralized decision making; public involvement was greatly increased, with stakeholders playing leadership roles; independent science reviews modified agency- and client-based science; accountability and transparency of decision making greatly increased; and flexible, adaptive management and joint learning replaced mechanistic decision making based on assumptions and mandates.

As noted earlier, the details of CALFED's long, complex and often tortured history have been well-documented. This brief analysis looks at but a small slice of this large process in order to discern how a collaborative dynamic emerged within such a hostile and resistant context and despite lack of voluntary engagement. While the process was voluntary in the sense that it was not legislatively required, participation in this process was not voluntary. The Governor and Interior Secretary did not invite the state and federal agencies under their authority to participate, they directed them to do so (Babbitt, 2005, p. 50; Ingram and Fraser, 2006, p. 92). Some agencies "hated CALFED" (Innes et al., 2006, p. 30) and their employees who were staffed to the process felt the repercussions of this animosity. As one CALFED participant put it, "Just because you agree that the way you were doing it in the past isn't working doesn't mean this proposed approach is the one you want" (Lurie, 2011).

Given their refusal to acknowledge their interdependencies and perceive incentives to work together, a mandate is likely the only way the various organizations involved in CALFED could have been brought together. However, it was an inauspicious beginning. How were commitment, good faith and perceptions of fairness instilled? Did the parties come to recognize their interdependence, feel a sense of urgency to address the issues, and conclude that collaboration was preferable to alternatives? If so, what enabled this transformation, however fleeting it might have been?

HOW VOLUNTARY QUALITIES WERE INSTILLED IN A MANDATED PROCESS

Despite initial resistance, the CALFED process was nonetheless able to instill a sense of urgency, interdependence, preferred alternative, and fairness among participants. At the same time, however, participant defection from the process was precluded and it appears that the combination of these enabling perceptions and constraining pressures were necessary to the progress of the process. As time revealed, when the mandate eventually weakened, many parties stopped collaborating but while the mandate was strong they were productive, achieving several notable accomplishments.

Sense of Urgency

Instilling a sense of urgency to the process was perhaps the easiest part of CALFED. Interior Secretary Babbitt and Governor Wilson, the conveners, imposed an ambitious task and a serious deadline that was vigorously enforced. Participants were instructed to develop a long-term, comprehensive solution over a three-year time frame. The magnitude of the expectations, the immediacy of the task, and the vigilant, at times forceful, oversight of the conveners afforded the parties little opportunity to resist or complain. The ambitious deadline provided a temporal framework for action that forced the stakeholders to focus immediately on ways to create an integrated, highly sophisticated planning and management document. Although the planning process took six years instead of three, the unmet deadline only seemed to increase the pressure on those involved to deliver a comprehensive plan.

Recognition of Interdependence and the Need to Work Together

Recognition of interdependence and the need to work together was instilled to some extent among CALFED participants through a number of procedural as well as political factors. For some participants, the mandate to participate merely forced them to behave for a limited time as if they were interdependent but when the mandate waned so did their inclinations to continue working together. For others, however, the process encouraged a recognition and acceptance of the scope and import of their interdependence. Few would have disputed the reality that their interests were intertwined and that independent actions taken by one would invariably, likely detrimentally, affect another. However, an understanding of both the full scope of their interdependency and, moreover, the nuances of their respective knowledge, needs and concerns was revealing to most.

CALFED's four common programs linking improvements in water quality, water supply, Delta infrastructure and the Bay-Delta ecosystem were a bold step forward. The programs physically connected the logical pieces. CALFED's planning required improvements in any one of the common program areas to be linked to improvements in the other programs. For instance, the Environmental Water Account, which set aside water for fish and wildlife purposes, also helped maintain water quality and allowed for increased water supply to be available to water contractors at times of the year during which water allocations might otherwise be reduced to maintain sufficient flow. The planning process provided ample evidence of how the various organizations, working together, could design programs and develop actions that none had the resources, technology or incentive to create on their own.

Although the directive to collaborate largely eliminated their choice whether or not to engage, agencies and non-governmental participants working together under the CALFED banner found that collaboration provided an environment and mechanisms for innovation. It encouraged and enabled learning, partly by breaking down prior notions about the nature of the problem and parties' objectives, but also by demonstrating possibilities that quickly shattered prior conceptions about the hopelessness of the process. New data and knowledge was generated through information sharing. Long-standing arguments over whether enough water was flowing through the Delta were replaced by joint efforts directed at finding ways to increase flows. There was better coordination of studies for water storage projects that saved both staff time and financial resources by eliminating duplication of efforts. The program also undertook studies and created modeling programs that might not otherwise have been designed and carried out.

CALFED was a new entity and a new process for all involved. Consequently, all participants were figuring it out together, a fact that appeared to have instilled some sense of ownership as well as shared purpose. Agency personnel on temporary assignment to CALFED needed to design new programs and approaches to solving a variety of problems outside of the normal operating procedures to which they were accustomed. The atmosphere provided a protected environment for entrepreneurial personalities to experiment with processes and ideas that might not be acceptable back in their home agencies due to resource constraints, constituent demands and organizational cultures. Participants were given latitude for crafting the process and being innovative about solutions. As Innes et al. (2006, p. 20) note, "Critical to the degree of success that CALFED had was the fact that the agencies had an agreed-on framework for working together on an agreed-on set of issues. They did not start with a set of detailed procedures nor with goals. No one had to pre-commit to anything." This flexibility provided the ability to be adaptive; if an element of the process did not work or was no longer needed, they could dispense with it.

Many participants brought an adversarial and competitive behavior to the process that needed to be transformed into a collaborative dynamic if CALFED had any chance of succeeding. CALFED's first Executive Director referred to the hardened positions of some participants as "religion," noting that they "were accustomed to arguing their case and standing behind rigid demands" (Innes et al., 2006, p. 33). "Education and communication is really what changed us away from that religion viewpoint," observed one agency staff person; "Even the most staunch religionist types that are still around have learned that they have to work with others because it just doesn't work anymore. Going to the Governor and saying, 'This is bad; we can't have this,' is no longer a tool that works effectively in California water issues" (Innes et al., 2006, p. 33).

CALFED had a central location, staff on assignment from participating agencies and an Executive Director to oversee planning and report to elected officials and policy-level executives in the different agencies. CALFED acted as a forum where people who might not otherwise come to know one another became acquainted and could better understand each other's organizations and interests. As a consequence, individuals became new resources for information and networking beyond CALFED meetings, advancing norms of trust and reciprocity. CALFED developed its own culture that, at least within the organization, galvanized support at a level that overrode home-agency identity and concomitant boundary issues. While this new identity introduced its own set of challenges (Lurie, 2011), it nonetheless provided a unifying mission and allegiances that helped participants focus on common objectives. They spoke with pride about what they termed "the CALFED way," the new norm of collaboration in addressing water issues in the state.

Part of the explanation for the tentative recognition of interdependence between parties is positive, rooted in learning, observing new possibilities, and the emergence of a new culture and norms among those directly involved in CALFED. Part of this recognition, however, was also externally enforced. That is, participants recognized and acted in an interdependent manner because they had no choice but to do so; the rules governing their behavior had changed. As one stakeholder commented,

> There are those in the environmental [and water supply] community that are very open and say, "I'm going to try and kill the stuff I don't like and promote the stuff I do like." And we need the Governor and the Secretary of the Interior

> cracking a whip over the rest of us, reminding us that the ground rules have changed. Cherry picking is not allowed. You accept the program as a whole. (Innes et al., 2006, p. 36)

In one instance, Secretary of the Interior Babbitt became personally involved in helping negotiate agreement among the agencies and stakeholders. Babbitt reportedly sent two participants "to the woodshed" at a critical point, directing them to undertake a side negotiation in a private room and emerge in half an hour to tell him whether a deal had been struck or whether their inaction effectively meant the end of CALFED. With the Secretary of the Interior and other parties waiting outside, the two deadlocked participants emerged with an agreement that formed the basis of what would become one of CALFED's innovative programs—the Environmental Water Account (Lurie, 2004b).

Recognition that Collaboration was the Preferred Alternative

While skepticism that CALFED would eventually succeed lingered throughout the process, most participants came to accept that, given the magnitude and interconnectedness of the issues, other options were not realistic. While parties may have felt that other paths would have served their individual organizational interests better, most involved had become committed to dealing with the issues as a whole. As CALFED passed its initial three-year deadline, enthusiasm was often replaced by criticism from water interest sectors; however, no one abandoned the effort. At one point a stakeholder representative, paraphrasing Winston Churchill's comments on democracy, described CALFED as ". . . the worst possible way to solve California's water problems, except for all the others" (Martin, 2000). The comment aptly captured what most participants had come to understand despite their ongoing reproaches; they needed to collaborate despite the enormous challenges associated with doing so.

The recognition of interdependence and need to work together certainly elevated the perceived value of collaboration relative to alternatives that might have been pursued had participation in CALFED not been mandated. At the same time, however, there were multiple ways in which the parties were also kept corralled. In other words, CALFED may have become the "preferred alternative" but it was sometimes the preferred alternative by default as other options were effectively precluded either by peer pressure, public expectations, or the frequently exercised clout of the conveners.

Highly public posturing by representatives of the different stakeholder groups occurred throughout most of the process. Side negotiations took place outside of the official CALFED parameters and different groups developed white papers and position statements that were submitted to media outlets and political channels in an effort to influence the process. Media, other stakeholder groups, and general public reactions to such self-interested behavior were typically harsh, labeling such tactics as corrosive to the best possible chance everyone had to resolve serious Bay-Delta issues. In a few instances, CALFED's executive director capitalized on public expectations of what had been billed a consensus process by invoking what was referred to as the "dead cat" scenario: a balky agency partner was asked if his or her organization wanted to be the one with the "dead cat" at its doorstep if its recalcitrance led to a deadlock and the subsequent collapse of the process (Lurie, 2011). As Ingram and Fraser (2006, p. 108) observed, "The water issue was of such high visibility for so long that no one wanted the blame for derailing agreement."

Peer pressure kept the various agencies and stakeholders engaged. As one participant commented, "The good part about CALFED . . . is that we set a ring. You step in that ring, you can fight like crazy. But we know the rules of the fight in the ring. You get outside that ring and you've got everybody that's in that ring against you" (Innes et al., 2006, p. 34). While it remained the case that all participating agencies retained their autonomy, agencies that took action outside the process were scorned.

Perceptions of Procedural Fairness

While most participants engaged reluctantly and skeptically, the process was structured to ensure that those involved were treated fairly and none had undue advantage. It did so in a number of ways, particularly by employing agreed-upon standards and criteria for decision-making, incorporating independent scientific review, and requiring that all proposals provide benefits that met objectives across CALFED's four major management goals. "Measuring and defending program balance seems to be almost an obsession for CALFED," noted Innes et al. (2006, p. 36). This sense of fairness in decision-making proved pivotal to sustaining collaborative behavior. As one stakeholder commented, "Most of the parties see that we are in a mode where everyone's interests are being accommodated to a sufficient degree to keep everyone together" (Innes et al., 2006, p. 34). CALFED also developed an independent science program to provide program-wide science review of proposed actions and it subjected this science program to its own periodic peer review.

The perceived fairness of the process, combined with the sense of urgency, interdependence and perceptions that collaboration was the preferred alternative, were essential factors encouraging participants to constructively collaborate. However, they were not sufficient to sustain the collaboration. What kept the parties corralled was also the maintenance of the mandate itself through traditional carrots and sticks, media attention, public expectations, and convener vigilance precluding non-collaborative behaviors or defection.

UNIQUE CHALLENGES OF MANDATED COLLABORATION

While the CALFED experience suggests that it is possible to instill to some extent the qualities associated with voluntary engagement when participation is mandated, it also highlights at least two significant process challenges that appear to be unique to mandated collaboration in public management: the imperative of sustaining the mandate, and the need to manage enduring home agency resistance.

The CALFED experience suggests that mandated processes may be more tenuous than voluntary processes, reflecting both the centrality of the directive in forcing participation as well as the lingering skepticism and resistance among the organizations involved. While voluntary processes can be self-sustaining (Wondolleck and Yaffee, 1997), mandated processes need additional "glue" to hold them together. This is an important area for further research given the reality that collaborative governance in the context of wicked problems requires extended time horizons and will inevitably be buffeted by changing political context and priorities.

Sustaining the Mandate

Both the progress of CALFED during its heyday and its experience in later years suggest that sustaining a mandate to collaborate is both critical and challenging. Failure to sustain the mandate will allow undercurrent resistance to resurface and participation to wane. Throughout its early years, the CALFED mandate was sustained through financial incentives, visible evidence of ongoing commitment and support by high-level officials, and intermittent cheerleading or cracking-of-the-whip by the conveners as needed.

Federal interest in CALFED changed in 2000 when George W. Bush became President (Ingram and Fraser, 2006; Lurie, 2011). Enthusiasm and oversight at the highest levels waned. Staff at one CALFED partner agency reportedly stated, "Things are different now. Under the former [Clinton] administration, CALFED was everything; under the new [Bush] administration, CALFED is just an interesting idea." In 2005, five years into implementation, anticipated federal support had not materialized, leaving both budget gaps and organizational issues. In 2008, after approximately US$4.7 billion in expenditures, state legislation to abolish CALFED's oversight entity, the California Bay-Delta Authority, was unopposed. In 2009, the Delta Reform Act repealed the California Bay-Delta Authority Act, ending what remained of the CALFED organization.

It was not clear how many of the CALFED partner agencies had truly embraced joint problem-solving, and several people perceived that no longer being under the watchful eyes of a highly engaged White House and Secretary of the Interior reduced cooperative behaviors of some of the federal partners (Lurie, 2011). Another observer explained that CALFED was everyone's Santa when its goodie bag was loaded; however, when there appeared to be no benefits left to dole out, cooperation and support deteriorated (Lurie, 2004b).

Managing Home Agency Resistance

A second challenge that appears magnified in a mandated process is the undercurrent of resistance among agency and organizational staff who were not involved in the process and hence did not experience the transformation in understanding, perspective and commitment described earlier. While tending the relationship between direct participants and their organizational constituencies, sometimes referred to as the "two table" problem, is a well-recognized challenge in any collaborative process (Carpenter and Kennedy, 1985; Moore, 1996; Susskind and Cruikshank, 1987), it is amplified and takes on a different dynamic in a mandated process. A voluntary process broadly engages organizations that are in agreement with the choice to collaborate and willingly send their representatives. The major challenge in a voluntary process is finding ways to transfer the learning that occurs about the issues, various parties' interests, and decision trade-offs back to the home agency or organization. In a mandated process, transferring this substantive learning is the least of the challenge. Rather, the greater challenge is instilling an appreciation of the overall value of the process and commitment to it; in other words, transforming the "mindset of a mandate" to the "mindset of choice" and this, at least in the CALFED experience, is extraordinarily difficult when blinders are firmly ensconced and resistance is so strong and pervasive.

Despite CALFED's progressive and safe environment for experimentation, there was a dark side to being on staff assignment to it. Different agency participants reported being passed over for promotions because they were "out of sight, out of mind" at their home agencies. Even more significantly, some perceived career threats and peer hostility at their home agencies due to ostensible breach of organizational boundaries and loyalties by agreeing to work with members of other organizations, some of which had a history of inter-agency hostilities. In this instance, being a collaborator was seen in pejorative terms by home agencies, leading to intra-agency resentment in addition to inter-agency antagonism (Lurie, 2004b).

CONCLUSION

Voluntary engagement in a collaborative governance process is the ideal. It assures understanding, commitment and good faith participation (Wondolleck, 2010). However, the CALFED experience suggests that it is possible for these qualities to be instilled to some degree in a mandated process. CALFED provides an instructive if painful demonstration of the power of a collaborative governance process, even when participation in it is not voluntary, to foster the dynamics that provide the essential foundation from which collaborative problem-solving can begin to emerge. Nevertheless, vigilance in keeping particularly recalcitrant parties at the table appears equally important to instilling the sense of urgency, interdependence, preferred approach, and fairness.

The central role of champions or collaborative capacity builders in voluntary collaborative processes is well established (Weber and Khademian, 2008b; Wondolleck and Yaffee, 2000). However, in mandated processes it appears that a substantively different yet equally central role is played by the convener-enforcer of the process. As Daniels and Walker note (2001, p. 64):

> It is unrealistic to merely announce that a collaboration is beginning and expect the current relationships and patterns of behavior to change. Collaboration requires innovative decision-building structures designed with considerable attention to the incentives that they create. If they do not establish clear rewards for collaboration and disincentives for competition, there is no reason to expect much change in behavior.

Process design and management needs to account for these particular needs when engagement in a process emerges from mandate rather than voluntary choice.

The CALFED experience also spotlights nuances to mandated processes that need to be better understood. This chapter's analysis takes but a first step towards building a framework for understanding the unique dynamics of mandated collaborative governance processes. In this one case, the imperative of sustaining the mandate and managing home agency tensions were apparent. This analysis is not meant to suggest that all mandated processes will experience the same tensions or should adopt the same strategies. It does suggest, however, that deliberate examination of the dynamics and consequences of mandated collaborative governance is needed. Policy-makers, public managers and process facilitators engaged in processes in which participation is mandated should consider ways in which essential collaborative process qualities might be compromised in the face of a mandate and develop issue- and context-appropriate approaches to instilling these qualities. However, for them to be able to do so requires expanded knowledge about the unique attributes, challenges and requirements associated with collaborative governance processes where engagement is not by individual or organizational choice.

More systematic research is needed to enhance understanding of the realities of mandated collaboration in public management. While there has been considerable attention to a broad array of advantages and disadvantages of compulsory participation in processes in the legal context (see, for example, Golann, 1989; Hedeen, 2005; Katz, 1993; Kirmayer and Wessel, 2004; Munro, 1999; Nelle, 1992; Smith, 1998; Winston, 1996; Wissler, 2002) this attention has not been matched in the public administration realm. The types of civil, family and criminal issues relevant to judicial review and the nature of the legal process differ in substantial ways from public issues and public management processes (Shapiro, 1981) and consequently this literature has limited reach within the public administration field. The predominate focus in the legal literature on mediator role and party self-determination and privacy is not aligned with the realities of wicked problems in public administration requiring vertical and horizontal knowledge-building in a transparent public process. Management of wicked problems requires "a fluid, continuous decision process" in which the "targets of decisions constantly morph and move" (Weber and Khademian, 2008a, p. 336). Civil disputes (e.g. personal injury, will probate, malpractice, contract, intellectual property, and business and labor), family disputes (e.g. divorce and child custody) and criminal disputes all involve situations in which the issues are well defined, the number of parties is limited—most often two—and the time required to settle is, for most, less than three hours (Wissler, 2002, p. 651). These are not unstructured, cross-cutting and relentless wicked problems requiring ongoing, adaptive processes that can consume years (Weber and Khademian, 2008a). The CALFED process, for example, was in place in some form for well over a decade. This gap in the collaboration literature addressing mandated public processes begs attention.

The magnitude of the San Francisco Bay-Delta problems, and the technical and scientific requirements for drafting a regional-scale, integrated plan, are well beyond what any one agency has the knowledge, resources or inclination to take on unilaterally. The sheer number of stakeholders, meetings and sub-groups that needed to be established and then interact over the six-year planning process in order to draft such a complex and comprehensive plan made it highly unlikely that any existing entity could either handle the responsibility alone or provide sufficient incentive or opportunity for all concerned agencies and stakeholders to convene in a collaborative process. In this case, the directive of high-level officials in a position of legitimate and overarching authority provided the necessary opportunity and incentives without which short-term, self-interested political behavior would have persisted and collaboration would not likely have occurred. This reality increasingly describes many large-scale and complex public issues, suggesting that greater attention be given to the distinctive characteristics and implications of mandated participation in collaborative governance processes.

REFERENCES

Ackoff, R. L. (1974). *Redesigning the Future: A Systems Approach to Societal Problems*. New York: Wiley.

Agranoff, R. (2006). Inside Collaborative Networks: Ten Lessons for Public Managers. *Public Administration Review* (December 2006 Special Issue): 56–65.

Agranoff, R. (2007). *Managing Within Networks: Adding Value to Public Organizations*. Washington, DC: Georgetown University Press.

Agranoff, R. and McGuire, M. (2003). *Collaborative Public Management: New Strategies for Local Governments*. Washington, DC: Georgetown University Press.

Alexander, E. R. (1995). *How Organizations Act Together: Interorganizational Coordination in Theory and Practice*. Luxemburg: Gordon and Breach Publishers.

Babbitt, B. (2005). *Cities in the Wilderness: A New Vision of Land Use in America*. Washington, DC: Island Press.

Bacow, L. S. and Wheeler, M. (1984). *Environmental Dispute Resolution*. New York: Plenum.

Bardach, E. (1998). *Getting Agencies to Work Together: The Practice and Theory of Managerial Craftsmanship*. Washington, DC: The Brookings Institution.

Bean, M., Fisher, L. and Eng, M. (2007). Assessment in Environmental and Public Policy Conflict Resolution: Emerging Theory, Patterns of Practice, and a Conceptual Framework. *Conflict Resolution Quarterly* 24(4): 447–468.

Bingham, G. (1986). *Resolving Environmental Disputes: A Decade of Experience*. Washington, DC: The Conservation Foundation.

Bingham, L. B. and O'Leary, R. (2006). Conclusion: Parallel Play, Not Collaboration: Missing Questions, Missing Connections. *Public Administration Review* (Supplement to Volume 66): 161–167.

Bolton, J. and Connaughton, J. L. (2005). *Memorandum on Environmental Conflict Resolution*. Washington, DC: Office of Management and Budget and President's Council on Environmental Quality.

Brock, J. (1991). Mandated Mediation: A Contradiction in Terms: Lessons from

Recent Attempts to Institutionalize Alternative Dispute Resolution Practices. *Villanova Environmental Law Journal* II: 57–87.
Brummel, R. F., Nelson, K. C. and Jakes, P. J. (2012). Burning Through Organizational Boundaries?: Examining Inter-organizational Communication Networks in Policy-mandated Collaborative Bushfire Planning Groups. *Global Environmental Change* 22: 516–528.
Carlson, C. (1999). Convening. In L. Susskind, S. McKearnan and J. Thomas-Larmer (eds.), *The Consensus Building Handbook: A Comprehensive Guide to Reaching Agreement* (pp. 169–197). Thousand Oaks, CA: Sage.
Carpenter, S. and Kennedy, W. J. D. (1985). Managing Environmental Conflict by Applying Common Sense. *Negotiation Journal* 1(2): 149–159.
Cheng, A. S. (2006). Build It and They Will Come?: Mandating Collaboration in Public Lands Planning and Management. *Natural Resources Journal* (46): 841–858.
Cohen, L. (1991). Mandatory Mediation: A Rose by Any Other Name. *Mediation Quarterly* 9(1): 33–46.
Cormick, G. W. (1980). The "Theory" and Practice of Environmental Mediation. *Environmental Professional* 2(1): 24–33.
Daniels, S. E. and Walker, G. B. (2001). *Working through Environmental Conflict: The Collaborative Learning Approach*. Westport, CT: Praeger.
Durant, R. (2004). Redefining Administrative Rationality. In R. F. Durant, D. J. Fiorino and R. O'Leary (eds.), *Environmental Governance Reconsidered*. Cambridge, MA: The MIT Press.
Dutterer, A. D. and Margerum, R. D. (2015). The Limitations of Policy-Level Collaboration: A Meta-Analysis of CALFED. *Society and Natural Resources* 28: 21–37.
Fisher, R., Ury, W. and Patton, B. (1991). *Getting to Yes: Negotiating Agreement without Giving In*. 2nd Edition. New York: Penguin Books.
Fredrickson, H. G. (2007). When Accountability Meets Collaboration. *PA Times* 30 (February): 11.
Golann, D. (1989). Making ADR Mandatory: The Constitutional Issues. *Oregon Law Review* 68: 487–568.
Gottlieb, R. (1988). *A Life of Its Own: The Politics and Power of Water*. New York: Harcourt Brace Jovanovich.
Graddy, E. A. and Chen, B. (2006). Influences on the Size and Scope of Networks for Social Services Delivery. *Journal of Public Administration Research and Theory* 16(4): 533–552.
Gray, B. (1989). *Collaborating: Finding Common Ground for Multiparty Problems*. San Francisco, CA: Jossey-Bass.
Hedeen, T. (2005). Coercion and Self-Determination in Court-Connected Mediation: All Mediations are Voluntary, but Some are More Voluntary than Others. *The Justice System Journal* 26(3): 273–291.
Heikkila, T. and Gerlak, A. K. (2005). The Formation of Large-scale Collaborative Resource Management Institutions: Clarifying the Roles of Stakeholders, Science, and Institutions. *The Policy Studies Journal* 33(4): 583–612.
Hundley, N. (2001). *The Great Thirst: Californians and Water, 1770s–1990s*. Berkeley, CA: University of California Press.
Huxham, C. (1996). Collaboration and Collaborative Advantage. In C. Huxham (ed.), *Creating Collaborative Advantage* (pp. 1–18). London: Sage.
Ingram, H. and Fraser, L. (2006). Path Dependency and Adroit Innovation: The

Case of California Water. In R. Repetto (ed.), *Punctuated Equilibrium and the Dynamics of U.S. Environmental Policy* (pp. 78–109). New Haven, CT: Yale University Press.

Innes, J. E., Connick, S., Kaplan, L. and Booher, D. E. (2006). Collaborative Governance in the CALFED Program: Adaptive Policy Making for California Water. Working Paper 2006–01. California State University, Sacramento: Center for Collaborative Policy.

Katz, L. V. (1993). Compulsory Alternative Dispute Resolution and Voluntarism: Two-Headed Monster or Two Sides of the Coin? *Journal of Dispute Resolution* (1): 1–55.

Kettl, D. (2006). Managing Boundaries in American Administration: The Collaboration Imperative. *Public Administration Review* (Supplement to Volume 66): 10–19.

Kirmayer, K. and Wessel, J. (2004). An Offer One Can't Refuse: Mediate. *The National Law Journal* (18 October) 27(12).

Kumar, S., Kant, S. and Amburgey, T. L. (2007). Public Agencies and Collaborative Management Approaches: Examining Resistance among Administrative Professionals. *Administration and Society* 39(5): 569–611.

Lawrence, R. L., Daniels, S. E. and Stankey, G. H. (1997). Procedural Justice and Public Involvement in Natural Resource Decision Making. *Society and Natural Resources* 10(6): 577–589.

Lax, D. A. and Sebenius, J. K. (1986). *The Manager as Negotiator*. New York: Free Press.

Leahy, I. (2006). Mandated Collaboration: An Assessment of Resource Advisory Committees. Communities and Forests. *The Newsletter of the Communities Committee of the Seventh American Forest Congress* 10(1): 1, 4–5.

Lewis, B. L., Boulahanis, J. and Matheny, E. (2009). Joined-up Governance: Mandated Collaboration in US Homeless Services. *International Journal of Public Sector Management* 22(5): 392–399.

Littleworth, A. L. and Garner, E. L. (1995). *California Water*. Point Arena, CA: Solano Press Books.

Lund, J., Hanak, E., Fleenor, W., Howitt, R., Mount, J. and Moyle, P. (2007). *Envisioning Futures for the Sacramento-San Joaquin Delta*. San Francisco, CA: Public Policy Institute of California.

Lurie, S. (2004a). Mandated Collaboration: The Case of the Forensic MOU. *Health Policy Canada* 24(3): 29–36.

Lurie, S. D. (2004b). Interorganizational Dynamics in Large-Scale Integrated Resources Management Networks: Insights from the CALFED Bay-Delta Program. Unpublished dissertation, Ann Arbor, MI: University of Michigan, School of Natural Resources and Environment.

Lurie, S. D. (2011). The CALFED Bay-Delta Program: Lessons from the Rise and Fall of a Large-Scale Ecosystem Management Network. *Journal of Natural Resources Policy Research* 3(3): 251–262.

Margerum, R. D. (2011). *Beyond Consensus: Improving Collaborative Planning and Management*. Cambridge, MA: The MIT Press.

Martin, G. (2000, 10 June). State Water Plan Taps into Art of Compromise. *San Francisco Chronicle*: A1.

McClurg, S. (1997a). *Layperson's Guide to California Water*. Sacramento, CA: Water Education Foundation.

McClurg, S. (1997b). *Sacramento-San Joaquin River Basin Study: Report to the*

Western Water Policy Review Advisory Commission. Albuquerque, NM: Western Water Policy Review Advisory Commission.

McClurg, S. and Newcom, J. (1998). *Layperson's Guide to the Delta*. Sacramento, CA: Water Education Foundation.

McGuire, M. (2006). Collaborative Public Management: Assessing What We Know and How We Know It. *Public Administration Review* (Supplement to Volume 66): 33–43.

Moore, C. W. (1996). *The Mediation Process: Practical Strategies for Resolving Conflict*. 2nd Edition. San Francisco, CA: Jossey-Bass.

Munro, M. M. (1999). Musings on the Consequences of Mandatory Mediation. *The Advocate* 57(2): 193–313.

Nabatchi, T. (2007). The Institutionalization of Alternative Dispute Resolution in the Federal Government. *Public Administration Review* 67(4): 646–661.

Nelle, A. (1992). Making Mediation Mandatory: A Proposed Framework. *Ohio State Journal on Dispute Resolution* 7(2): 287–313.

O'Leary, R. and Bingham, L. B. (eds.) (2003). *The Promise and Performance of Environmental Conflict Resolution*. Washington, DC: Resources for the Future.

O'Leary, R. and Raines, S. S. (2001). Lessons Learned from Two Decades of Alternative Dispute Resolution Programs and Processes at the U.S. Environmental Protection Agency. *Public Administration Review* 61(6): 682–692.

Raelin, J. A. (1980). A Mandated Basis of Interorganizational Relations: The Legal-Political Network. *Human Relations* 33(1): 57–68.

Rieke, E. A. (1996). The Bay-Delta Accord: A Stride Toward Sustainability. *University of Colorado Law Review* 67(2): 341–369.

Reisner, M. (1993). *Cadillac Desert: The American West and its Disappearing Water*. New York: Penguin Books.

Rittel, H. W. J. and Webber, M. M. (1973). Dilemmas in a General Theory of Planning. *Policy Sciences* 4: 155–169.

Rodriguez, C., Langley, A., Beland, F. and Denis, J.-L. (2007). Governance, Power, and Mandated Collaboration in an Interorganizational Network. *Administration & Society* 39(2):150–193.

Sandfort, J. (1999). The Structural Impediments to Human Service Collaboration: Examining Reform at the Front Lines. *Social Service Review* 73(3): 314–339.

Schneider, A. L. (2009). Why do Some Boundary Organizations Result in New Ideas and Practices and Others only Meet Resistance?: Examples from Juvenile Justice. *The American Review of Public Administration* 39(1): 60–79.

Shapiro, M. (1981). *Courts: A Comparative and Political Analysis*. Chicago, IL: The University of Chicago Press.

Smith, G. (1998). Unwilling Actors: Why Voluntary Mediation Works, Why Mandatory Mediation Might Not. *Osgoode Hall Law Journal* 36(4): 847–885.

Smith, P. D. and McDonough, M. H. (2001). Beyond Public Participation: Fairness in Natural Resource Decision Making. *Society and Natural Resources* 14(3): 239–241.

Susskind, L. and Cruikshank, J. (1987). *Breaking the Impasse: Consensual Approaches to Resolving Public Disputes*. New York: Basic Books.

Susskind, L., McKearnan, S. and Thomas-Larmer, J. (1999). *The Consensus Building Handbook: A Comprehensive Guide to Reaching Agreement*. Thousand Oaks, CA: Sage.

Thomson, A. M. and Perry, J. L. (2006). Collaboration Processes: Inside the Black Box. *Public Administration Review* (Supplement to Volume 66): 20–32.

U.S. Department of Commerce (2007). National Oceanic and Atmospheric Administration. Advancing NOAA's Priorities Through Regional Collaboration. Washington, DC: U.S. Department of Commerce.

U.S. Institute for Environmental Conflict Resolution (2006). ECR Performance Evaluation: An Inventory of Indicators. Tuscon, AZ and Washington, DC: U.S. Institute for Environmental Conflict Resolution.

Van de Wetering, S. B. and McKinney, M. (2006). The Role of Mandatory Dispute Resolution in Federal Environmental Law: Lessons from the Clean Air Act. *Journal of Environmental Law and Litigation* 21(1): 1–45.

Weber, E. P. (2003). *Bringing Society Back In: Grassroots Ecosystem Management, Accountability, and Sustainable Communities*. Cambridge, MA: The MIT Press.

Weber, E. P. and Khademian, A. M. (2008a). Wicked Problems, Knowledge Challenges, and Collaborative Capacity Builders in Network Settings. *Public Administration Review* 68(2): 334–349.

Weber, E. P. and Khademian, A. M. (2008b). Managing Collaborative Processes: Common Practices, Uncommon Circumstances. *Administration & Society* 40(5): 431–464.

Winston, D. S. (1996). Participation Standards in Mandatory Mediation Statutes: "You Can Lead A Horse to Water . . .". *Ohio State Journal on Dispute Resolution* 11: 187–206.

Wissler, R. L. (2002). Court-Connected Mediation in General Civil Cases: What We Know from Empirical Research. *Ohio State Journal on Dispute Resolution* 17(3): 641–704.

Wondolleck, J. M. (2010). A Crack in the Foundation?: Revisiting ECR's Voluntary Tenet. *Conflict Resolution Quarterly* 27(3): 321–343.

Wondolleck, J. M. and Yaffee, S. L. (1997). Sustaining the Success of Collaborative Partnerships. Working Paper. Ecosystem Management Initiative. School of Natural Resources & Environment. Ann Arbor, University of Michigan.

Wondolleck, J. M. and Yaffee, S. L. (2000). *Making Collaboration Work: Lessons from Innovation in Natural Resource Management*. Washington, DC: Island Press.

10. Politicians and collaborative governance: the new logic of support

Edward P. Weber

In 1991, John Scholz asked: if cooperative regulatory enforcement produces better policy effectiveness, why do the beneficiaries and other policy supporters not favor the most effective means of administrating their policies (1991, 116)? He ultimately concludes that optimal institutional choices at the administrative level generate so much uncertainty in the broader political game that political actors prefer regulatory deterrence and policy ineffectiveness to cooperation and policy effectiveness. Other literature argues similarly that politicians are comfortable with the existing hierarchical, command-and-control structure of bureaucracies (orthodox public administration) because they offer a good degree of certainty in delivering public goods and services to constituents important in the electoral equation (see Knott and Miller 1987). Further, the political science and public administration literatures have long advised against devolving authority too much, whether to collaboratives or to agency clienteles, for fear of agency and/or community capture at the expense of broad public interests (e.g., Foss 1960; Kaufman 1967; McConnell 1966).

Finally, the principal-agent and New Economics of Organization (NEO) literature posit that hierarchical elected superiors cannot trust subordinates in the bureaucracy because they are self-interested and have different preferences than the politicians do. This often leads bureaucrats to shirk, thus confounding politicians' policy goals. The uncertainty leads hierarchical superiors to use their authority to write contracts restricting subordinates' discretion (e.g., annual appropriations, detailed laws, budgets, etc.). The same behavioral expectations apply to the hierarchical relationship between agency experts and the regulated community. In both cases opportunities for subordinates to collaborate or have the discretion to make their own decisions either do not exist or are extremely limited in nature (Moe 1984; Weingast 1984).

The logic tying all these approaches together is that there will be fewer devolved, collaborative governance arrangements than there would otherwise be, especially at the administrative and political levels furthest removed from central political authority (i.e., local or place-based efforts). This is because politicians do not see it as in their best interest to promote them either by passing laws or granting the discretion necessary for their ultimate success. This is a limitation on the number of collaborative governance (CG) arrangements in operation. And when we think about the time these analyses were written—the 1950s through the early 1990s—they made sense; there were not many CG arrangements in the U.S. at any level.

But this conventional wisdom has been sorely tested over the past 20 to 25 years as CG arrangements have exploded in use at the community, or small-scale (e.g., watershed), place-based level, especially in the natural resources policy arena and especially in rural areas of the American West (Margerum 2011; Weber 2000; Wondolleck and Yaffee 2000). What has changed? Why are elected officials now more willing to accept, endorse and promote collaborative governance arrangements at the rural, place-based level in the American West?

The analysis will explore the new logic of support for CG arrangements from the perspective of politicians.[1] Chief among the reasons for explaining this change in how elected U.S. officials view collaborative governance are:

- How the federal environmental superstructure of laws and regulations decrease the uncertainty associated with CG outcomes for liberal-left politicians in the Democratic Party, thereby decreasing the chance of industry capture.
- CG offers conservative Republican Party politicians affiliated with rural areas of the western U.S. the opportunity to allow their constituents to achieve more of their primary policy goals and to show support for conservative political principles.
- The presence of traditionally adversarial policy watchdogs (e.g., nongovernmental organizations (NGOs)) inside CG efforts decreases the uncertainty associated with outcomes. The same logic applies to such groups outside collaboratives provided trust-based relationships with such watchdogs are in place.
- Practice and experience associated with hundreds of place-/community-based CG efforts support the expectation that outcomes adhere to a broad-based public interest, thus decreasing uncertainty and the probability of "capture" by any one set of interests.
- The reality that fighting against broad-based consensus outcomes can be politically risky, especially in an era of national gridlock.

- Continuation of national gridlock leads stakeholders, including politicians, to seek out alternatives to the traditional legislatively based policy process.

The combination of these elements is leading elected officials to grant agencies more discretion to engage and promote CG. By giving agency officials either formal or tacit approval for CG, we find that bureaucrats have their own reasons for deciding to embrace and pursue CG.

THE FEDERAL "ENVIRONMENTAL SUPERSTRUCTURE" DECREASES POLITICAL RISKS FOR LIBERAL POLITICIANS

As air and water pollution mounted in the wake of the U.S.'s industrial expansion after World War II, a new environmental movement emerged at the national level starting in the 1960s. Focused primarily on protecting human health and correcting the market failures that created the pollution, the national movement also arose in response to the lack of effective environmental protection legislation in the vast majority of the 50 state governments. Concerned that little or no real progress would be made attacking the problem state-by-state, environmentalists instead focused their efforts on converting elected politicians at the national, or federal, level government to their cause (Weber 2000).

Environmentalists met with remarkable legislative success during the 1960s and 1970s, as the U.S. Congress proceeded to pass, and both Democrat and Republican Presidents signed into law, dozens of major laws protecting the environment and natural resources from harm and overexploitation. Starting with the Wilderness Act of 1964, this federal, top-down, command-and-control-oriented superstructure of laws supersedes state-based legislation and forces them to adhere to national directives. The federal superstructure of environmental law also includes, among many others, the Wild and Scenic Rivers Act (WSRA, 1968), National Environmental Policy Act (NEPA, 1970), Clean Air Act (CAA, 1970), Clean Water Act (CWA, 1972), Marine Mammal Protection Act (MMPA, 1972), Endangered Species Act (ESA, 1973), National Forest Management Act (NFMA, 1976), and Federal Lands Policy and Management Act (FLPMA, 1976).

The net effect of this national legal superstructure is to constrain and limit the policy choices for states and any community-level initiatives, including collaboratives, thus providing significant, predetermined protections for nature and natural resources. In political terms, and as the brief interlude of compromise and consensus on this "environmental superstructure" turned to rancor and conflict starting in the 1980s, these "limits" fit firmly within the larger political portfolio of liberal-left politicians in the Democratic Party. Thus, the superstructure gives them greater security that outcomes produced by rural, place-based CG arrangements will necessarily include the kinds of significant protections for the environment that they and their supporters prefer. This is something of a confirmation of the overall logic of the NEO. But instead of specific "rational" contracts to control subordinate behavior, it is the aggregation of multiple prior laws as contracts that, when taken as a whole, create enough structured controls that superiors (in this case liberal Democrats at the state and federal levels) are more willing to loosen the reins and afford subordinates in local communities (or, for example, watersheds) the discretion needed to craft their own deals for managing a specific area.

Two examples suffice to make the broader point. If a CG effort, in cooperation with the appropriate federal agency (e.g., the U.S. Forestry Service (USFS), the Bureau of Land Management (BLM)), chooses to log or conduct other extractive activities on federal public lands they cannot avoid NEPA Section 102 requirements. More specifically, Section 102 requires "agencies to incorporate environmental considerations in their planning and decision-making through a systematic interdisciplinary approach," including the use of detailed environmental impact statements (EIS) "assessing the environmental impact of, and alternatives to, major federal actions significantly affecting the environment" (EPA 2015).

Another example of these limits, or boundaries on decision-making, involves the Endangered Species Act (ESA) of 1973. Although passed by a near consensus vote in the U.S. Congress, within a few short years Republican Senate Minority Leader Howard Baker (R-TN) tested its scope and authority in the infamous snail darter habitat case in Tennessee. The resulting Supreme Court decision in *TVA v. Hill* (1978) affirmed that the plain language of ESA's Section 7, along with the law's legislative history, gave the highest priority to the preservation of *all* endangered or threatened species, even "just a small fish," as argued by TVA's lawyers. In short, the ESA did not pick and choose among species according to society's economic valuations; rather, it afforded protection to all species once science determined they were either threatened or endangered.

The flip side of the national environmental superstructure for liberal politicians is that allowing, or endorsing, collaborative governance initiatives, with their typical focus on the tripartite mission of environment, economy, and community, gives them an opportunity to display support for the economic, land-based livelihoods so often critical to rural western economies. At the same time, they can claim they are saving such stakeholders, who typically are the regulated communities whose behaviors are being targeted by environmental laws, from a worse fate—stricter, less flexible, higher cost regulations vis-à-vis the more customized, lower-cost outcomes possible from collaboratives (Weber 2003). The key point here is that such politicians do not see the ESA goal of species recovery as being sacrificed for the sake of collaboration; instead, collaboration is viewed as simply another means to the primary ESA end of recovery.

A good example of this logic involves leading Democrats in Colorado and their reactions to the U.S. Fish and Wildlife Service (USFWS) listing of the Gunnison sage grouse as threatened under the ESA in November 2014. Counties in the bird's primary habitat in western Colorado had for years been working collaboratively with state and federal wildlife officials, local landowners, and environmentalists to adopt practices and protect critical habitat in order to forestall the ESA listing. Colorado's top state-level politician, Governor John Hickenlooper and U.S. Senators Michael Bennet and Mark Udall, all Democrats, were strong supporters of the local collaborative efforts. Governor Hickenlooper was disappointed in the USFWS decision, and called the decision "discouraging . . . it complicates our good-faith efforts to work with local stakeholders on locally driven approaches." Senator Bennet, for his part, felt that the USFWS had "pulled the rug out from communities already committed to saving grouse," while Senator Udall argued that formal ESA protection "threatens to unravel much of the grassroots and science-based progress Colorado has made preserving the Gunnison sage grouse" (Finley 2014).

COLLABORATIVE GOVERNANCE OFFERS OPPORTUNITIES TO CONSERVATIVE POLITICIANS

Elected officials occupying the conservative side of the political spectrum, including those with libertarian tendencies, are generally associated with the Republican Party. They, too, are finding philosophical and practical reasons to support collaborative place-based governance in rural western areas. The political philosophical case is grounded in the fact that the kinds of small-scale, place-based collaboratives in question match the conservative idea of small government, or that the best level of government is the one that governs closest to home. This increases the chance that local constituents will have, in the best cases, substantial influence over public policy decisions, and, at a minimum, expanded opportunities to deliberate with other stakeholders and have their voices and needs heard (see Kemmis 1990). As part of this, there is value in CG from the conservative side because it gives key conservative constituencies such as farmers, ranchers, and loggers greater liberty to determine, or control, just how legislative and regulatory goals will be achieved. And this opportunity for greater control increases the chance that private property rights considerations can shape or somehow influence eventual consensus agreements. Linda Evans Parlette, a Republican State Senator (2000–present) for the rural 12th legislative district in Washington State, captures this sentiment:

> It's not hard to support these local efforts at cooperation among farmers and environmentalists, the agencies, and others. The people living in these [rural] areas like action and like to have some control over decisions that matter to their everyday lives—and that's what these endangered species [in this case, fish,] decisions are. They can be the difference between being reasonably profitable on the farm and going out of business. It [collaboration] is much better, by far, than just having the agencies show up and tell everyone what to do. (Interview October 2001)

More practically, the very presence of the national environmental superstructure gives conservative stakeholders and their Republican Party allies good incentive to engage and support place-based CG. This is because the environmental superstructure constrains their choices by forcing them to give due consideration to environmental values even if they add costs or otherwise conflict with their preferred values or business plans. This reality gives conservative politicians, and their constituents, greater appreciation for place-based CG as a different type of policy venue that increases the probability of flexibility and innovation in the application of top-down, command-and-control-oriented environmental protection laws. The flexibility and innovation, in turn, can lead to lower compliance costs and additional income gains vis-à-vis the existing environmental superstructure for the same conservative constituencies noted above.

We see this dynamic playing out with the Deschutes River Conservancy (DRC) and the Deschutes Partnership in Oregon State, located in the Pacific Northwest region of the U.S. Established in 1996 by federal legislation sponsored by Oregon's Republican U.S. Senator Mark Hatfield, the DRC is an NGO with the primary mission of improving and protecting instream flows on the oversubscribed Deschutes and its tributaries for the benefit of fish, riparian zones, and the environment more generally. Of primary concern are Columbia River salmon and steelhead stocks that had been blocked in 1964 from upstream migration to the middle and upper Deschutes Basin by the Pelton-Round Butte hydropower dam. Senator Hatfield's legislation specified that the Board of Directors include a broad cross-section of stakeholders, including recreation/tourism, livestock grazing, environmentalists, irrigation, hydropower, timber, the Confederated Tribes of Warm Springs, U.S. Departments of Interior and Agriculture, State of Oregon, local governments in the river basin, and four at-large citizen representatives. It also required the Board to operate according to consensus-based decision rules. In its first ten years, among other accomplishments, it succeeded in passing the 100 cubic feet per second (cfs) milestone of restored flow in the Middle Deschutes downstream of the city of Bend, launching the largest water conservation project in the state's history (the Swalley Main Canal Piping Project), and striking a series of unprecedented agreements with irrigation districts to transfer part of their water rights to instream uses (River Voice 2007). As Republican U.S. Congressman Greg Walden, the elected representative from eastern Oregon State, notes:

> In the Deschutes Basin, you've had the Deschutes River Conservancy operating that brings everybody to the table—environmentalists, government officials, and farmers to say how we increase streamflows and still make sure we have water for agriculture. It's been a very successful process. Not easy, but very successful. (River Voice 2007)

Ongoing problems with fish recovery, however, prompted the DRC in 2007 to join together with three other local organizations—the Deschutes Land Trust, the Upper Deschutes Watershed Council, and the Crooked River Watershed Council—to form the collaborative Deschutes Partnership. The Partnership adopted a mission of whole, integrated, strategic watershed restoration and focused their initial efforts on the 40-mile-long Whychus Creek drainage, particularly on Camp Polk Meadows and areas upstream of Camp Polk. Whychus Creek was an easy choice given that sections of the stream often were dry toward the end of the irrigation season in August and September. It was also driven by the fact that the channelization (i.e., straightening) of 18 miles of stream by the U.S. Army Corps of Engineers after a major flood in 1964 destroyed what had historically been the Creek's best, most productive fish nursery for steelhead, which had been listed under the ESA in 1999. In short, the biological potential for recovering and re-establishing healthy habitat was high (Deschutes Partnership 2013b).

The record of success for the Deschutes Partnership in achieving virtually all of their original restoration goals in the first several phases of Whychus Creek restoration (years 2009 through 2015) is a matter of record (see Deschutes Partnership 2013a; Weber 2014). But the main purpose of this part of the chapter is how this collaborative effort played for conservative interests and conservative-minded elected officials. The chief outcomes, and overall gains, in this regard accrued to the 180 farmers and ranchers of the Three Sisters Irrigation District (TSID), an essential player in the Partnership's larger collaborative restoration efforts. Trying to stay ahead of ESA demands for the listed steelhead stocks on Whychus Creek,[2] TSID embarked on an ambitious plan to pipe and pressurize their irrigation system, while also adding and integrating small, low-head hydropower plants into the system for the purposes of generating both electricity and revenue. The potential for efficiency gains from the new system was significant. In a typical case in the old gravity flow irrigation system, TSID would divert a "cup" of water; yet only deliver roughly half a "cup" to their members. This was due to the highly porous fractured basalt geology of the area, which lost anywhere from 30 to 60 percent of each "cup" diverted from instream flows. As of June 2015, the new pressurized system was delivering the following benefits:

- TSID members are receiving their "old" half a cup, putting ¼ of a cup back into Whychus instream flows, and delivering another added, or bonus, ¼ cup to their typical member. Put differently, almost every farm is now receiving 50 percent more water than previously *and* streamflows are getting guaranteed flows much higher than before.
- The US$50 million in TSID irrigation system upgrades are being financed from the proceeds from the instream water sales and the new hydropower electricity sales.
- Water pressurization has removed water pumping costs from the farming equation, with a typical 100-acre spread saving around US$20,000 per year in power costs.
- The new efficiency of the system—delivering 75 percent of water rights flows instead of only 50 percent—creates greater certainty of delivery for more TSID members, specifically those with junior water rights claims in the prior appropriations regime. This means that more constituents get more certainty over their long-range business planning process, thus increasing the probability that they can not only stay in business, but increase their profit margins—but only *after* helping the environment with the added instream flows. (Interviews August and September 2013; Weber 2014)

Finally, there is the fact of ongoing cultural change in many agricultural communities across the western U.S. that give rural-based politicians new incentives to consider and support place-based CG. Younger farmers and ranchers having grown up with contemporary environmentalism and the many parameters imposed on their business practices by the federal environmental superstructure, as well as additional state-based protection mandates. As a result, they are more willing to embrace, or at a minimum, less willing to fight and more willing to incorporate environmental regulations as the normal cost of doing business. Speaking in 1998, Republican State Representative (WA) Dave Mastin notes that:

> [t]here's a big difference between age groups. You talk to the 30-to-50-year-old farmers who grew up in a little different environment than the 60-year and older farmers, and they're much more willing because it's part of the culture in which they grew up, the expectations of how things are done. The era in which you grew up influences how you view things. (Interview June 1998)

Or as Sid Snyder, Democrat Majority Leader of the Washington State Senate, found: "Farmers aren't always happy with existing [environmental protection] laws. They may grate and be seen as a general nuisance, but the tendency today is not to try to overturn the laws, but to seek more autonomy in how they can reach these legally imposed goals, not change them" (interview October 1998).

Such sentiments lead in the direction of a more local implementation-focused problem-solving venue that can customize and adapt solutions based on local conditions. Given that this is considered a strength of CG arrangements, it fits into the logic of why more politicians are now more willing to support or allow place-based collaboratives.

INCREASED CERTAINTY GIVEN THE PASSAGE OF TIME AND POLICY WATCHDOG ROLES

Key parts of the first two rationales explaining why elected officials from both sides of the political spectrum, whether Democrats or Republicans, are now more likely to support CG do not get us very far. This is because both the federal environmental superstructure and the match for Republicans with conservative political philosophy have been in existence for many more years than the emergence and use of place-based CG, which dates to roughly 20 to 25 years ago in the western U.S. Thus, they are not sufficient by themselves. Other elements needed to come into play in order for both conservative and liberal politicians to exercise their discretion in support—active or tacit—of collaboratives.

Part of this is likely due to the fact that despite the passage of so many environmental protection laws and new, more environmentally friendly management directives to federal land management agencies, it takes time to see how they will be implemented and enforced, both by agencies and the courts. It is not uncommon for major parts of national environmental protection laws to take ten or more years to conduct the necessary administrative rulemaking procedures, fight the almost inevitable court battles, and reach final policy implementation. The first major court battle—*TVA v. Hill*—over the ESA in 1978, as previously discussed, signaled that science, not economics, would prevail in determining species listings, thus clarifying that the law would "have teeth" (Mann and Plummer 1995). The failure of the Reagan Administration in the 1980s to overturn, weaken, and otherwise inflict long-term damage to the standards associated with the environmental superstructure indicated that these laws would continue providing protection well into the future. Supreme Court decisions in 1988 on the northern spotted owl (*Northern Spotted Owl v. Hodel*) and in favor of an expanded definition of ESA harm to include habitat modifications in 1995 (*Babbitt v. Sweet Home*) further signaled the strength of the 1973 ESA.

Another important example involves Section 303(d) of the CWA. It requires states to identify waters that are impaired by pollution, even after application of CWA-mandated point-source pollution controls. For "impaired" waters, states must establish a total maximum daily load (TMDL) of pollutants to ensure that water quality standards can be attained. Yet, for budgetary and other reasons, EPA did little to enforce 303(d) until prompted by a number of lawsuits won by environmentalists in the early to mid-1990s. After issuing a TMDL guidance document in 1997, EPA and states have established more than 48,000 TMDLs.[3]

The inclusion of key organized interests inside a collaborative who see their roles as watchdogs, or enforcers, of particular policy preferences also matters to politicians and to stakeholders working in collaboratives. This did not used to be the case, especially for environmentalists. One of the earliest place-based CG efforts, the Quincy Library Group (QLG), saw national environmental groups, including the Sierra Club[4] and the Natural Resources Defense Council, attempting to disrupt and destroy this CG arrangement "because it challenged their version of adversarial environmentalism" (interview March 1998), leading QLG participants to seek federal legislation as a protective measure. The lesson reverberated throughout other western natural resource collaboratives, with many believing that "it is in our best interest to keep our heads low, stay below the [political] radar of national environmentalists so that we don't get our heads chopped off" (interviews March and June 1998, and January 1999).

Yet, as time has worn on, we see more environmental advocates, who typically have preferred legislation and litigation as tactics, joining in CG arrangements. Hence, Trout Unlimited, a major national advocacy group for protecting coldwater fisheries, became a central stakeholder in the highly successful Blackfoot Challenge collaborative in Montana State, while a member of the national Defenders of Wildlife has been instrumental in the Lakeview Stewardship Group in Oregon State, and the National

Wildlife Federation is part of the Clark Fork Coalition and is also working collaboratively with ranchers on voluntary greater sage-grouse protection in Montana State (interview October 2013). As these barriers have broken down it has reduced the uncertainty of consensus agreements even further, since key, often primary litigators are part of collaborative agreements instead of on the outside looking in. Moreover, it has reduced political risk for elected officials because key elements of their constituencies are less likely to pressure them for alternative solutions and policies contrary to the collaboratively produced outcomes.

This point on reduced uncertainty and lower political risk applies equally well to policy watchdogs as interested observers *outside* the collaborative as long as they have informal, trust-based lines of communication and consultation with like-minded interests inside a collaborative. Rob Caldwell, an environmental lawyer in Washington State with a well-established reputation as an environmental advocate within the larger statewide advocacy community, explained it as follows:

> I have built relationships over the years with many members of Washington's [environmental] advocacy community and have a track record of fighting for a cleaner environment. So they cut me some slack and respected me when I asked them to stand back and not litigate while we cooperated with farmers, irrigators, local elected officials, and agencies on how best to save the fish [salmon and steelhead] in the Walla Walla. This gave me the space to come up with a successful [collaborative] deal, but it also served as a reminder to everyone that the Sierra Club Legal Defense Fund and others, if the deal didn't have enough protection built in, could and would act [using litigation]. (Interview August 2002)

A member of the Deschutes Partnership collaborative on Whychus Creek in Oregon's Deschutes River Basin agrees:

> we work hard to build and maintain good relationships with these "litigators" not in the collaborative, and in our case we keep in touch with them to make sure they know our goals and our successes in protecting the environment. We're absolutely convinced that this informal consultation leads them to leave us alone so they can focus their energies on other, more problematic [environmental] policy areas where they are more needed. (Interview September 2013)

BROAD-BASED PUBLIC INTEREST SOLUTIONS AND THE ERA OF GRIDLOCK

A chief promise of collaborative governance is that it will produce outcomes responsive to a broad public interest. Tied closely to the design rules of inclusiveness, consensus decisions, broad-based missions, often in the form of "environment, economy, and community," and a dedication to mutual gain outcomes, the general lack of experience with place-based collaboratives prior to the 1990s made the broad public interest idea more theoretical than real. It was understandably difficult in a world of conflict and adversarial-based politics to conceive of much less trust that win-win-win outcomes from collaboratives might be the rule, rather than the exception. But as we see more CG in action, there is now greater certainty that broad public interest/mutual gain outcomes are a reasonable expectation for such efforts. Put differently, the long-established fear of capture by industry, other development-oriented interests, or any one set of interests is less probable than before provided the CG in question adheres to the institutional design principles noted above (see also Weber 2003). This allows politicians interested in broad public interest outcomes and solutions to support collaboratives with less political risk than before.

Correlated with this is that when you have all the stakeholders saying "yes, this is what we want," it makes less sense for an elected official to fight against it. As Democrat Alan Unger, a local elected Commissioner in Deschutes County (Oregon), argues: "Why would I fight this? With all the players from across the political spectrum on board I become more interested in whether they are getting the main problems solved, and if they are, then I applaud them for working so hard on behalf of our community" (interview September 2013). Another way to put this is that with a well-designed, inclusive CG arrangement there is less chance that organized interests seeking parochial, self-interested outcomes will be knocking on politicians' doors asking for something different, hence there is less political pressure on elected officials to respond to such "narrow" policy requests. Washington State Republican Dave Mastin, an elected member of the state-level House of Representatives, appreciates being in the middle of collaborative consensus-based groups:

> In many respects they make my life easier. They work out the tough issues amongst themselves and figure out solutions that everybody can live with, and that means they spend less time pushing me to do this or do that just for them. And so sure, when we get together they make requests that they think the state[-level] can help with, but instead of me having to put all the pieces together, they [collaborate and] do it for me in many cases. (Interview June 1998)

The promise of broad public interest outcomes necessarily implies that problems are being addressed with new programs and policies, and actions being taken to better manage and resolve them. Of course, during times when legislatures and Congress are able to produce similar outcomes, and have executives sign them into law, the valued added by place-based

CG arrangements on this count is diminished. But this problem-solving dynamic takes on added importance during times of political gridlock in traditional political institutions, such as what has been the norm for Congress over the past 25 years in environmental and natural resource politics, and, more recently, across many other policy areas (Klyza and Sousa 2008). As Gerald Seib, a *Wall Street Journal* columnist writing on race relations in the aftermath of the June 2015 murders of nine African-Americans in a Charleston, South Carolina church, observes: "[s]olving problems generally requires creating either compromise or consensus, and government leaders often seem to have lost the ability to do either these days. So solutions are starting to emerge elsewhere" (Seib 2015).

In short, in many situations today new policy solutions are not coming out of traditional, or primary state- and federal-level executive branch- or legislative-based policy venues, yet problems still persist, and in many cases are growing more severe and having significant effects at the local scale. This creates strong incentives for stakeholders tied to local, community-based settings to press elected state- and federal-level officials for permission and support, or at minimum a pledge of non-interference, as they collaborate in search of new broad-based solutions. At the same time, gridlock at higher representative levels of government in the U.S. creates an opportunity for politicians at those same levels, and for local elected politicians as well, because endorsing, promoting, or deferring to collaboratives that hold the potential for more effective, and actual, problem-solving progress is something they can then claim at least some credit for much in the same way Mayhew (1974) found that members of the U.S. Congress did with their legislative successes. This is because these new, small-scale, place-based governance arrangements promise to break the logjam on the kinds of public policy problems many, if not most, stakeholders already agree on, but by doing so in what is perceived as a fair, judicious manner given the expected win-win-win (mutual gain) outcomes.

POLITICIANS AND BUREAUCRACIES: MORE DISCRETION EQUALS MORE COLLABORATIVE GOVERNANCE

Given the changes in context and incentives for elected officials at state, local, and federal levels of government in the U.S. to engage and support place-based collaborative governance vis-à-vis the past, it is not surprising to see also that politicians are now more willing to grant federal and state bureaucratic agencies more discretion to do the same. This evidence challenges not only the Scholz (1991) logic, but also the NEO literature and the classic political science and public administration literatures that have long advised against devolving authority to local, place-based efforts, whether to collaboratives or otherwise, for fear of agency and/or community capture. Yet, as Leong et al. (2011, 236) note, and as growing numbers of agency officials recognize: "As large-scale societal changes continue to affect the way people experience and value public lands, effectively incorporating collaborative conservation will be increasingly important in management." This is occurring in two primary ways: legislative sponsorship, and agency-initiated CG.

Legislative sponsorship is just as it sounds—elected representatives choose and fund collaborative governance as their preferred mechanism for policy implementation and problem-solving. A major step forward at the federal level in the U.S. occurred in 2009, when Congress passed the Omnibus Public Land Management Act. Title IV of the Act established the Collaborative Forest Landscape Restoration Program (CFLRP) in order "to encourage the collaborative, science-based ecosystem restoration of priority forest landscapes" and to promote an idea of an "all lands approach" to forest stewardship that necessarily involves requisite state agencies and private landowners at the landscape-scale (U.S. Forest Service 2009). The larger purpose of CFLRP is about creating and providing long-term (ten-year) funding for collaboratives to:

- encourage ecological, economic, and social sustainability;
- leverage local resources with national and private resources;
- facilitate the reduction of wildfire management costs, including through re-establishing natural fire regimes and reducing the risk of uncharacteristic wildfire;
- demonstrate the degree to which various ecological restoration techniques achieve ecological and watershed health objectives; and
- encourage utilization of forest restoration by-products to offset treatment costs, to benefit local rural economies, and to improve forest health. (U.S. Forest Service 2015)

Another example involves salmon recovery efforts in Puget Sound, Washington. A grass-roots collaborative effort across 16 watersheds in the region involved technical experts, tribes, local citizens, environmentalists, businesses, and agencies (state, federal, and local) in order to produce a plan to protect and restore weakened salmon runs. The National Oceanic and Atmospheric Administration (NOAA) adopted the Shared Strategy plan in January 2007, and then the state of Washington followed with legislation in January 2008 creating the Puget Sound Partnership to manage collaboratively the ongoing salmon recovery efforts based on the plan (Puget Sound Partnership 2015; Weber et al. 2010).

And while more such legislative examples can be discussed (e.g., see Koontz et al. 2004; Sirianni 2010), there are also growing numbers of examples in other countries. The European Union (EU), frustrated by the ineffectiveness of many of its environmental laws, has pushed new initiatives over the past ten to 15 years that are local and collaborative in nature. Chief among them is the EU Water Framework Directive, passed in 2006, which "devolves policies . . . to local collaborative decision-making bodies on natural as opposed to territorial scales" (Newig and Fritsch 2008). New Zealand has also become a prominent practitioner of place-based collaborative governance sponsored by elected officials. Starting in 2005, the Canterbury Regional Government, Environment Canterbury, started regional collaboration with major stakeholders, including the Maori, considered New Zealand's indigenous people, to craft a watershed-based collaborative approach to water resource management (Holling and Gunningham 2011). After several years and success in creating a guidance document containing ten principles supporting an environment-economy-community approach, however, the effort to push collaborative governance down into the ten individual watersheds within Canterbury failed. The central, national government stepped in after this in 2010 and promulgated that Canterbury would proceed with place-based water management collaboratives. The innovative, government-sponsored design took effect in 2012 and, by most measures, has met with considerable success in getting consensus agreement on strategic watershed plans thus far (Jenkins 2013; Memon et al. 2012).[5]

The discretion granted by politicians to agencies for conducting place-based CG is also allowing individual agencies to pursue CG on their own initiative. Although there are a number of reasons why various agencies are more supportive of CG today than in the past, three are central. First, there is growing recognition on the part of key agency decision-makers that many of their natural resource-based problem sets are wicked in character. This means that they are unstructured and that causes and effects are extremely difficult to identify and model, thus adding complexity and uncertainty, and engendering a high degree of conflict because there is little consensus on the problem or the solution (Rittel and Webber 1973; Roberts 2002). They are cross-cutting in that the wicked problem space is comprised of multiple, overlapping, interconnected subsets of problems that cut across multiple policy domains and levels of government. Wicked problems, in other words, cut across hierarchy and authority structures within and between organizations, and across policy domains, political and administrative jurisdictions, and political "group" interests, which induce interdependence. The probability therefore that any one actor can resolve a wicked problem on their own is slim to none. Wicked problems are also relentless; they are not going to be solved once and for all despite all the best intentions and resources directed at the problem, and efforts to solve the wicked problem will have consequences for other policy arenas, as well. Similar to a stone dropped in the water, the ripples spread rapidly to impact other issue areas, thus adding new complications to an already complex situation (Weber and Khademian 2008).

Second, across the board in contemporary bureaucracies there is greater emphasis on evidence-based approaches to problem-solving and outcome measurement (Kamarck 2007). Well-designed place-based collaboratives incorporate this element, including robust monitoring regimes, because they know that as newly established alternative problem solving institutions they bear this burden more so than established institutions, that the uncertainty associated with the wicked character of so many of their problems demands it, and that continual information feedback loops are necessary for adaptive management, which is also central to the CG concept (Koontz and Thomas 2006; Weber 2003).

Third, there is the simple fact of declining agency budgets relative to the past. Put simply, many agencies realize that they cannot do as much as they need to do given their statutory responsibilities and CG offers an opportunity to leverage agency resources by catalyzing private- and non-profit-sector resources on behalf of public problems (Kettl 2006; Weber 2003).

As with legislatively sponsored CG, there are many examples of this dynamic in practice, a few of which will suffice to make the point. In Oregon, the legislature created the framework in support of place-based collaborative watershed councils in 1998. Yet, the original framework was changed in 2013 by the agency in charge, the Oregon Watershed Enhancement Board (OWEB), in favor of a policy promoting new, strategic collaboratives that tie together watershed councils with other restoration-oriented non-profits and agencies within the same place, while also pushing the smallest councils to join forces with other councils in close proximity. The new "focused investment partnerships" for watersheds also require comprehensive strategic management plans with measurable milestones and outcomes, long-term six-year funding cycles, and the agency's commitment to CG after initial funding expires if planning milestones are being met and a follow-on collaboratively produced strategic plan meets with approval (OWEB 2014).

The U.S. National Park Service, the BLM, and the USFWS, for their part, have created internal collaborative governance units designed to promote both communities of practice and greater collaboration with communities closest to their public lands (Leong et al. 2011; Rogers and Weber 2010).

In 2006 the Greater Sage-grouse Comprehensive Conservation Strategy was developed by a consortium of western wildlife agencies to combat threats to the bird. The Western Association of Fish and Wildlife Agencies (WAFWA) and federal agencies including the BLM, USFS, USFWS, Natural Resources Conservation Service, U.S. Geological Survey, and the Farm Services Agency joined together under a Memorandum of Agreement (MOA) in 2008. Through the efforts of this coalition of agencies, states and their associated wildlife agencies have engaged local communities and taken on voluntary, collaborative conservation efforts to preserve the species (Finley 2014).

The larger pattern of agency-initiated collaboratives, and their growth over time, is well illustrated by forest-based collaboratives involving the Oregon Department of Forestry, along with many other agencies, including, but not limited to, BLM, USFS, the Oregon Water Resources Department, and place-based citizens groups. As of November 2014, there were 25 forest collaboratives throughout the state, with three of these established during the 1990s, another six between 2000 and 2005, and 16, or almost two-thirds of the total, initiated from 2006 through 2014 (University of Oregon 2015).

CONCLUSION

As outlined early on in this chapter, the long-established conventional wisdom on politicians' preferences for institutional arrangements comes in several forms. All the same, the central logic associated with these various approaches to elected officials and the delegation of authority and control to either bureaucratic subordinates, an agency's organized clienteles, or local citizens, more generally, is that politicians prefer control and certainty with respect to policy outcomes. These preferences lead them to choose *not* to devolve authority in cases where uncertainty is the rule, preferring instead to lock in control via specific contracts and rules for organizing public administration. In cases where electeds do choose to devolve authority to communities, or subgovernments, it is because they are responsive to specific clienteles and/or interests that have enough control and power to create certainty as regards the kinds of narrow, self-interested policy outcomes that accord with the politicians' desires.

Taken together, the conventional wisdom tells us that there will be fewer devolved, collaborative governance arrangements than there would otherwise be, especially at the administrative and political levels furthest removed from central political authority (i.e., local or place-based efforts). This is because politicians do not see it as in their best interest to promote them, with their focus on broad public interest-type outcomes, either by passing laws or granting the discretion necessary for their ultimate success. This necessarily limits the number of collaborative governance arrangements in operation.

But the past 25 years in the American West has seen significant growth in the engagement and operation of place-based, collaborative governance arrangements in the natural resources policy arena, many with strong support from politicians. This suggests that there is a new, different, and competing logic that applies to how elected officials view the idea of place-based CG efforts. Instead of avoidance, and for the series of reasons listed above, it is now perhaps just as likely for politicians to embrace and support, or at least allow, the collaborative dynamic to play out and, if consensus agreements are reached, to support them.

This is not to say that the new logic of support for CG by politicians is now the dominant logic and that it has completely replaced the old conventional logics associated with institutional choice. There are still a significant number of scenarios in which elected officials will be unlikely to either prefer or promote collaborative governance, including, as Putnam and Wondolleck (2003) tell us, cases where the issues involve high stakes and are distributional in nature, which often means that the cost of negotiating and settling is higher than the cost of fighting. In other cases there is little or no opportunity for a collaborative effort, grounded as they often are in innovative solutions that creatively bridge differences in stakeholder interests. In one instance, the presence of significant blocks of "value" voters with belief in the absolute sanctity of certain principles (e.g., the abortion debate over right to life versus freedom of a woman's right to choose), especially when in opposition to each other, leaves little to no room for collaboration or compromise (Amy 1987; LeBaron and Carstarphen 1999). In another example, settled law and existing policies can constrain the collaborative option for politicians in situations where the likely solutions either run contrary to existing legislation or the power to act is held in another branch or level of government (Agranoff 2007).

Further, and as implied above, the existence of power imbalances and domination of a local community and/or economy, particularly when this power rests in the hands of a stakeholder group critical to an elected official's electoral coalition, makes politicians much less likely to support collaborative governance arrangements. As Daniels and Walker (2001) note, "without interdependence, [or mutual dependence,] there is little need or opportunity for meaningful [collaborative] interaction" (31; see also Innes and Booher 2009). Sources of interdependence can include shared need for the natural resource(s) in question and/or the benefits anticipated from sharing risks, uncertainty, and costs (Ostrom 1990; Thomson and Perry 2006). Interdependence, in fact, is one of the few antecedent conditions with little counter-evidence against its essential necessity to successful collaborative formation (Emerson et al. 2012).

Finally, as noted in the opening chapter of this volume, political and public support for CG arrangements may well wax and wane over the course of multiple elections to the extent that there is turnover among elected officials. Put differently, different politicians are likely to pursue different policy and governance priorities (Heikkila and Gerlak 2005; Kallis et al. 2010; Owen 2007).

Even with these challenges, the main point here is that the significant growth in natural resources-based collaboratives in the American West did not occur in a political vacuum (Dietz 2013). In short, elected officials at all levels of government in the U.S.—local, state, and federal—have found reasons to overcome their concerns about control, devolution, and uncertainty to both actively and tacitly support place-based collaboratives in many, but not all, cases. In this sense, the political choice dynamic still limits the overall number of collaboratives in operation. This is most likely a good thing, since place-based collaborative governance is like any other policy-making institution—it is not perfect and is only likely to be effective in some, but not all circumstances.

NOTES

1. This research relies on a mix of primary documents and secondary source materials, along with field interview data taken from nine separate research projects focused on small-scale, place-based collaborative governance arrangements in the western U.S. The various projects, and over 100 semi-structured, open-ended interviews that this chapter relies on, were conducted between the years 1998 and 2013, but not on the specific topic of the "new logic of politics" as applied to collaborative governance efforts. Instead, the "new logic of politics" began to appear as a recurrent theme within the open-ended responses of collaborative governance stakeholders, including politicians, to the extent that by 2013 I started searching for additional empirical examples to see if, indeed, there was something more to the apparent phenomenon. The evidence in this chapter is the result of that search. But, as the concluding section here makes clear, these claims are suggestive and do not seek to establish the overall frequency at which the "new logic of politics" applies to collaboratives. That is a task for future research.
2. In 1982, Congress amended the ESA by including an "experimental" designation in Section 10(j) of the Act. Section 10(j) allows the Secretary of the Department of Interior to designate a reintroduced species as threatened, while not triggering the protections that normally apply to species that are threatened and giving the agency flexibility and discretion in managing that species. This designation allows agencies to re-establish self-sustaining populations in regions that are outside the species' current range when doing so fosters its conservation and recovery.
3. State 303(d) lists, as of 2013, identified over 39,000 water bodies as not meeting water quality standards and in need of a TMDL.
4. This opposition came despite the presence of local Sierra Club members being involved in the QLG.
5. The successes in Canterbury have led New Zealand's central government to promote

collaborative governance and consensus-based agreements as a standard approach to resolving natural resource issues at the national level (e.g., *Land and Water Forums*) and all other regions of the country, including Auckland (Weber 2013).

REFERENCES

Agranoff, R. (2007). *Managing within networks : adding value to public organizations*. Washington, DC: Georgetown University Press. Retrieved from http://www.loc.gov/catdir/toc/ecip071/2006031171.html

Amy, D. (1987). "The politics of environmental mediation." *Ecology Law Quarterly*, *11*(1), 1–19.

Daniels, Steven, and Walker, Gregg B. (2001). *Working through environmental conflict : the collaborative learning approach*. Westport, CT: Praeger.

Deschutes Partnership. (2013a). "Whychus Creek revived through combined efforts," (15 August). Retrieved from http://www.deschutesriver.org/blog/2013/08/15/whychus-creek-revived-through-series-of-restoration-projects/

Deschutes Partnership. (2013b). "History." Retrieved from http://www.deschutes partnership.org/about-us/history/

Dietz, T. (2013). "Bringing values and deliberation to science communication." *Proceedings of the National Academy of Sciences*, *110* (Supplement 3), 14081–14087.

Emerson, K., Nabatchi, T., and Balogh, S. (2012). An integrative framework for collaborative governance. *Journal of Public Administration Research and Theory*, *22*(1), 1–29.

Environmental Protection Agency. (2015). "National Environmental Policy Act (NEPA)." Retrieved from http://www.epa.gov/compliance/basics/nepa.html

Finley, Bruce. (2014). "Gunnison sage grouse gets federal protection to prevent extinction." *Denver Post* (November 11). Retrieved from http://www.denverpost.com/environment/ci_26922049/gunnison-sage-grouse-get-federal-protection-prevent-extinction

Foss, Philip O. (1960). *Politics and Grass*. Seattle, WA: University of Washington Press.

Heikkila, T., and Gerlak, A. K. (2005). "The formation of large-scale collaborative resource management institutions: clarifying the roles of stakeholders, science, and institutions." *Policy Studies Journal*, *33*(4), 583–612.

Holling, C., and Gunningham, N. (2011). "Natural resources, new governance and legal regulation: when does collaboration work?" *New Zealand Universities Law Review*, *24*, 309–327.

Innes, J. E., and Booher, D. E. (2009). *Planning with complexity : an introduction to collaborative rationality for public policy*. New York: Routledge.

Jenkins, Bryan. (2013). Progress of the Canterbury Water Management Strategy and some emerging issues. Waterways Centre for Freshwater Management, Canterbury and Lincoln Universities.

Kallis, G., Kiparsky, M., and Norgaard, R. (2010). "Collaborative governance and adaptive management: lessons from California's CALFED water program." *Environmental Science and Policy*, *12*(6), 631–643.

Kamarck, Elaine. (2007). *The end of government as we know it*. Washington, DC: Lynne Reiner Publishers.

Kaufman, Herbert. (1967). *The Forest Ranger*. Washington, DC: Resources for the Future.
Kemmis, Daniel. (1990). *Community and the politics of place*. Norman, OK: University of Oklahoma Press.
Kettl, Donald F. (2006). "Managing boundaries in American administration: the collaboration imperative." *Public Administration Review*, *66*(1), 10–19.
Klyza, Christopher M., and Sousa, David J. (2008). *American environmental policy, 1990–2006: beyond gridlock*. Cambridge, MA: The MIT Press.
Knott, Jack H., and Miller, Gary J. (1987). *Reforming bureaucracy*. Englewood Cliffs, N.J.: Prentice-Hall.
Koontz, T. M., Steelman, T. A., Carmin, J., Korfmacher, K. S., Moseley, C., and Thomas, C. W. (2004). *Collaborative environmental management: what roles for government*. London: Routledge.
Koontz, Thomas M., and Thomas, Craig W. (2006). "What do we know and need to know about the environmental outcomes of collaborative management?" *Public Administration Review*, *66*(1), 111–121.
LeBaron, M., and Carstarphen, N. (1999). "Finding common ground on abortion." In L. Susskind, S. McKearnon, and S. Carpenter (eds.), *Consensus building handbook: a comprehensive guide to reaching agreement* (pp. 1031–1050). Thousand Oaks, CA: Sage.
Leong, Kirsten, Emmerson, David P., and Byron, Rebecca R. (2011). "The new governance era: implications for collaborative conservation and adaptive management in Department of the Interior agencies." *Human Dimensions of Wildlife*, *16*: 236–243.
Mann, Charles C., and Plummer, Mark L. (1995). *Noah's choice: the future of endangered species*. New York: Knopf.
Margerum, Richard D. (2011). *Beyond consensus: improving collaborative planning and management*. Cambridge, MA: The MIT Press.
Mayhew, David R. (1974). *Congress: the electoral connection*. New Haven, CT: Yale University Press.
McConnell, Grant. (1966). *Private power and American democracy*. New York: Vintage Books.
Memon, A., Duncan, R., and Spicer, A. (2012). "The Hurunui-Waiau Zone Implementation Programme as a collaborative planning process: a preliminary review." Environment Canterbury Regional Council, Report No. R12/46.
Moe, Terry M. (1984). "The new economics of organization." *American Journal of Political Science*, *28* (November), 739–777.
Newig, Jens, and Fritsch, Oliver. (2008). "Environmental governance: participatory, multi-level -- and effective?" UFZ Discussion Paper 15 (November). Retrieved from http://www.econstor.eu/bitstream/10419/44744/1/604559410.pdf
Oregon Watershed Enhancement Board. (2014). "Focused investment partnerships." Retrieved from http://www.oregon.gov/OWEB/docs/FIP/FI_definition_solicitation_criteria.pdf
Ostrom, Elinor. (1990). *Governing the commons: the evolution of institutions for collective action*. New York: Cambridge University Press.
Owen, D. (2007). "Law, environmental dynamism, reliability: the rise and fall of CALFED." *Environmental Law*, *37*, 1145–1204.
Puget Sound Partnership. (2015). "Salmon recovery in Puget Sound." Retrieved from http://www.psp.wa.gov/SR_status.php

Putnam, L. L., and Wondolleck, J. M. (2003). "Intractability: definitions, dimensions, and distinctions." In R. J. Lewicki, B. Gray, and M. Elliot (eds.), *Making sense of intractable environmental conflicts: concepts and cases* (pp. 35–59). Washington, DC: Island Press.

Rittel, Horst, and Webber, Melvin. (1973). "Dilemmas in a general theory of planning." *Policy Sciences*, *4*(2), 155–169.

River Voice. (2007). "History of the Deschutes River Conservancy." *1*(4) (Summer). Retrieved from http://www.deschutesriver.org/DRC%20Sum07.pdf

Roberts, Nancy C. (2002). *The transformative power of dialogue.* New York: JAI Press.

Rogers, Ellen, and Weber, Edward P. (2010). "Thinking harder about outcomes for collaborative governance arrangements." *American Review of Public Administration*, *40*(5) (September), 546–567.

Scholz, John T. (1991). "Cooperative regulatory enforcement and the politics of administrative effectiveness." *American Political Science Review*, *85*, 115–136.

Seib, Gerald. (2015). "The Charleston shooting." *Wall Street Journal* (23 June), A4.

Sirianni, Carmen. (2010). *Civic democracy: engaging citizens in collaborative governance.* Washington, DC: The Brookings Institution.

Thomson, Ann M., and Perry, James L. (2006). "Collaboration processes: inside the black box." *Public Administration Review*, *66* (Supplement 1), 20–32.

University of Oregon. (2015). "Graphic depicting forest collaboratives in Oregon." Retrieved from http://ewp.uoregon.edu/sites/ewp.uoregon.edu/files/Collaboratives_OR_112014.pdf

U.S. Forest Service. (2009). "Omnibus Public Land Management Act of 2009: Title IV—Forest Landscape Restoration." Retrieved from http://www.fs.fed.us/restoration/documents/cflrp/titleIV.pdf

U.S. Forest Service. (2015). "Collaborative Forest Landscape Restoration Program overview." Retrieved from http://www.fs.fed.us/restoration/CFLRP/overview.shtml

Weber, Edward P. (2000). "A new vanguard for the environment: grass-roots ecosystem management as a new environmental movement." *Society and Natural Resources*, *13*(3), 237–259.

Weber, Edward P. (2003). *Bringing society back in: grassroots ecosystem management, accountability, and sustainable communities*. Cambridge, MA: The MIT Press.

Weber, Edward P. (2013). "Building capacity for collaborative water governance in Auckland." For the Water Management Strategy and Policy Team, Auckland Council, a Regional Government in New Zealand (June).

Weber, Edward P. (2014). "Learning from collaborative restoration efforts: the case of Whychus Creek." White Paper for the Deschutes Partnership (Bend, Oregon).

Weber, Edward P., and Khademian, Anne M. (2008). "Wicked problems, knowledge challenges, and collaborative capacity builders in network settings." *Public Administration Review*, *68*(2) (March–April), 334–349.

Weber, Edward P., Leschine, Thomas M., and Brock, Jon. (2010). "Civic science and salmon recovery planning in Puget Sound." *Policy Studies Journal*, *38*(2) (May), 235–256.

Weingast, Barry R. (1984). "The congressional-bureaucratic system: a principal agent perspective (with applications to the SEC)." *Public Choice*, *44*, 147–191.

Wondolleck, Julia M., and Yaffee, Steven L. (2000). *Making collaboration work: lessons from innovation in natural resource management.* Washington, DC: Island Press.

11. The role of power in collaborative governance

Jill M. Purdy

Every collaboration is, at some level, about power. Power is a vital resource needed to convene parties, to frame problems, to negotiate meanings, to make decisions, and to take action. However, it is not a fixed resource nor an objective quality, rather power is a perceived quality that emerges from contextual and relational dynamics. Power is interactive in nature. Any observation about the power of an individual, group, organization or nation-state is made through an assessment of the observed party in relation to at least one other party and in consideration of multiple levels of social organization. In collaborative governance contexts, power dynamics emerge from a complex web of varied understandings about the interdependencies between participants' interests, resources, and influence. Scholars have been challenged to develop theories about power that apply to such highly complex and variable contexts in which participants, social structures, and processes can change (Huxham and Vangen, 2000), resulting in limited scholarship on the topic (Huxham and Vangen, 2005).

This chapter considers the nature of power within the context of environmental collaboration to develop a deeper understanding of it and our ability to influence power dynamics. A thorough analysis of power must consider both episodic and structural issues that extend from everyday interactions to broader social structures, norms, and sanctions (Clegg, 1989). Episodic power describes the use of power in interactions among individuals related to conversations, conflicts, and non-confrontations. For example, an employee who has exclusive knowledge of how a database system works has a type of episodic power that can influence daily interactions by enabling him/her to bargain with those who seek information from the system. S/he may freely share knowledge about the system with everyone or withhold it to create a dependency that allows him/her to receive something in return for his/her expertise. Thus from an episodic perspective, parties to collaborative governance can be analyzed in terms of their sources of power and their orientations toward power.

This approach recognizes how perceptions of power affect the beliefs and actions of individual actors, drawing attention to discrete acts of strategic mobilization (Clegg, 1989) such as persuasion and coercion.

In contrast, structural power is linked to more macro rules and practices that inform how actors are perceived in the social order. For example, the power of labor unions may vary significantly in different countries based on labor's status in each society. Union membership conveys a very different status in Norway, where more than 50% of employees belong to unions and unions participate in collective bargaining at the national level (Ministry of Labour and Social Affairs, 2011), compared to the United States, where 11% of employees belong to unions and collective bargaining is decentralized (Pew Research Center, 2015). The view that unions are valuable in society is largely taken for granted in Norway, while public opinion of unions in the United States is almost evenly split between positive and negative views (Pew Research Center, 2015). From a structural perspective, power is determined not by individual actions and dependencies but by legitimacy within the social order, yielding variations in participation and acknowledgment that go unchallenged and can hamper reaching agreements that can achieve broad acceptance and be sustained. The structural approach to power also recognizes that collaborative governance networks may be challenged to obtain legitimacy within the broader social context (Provan et al., 2008) and thus participants may be more strongly influenced by the institutional logics of their fields or societal sectors. This focus draws attention to the structural aspects of power that works through routine, taken-for-granted practices that advantage particular groups (Clegg, 1989) such as dominant technologies or culturally accepted definitions of race or gender.

Scholarly research on power in collaborative governance settings has emphasized the episodic perspective, yielding valuable progress in understanding how to manage power asymmetries in collaborative processes. However, institutional norms deeply ingrained in social structures may generate disruptive power dynamics that cannot be overcome through effective process management. This analysis draws upon literature from several disciplines including organization theory, public administration, and political economics to offer a multi-level perspective on the role of power in collaborative governance processes.

APPROACHES TO GOVERNANCE OF RESOURCES

While a variety of governance approaches exist, most efforts to address shared problems or common resource issues fall into one of two categories.

The first is a rational-legal approach that relies on regulatory authority or private property rights as forms of power that compel stakeholders to act in accordance with specific rules (Weber et al., 1946). This approach emphasizes formalized legal processes that rely on the larger governance structures of the region or nation, emphasizing structural aspects of power that reinforce existing institutionalized systems of governance. Such an approach is being used by the Wild Olympics coalition in the western part of Washington state in an attempt to preserve forests and watersheds in their natural state. The non-governmental conservation organizations that comprise the coalition have introduced legislation at the federal level seeking to protect the Olympic Peninsula by adding 'wilderness' and 'wild and scenic river' designations that would limit road access and the logging of old growth timber (State News Service, 2015). This approach involves a coalition of like-minded groups, but does not include collaboration among all stakeholders with interests related to the resources in question, notably excluding some community members who disagree with the policies being proposed (Underwood et al., 2014).

The second type of governance approach emphasizes collaborative processes where stakeholders together determine their desired course of action. Such processes may provide an avenue for discussion and negotiation that leads to a rational-legal outcome, or they may rely on less formalized mechanisms where stakeholders hold each other accountable for upholding the common good. Informal collaborative approaches have been used around the world for centuries to manage common pool resources such as fisheries (Ostrom, 1990). Ostrom's Nobel prize-winning research on common pool resource management identified a number of design principles that characterize stable collaborative governance approaches. Two of these principles are particularly relevant to understanding power in environmental collaboration: (1) the importance of collective choice arrangements that allow participation in decision making, and (2) the recognition of community self-determination by higher-level authorities (Ostrom, 1990). The first principle highlights episodic aspects of power, recognizing the importance of sufficiently equal power relations within a collaboration to allow balanced participation in processes. The second principle acknowledges structural aspects of power that reside at higher levels of social organization, indicating that collaborative governance efforts must be accepted or sanctioned by wider authorities such as government. Although such approval is sometimes taken for granted, particularly when government entities participate in collaborative processes, the legal foundation for collaborative governance is by no means uncontested. For example, a 1935 ruling of the Supreme Court of the United States still stands which stated that government agencies could not delegate their authority to associations or groups that would in effect act as legislative bodies (Bingham, 2008). Nevertheless, collaborative public management and related governance processes have grown despite a lack of legislation that specifies the rights and limits of citizens to participate in governance rather than government (Kettl, 2002).

A key distinction between these two approaches to collaborative governance is the emphasis each places on different aspects of power. The rational-legal approach relies on the power in the existing roles, structures, and institutions of society to advance the preferred actions and outcomes of a group, reinforcing the existing power dynamics within a social system. In contrast, the collaborative approach incorporates both episodic and structural elements, yielding opportunities for episodic use of power within the power dynamics of a particular social system. This yields additional complexity as episodic efforts to garner and exert power around a specific resource issue are themselves nested in a broader structural context for power that includes elements such as electoral politics, socioeconomic class distinctions, and industry- or sectoral-level influence (Holm, 1995). Advancing our understanding of collaborative environmental governance requires attending carefully to both aspects of power as well as how they intersect.

THE NATURE OF POWER

The term 'power' encompasses many meanings, from the idea that power is actor-based activity intended to influence, to the Foucauldian notion that power is a force embedded in discourse and elements of everyday life. Göhler (2009) notes the distinction between 'power to' and 'power over,' highlighting that 'power to' is a capability or precondition, while 'power over' involves exercised power. Huxham and Vangen (2005) extend this perspective by adding the idea of 'power for,' which emphasizes the sharing or expansion of power to reduce power imbalances or advance a position that is not self-interested. To be useful for the purpose of understanding episodic and structural aspects of power in collaborative contexts, a definition of power must accommodate views of power as potential and as action as well as the full range of power motives from coercive to altruistic. Power is present in every social interaction, it incorporates both repressive and productive elements, and it operates on multiple levels of social organization simultaneously. Thus, power in this chapter will be treated as having social and relational aspects that incorporate both capacity and action, such that "power is the medium in social relations to structure fields of action" (Göhler, 2009, p. 36).

EPISODIC ASPECTS OF POWER

The literature on collaborative governance reveals numerous insights about the nature of power at the level of interactions among parties to a governance process. Some insights from this research address the 'power to' dimension related to perceptions of the capacity for power among actors. For example, Huxham and Vangen (2005) note that power imbalances among partners are a potential threat to collaboration because they may generate distrust among participants. Concerns about 'power over' come into play when participants have difficulty agreeing on a shared purpose and they have different levels of power (Bryson and Crosby, 2008). Under these conditions, collaborative governance becomes more difficult because of the threat that some actors may attempt to impose their will on others.

To fully understand episodic aspects of power, we must consider why actors are perceived to possess the capacity to take action or the ability to coerce others to accept their will. Participants in collaborative governance processes most commonly represent organizations or affiliated groups of like-minded people, thus I use a framework here that addresses organizational power rather than personal sources of power. This framework, developed by Hardy and Phillips (1998), proposes that power in collaborative contexts is generated primarily through the authority, resources, and discursive power held by organizational actors. Each of these three forms of episodic power is discussed in greater detail below.

Authority refers to the socially validated right to make a decision or take action on behalf of others. While it may be derived from coercion, authority is more commonly understood as a delegation of power by those who are governed, through social and political structures that are sanctioned and legitimate. For example, government agencies have the authority to establish and enforce rules because citizens share a belief in the "rationalization and the regulation of human activity by legal and bureaucratic hierarchies" (Friedland and Alford, 1991, p. 248). Private organizations and non-governmental organizations (NGOs) rely on corporate governance structures and the strength of institutional structures such as the law to vest authority in designated actors.

Resources serve as a form of episodic power because they can be used to influence dependency relations among organizations. Whether resources are human, technical, financial, informational, or cultural, they represent the ability of actors to grant or withhold something that other actors desire. The value of resources as a form of power is not absolute; it is specific to the episodic domain in which actors have an interest and the needs of those actors in relation to each other. For example, scientific knowledge might prove to be a more valuable resource in solving an environmental challenge than having access to money. However, perceptions of resources as well as actual resources are relevant to how actors perceive power. Kanter notes that "people who are thought to have power already . . . who look like they can command more of the organization's resources . . . may also be more influential and more effective in getting the people around them to do things and feel satisfied about it" (1977, p. 168–169). Although Kanter's research focused on individuals rather than organizations, it reminds us that the appearance of power can prompt actors to behave in ways that are not reflective of the actual dependency relationships between them.

Discursive legitimacy is a form of power that recognizes the ability of an organization to represent a discourse or speak on behalf of an issue in the public sphere (Hardy and Phillips, 1998). The ability to manage meaning by influencing how information is presented is particularly important in collaborative governance because the process involves complex negotiations around developing shared understandings (Huxham and Vangen, 2005). Expertise in shaping meanings yields discursive power; Hallett (2003) describes this as "the power to define the situation" (p. 133). Furthermore, discursive power represents access to a means of catalyzing social groups. Grass-roots organizations that generate social movements such as 'Occupy Wall Street' provide a familiar example of discursive power in action; however, other organizations have access to this form of power as well through the values or principles they represent. Government agencies may represent the principle of democracy or the rule of law, corporations may represent the desire for prosperity and economic well-being, and non-profit organizations may represent values such as equality, sustainability, or freedom from want. Like other forms of power, discursive power exists in the eye of the beholder. For example, an organization that presumes to have discursive power linked to the value of equality is unlikely to be powerful in a social context where significant social inequities are accepted as the norm. Conversely, an organization that serves or is comprised of individuals with low power (such as children, the poor, or immigrants) can have considerable discursive power by speaking on behalf of a value such as compassion if other actors see this value as important.

When evaluating power dynamics in collaborative governance contexts, the three forms of power described by Hardy and Phillips (1998) can be juxtaposed with the three power orientations described by Huxham and Vangen (2005) to create a framework for assessing possible power responses of actors based on their perceived characteristics. Identifying the placement of an actor within the framework requires careful assessment because forms of power and power orientations are subjective characteristics that involve an element of choice. As noted above, forms of power are not absolute and depend in part on perceptions or attributions within

Table 11.1 Actor capacities based on forms of power and power orientations

		Power orientations		
		Power over	Power to	Power for
Forms of power	*Authority*	Impose unilateral decision	Decide how to decide	Endorse collaborative efforts
	Resources	Take action independently	Participate in decision making	Provide means for broad participation
	Discursive power	Create social pressure for a given action	Manage meaning or sanction a decision	Represent those who cannot participate

contexts, thus actors and observers make judgments about which forms of power are present and to what degree various actors have them. Power orientations are largely a matter of choice by the actor, although social and cultural influences as well as past experience can strongly influence the orientation an actor brings to a common resource problem.

Table 11.1 provides examples of potential power moves that arise from the various combinations of power forms and power orientations. It identifies the capacity for action that is generated by power when taken at its most extreme. The framework is not predictive of the actions that actors will take; rather it illustrates the range of possibilities that are available to them. The actions taken by an actor are dependent on their assessment of the power of other actors as well as the costs and benefits of taking action. For example, the first row of Table 11.1 indicates that actors who are perceived to have authority may have the capacity to impose a unilateral decision, as in the case of a regulatory agency that has the ability to promulgate regulations in a particular domain. However, they may not choose to exercise that capacity and may instead elect a collaborative approach rather than a rational-legal one. Such a choice was made by the Federal Energy Regulatory Commission (FERC), the US federal agency responsible for governing the electric power system, when it was rewriting the laws for hydroelectric power project relicensing in the United States. Rather than drafting regulations and limiting stakeholder involvement to a public comment period, FERC engaged in collaborative governance through a series of meetings across the country that culminated in stakeholder drafting of the new regulations (Purdy, 2012).

As the second row of Table 11.1 shows, actors with access to resources have the ability to select the degree to which they wish to influence the dependencies among stakeholders in a common resource context.

Depending on their assessments of the power of others and their own preferences, these actors may act unilaterally or may level the playing field to support broad participation in collaborative governance. In the hydroelectric relicensing example, FERC expended its own resources to travel to thirteen locations throughout the country near hydroelectric facilities to facilitate the participation of Native American tribes, and designated 50% of all meetings specifically for tribal participation (Purdy, 2012). Finally, the third row of Table 11.1 illustrates ways in which actors with discursive power are able to influence public opinion and change the nature of the discourse around a common resource issue. For example, NGOs such as Greenpeace walked out of United Nations climate change talks in Warsaw, Poland in 2013 to indicate growing global frustration with slow progress on an agreement (Twidale and Chestney, 2013). Some attribute agreement on greenhouse gas emissions at the 2014 talks in Lima to 'peer pressure' that resulted from this action (Davenport, 2014).

Episodic aspects of power are concerned with elements of influence that are specific to the actors, contexts, and relationships associated with a particular common resource issue. These perceptions and calculations of power occur through interactions that are relatively immediate to the situation and to their interest and actions. However, the situation itself is infused with power dynamics that emerge from the taken-for-granted practices and processes that are fundamental aspects of social organization. These forms of power may be invisible even to the actors themselves. Power in the forms of discipline and domination (Lawrence, 2008) is hidden in the technologies, physical settings, and practices that we use to form understandings of the world. Only when we consider the role that institutions play in society can we begin to see some of the less visible aspects of power that position actors in the social order and limit or control what they are able to create. These structural aspects of power will be considered next.

STRUCTURAL ASPECTS OF POWER

The forms of power available to organizations, such as those described above, are derived from wider social systems that are organized through sectors, fields, professions, and institutions. When different organizations and actors come together, they bring with them understandings about how to think, decide, and act that are derived from the systems of social organization in which they operate (Gray and Purdy, 2013). These systems generate patterns of relations that appear as structures and have a significant if often unrecognized effect on power dynamics among organizations. The structural approach to power acknowledges that "interorganizational power relations cannot be fully understood without attention to the larger pattern of societal dominance" (Benson, 1975, p. 233).

Scholars of collaborative governance have recognized the importance of social context in determining the dynamics and outcomes of collaborative processes (Ansell and Gash, 2008; Emerson et al., 2012). The importance of power in the political-economic context of natural resource negotiations has been affirmed (Layzer, 2008), but research specifically examining how higher-order social groups and institutions influence the power dynamics of collaborative governance is less common. The limited nature of inquiry into structural aspects of power is a concern because power is first and foremost a structural phenomenon (Pfeffer, 1981). The impact of structure is evident when collaborations draw upon the institutional rules and resources of their members, influencing the problem definition, who participates, and what practices are used (Phillips et al., 2000). In this section, I will consider structural aspects of power by describing the organization of societies into institutional orders and by examining how the institutional logics predominant in modern Western societies affect attributions and understandings of power during collaboration.

In the past decade, a significant body of research has advanced the institutional logics approach introduced by Friedland and Alford (1991) as a means of understanding the core beliefs and norms that constitute society and that affect both the means and ends of human and organizational behavior. Thornton and Ocasio defined institutional logics as "the socially constructed, historical patterns of material practices, assumptions, values, beliefs, and rules by which individuals produce and reproduce their material subsistence, organize time and space, and provide meaning to their social reality" (2008, p. 101). These patterns of practices and belief systems take on the character of structural features as they increasingly are taken for granted and the logics become rule-like norms that habitually and subconsciously guide cognition and behavior. Friedland and Alford (1991) initially identified five institutional orders that characterize social systems, but subsequent theorizing has suggested that the inter-institutional system that guides meaning and action consists of seven institutional orders, each with its own logic: market, corporation, profession, state, family, religion, and community (Thornton et al., 2012). This system integrates structural, normative, and symbolic dimensions of institutions and defines the orders as ideal types that can be used for analysis.

The inter-institutional system is linked to the structural aspects of power in two ways. First, the orders of the inter-institutional system are not equally powerful in a society, and the relative status of an institutional order in a society is reflected in power and status dynamics that play out in the social interactions of actors who represent that order. Second, each institutional order is linked to a particular source of legitimacy, and actors consciously or unknowingly seek to maintain legitimacy within their dominant institutional order even as they work across the inter-institutional system. Each of these connections between power and the inter-institutional system is considered below.

The first link between the inter-institutional system and power relates to the ranking of the orders within a social system. Logics are not equally prominent nor equally valued; the orders and their logics operate within a hierarchy that varies across societies such that some logics play a greater role than others in influencing values, beliefs, activities, and norms. In countries such as the United States and the United Kingdom where market capitalism is a significant force in everyday life (Hall and Soskice, 2001), the market logic may dominate interactions. In countries where the state, the community, or religion are the most prominent features of daily life, those logics may dominate. The presence of such a hierarchy and the relative status of the institutional orders can be seen in the case of an organization such as the Moorish Nation, an American religious organization that disavows the sovereignty of the nation-state and asserts the authority of Islam instead. The existence of this organization is protected in the United States because religion as an institutional order is relatively important; however, the pre-eminence of the state order over religion is clear because Moorish Nation members who violate property laws are jailed (Gordon, 2015). One can imagine a very different response in North Korea, where the state dominates daily life and religion is repressed (Evans, 2015), or in Sudan, where religion dominates the state in the form of sharia law (Otto, 2010).

While the hierarchy of logics is most easily illustrated by considering differences between countries, variations in the priority of logics occur within nation-states. Logics may be close or quite distant from each other in terms of their status within a social context. Different regions and sub-populations may prioritize logics differently within a country context. The key insight here is that the logics approach offers a means of assessing how the social context of a situation may impose structural differences in power based upon the status of logics within the inter-institutional system. This is important to collaborative governance because any stakeholder who is closely aligned with a particular logic will enjoy the structural privilege of the assumptions that are linked to the logic that is dominant in the context. Problems and solutions that are framed according to the dominant logic may receive more attention or resources, and decisions by a collaborative group may prioritize the values of the dominant order above those of other orders. Actors representing other less dominant social orders may face difficulty in gaining acceptance of their viewpoints. As a result, collaborative

Table 11.2 Bases of legitimacy for institutional orders

Institutional order	Source of legitimacy
Family	Loyalty
Community	Trust and reciprocity
Religion	Faith
State	Democratic participation
Market	Economic value
Professional	Expertise
Corporation	Market position

Source: Adapted from Thornton et al., 2012.

governance efforts are imbued with a power dynamic that is constructed according to priorities within an inter-institutional system that appears fixed and structural in nature. Efforts to level the playing field among participants in a particular collaboration may be unable to counter the fundamental bias of the context that is rooted in the inter-institutional system. The problems that get brought to collaboration and the ways in which they are framed are strongly influenced by the existing power structure of a society based on orders of its inter-institutional system.

The second linkage between power and the inter-institutional system is related to the legitimacy of an organization's connection with a particular logic. Organizations are typically aligned with a logic and must remain legitimate within that logic to have access to resources and to be sheltered from external pressures (Deephouse and Suchman, 2008). For example, NGOs are usually aligned with the community logic, while businesses are linked to the market logic, and government agencies to the state logic. An NGO that focuses too heavily on fundraising rather than achieving its mission risks losing credibility, and that loss of legitimacy can lead to the loss of resources, authority, and discursive power.

Each institutional order is associated with a particular basis of legitimacy as shown in Table 11.2. Family is associated with loyalty, community with trust and reciprocity, and religion with faith, while the state is associated with democratic participation, the market with economic value, the professions with expertise, and corporations with market position (Thornton et al., 2012). Organizations are judged by a variety of external observers as to whether their activities, policies, representatives, and systems reflect the basis of legitimacy for the logic with which they are associated (Deephouse and Suchman, 2008). Legitimacy is especially important when a participant to collaborative governance has discursive power as a primary form of episodic power, because loss of legitimacy eliminates that organization's ability to speak on behalf of an issue or audience and reduces its status to that of bystander.

Actors participating in collaborative governance may be fully engaged in the episodic aspects of working together but their behavior is influenced by their beliefs about what will be seen as legitimate within their own dominant institutional order. As a result, a business organization may insist on prioritizing the use of economic criteria to evaluate proposals, while environmentalists may contend that scientific knowledge and expertise should be the basis of judgment, and a governmental agency may focus on regulatory alignment and citizen acceptability as most important. Managing power at the episodic level can ensure that parties have a fair hearing within the context of a collaboration, but the pressures for each organization to remain legitimate within its own institutional order may prevent them from making concessions or compromising with each other. If participants representing lower-status institutional orders utilize their preferred modes of expression, or if they frame information from perspectives that are not familiar to higher-status participants, their contributions may be devalued even if given equal opportunity to participate. For example, Indigenous peoples who act according to their cultures during collaborative processes (through language, appearance, facial expression, ceremony, relational patterns, or world view) may find that other participants focus on areas of difference or frame Indigenous people as 'others' thereby reducing attention to the meanings being conveyed and diminishing Indigenous peoples' power. Alternately, lower-status participants may be required to participate in collaboration via dominant modes that are foreign or antithetical to their own institutional order, which also reduces their power to convey meaning and influence the proceedings. As a result, lower-status participants face fundamental structural barriers to power.

If pressures to remain legitimate within one's own institutional order are significant, one may ask how any collaborative governance process could succeed since no participant would tolerate legitimacy threats in order to reach agreement. Scholars have noted that organizations can shield some of their practices from external observers by decoupling (Meyer and Rowan, 1977; Oliver, 1997), which separates their actual activities from their espoused identity. Decoupling separates organizational structures from organizational practices and can be seen when an organization issues policies but does not abide by them internally, or when it revises underlying processes without a visible change to operational outputs (Boxenbaum and Jonsson, 2008). Indigenous peoples may decouple by using agents to represent their interests whose appearance, modes of expression, and cultural behaviors are aligned with more dominant institutional orders. Some organizations reduce legitimacy pressures in other ways. Elite actors may have sufficient resource streams and power sources that are not controlled by external observers to set aside concerns about legitimacy (Greenwood and Suddaby, 2006). Finally, some organizations may operate in contexts where the legitimacy of certain practices is ambiguous (Goodrick and Salancik, 1996) or the institutional context is complex or changing (Greenwood et al., 2011), which creates greater organizational discretion to act because the parameters of legitimacy are unclear or in transition.

CHALLENGES OF POWER IN ENVIRONMENTAL COLLABORATION

Although the use of collaborative approaches to governance has increased in recent years, problems with power in collaboration persist. Existing power dynamics between parties can heavily influence the interactions of parties (Helms and Oliver, 2015) or amplify power struggles (Walker and Hurley, 2004). Some parties may withhold information or effort to gain or retain power in collaboration (Gray and Schruijer, 2010). Power issues can also be more subtle, when representatives of some communities are not organized in a way that allows them to fully participate, or when the interests of some stakeholders are not noticed or not acknowledged. Scholars have identified practices that can improve positive outcomes for collaboration, including having a powerful actor convene the parties (Wood and Gray, 1991), supporting voluntary participation (Genskow, 2009), and using procedures that treat stakeholders equally (McKinney and Field, 2008); however, these are focused primarily on influencing the episodic aspects of power rather than the structural aspects. Such solutions do not address challenges that are embedded in the structure of the social system, such as the established models for how problems are recognized and framed that are typically derived from the dominant institutional orders, reducing or eliminating recognition of the concerns of lower-power orders. Stakeholders grappling with issues such as whaling must contend with different and incommensurable frames such as species sustainability, cultural heritage, subsistence and economic power, animal rights, and the sovereignty of Indigenous peoples. Beyond the difficulties of collaborating across such varied perspectives, the distributive, zero-sum nature of this problem makes a compromise solution impossible, as some parties are unwilling to accept a complete ban on whaling while other parties are unwilling to accept the killing of a single whale. Such problem structures are not uncommon in environmental contexts where naturally-occurring critical values (such as extinction thresholds) impose absolute limits on solutions and serve as barriers to compromise and creative, win-win solutions.

This chapter's examination of both episodic and structural power suggests that collaboration is unlikely to succeed unless two conditions are met. First, parties to collaboration require a context for interaction that insulates them from the demands of their dominant institutional logics and supports their ability to create a shared institutional logic which supersedes their dominant logics. This is a daunting challenge considering that common resource issues typically bring together stakeholders representing at least four different institutional orders and their respective logics: the state logic (government agencies), the professional logic (scientists), the market logic (businesses), and the community logic (NGOs and geographic groups). Overcoming the dominance of any one of these logics is difficult, and the state logic is particularly dominant with respect to environmental issues for several reasons. Governments and the rule of law are typically strong institutions in developed countries, and are generally tasked with preserving the public good. In addition, global pressure on nation-states has increased to address critical problems and governments are exercising regulatory authority at multiple levels to address concerns about diminishing resources. This may mean that stakeholders affiliated with the state logic are likely to hold disproportionate power that they are unwilling to relinquish no matter the specifics of the situation.

However, the relative power of the actors does not determine whether a relationship is collaborative (Gray, 1989). Instead collaboration is dependent on settings where roles and practices are not predetermined by markets or hierarchies (Phillips et al., 2000). To successfully construct a shared context for engaging in collaboration, actors who are guided by different dominant logics need to "build upon, work around, recombine, reinvent and reinterpret logics and institutional arrangements" (Djelic and Quack, 2008, p. 308). Actors must overcome the assumptions embedded in their own institutional logics about how problems should be framed, how information should be interpreted, and how they should relate to each other when working together. To construct a collaborative field for managing resource issues, the group must recognize or create cultural, symbolic, and material elements that are mutually valued by participants. The collaboration must also offer sufficient legitimacy to allow participants to violate at least partially the dictates of their own logics and support systems that shield them from critical external observers. A social learning approach to collaboration that arises from self-governance allows the creation of loosely coupled arrangements that can be customized to address the complexity and uncertainty of sustainability challenges (Paquet, 2004).

A second important condition for collaborations that stems from this analysis of power is the acceptability of the collaborative effort itself. Collaborative governance networks are one option among several alternatives that can be used to address common pool resource issues (Hanemann and Dyckman, 2009), and rational-legal approaches may be preferred because they are more deeply institutionalized or they offer less risky paths to preferred outcomes (Layzer, 2008).

Environmental collaborations in particular face a difficult task in changing understandings of how people should behave and how resources should be managed because they are complex, multi-jurisdictional, and often poorly suited to compromise solutions that would be acceptable to all participants. Progress on problems such as climate change is difficult to achieve through collaborative approaches, not only because power dynamics and institutional logics make finding solutions difficult, but because collaborations may identify solutions that challenge the basis and order of the inter-institutional system itself. Helms and Oliver note that "when institutional constituents resolve conflict in ways that radically alter how they relate to one another, fields change. Radical settlements can also lead to major redistributions of power among field members" (2015, p. 473). Changes in the institutional order occur more commonly and easily through "institutional shocks" such as natural disasters and similar catastrophic events than through deliberate incremental change through sustained collective action (Wijen and Ansari, 2007). Nevertheless, gradual change is occurring in many democracies where it is no longer assumed that the nation-state should dominate governance or that relations between society and government should be uniform and at arms length (Paquet, 2007). Accountabilities in environmental governance are not uni-directional; instead they are multi-directional among all the relevant stakeholders, leading to effective and creative social learning (Paquet, 2007). Collaborative efforts that recognize and embrace this intelligent accountability take a step toward overcoming the hierarchical dominance structure of institutional orders.

CONCLUSION

Collaborative governance efforts are not merely vessels in which power dynamics play out. They are arenas for the social construction of power, and they influence participants' subsequent forms of power and orientations toward power. The process of collaboration has the potential to yield new and changed relationships that affect access to information, levels of trust, and participants' placement in a network of organizations. The outcomes of collaborative governance processes may expand or diminish an organization's access to authority, resources, or discursive power, or precedents may be set that reposition actors relative to the issues and the future sources of power related to them. Despite the difficulty of studying a dynamic, relational, multi-level concept such as power, further research is needed to understand the episodic and particularly the structural aspects of power that affect and are affected by collaboration.

REFERENCES

Ansell, C., and Gash, A. (2008). Collaborative governance in theory and practice. *Journal of Public Administration Research and Theory*, 18(4), 543–571.

Benson, J. K. (1975). The interorganizational network as a political economy. *Administrative Science Quarterly*, 20(2), 229–249.

Bingham, L. B. (2008). Legal frameworks for governance and public management. In L. B. Bingham and R. O'Leary (eds.), *Big ideas in collaborative public management* (pp. 247–269). Armonk, NY: M. E. Sharpe.

Boxenbaum, E., and Jonsson, S. (2008). Isomorphism, diffusion and decoupling. In R. Greenwood, C. Oliver, K. Sahlin and R. Suddaby (eds.), *The SAGE handbook of organizational institutionalism* (pp. 78–98). Thousand Oaks, CA: SAGE.

Bryson, J. M., and Crosby, B. (2008). Failing into cross-sector collaboration successfully. In L. B. Bingham and R. O'Leary (eds.), *Big ideas in collaborative public management* (pp. 55–78). Armonk, NY: M. E. Sharpe.

Clegg, S. R. (1989). *Frameworks of power*. Thousand Oaks, CA: SAGE.

Davenport, C. (2014, 14 December). A climate accord based on global peer pressure. *New York Times*. Retrieved from http://www.nytimes.com/2014/12/15/world/americas/lima-climate-deal.html

Deephouse, D. L., and Suchman, M. (2008). Legitimacy in organizational institutionalism. In R. Greenwood, C. Oliver, K. Sahlin and R. Suddaby (eds.), *The SAGE handbook of organizational institutionalism* (pp. 49–77). Thousand Oaks, CA: SAGE.

Djelic, M. L., and Quack, S. (2008). Institutions and transnationalization. In R. Greenwood, C. Oliver, K. Sahlin and R. Suddaby (eds.), *The SAGE handbook of organizational institutionalism* (pp. 299–323). Thousand Oaks, CA: SAGE.

Emerson, K., Nabatchi, T., and Balogh, S. (2012). An integrative framework for collaborative governance. *Journal of Public Administration Research and Theory*, 11(1), 1–29.

Evans, S. (2015, 3 August). North Korea and Christianity – uneasy bedfellows. BBC News. Retrieved from http://www.bbc.com/news/world-asia-pacific-33740261

Friedland, R., and Alford, R. R. (1991). Bringing society back in: Symbols, practices and institutional contradictions. In W. W. Powell and P. J. DiMaggio (eds.), *The new institutionalism in organizational analysis* (pp. 232–263). Chicago, IL: University of Chicago Press.

Genskow, K. D. (2009). Catalyzing collaboration: Wisconsin's agency-initiated basin partnerships. *Environmental Management*, 43(3), 411–424.

Göhler, G. (2009). 'Power to' and 'power over.' In S. Clegg and M. Haugaard (eds.), *The SAGE handbook of power* (pp. 27–39). Thousand Oaks, CA: SAGE.

Goodrick, E., and Salancik, G. R. (1996). Organizational discretion in responding to institutional practices: Hospitals and cesarean births. *Administrative Science Quarterly*, 41(1), 1–28.

Gordon, M. (2015, 12 November). Woman claims right to reside in pricey Piper Glen home. *Charlotte Observer*. Retrieved from http://www.charlotteobserver.com/news/local/ crime/article44522178.html

Gray, B. (1989). *Collaborating: Finding common ground for multiparty problems*. San Francisco, CA: Jossey-Bass.

Gray, B., and Purdy, J. (2013). Conflict in cross sector partnerships. In M. Seitanidi and A. Crane (eds.), *Social partnerships and responsible business: A research handbook* (pp. 205–225). London: Routledge.

Gray, B., and Schruijer, S. (2010). Integrating multiple voices: Working with collusion in multiparty collaborations. In C. Steyaert and B. von Looy (eds.), *Relational practices: Participative organizing* (pp. 121–135). Bingley, UK: Emerald Group Publishing.

Greenwood, R., and Suddaby, R. (2006). Institutional entrepreneurship in mature fields: The big five accounting firms. *Academy of Management Journal*, 49(1), 27–48.

Greenwood, R., Raynard, M., Kodeih, F., Micelotta, E. R., and Lounsbury, M. (2011). Institutional complexity and organizational responses. *The Academy of Management Annals*, 5(1), 317–371.

Hall, P. A., and Soskice, D. (2001). *Varieties of capitalism: The institutional foundations of comparative advantage*. New York: Oxford University Press.

Hallett, T. (2003). Symbolic power and organizational culture. *Sociological Theory*, 21(2), 128–149.

Hanemann, M., and Dyckman, C. (2009). The San Francisco Bay-Delta: A failure in decision making capacity. *Environmental Science and Policy*, 12(6), 710–725.

Hardy, C., and Phillips, N. (1998). Strategies of engagement: Lessons from the critical examination of collaboration and conflict in an interorganizational domain. *Organization Science*, 9(2), 217–230.

Helms, W. S., and Oliver, C. (2015). Radical settlements to conflict: Conflict management and its implications for institutional change. *Journal of Management and Organization*, 21(4), 471–494.

Holm, P. (1995). The dynamics of institutionalization: Transformation processes in Norwegian fisheries. *Administrative Science Quarterly*, 40(3), 398–422.

Huxham, C., and Vangen, S. (2000). Leadership in the shaping and implementation of collaboration agendas: How things happen in a (not quite) joined-up world. *Academy of Management Journal*, 43(6), 1159–1175.

Huxham, C., and Vangen, S. (2005). *Managing to collaborate: The theory and practice of collaborative advantage*. New York: Routledge.

Kanter, R. M. (1977). *Men and women of the corporation*. New York: Basic Books.

Kettl, D. F. (2002). *The transformation of governance: Public administration for twenty-first century America*. Baltimore, MD: Johns Hopkins University Press.

Lawrence, T. B. (2008). Power, institutions and organizations. In R. Greenwood, C. Oliver, K. Sahlin and R. Suddaby (eds.), *The SAGE handbook of organizational institutionalism* (pp. 170–197). Thousand Oaks, CA: SAGE.

Layzer, J. A. (2008). *Natural experiments: Ecosystem-based management and the environment*. Cambridge, MA: The MIT Press.

McKinney, M., and Field, P. (2008). Evaluating community-based collaboration on federal lands and resources. *Society and Natural Resources*, 21(5), 419–429.

Meyer, J. W., and Rowan, B. (1977). Institutionalized organizations: Formal structure as myth and ceremony. *American Journal of Sociology*, 83(2), 340–363.
Ministry of Labour and Social Affairs (2011). Joint responsibility for a good and decent working life. Oslo: Report to the Storting. Meld. St. 29.
Oliver, C. (1997). Sustainable competitive advantage: Combining institutional and resource-based views. *Strategic Management Journal*, 18(9), 697–713.
Ostrom, E. (1990). *Governing the commons: The evolution of institutions for collective action*. Cambridge, UK: Cambridge University Press.
Otto, J. M. (2010). *Sharia incorporated: A comparative overview of the legal systems of twelve Muslim countries in past and present*. Amsterdam: Amsterdam University Press.
Paquet, G. (2004). *The governance of sustainability: a social learning approach*. Ottawa: First National Capital Colloquium on the Governance of Sustainable Development.
Paquet, G. (2007). Intelligent accountability. *Optimum Online: The Journal of Public Sector Management*, 37(3), 1–15.
Pew Research Center (2015, 27 April). Mixed view of impact of long-term decline in union membership. Retrieved from http://www.people-press.org/2015/04/27/mixed-views-of-impact-of-long-term-decline-in-union-membership/
Pfeffer, J. (1981). *Power in organizations*. Marshfield, MA: Pitman.
Phillips, N., Lawrence, T. B., and Hardy, C. (2000). Inter-organizational collaboration and the dynamics of institutional fields. *Journal of Management Studies*, 37(1), 23–43.
Provan, K. G., Kenis, P. N., and Human, S. E. (2008). Legitimacy building in organizational networks. In L. B. Bingham and R. O'Leary (eds.), *Big ideas in collaborative public management* (pp. 121–137). Armonk, NY: M. E. Sharpe.
Purdy, J. M. (2012). A framework for assessing power in collaborative governance processes. *Public Administration Review*, 72(3), 409–417.
State News Service (2015, 4 June). Wild Olympics: Senator Murray and Representative Kilmer renew push to designate wilderness, protect rivers on Olympic Peninsula. Washington Newswire.
Thornton, P. H., and Ocasio, W. (2008). Institutional logics. In R. Greenwood, C. Oliver, K. Sahlin and R. Suddaby (eds.), *The SAGE handbook of organizational institutionalism* (pp. 99–128). Thousand Oaks, CA: SAGE.
Thornton, P. H., Ocasio, W., and Lounsbury, M. (2012). *The institutional logics perspective: A new approach to culture, structure and process*. New York: Oxford University Press.
Twidale, S., and Chestney, N. (2013, 21 November). Green groups quit Warsaw climate talks over lack of progress. Retrieved from http://www.reuters.com/article/2013/11/21/us-climate-talks-ngo-idUSBRE9AK0OM20131121#Ic7HKyOl75pOkoaI.97
Underwood, D. A., Friesner, D., and Cross, J. (2014). Toward an institutional legitimation of sustainability. *Journal of Economic Issues*, 48(3), 871–885.
Walker, P. A., and Hurley, P. T. (2004). Collaboration derailed: The politics of 'community-based' resource management in Nevada County. *Society and Natural Resources*, 17(8), 735–751.
Weber, M., Gerth, H. H., and Mills, C. Wright (1946). *From Max Weber: Essays in sociology*. New York: Oxford University Press.
Wijen, F., and Ansari, S. (2007). Overcoming inaction through collective

institutional entrepreneurship: Insights from regime theory. *Organization Studies*, 28(7), 1079–1100.
Wood, D. J., and Gray, B. (1991). Toward a comprehensive theory of collaboration. *The Journal of Applied Behavioral Science*, 27(2), 139–162.

PART IV

Organizations, stakeholders and governance

12. Collaboration across boundaries in the Indian Forest Service

Daniel H. Nelson, Rosemary O'Leary, Larry D. Schroeder, Misty Grayer and Nidhi Vij

COLLABORATION ACROSS BOUNDARIES IN THE INDIAN FOREST SERVICE

Collaboration has been touted as an effective leadership and management strategy to help solve issues that span boundaries (O'Leary et al., 2006). The forest sector in most countries, but particularly in India, provides excellent examples of problems that span boundaries that cannot be solved by single organizations. Thus, the Indian Forest Service (IFS) should be a fertile environment for collaboration. At the same time, there are many reasons why some members of the IFS are unwilling or unable to engage in collaborative endeavors. The objective of this chapter is to provide a balanced analysis of the use of collaborative management and leadership strategies by senior officials of the IFS with an emphasis on the challenges of collaboration.

We begin with a brief review of the literature that guided our research concerning why people, organizations, and jurisdictions collaborate, followed by an overview of the context of forest management in India, emphasizing the types of issues commonly faced by higher level executives in the IFS. (For a full discussion of the literature on the challenges to collaboration, see Chapter 1 of this book.) We then present and discuss our findings based on a survey of 180 senior officials in the IFS. The chapter concludes with a summary of our major findings concerning the challenges of collaboration, a new "Need-Attitude-Skillset" theory of collaboration, and a discussion of future directions for collaborative public management research.

WHY COLLABORATION MIGHT OR SHOULD OCCUR BASED ON THE LITERATURE

Today the term "collaboration" is widely used in all sectors around the world—public, private, and nonprofit. In line with Agranoff and McGuire's work (2003), we define collaboration as the process of facilitating and operating in multi-organizational arrangements to solve problems that cannot be solved or easily solved by single organizations, and add that collaboration can include the public. Vangen et al. (2015) and Vangen and Huxham (2003) call this the difference between collaborative governance and governing collaborations.

Several practical and theoretical reasons account for the increase in public and nonprofit collaboration both in the literature and in practice. First, on the practical side, most challenges are complex and larger than the purview of one organization, requiring new approaches to addressing public issues. Think of any major public policy challenge: housing, poverty, economic development, education, pollution, to name a few. In order to address any one of these challenges effectively, a "full court press" is needed with collaboration across boundaries (Huxam, 1993; O'Leary et al., 2006). Indeed, prior research tells us that organizations may collaborate in order to maximize *collaborative advantage*, which may result when agencies collaborate to produce creative and innovative solutions that one agency alone could not produce (Huxham, 1993).

Second, the desire to improve the effectiveness and performance of programs encourages public and nonprofit leaders, in particular, to identify new ways of providing services (Agranoff and McGuire, 2001; Bingham and O'Leary, 2008; Goldsmith and Kettl, 2009; O'Leary and Bingham, 2009). A limited body of literature concludes that collaboration may have an impact on management, program, and client outcomes (see, e.g., Gazley et al., 2010; Choi and Choi, 2012; Selden et al., 2006).

Third, technology is helping public and nonprofit organizations and personnel share information in a way that is integrative and interoperable, with the outcome being a greater emphasis on collaboration (Pardo et al., 2010). Finally, citizens are seeking additional avenues for engaging in governance, which can result in new and different forms of collaborative problem-solving and decision-making (Nabatchi et al., 2012; O'Leary et al., 2006).

On the theoretical side, there are many reasons why public and nonprofit organizations collaborate, despite the fact that most scholars of interorganizational collaboration agree that organizations prefer autonomy to interdependence (Bryson et al., 2006; Hudson et al., 1999; Rogers and Whetten, 1982). *Resource dependency* is the most well developed theory of interorganizational partnership. The basic assumption of resource dependency theory is that individual organizations do not have all the resources they need to achieve their goals, and, thus, must acquire resources, such as money, people, support services, technological knowledge, and other inputs, in order to survive (Pfeffer and Salancik, 1978). That is, organizations must rely on a variety of inputs from the collection of interacting organizations, groups, and people in the external environment (Gazley and Brudney, 2007; Mitchell, 2014; Sowa, 2009).

As a consequence of resource-dependent activities, exchange relationships develop (Levine and White, 1961). Although resource exchange theory is based on the notion of dependency, even relatively independent organizations may collaborate to take advantage of available resources (Ansell and Gash, 2007; Emerson et al., 2012; Foster and Meinhard, 2002; Gazley and Brudney, 2007; Graddy and Chen, 2006; Gray, 1989; Gray and Wood, 1991; Mitchell, 2014; Pfeffer and Salancik, 1978; Sowa, 2009).

A second reason found in the literature to suggest why organization leaders choose to collaborate is *common purpose*. Organizations form network linkages in order to achieve similar, compatible, or congruous goals (e.g. Gray, 1989; Rogers and Whetten, 1982). Issues that were previously thought of as single agency issues are now increasingly understood to have broad linkages and to be interconnected with other issues (Bryson et al., 2006; O'Leary et al., 2006). Accordingly, many groups or organizations have some partial responsibility to address public challenges (Crosby and Bryson, 2005) and are using collaboration to do so.

Related to common purpose is the notion of *shared beliefs*. A similarity in values and attitudes make the formation of interorganizational linkages more probable (Aldrich, 1979; Alter and Hage, 1993) and make these linkages more stable over time (Van de Ven et al., 1975). A common belief system, including norms, values, perceptions, and worldviews, provides "the principal 'glue' to hold together networks of actors" (Fleishman, 2009; Sabatier, 1993, p. 27).

In addition to shared beliefs, organizations also sometimes pursue their *political interests* through collaborative arrangements (Gazley and Brudney, 2007; Heclo, 1978; Kickert et al., 1997; Mitchell, 2014; Sabatier, 1993; Sowa, 2009). Through participation in a policy network, for example, organizations may promote the views or desires of their members or constituency; gain access to political officials or decision processes and cultivate political alliances; gain political legitimacy or authority; and promote organizational policies or programs.

Catalytic actors, or leadership both within the organization and by network leaders or coordinators, can provide other important incentives for the formation of collaborative linkages (Agranoff and McGuire, 2001; Bardach, 1998; Kickert et al., 1997; O'Leary et al., 2012). Thus, individuals acting as leaders or catalysts may provide incentives for organizations to collaborate (Emerson et al., 2012). Sometimes this takes the form of an individual whose sense of what it means to be a highly professional actor includes the imperative to collaborate (McGuire, 2009).

SETTING THE STAGE: FOREST MANAGEMENT IN INDIA

Inherent in forest management around the world are tensions related to defining the benefits of the forest, identifying who can claim these benefits, and how these benefits are allocated among numerous stakeholders. The fact that the effect of these decisions is manifested over an exceptionally long duration only serves to add a further degree of complexity to an already difficult situation. In such instances, one might anticipate that collaborative problem-solving could be utilized as an effective leadership and management strategy in addressing these challenges.

Balancing multiple competing claims for the conservation and sustainable use of the forest and wildlife is center to the challenges faced by the IFS. The IFS is placed in the difficult and important position of both administering national policy that addresses large global and national spanning issues, such as climate change, while also serving as the public face for government regarding environmental matters and the literal "face" of government with forest-dependent communities. It is important to remember that while some issues have drastically changed in the recent past, the roots of many of these challenges stem from the allocation of property rights and the tension between the "state" and forest-dependent communities. The 1988 Forest Policy and the Joint Forest Management resolution of 1990 can be viewed as more recent attempts to devolve power by delegating responsibilities and rights to "participatory committees" at the village level, although there is concern that these committees are tightly controlled by government staff and do not always represent the actual users of the forest (Sundar, 2001).

Finally, it is important to note that the work undertaken by the IFS is taking place in a rapidly evolving environment of both state and non-state actors. An increasing number of domestic and international NGOs, with their own goals and objectives related to the forests and wildlife, has entered the stage (Ebrahim, 2001) and the IFS is increasingly relying on them to work with local forest-dependent communities (Daftary, 2014). The press and other social media outlets are proving to be a voice that can challenge government policies. The desired economic growth of this large and increasingly populous country will further escalate the need to develop policies that address conflicting demands from various government ministries and departments on India's natural resources. Where the IFS once operated as a soloist, serving as one of the stronger and more respected voices representing environmental issues in India, it now finds itself part of a large choir and accompanying orchestral arrangement that requires the service to identify new ways to find and more effectively contribute its voice.

The pressure to pursue economic development in an environmentally sustainable way is one of the key challenges faced by the government of India today (Planning Commission, Government of India, 2013). The challenges are enormous, as a recent report credits environmental degradation costing India US$80 billion per year or 5.7 percent of its economy (World Bank, 2014). The report goes on to recommend that India needs to value its natural resources and ecosystem services to better inform policy and decision-making.

In an effort to develop a consistent policy arena that allowed for a unified approach to these difficult challenges, the National Environmental Policy was created in 2006 to extend the coverage and help fill in the gaps of several pre-existing policies including the National Forest Policy, 1988; the National Conservation Strategy and Policy Statement on Environment and Development, 1992; the Policy Statement on Abatement of Pollution, 1992; the National Agriculture Policy, 2000; the National Population Policy, 2000; and the National Water Policy, 2002. The breadth of these various policies demonstrates the need for collaboration among multiple government agencies to address boundary spanning environmental issues (Ministry of Environment and Forests, 2006). In fact the National Environmental Policy states:

> Conservation of the environment requires the participation of multiple stakeholders, who may bring to bear their respective resources, competencies, and perspectives, so that the outcomes of partnerships are superior to those of each acting alone. Implementing and policy making agencies of the Government, at Central, State, Municipal, and Panchayat levels; the legislatures and judiciary; the public and private corporate sectors; financial institutions; industry associations; academic and research institutions; independent professionals and experts; the media; youth clubs; community based organizations; voluntary organizations; and multilateral and bilateral development partners, may each play important roles in partnerships for the formulation, implementation, and promotion of measures for environmental conservation.

In an effort to better address pressing intersectional environmental issues that require collaboration among various government departments, the Government of India is exploring the establishment of a Department of Environment in the States, inter-ministerial standing committees and working groups in specific environmental domains at the central and state government levels, as well as a high-powered body called the National Environment and Forestry Council (NEFC) with the Prime Minister as the chairperson, and State Environment and Forest Councils (SEFCs) to align efforts at the state level (Planning Commission, Government of India, 2013).

THE INDIAN FOREST SERVICE

While the Ministry of Environment, Forestry and Climate Change is the government organization in charge of planning, promoting, and overseeing the implementation of policies pertaining to the environment, it is the responsibility of the IFS to implement these policies. The IFS is mandated with the implementation of India's National Forest Policy, while the responsibility for managing the forests, the charge of the provincial governments since 1935, remains with the State Forest Departments under the direction of their respective state governments (Ministry of Environment, Forests and Climate Change (MoEFCC), 2015). It is important to note, however, that the senior positions of all the State Forest Departments are headed by IFS officers. Hence, a primary determinant of the extent of collaboration in the forestry and related environmental sectors depends greatly on the perceptions of higher-ranking officers within the IFS regarding its efficacy and the challenges of its implementation.

India has a record of forest management through a public administration system that spans more than 150 years. The IFS, re-constituted in 1966 under the All India Service Act, 1951, provides forestry services throughout the country through the allocation of officers to 24 state and joint-state cadres that manage the forests under the respective state governments. The IFS is the newest and smallest member of the All India Services of the Indian government, which consists of the Indian Administrative Service and Indian Police Service, and is currently authorized to have a strength of 3,131 officials (IFS, 2015), although the present strength is 2,646 (Civil List, 2015). The career of an IFS officer will largely consist of serving in senior leadership positions within various levels of the state and central government. While initially established to manage, protect, and develop the forest, the IFS has seen its responsibilities expand to include a number of inter-sectoral issues such as environmental conservation, rural development, wildlife management, and social forestry.

IFS officials are career civil servants. There are only two ways to join the IFS. The most direct route is achieved through the all-India-level competitive examination that is conducted by the Union Public Service Commission, which consists of a written examination, an interview, a walking test (25 km for men and 14 km for women in four hours in Delhi Zoological Park) and a standard medical fitness test (IGNFA, 2015; and rule NO. 17011/03/200-IFS-II (Ministry of Environment and Forests (MoEF), 2001)).The second, and less direct, route is through promotion and appointment within the State Forest Services. As per regulation, two-thirds of the IFS is reserved for "direct recruits" who score well on the UPSC examination with the remainder reserved for "promotes" from the State Forest Service (IFS, 2015). Given the extremely competitive recruitment process, the minimum requirement of a bachelor's degree is often exceeded with the bulk of all recruits holding postgraduate degrees, particularly in the areas of science, engineering, agriculture and forests (IGNFA, 2015). Once an individual is recruited, they attend an extensive induction training program under the direction of the Indira Gandhi National Forest Academy (IGNFA), which serves as the staff college for the IFS with an original focus on the training of promotees, but which has relatively recently expanded its management of a more robust mid-career training effort. While extremely competitive to enter, promotions within the service are largely a function of the officers' time in the service rather than primarily on merit.

In a previously published study Kumar et al. (2007) concluded that "attitudinal inertia" of members of the IFS make them resistant to collaborative management techniques. Their study focused on forest managers in four Indian states—Andhra Pradesh, Haryana, Himachal Pradesh and West Bengal—and specifically on the attitudes of those managers towards the implementation of community-based forest management (CBFM). CBFM requires a great deal of participation by local communities in or nearby forests and, hence, requires a collaborative approach to management. Thus, their findings based on multivariable analysis of manager attitudes using personality, organizational, external environmental, and socialization factors suggest that, despite its potential advantages, members of the IFS may perceive collaboration—at least collaboration with the public—negatively.

RESEARCH QUESTIONS

Our research approach was inductive and exploratory in an attempt to answer several questions; two of which are the subject of this chapter: (1) To what extent, if any, do senior IFS officers use collaboration as a management and leadership strategy? (2) If they do use collaboration as a management and leadership strategy, what are consequences of, and challenges to, those collaborations?

Based on the literature and our familiarity with the IFS we entered the research with some a priori expectations. First, we thought some officers would use collaboration as a management and leadership strategy, but on a very limited basis given the hierarchical and regimented organization culture in which they work. Second, we anticipated that a strong explicit mandate from a superior in the agency, a formal department policy, or Parliamentary Act would be needed to catalyze collaboration. Third, we expected that relational (people) factors would be the greatest impediment to collaboration. Fourth, we anticipated that IFS officers would indicate that the skillset of the successful collaborator in their environment would primarily entail the ability to wield strong positional power and authority.

DATA AND METHOD

The data used in our analysis were collected from senior IFS officers over the period from April 2012 through May 2014. The officers were all attending executive training sessions at the Maxwell School, Syracuse University. Paper surveys were distributed to each officer prior to the inauguration of the training program. Thus the responses reflect only their opinions and experiences with collaborative leadership prior to the program.

The surveys consisted of 12 open-ended questions concerning the respondent's experience with and perception of collaborative management and leadership along with 12 close-ended questions. The bulk of these questions had been previously used in analyses of senior civil servants and leaders in the U.S. federal government Senior Executive Service (SES) by O'Leary and Gerard (2012a) and local governments through the International City/County Management Association (ICMA) by O'Leary and Gerard (2013). The questions ultimately included were first pre-tested on a group of 83 senior civil servants in the Government of India, including 19 members of the IFS. A code-book was constructed to ensure that the codes assigned to the various open-ended responses would be consistent across the coders.

The resulting data set consists of 180 observations from the IFS officers. Each of the senior IFS officers who participated in the training had generally been in the IFS for 26–28 years and therefore had extensive management experience. In a similar vein, none of the respondents was younger than 45 years with nearly 90 percent of the participants in the 46–55 year age range. The respondents were predominantly male (probably reflecting the hiring practices of the government during the mid-1980s) with only about 8 percent female. All of the participants in the survey have university degrees with many having earned advanced degrees. The participants also represent 25 Indian states. These demographic and experience characteristics are, therefore, quite different from the participants in the Kumar et al. (2007) study where "forest managers" in only four states were included in the study. The participants in the analysis here have job titles such as "Conservator of Forests" (CF), "Chief Conservator of Forests" (CCF), or "Additional Principal Chief Conservator of Forests" (APCCF). As such, they are serving in key senior leadership positions, dealing with a wide range of natural resource management issues that definitely would suggest that with their responsibilities, collaborative leadership and management qualifications are needed.

FINDINGS

Forest Service officials surveyed agreed that many activities and responsibilities of the department cannot be fulfilled without collaboration. Collaboration generally is seen by these public servants as a strategy to solve complex environmental and sustainability-related challenges arising in issues that go beyond just managing wildlife and their habitats. Examples include common property resources and global climate change. In the Indian context, human dimensions play an important role, and, therefore, in the conservation of forests, it is essential that issues such as rural livelihood, security, and participatory governance of resources are also addressed. Thus, a collaborative approach often involves local governments, district administration, nonprofit organizations, and civil society organizations. These ideas were echoed in the 2013 Twelfth Year Plan where it was urged that managers of the environment and the forests have to work in tandem with different Ministries including Agriculture, Revenue, Rural Development, Panchayati Raj, Tribal Affairs, and Renewable Energy, to name a few (Planning Commission, Government of India, 2013).

In our study, 92 percent of the forest officials we surveyed said they use collaboration as a management strategy. These officers perceived collaboration as a potential means of protecting, conserving, and managing sustainable forests and increasing the livelihoods of forest dependent communities. The remaining officers were split between those who did not collaborate because they felt there was no need to do so based on their current job duties (5 percent) and 3 percent who did not respond to the question. Those who said they did not collaborate clarified that their current positions were focused on specific duties, such as handling satellite data of forests, or were on central deputation to other departments, and therefore did not require collaboration. One non-collaborating respondent

Table 12.1 Reasons to collaborate

Reason to collaborate	Responses (%)
Impact: Improve outcomes by leveraging resources and catalyzing innovations	42
Process: Improve the techniques used to solve problems	19
Mandate: Implicit in the organization's culture, or explicit mandates from a superior or agency policy	13
Relational: A way to build better relationships and credibility	8
Other and miscellaneous	18

expressed his view that collaboration can be done only at the central government level.

When reviewing the responses of IFS officers who reported choosing collaboration as a management and leadership strategy, four main categories emerged for why they would choose to collaborate, in the following order, with a fifth category comprised of many different "miscellaneous" reasons (Table 12.1).

Forty-two percent of the officials said that collaboration could yield better outcomes than traditional command and control/hierarchical management strategies. They indicated that collaboration can lead to more effective and efficient utilization of resources, and promote new ideas and innovation in inputs, outcomes, and processes. This can lead to more effective goal achievement in comparison to working alone, they told us. The forest officials indicated that collaboration could address mutual deficiencies of organizations and could create synergies. It could be an opportunity to access resources, knowledge, expertise, and experiences available outside the organization. They described real and potential opportunities to leverage financial resources, jump-start new and diverse ideas for addressing complex issues, and develop sustainable technologies. Collaboration is preferred, they said, when the scale of the problem is large and overlaps political and geographic boundaries (e.g. when dealing with issues involving communities located inside the core zone of national parks and sanctuaries) and when challenges are seen as impossible to be effectively addressed by a single authority. Box 12.1 contains two examples of collaboration with the intent of fostering better outcomes found in their survey responses.

Further, 19 percent of the respondents saw collaboration as a way to improve problem-solving and learning, and to build capacity for themselves and the organization. IFS officials collaborate with the central and state governments and technical experts from different fields such as corporations,

BOX 12.1 COLLABORATION WITH THE INTENT OF FOSTERING BETTER OUTCOMES (EXCERPTS FROM SURVEY RESPONSES)

"Participatory Watershed Management was initiated through collaboration between the social forestry department and farmers in two districts of Maharashtra-Raigad and Yavatmal. The objective was to enhance the livelihood of farmers through effective management of land and water resources. It started through constant dialogues and organizing awareness campaigns and training for the farmers and the field staff."

***

"In an eco-restoration and livelihood security project in Kerala [the southern Indian state] forest, revenue, police, and local government departments were to collaborate. The project director reached out to various departments in order to solicit resources for a common good. The organization that led in the process is known as Attappady Hills Area Development Society (AHADS). The project was funded by the Japan Bank for International Cooperation (JBIC)."

nonprofit organizations, village administrations, and local committees. The best collaborations enable them to understand problems and issues from different perspectives and allow for mutual feedback. The IFS officials reported collaborating with research institutes and universities to advance forest research and development. Box 12.2 contains the most salient examples of collaboration for problem-solving found in the survey responses.

IFS collaboration can also be mandated. Explicit mandates can come from an employer, formal ministry policy, and parliament. However, the vast majority of IFS officials who indicated mandates as a reason to collaborate wrote about implicit mandates rooted in personal beliefs of the "right thing to do," as well as organization values, culture, or mission statements, as opposed to explicit mandates stemming from employers or ministry directives. See Box 12.3 for excerpts from survey responses and Box 12.4 for information about Joint Forest Management, a specific case of mandated intersectoral collaboration.

Only 8 percent of the senior forest officials queried said that collaboration can also improve relations. Challenges which come from the bureaucratic administrative structure of the IFS limit the scope of collaboration. Working within the Ministry and adhering to directives from above at times poses constraints. The nature of work may be limited to coordinating activities between different departments. Attempts to collaborate are hindered when other departments do not respond as expected. At times a pervasive "silo culture" of working in government departments makes collaboration a difficult proposition, see Box 12.5.

BOX 12.2 COLLABORATION WITH THE INTENT OF FOSTERING PROBLEM-SOLVING (EXCERPTS FROM SURVEY RESPONSES)

"The Forest Department (FD) officials collaborated with non-profit organizations in a drive to save injured birds during the uttarayan (kite) festival in Gujarat. The FD became instrumental in bringing together non-profit organizations at a common table for the cause. Technology such as internet and mobile phones were used to inform and spread awareness through text messages and websites. A voluntary helpline was set up for information sharing, receiving people's calls and transferring those calls to volunteers to pick up injured birds at the nearest established hospitals."

***

"Forest Protection is a major and serious problem. Gangs of smugglers cut down forest trees to earn quick money. The problem cannot be solved by the department alone. It started by dialogue and discussion with villagers and resulted in the formation of Joint Forest Protection Committees in 78 villages. NGOs were given the power of governance and accountability. Villagers came out in large numbers to stop illegal activities as villages are located in and around forests."

***

"The Forest Department in Gujarat collaborated with the Wildlife Trust of India, the Coast Guard, and Tata Chemical Industries Limited to protect whale sharks. Whale Sharks have come under threat due to large-scale fishing. Religious leaders, political leaders, fisheries, maritime boards, police and revenue departments were also included in the collaborative network."

WHAT MAKES COLLABORATION WORK?

Senior IFS officers face a tide of challenges. With a finite budget, they need to balance long-term ecological goals with short-term political objectives, while confronting the swelling needs of an increasing population. Given the complexities of this situation, we desired to learn what senior leadership within the IFS think about the factors that affect whether a collaboration will be successful or not. The top factors which IFS officers credited as playing a significant role for successful collaboration were communication, trust, and motivation. These factors were closely followed by the value of a common ideology or mission among collaborators, supportive governance, and strong leadership. Less frequently referenced were the size or scale of the collaborative effort or the need for strong authority. See Figure 12.1.

BOX 12.3 MANDATED COLLABORATION (EXCERPTS FROM SURVEY RESPONSES)

	Implicit mandates
Personal belief	"Collaboration across sectors is the need of the hour in the present context of governance if delivery of services is to be guaranteed to the citizens."
Organization culture	"Collaboration is one of the management strategies because protection and conservation of the forest requires support from people at large and from different government departments like the finance department, police, and administration."
Mission/value	"We as government cannot work in isolation, government works for people. Being in social forestry, we have to work outside government forests in community or private lands."
	"[Our job is] to implement cross-sectional programs like forestation on non-forestry lands, watershed programs which extend beyond boundaries, (and) people-oriented programs where the village/block is a unit of implementation."
	Explicit mandates
Directive	"Collaboration with other agencies is decided by the board of directors of . . . . in accordance with the by-laws of the organization."
	"Collaboration is done by the Central Government of India."

BOX 12.4 MANDATED COLLABORATION: JOINT FOREST MANAGEMENT AND PLANNING (EXCERPT FROM SURVEY RESPONSES)

"The objective was to develop a forest sector policy and strategy for the state. A policy analysis and planning unit was set up and it was decided to have a multidisciplinary approach to various aspects affecting the forest sector – land and water – and in consultation with all stakeholders. Land using departments, such as Agriculture, Horticulture, Animal Husbandry, Forests, Planning and ultimate end users – local communities – including NGOs, CBOs, and politicians, were included."

BOX 12.5 CONSTRAINTS TO COLLABORATION (EXCERPTS FROM SURVEY RESPONSES)

"It (collaboration) gives new ideas, opportunities to solve problems within your own organization. However, the scope is limited. In the Forest Service everything is regimented. Most of the time, we work within the department and cope with the orders coming from top. In rare cases we collaborate with Rural Development, Police, and the Revenue Department."

***

"[A]t the government level, there is a habit of working within your own compartment. So collaboration becomes a difficult proposition. It requires an open mind and an enabling atmosphere to collaborate. Both are in short supply in the government set up."

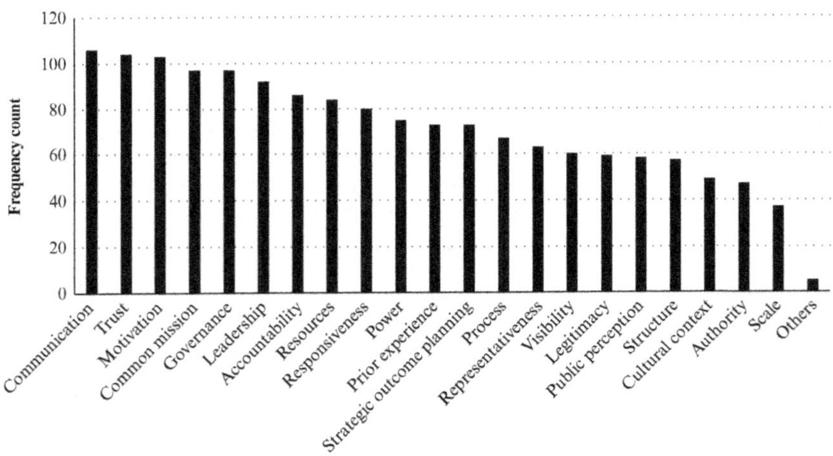

Figure 12.1 Factors affecting the success of collaboration reported by senior IFS officials

NEGATIVE CONSEQUENCES OF COLLABORATION

The popularity of collaboration implies advantage, but this is not always the case. Our IFS respondents also recognized that the consequences of collaboration are not always positive. Table 12.2 summarizes four general categories of negative effects of collaborative efforts. Although there was not a substantial difference in the relative sizes of these general categories, relational issues (e.g. conflicts and erosion of trust) were most often mentioned among the negative effects of

Table 12.2 Negative consequences of collaboration

Negative consequences of collaboration	Responses (%)
Relational issues including conflicts and erosion of trust	30
Impeding of process due to time needed and burden it places on collaborating participants	27
Poor outcomes including suboptimal results, loss of resources, and interests that go unfulfilled	20
Other and miscellaneous	23

collaboration. Quite a few respondents specifically mentioned that, in spite of efforts to collaborate, these efforts still led to conflicts including interorganizational conflicts. Respondents also stated that the collaborative process can be very time-consuming and slow and, therefore, inefficient.

CHALLENGES TO COLLABORATION

While the participants recognized that there can be both positive and negative consequences from collaboration, it is also clear from their responses that they perceived that the challenges in establishing and sustaining inter-departmental and inter-sectoral collaborations in India are great (Saxena, 2007). IFS officers struggle with limited fiscal and human resources within a rigid and hierarchical organizational structure that prioritizes existing processes over change (Rastogi, 1999; Sundar, 2001). There can be significant misalignment of stakeholder interests based on many things, including organizational cultures (O'Leary and Vij, 2012b), as well as the time horizons for realizing outcomes of a common mission. It is the case that stakeholders are many and the accountability of individual stakeholders can be low, which may further delay the decision-making and mask the progress and desires of committed individuals. This entire situation is further complicated by a complex political environment along with frequent transfers of IFS officers between positions that has a negative effect on communication and trust with stakeholders.

We reviewed our findings with other non-surveyed IFS officers and other key informants. These additional interactions indicated that the major barriers to collaboration are concentrated at the implementation stage. The large number of stakeholders, multiple interested parties, and the constant change of representatives for these groups, lead to low trust

Table 12.3 Challenges to collaboration

Challenges to collaboration	Responses (%)
Relational, including reaching consensus and buy-in by stakeholders, lack of mutual trust and lack of communication	32
Organizational, particularly lack of shared mission and goals	21
Personal, particularly the characteristics of the actors	17
Logistical, particularly lack of time and other resources making it difficult to follow up in the process	12
Political, especially ability to set agenda	5
Other and miscellaneous	13

and a lack of transparency. Sometimes the responsibility of an organization to implement a collaborative agreement may shift to a person who does not see the project through to its end. All of these factors can lead to a delay in the decision-making progress and the alienation of some stakeholders. The environment outlined above was sometimes cited as a catalyst for desperate action taken by an IFS officer to push through a specific collaborative agenda, but these results were isolated to specific individuals, times, and conditions and highlight the challenges faced by the system more than the success of an individual project.

Relational and organizational challenges were credited for over 50 percent of all obstacles to collaboration, 32 percent and 21 percent respectively (Table 12.3). Another third was split fairly evenly between logistical constraints (12 percent) and personal constraints (17 percent). Surprisingly, only 5 percent of respondents cited politics as a challenge to collaboration. Given the degree of political involvement in the forestry sector, we are unclear as to why political attributes were hardly noted by respondents as a challenge to collaboration and wish to explore this further in future surveys.

WHAT MAKES AN UNSUCCESSFUL COLLABORATOR?

Much has been written about the skillset of the successful collaborator. People ("relational") are what make collaboration work, yet they are also the major challenge to collaboration, according to the IFS officers we surveyed. This finding is identical to the findings of the SES and ICMA studies of O'Leary and Gerard (2012a, 2013). One way to look at this finding is that a specific collaboration is only as good as the people at the table representing the jurisdictions and organizations. But the role of the individual to make or break collaborations has largely been given short shrift in the literature. Much of the published research is on networks of organizations, with little mention of the fact that while organizations and jurisdictions collaborate, it is always in the form of individuals—an obvious yet important observation. For example, early research by Huxham examined organizations' "collaborative capability" (1993) but emphasized that she was focusing "not on collaboration . . . between individuals, but on collaboration . . . between organizations" (Huxham and Vangen, 1996, p. 1).

Four years later, Huxham shifted her lens to include, in part, the people who represent their organizations in collaborations, writing that the relationships between individual participants in collaborations are often fundamental to getting things done (Huxham and Vangen, 2000, p. 341, 2005, p. 74). In a later work, Huxham explained:

> Collaborations are, of course, enacted by individuals . . . [T]hese individuals are generally linked to the various organizations that form the collaboration. Commonly, they are acting in a representative function. In the course of collaborative activities, such individuals tend implicitly (and often unwittingly) to converse about their aims, and those of their partners at three levels: the level of the collaboration; the level of the participating organizations; and the level of the participating individuals. (Huxham and Vangen, 2005, p. 84)

Indeed, throughout Huxham's large body of pioneering work on collaboration are repeated findings about, and references to, the difficulties and challenges involved for the individuals who represent the organizations that collaborate. This sentiment is echoed by Frederickson (2007). Clearly, the success of collaborations with the IFS are deeply dependent on the knowledge, attitude, motivation, and skillset of the people on the front lines of collaboration.

Tied in with this is the importance of dealing with the conflict that is associated with collaboratively developing and administering policies in a pluralistic society where resources are scarce, population density is high, and demands exceed what any one government official can do. While we expected IFS officers to identify conflict resolution skills including negotiation as important, we did not expect communication skills to be identified as the most important individual attribute of a successful collaborator, but they were. Coming in second was leadership. Coming in third was an open mind.

Among the major challenges to collaboration cited by our informants is what we call the "anti-skillset" or the skillset of the unsuccessful collaborator. A public official who is not an effective communicator, who believes in the "great man" theory of leadership, who refuses to share power and credit, who is not open, who can't build a team, who works without vision and goals, who is untrustworthy, who lacks empathy, and who gives up easily is the "anti-collaborator." In the worst case scenario this person might be dishonest, disrespectful, and believe in "one right way" to solve society's most pressing public problems.

Phrased in the positive, based on our study three factors are needed to overcome barriers to collaboration: need, attitude, and skillset.

Need. IFS officers collaborate on issues that have broad linkages to other organizations and are interconnected with other issues/common purpose. Typically other groups or organizations have some partial responsibility to address, or interest in addressing, parts of the same public challenges. Intricately interwoven with this idea of common purpose is resource dependency: the fact that IFS does not have all the resources it needs to achieve its common goals, and thus, must acquire resources, such as money, people, support services, technological knowledge, and other inputs. Hence, there must be a need to collaborate, but need itself is not enough.

Attitude. The IFS officers we surveyed who report collaborating successfully expressed strong personal motivation to improve government, to positively affect the problem-solving process, to better serve the citizens of India, and to build better relationships. They wrote and spoke in terms of the public interest, a desire to foster improved outcomes and to utilize resources that will benefit the clients they serve: a form of public service motivation (PSM) that surprised us. As most IFS officers are biophysical scientists, we anticipated more technical and scientific rationale for their collaborations, rather than PSM. The PSM literature suggests that officials working in government are attracted to the public sector due to a concern for the public interest, and they are more likely to seek improved outcomes and resources that will benefit the citizen-clients that they serve (Perry and Wise, 1990; Perry et al., 2010). How might they do this in an environment of scarce resources working with others who share a common purpose? One way is by seeking collaborative advantage (Huxham, 1993). When these officers choose collaboration as a management and leadership strategy, it is because they believe that it will produce creative and innovative solutions that one agency could not produce alone. Hence, a passion to serve the public, plus an attitude that sees collaborative advantage, form the second part of the puzzle explaining why IFS officers choose collaboration as a management and leadership strategy. The absence of this attitude can be an impediment to collaboration.

Skillset or Individual Attributes. Our 180 respondents provided a comprehensive list of skills and, more importantly, described the attributes and mindset of the collaborative leader. Successful collaboration requires an individual with an intricate set of relational attributes, including communication skills, leadership skills, and an open mind.

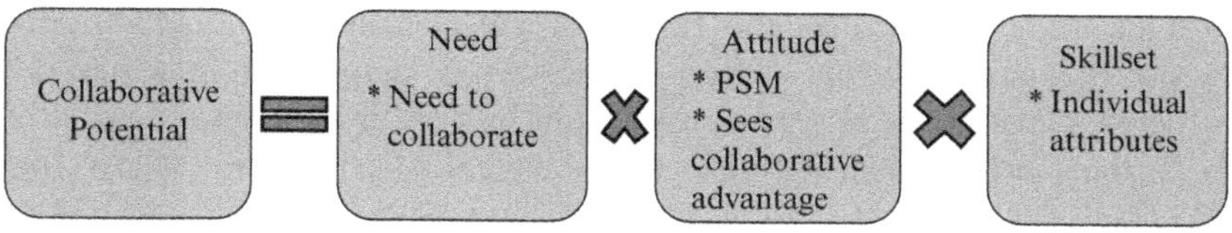

Figure 12.2 The Need-Attitude-Skillset theory of successful collaboration

Putting all this together yields what we call the Need-Attitude-Skillset theory of collaboration. We offer a simple hypothesis for future research, based on this theory: the greater the combined need, attitude and skillset of collaborators, the greater the odds of successful collaboration, see Figure 12.2.

CONCLUSION

This study presents a unique insight, as possibly the only survey available that has explored the perceptions of IFS officers serving in senior positions across India. Our findings produce important contributions to the ongoing discussion of the use of collaboration as a leadership and management strategy to address environmental challenges. To fit the theme of this book, we primarily analyzed the challenges to collaboration in this chapter. Yet, as suggested by the current collaboration and networks literature, an overwhelming majority of the forest officials we surveyed reported using collaboration as a management and leadership strategy. The "ocean" in which they "swim" is one of common purpose and resource dependency. When they are open to collaboration, the attitudes they exhibit are part PSM and part a sense of collaborative advantage. The skillset they tout is a set of individual attributes including effective communication, leadership, and an open mind. In order to collaborate effectively, IFS officers are likely to rely on conflict management skills, which is not surprising in the tumultuous culture of India. It would therefore be beneficial to the IFS to explore options for increasing these topics within their internal training programs.

We proposed a three-part Need-Attitude-Skillset theory of collaboration consisting of: (1) the need to collaborate (e.g. from scarce resources); (2) an attitude consisting of PSM and the ability to see collaborative advantage; and (3) the skillset (personal attributes) to carry it out. We are not arguing that all three parts are needed for successful collaboration. Rather, we hypothesize that the greater the combined need, attitude and skillset, the greater the odds of successful collaboration across boundaries. Conversely, the lower the combined need, attitude and skillset, the less likely the odds of successful collaboration across boundaries.

This study provided insights from senior leaders across India in an area where data are extremely limited. While specific data are from senior IFS officers' perceptions of management and leadership strategies associated with their environmental and forest management efforts, we believe that the results may be generalizable to other All India Services given that these services use a common recruitment process. Our research on the use of collaboration as a management and leadership strategy by IFS officials demonstrates that collaboration can take place even in a regimented, hierarchical institutional environment, but that it is not always successful, as significant impediments exist. More important than strong authority, pressure, and mandates are: (1) a need to collaborate; (2) a passion to serve the public coupled with an attitude that sees collaborative advantage; and (3) the individual skillset to carry out the collaboration.

ACKNOWLEDGMENT

Syracuse University MPA student Tari Lestari and SUNY Environmental Science and Forestry PhD candidate Chandrani Ghosh are thanked for their assistance with this research.

REFERENCES

Agranoff, R. and McGuire, M. (2001). "Big Questions in Public Network Management Research." *Journal of Public Administration Research and Theory*, *11*(3), 295–326.

Agranoff, R. and McGuire, M. (2003). *Collaborative Public Management: New Strategies for Local Governments*. Washington, DC: Georgetown University Press.

Aldrich, H. E. (1979). *Organizations and Environments*. Englewood Cliffs, NJ: Prentice-Hall.

Alter, C. and Hage, J. (1993). *Organizations Working Together*. Newbury Park, CA: Sage.

Ansell, C. and Gash, A. (2007). "Collaborative Governance in Theory and Practice." *Journal of Public Administration Research and Theory*, *18*(4), 543–571.

Bardach, E. (1998). *Getting Agencies to Work Together: The Practice and Theory of Managerial Craftsmanship*. Washington, DC: Brookings Institution.

Bingham, L. B. and O'Leary, R. (eds.). (2008). *Big Ideas in Collaborative Public Management*. Armonk, NY: M. E. Sharpe.

Bryson, J. M., Crosby, B. C., and Stone, M. M. (2006). "The Design and Implementation of Cross-Sector Collaborations: Propositions from the Literature." *Public Administration Review*, *66*(6), 44–55.

Choi, C. G. and Choi, S. O. (2009). "Collaborative Partnerships and Crime in Disorganized Communities." *Public Administration Review*, *72*(2), 228–239.

Civil List for the Indian Forest Service. (2015). Accessed 16 November 2015 from http://ifs.nic.in/record.aspx
Crosby, B. C. and Bryson, J. M. (2005). *Leadership for the Common Good: Tackling Public Problems in a Shared-Power World*. San Francisco, CA: Jossey-Bass.
Daftary, D. (2014). Development in an Era of Economic Reform in India. *Development and Change*, *45*, 710–731. DOI: 10.1111/dech.12101.
Ebrahim, A. (2001). NGO Behavior and Development Discourse: Cases From Western India. *Voluntas: International Journal of Voluntary and Nonprofit Organizations*, *12*(2), 79–101. Retrieved from http://www.jstor.org/stable/27927714
Emerson, K., Nabatchi, T., and Balogh, S. (2012). "An Integrative Framework for Collaborative Governance." *Journal of Public Administration Research and Theory*, *22*(1), 1–29.
Fleishman, F. (2015). "Understanding India's Forest Bureaucracy: A Review." *Regional Environmental Change*, August, 1–13. DOI: 10.1007/s10113-015-0844-8. Retrieved from http://link.springer.com/article/10.1007/s10113-015-0844-8?wt_mc=email.event.1.SEM.ArticleAuthorOnlineFirst#
Fleishman, R. (2009). "To Participate or Not to Participate? Incentives and Obstacles for Collaboration." In R. O'Leary and L. B. Bingham (eds.), *The Collaborative Public Manager*. Washington, DC: Georgetown University Press.
Foster, M. K. and Meinhard, A. G. (2002). "A Regression Model Explaining Predisposition to Collaborate." *Nonprofit and Voluntary Sector Quarterly*, *31*(4), 549–564.
Frederickson, H. G. (2007). "Bureaucrats Without Borders: Public Management and the End of Geography." The Donald C. Stone Lecture at the Annual Conference of the American Society for Public Administration, Washington, DC.
Gazley, B. and Brudney, J. L. (2007). "The Purpose (and Perils) of Government-Nonprofit Partnership." *Nonprofit and Voluntary Sector Quarterly*, *36*(3), 389–415.
Gazley, B., Chang, W. K., and Bingham, L. B. (2010). "Board Diversity, Stakeholder Representation, and Collaborative Performance in Community Mediation Centers." *Public Administration Review*, *70*, 610–620.
Goldsmith, S. and Kettl, D. (2009). *Unlocking the Power of Networks: Keys to High-Performance Government*. Washington, DC: The Brookings Institution.
Graddy, E. A. and Chen, B. (2006). "Influences on the Size and Scope of Networks for Social Service Delivery." *Journal of Public Administration Research and Theory*, *16*(4), 533–522.
Gray, B. (1989). *Collaborating: Finding Common Ground for Multiparty Problems*. San Francisco, CA: Jossey-Bass.
Gray, B. and Wood, D. (1991). "Collaborative Alliances: Moving from Practice to Theory." *Journal of Applied Behavioral Science*, *27*(2), 3–22.
Heclo, H. (1978). "Issue Networks and the Executive Establishment." In A. King (ed.), *The New American Political System*. Washington, DC: American Enterprise Institute for Public Policy Research.
Hudson, B., Hardy, B., Henwood, M., and Winstow, G. (1999). "In Pursuit of Inter-Agency Collaboration in the Public Sector: What is the Contribution of Theory and Research?" *Public Management*, *1*(2), 235–260.
Huxham, C. (1993). "Pursuing Collaborative Advantage." *The Journal of the Operational Research Society*, *44*(6), 599–611.
Huxham, C. and Vangen, S. (1996). "Working Together: Key Themes

in the Management of Relationships Between Public and Non-Profit Organizations." *International Journal of Public Sector Management*, *9*(7), 5–17.

Huxham, C. and Vangen, S. (2000). "Leadership in the Shaping and Implementation of Collaboration Agendas: How Things Happen in a (Not Quite) Joined-up World." *Academy of Management Journal*, *43*(6), 1159–1175.

Huxham, C. and Vangen, S. (2005). *Managing to Collaborate: The Theory and Practice of Collaborative Advantage*. London: Routledge.

IFS (2015). India Forest Service Welcome. Retrieved from http://ifs.nic.in/welcome-full.aspx

IGNFA (2015). Indian Forest Service. Retrieved from http://www.ignfa.gov.in/IndianForestService/tabid/56/language/en-US/Default.aspx

Indian Forest Service (2015). "Indian Forest Service: An Introduction." Retrieved from http://ifs.nic.in/welcomefull.aspx

Kickert, W. J. M., Klijn, E.-H., and Koppenjan, J. (1997). *Managing Complex Networks: Strategies for the Public Sector*. New York and London: Sage.

Kumar, S., Kant, S., and Amburgey, T. L. (2007). "Public Agencies and Collaborative Management Approaches: Examining Resistance Among Administrative Professionals." *Administration and Society*, *39*(5), 569–611.

Levine, S. and White, P. E. (1961). "Exchange as a Conceptual Framework for the Study of Interorganizational Relationships." *Administrative Science Quarterly*, *5*, 583–610.

McGuire, M. (2009). "The New Professionalism and Collaborative Activity in Local Emergency Management." In R. O'Leary and L.B. Bingham (eds.), *The Collaborative Public Manager*. Washington, DC: Georgetown University Press, 71–93.

Ministry of Environment and Forests (MoEF) (2001). Rule No. NO. 17011/03/200-IFS-II-T. Accessed 16 November 2015 at http://www.moef.nic.in/sites/default/files/fellowships/17011%20IFS.pdf Environment Policy

Ministry of Environment and Forests (2006). *National Environment Policy*. New Delhi: Government of India.

Ministry of Environment, Forests and Climate Change (MoEFCC) (2015). About the Ministry. Retrieved from http://www.moef.gov.in/division/ifs.

Mitchell, G. E. (2014). Collaborative propensities among transnational NGOs registered in the United States. *The American Review of Public Administration*, *44*(5), 575–599.

Nabatchi, T., Gastil, J., Weiksner, M., and Leighninger, M. (eds.). (2012). *Democracy in Motion: Evaluating the Practice and Impact of Deliberative Civic Engagement*. New York: Oxford University Press.

O'Leary, R. and Bingham, L. B. (eds.). (2009). *The Collaborative Public Manager*. Washington, DC: Georgetown University Press.

O'Leary, R. and Gerard, C. (2012a). *Collaboration across Boundaries: Insights and Tips from Federal Senior Executives*. Washington, DC: IBM Center for the Business of Government.

O'Leary, R. and Vij, N. (2012b). "Collaborative Public Management: Where Have We Been and Where Are We Going?" *American Review of Public Administration*, *42*, 507–522.

O'Leary, R. and Gerard, C. (2013). "Collaborative Governance and Leadership: A 2012 Survey of Local Government Collaboration." Chapter 6 in the *Municipal Yearbook 2013*. Washington, DC: The International City/County Management Association, 43–56.

O'Leary, R., Gerard, C., and Bingham, L. B. (2006). "Introduction to Special Issue on Collaborative Public Management." *Public Administration Review*, *66*(6), 6–9.
O'Leary, R., Choi, Y., and Gerard, C. (2012). "The Skill Set of the Successful Collaborator." *Public Administration Review*, *72*(s1), 70–83.
Pardo, T. A., Gil-Garcia, R. A., and Luna-Reyes, L. F. (2010). "Collaborative Governance and Cross-Boundary Information Sharing: Envisioning a Networked and IT-Enabled Public Administration." In R. O'Leary, D. Van Slyke, and S. Kim (eds.), *The Future of Public Administration Around the World: The Minnowbrook Perspective*. Washington, DC: Georgetown University Press.
Perry, J. L. and Wise, L. R. (1990). "The Motivational Bases of Public Service." *Public Administration Review*, *50*(3), 367–373.
Perry, J. L., Hondeghem, A., and Wise, L. R. (2010). "Revisiting the Motivational Bases of Public Service: Twenty Years of Research and an Agenda for the Future." *Public Administration Review*, *70*(5), 681–690.
Pfeffer, J. and Salancik, G. R. (1978). *The External Control of Organizations: A Resource Dependence Perspective*. Stanford, CA: Stanford University Press.
Planning Commission – Government of India (2013). *Twelfth Five Year Plan, 2012–2017: Faster, More Inclusive and Sustainable Growth, Volume 1*. New Delhi: Government of India.
Rastogi, A. (1999). "Conflict Resolution: A Challenge for Joint Forest Management in India." *Indian Forester*, *125*(6), 573–580.
Rogers, D. L. and Whetten, D. A. (1982). *Interorganizational Coordination: Theory, Research, and Implementation*. Ames, IA: Iowa State University Press.
Sabatier, P. (1993). "Policy Change Over a Decade or More." In P. A. Sabatier and H. C. Jenkins-Smith (eds.), *Policy Change and Learning: An Advocacy Coalition Framework*. Boulder, CO: Westview Press.
Saxena, N.C. (2007). "Strengthening Environmental Coordination in India." *Sustainable Mountain Development*, *53*, 19–21.
Selden, S. C., Sowa, J. E., and Sandfort, J. (2006). "The Impact of Collaboration in Early Child Care and Education on Management and Program Outcomes." *Public Administration Review*, *66*(3), 412–425.
Sowa, J. E. (2009). "The Collaboration Decision in Nonprofit Organizations: Views From the Front Line." *Nonprofit and Voluntary Sector Quarterly*, *38*(6), 1003–1025.
Sundar, N. (2001). "Is Devolution Democratization?" *World Development Elsevier*, *29*(12), 2007–2023.
Van de Ven, A. H., Emmett, D. C., and Koening, Jr., R. (1975). "Frameworks for Interorganizational Analysis." *Organization and Administrative Sciences*, *5*, 113–129.
Vangen, S. and Huxham, C. (2003). "Enacting Leadership for Collaborative Advantage: Dilemmas of Ideology and Pragmatism in the Activities of Partnership Managers." *British Journal of Management*, *14*(S1), S61–S76.
Vangen, S., Hayes, J. P., and Cornforth, C. (2015). "Governing Cross-Sector, Inter-Organizational Collaborations." *Public Management Review*, *17*(9), 1237–1260.
World Bank (2014). India: Green Growth – Overcoming Environment Challenges to Promote Development. Retrieved from http://www.worldbank.org/en/news/feature/2014/03/06/green-growth-overcoming-india-environment-challenges-promote-development

13. Towards a Joint Maintenance Approach for floodplain management in the Netherlands: tensions and possibilities

Jeroen F. Warner, Jan M. Fliervoet and Antoine J. M. Smits

INTRODUCTION

In 1995 the mid-Netherlands experienced flooding on the river Rhine. Over 200,000 people were pre-emptively evacuated in the southeast Netherlands and bordering areas in Germany. Next to an urgent dike repair programme, the Netherlands decided to make horizontal space for rivers post-flood rather than constrain them more – a rather radical change of direction in a densely populated country. This engendered an extensive planning and implementation programme for Dutch waters: 'Making Space for the River' (2015) (Rijke et al., 2012; Warner et al., 2012). Now that the implementation of the programme of work is about to be finalized, a new phase is called for, the floodplain maintenance phase. This phase is to be embedded in the recently formulated long-term objectives stated in the Dutch Delta Programme, a middle- and long-run strategy (2050–2100) to keep the Netherlands flood- and drought-free in the face of extreme climate-change scenarios.

Actors in Dutch land-use policy know they will continuously encounter each other in different policy domains and in different 'games'. This means they will have to invest in good working relations in addition to substantive negotiation and strategy (Warner et al., 2010). Since the 1970s, a range of stakeholders have demanded and obtained a place at the negotiation table in river planning and implementation. Rivers became valued for more than just their production and drain function, giving rise to multi-functional river widening and deepening projects, while managers now ventured 'behind the dikes' to integrate land and water management (Immink, 2007). River managers learned not to fear or ignore citizens, and new forms of participatory planning developed, such as Radboud University's

Joint Planning Approach (JPA), banking on the strong bonds many people feel with the river (De Groot and Warner, 2011).

While that brought some encouraging results for river interventions, how does this work during the post-implementation stage, and what should be done if this stage produces unforeseen problems? Maintenance of floodplains is a slow and politically unexciting process: it rarely brings photo opportunities, and long-term visioning exceeds customary political horizons. Moreover, maintenance activities in Holland are fragmented as the actor configuration has been changing.

The key problems concerning collaborative governance related to the maintenance of multi-functional floodplains are:

1. absence of a shared vision on how to maintain multi-functional floodplains in the Netherlands (Fliervoet et al., 2013); and
2. the near-absence of collaborative relationships between water agencies and nature conservation organizations (Fliervoet et al., 2016).

We shall illustrate our points with the help of three Dutch case studies, contrasting 'joint' and 'non-joint' maintenance, and completed and non-completed projects:

- Saeftinghe (non-joint, managed by just one nature conservation organization; completed).
- *Munnikenland* (joint collaboration regarding the maintenance; completed).
- *Rijnwaardense Uiterwaarden* (joint collaboration regarding the maintenance; not completed).

The cases comprise recent multi-purpose river rehabilitation programmes in the flood-prone Netherlands. The actors mainly comprise institutional stakeholders, although local actors did not necessarily stay away. Interviews, participant observations, video recordings and reports, including governmental as well non-governmental documents, were used to explore the case studies. Based on these case studies we set out to answer the following research questions:

- Which lessons could be learned from past multi-purpose river rehabilitation programmes to facilitate ongoing and future collaboration concerning the maintenance of multi-functional floodplains?
- (How) can joint planning as a working methodology strengthen collaborative processes in maintaining multi-functional floodplains (Joint Maintenance Approach)?

Briefly, we explore if the working methodology of JPA could be introduced in collaborative processes to strengthen partnerships between diverse actors and sectors in the currently fragmented maintenance of multi-functional floodplains.

BACKGROUND: PARTICIPATION DESPITE CONFLICT

Involving multiple stakeholders provides a kind of safety net by tapping the coping capacity of a wider range of actors in tackling highly complex issues. Integrated or Adaptive Water Management is beset by uncertainties, which makes planning less than linear. In this context, Faysse (2006) notes that public-sector actors tend to have a double rationale for encouraging public involvement: (1) local stakeholders are more knowledgeable about the details of a policy issue, so that tapping their knowledge can improve the quality of the project; (2) multi-stakeholder involvement fosters a support base, which makes it easier for authorities to implement projects, reducing the likelihood of costly public protest and litigation. While this perspective focuses on how an issue can best be 'sold' and governed, policy-affected stakeholders may be more concerned with reducing policy uncertainty, and increasing the chances of a positive benefit in their everyday lives (or resisting negative impact).

Given the contextual developments in Dutch river planning towards integration and adaptivity in the past few decades, top-down planning will not suffice for many water management problems, which present themselves as 'political' or 'wicked', beset by uncertainties, unexpected dynamics and complexities (Kooiman, 1993; from climate change and systemic risk to political oscillations) and disparities over the values of land, water and nature. This has given rise to a deliberative turn in planning (Healey, 1997; Innes and Booher, 2003). At the turn of the century, multi-stakeholder participation and planning reached their heyday, especially in the Netherlands.

As a result, however, Dutch policy-making was slow to get started and hard to stop or change course once given the go-ahead. Short of emergency legislation, any policy plan has to clear many participatory and legislative obstacles to reach the finishing line. This sluggish pace is annoying and potentially costly to all involved, and many would like to find ways to accelerate the planning processes. An obvious candidate would be more straightforward and efficient planning, which suggests more power-driven forms of management. We will first examine an example of a top-down Dutch riverine maintenance arrangement that is *neither* multi-stakeholder nor mono-functional: self-management in the Sunken Land of Saeftinghe.

SAEFTINGHE

In Europe, land owners are supposed to keep a watercourse associated with the land up to a minimum standard, and more recently have received incentives to enhance its environmental quality. In Holland, non-public stakeholders, especially agricultural and nature organizations, are quite well represented in river management. They have the right to 'self-realize' publicly agreed interventions with a view to enhance safety from flooding. In the Netherlands, maintenance activities with regard to flood protection and nature restoration are likewise mostly fragmented, performed on a small scale (land owner scale) and based on single-sectoral perspectives. A wide range of governmental organizations are involved, which indicates the dependency of non-governmental organizations (NGOs), and integrated maintenance objectives are still missing.

An example is the Sunken Land of Saeftinghe, located in the tidal area of the Scheldt estuary, in the Dutch province of Zeeland, right next to Belgium (see Figure 13.1). A protected area under the Ramsar Treaty in 1995, and Natura 2000 in 2009, it is one of the very few European deltas that has a full gradient from salt- to freshwater, and it functions as an important hibernation area for birds. Historically, the reclaimed area's main economic activities have been agriculture and peat extraction, run by private landlords. Saeftinghe was supposed to buffer the city of Antwerp from flooding from the Western Scheldt (Nienhuis, 2008) but it flooded repeatedly and after the particularly destructive All Saints' Flood of 1570 the owners decided not to recover it. Human settlement ended in 1584 when the dikes were cut for strategic reasons: to avoid the cities of Gent, Bruges and Antwerp being occupied by Spanish troops (De Kraker, 1997).

Keeping the area flooded created space for both excess water and for sediment to accrete; a historic example of a 'natural' solution to accommodate flood risk. Due to continued diking, canalization and constant dredging to facilitate deepening the fairway to Antwerp international port, river sediment has no natural accretion space and salt marshes are eroding.

While 2,500 out of the total 3,500 ha area are state owned, the whole territory is run by an environmental management non-profit NGO, Het Zeeuwse Landschap (HZL) (Jacobusse and Decleer, 2003). The area, with a view on the reactors at Doel, across the border in Belgium, has a small marina, but conserving the environment is the key concern. HZL works with social partnerships such as recipients of psychiatric care to maintain

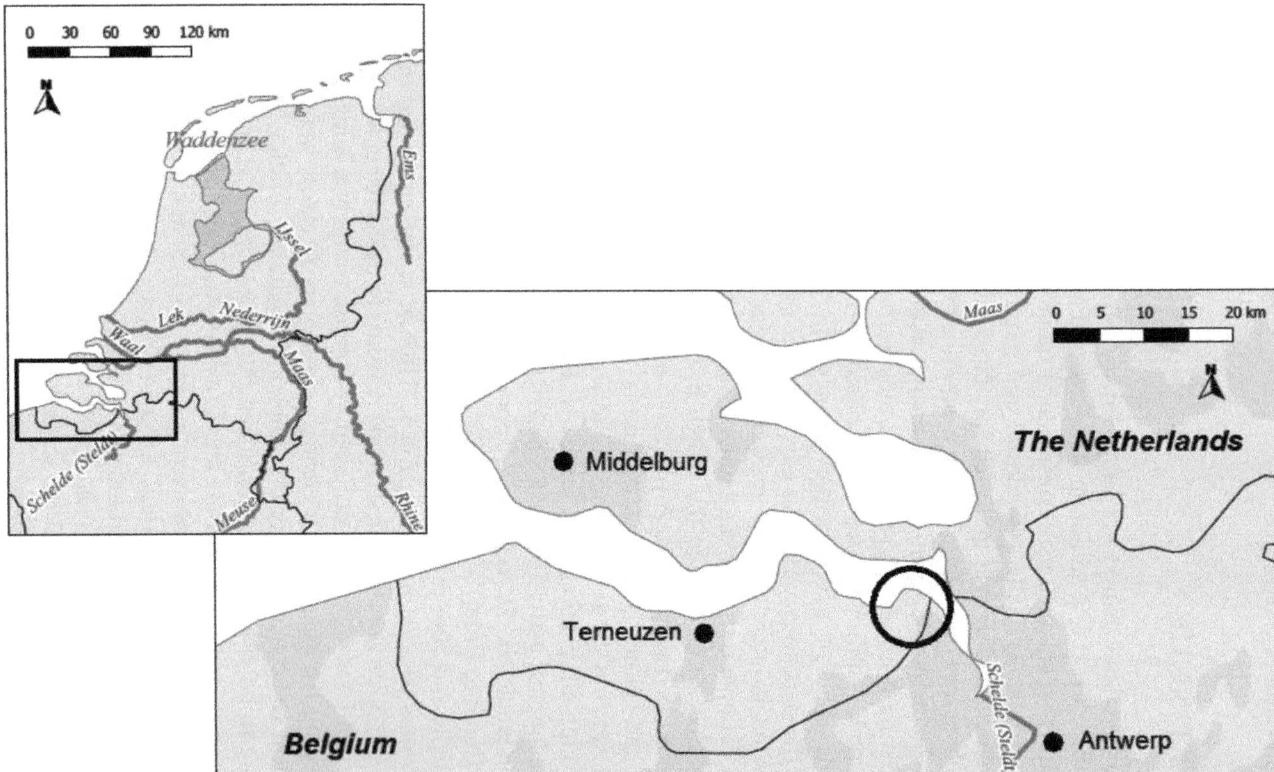

Figure 13.1 *The location of the Sunken Land of Saeftinghe (black circle) near the city of Antwerp in Belgium*

the area.[1] Dutch and Flemish environmental organizations in the HZL headquarters signed the 'Saeftinghe Treaty' for the joint rehabilitation of the transboundary area.

Other local actors however have accused HZL of acting as a commercially minded landlord making deals with local business. In 1995 the landlord of the only local café managed to obtain a monopoly on such services and international business (Dow Chemical, based in nearby Terneuzen). This did not sit well with local farmers and citizens.[2]

As the main attraction of the sparsely inhabited region, ecological tourism has economic importance; HZL promotes ecological tourism, presenting an adventurous group trek through the area at ebb tide. Individuals are banned from the grounds, for their own safety and so as not to disturb plants and animals. Locals from nearby Emmadorp opposed the establishment of a visitor centre, and the fact they lost their right to roam in the natural area (Speelmansgat and De Uitslopen) and need to apply and pay for an entry pass with HZL.

A local stakeholder survey (Muhlig, 2011) suggests that local stakeholders do not appreciate their 'backyard' being run in a top-down, technocratic way by an organization that is not local. Conflicts basically remain unmanaged. However, the small scale and low stakes prevent escalation and promote indifference.

In a larger watercourse, however, used by various stakeholders, this self-management is not so straightforward and governments at various levels tend to engage. Where national levels have given space, lower-level authorities have enthusiastically stepped in. Unlike the national level, these authorities tend to be open to collaborative efforts in land-use planning. This has created opportunities for 'joint maintenance' of floodplains in multi-functional settings in the central Netherlands. Below, we look at two examples of attempts to realize this, mindful of the above considerations.

INTRODUCING THE JOINT PLANNING APPROACH

In the context of the transregional Freude am Fluss project, funded under the Interreg IIIb facility, a Joint Planning Approach (JPA) was developed by Nijmegen University's Centre for the Sustainable Management of Resources (CSMR). The European-funded project developed an approach to truly involve key stakeholders in river management in all planning stages: joint fact-finding, joint design, joint institutions, joint options, joint decision making and joint implementation. The underlying philosophy was that by facing flood risk and people's varying interests in tackling this head-on, participatory arrangements would be possible that provided something for everyone.

Freude am Fluss explored innovative approaches to river management in France, Germany and the Netherlands that do not see flood risk and public engagement as a problem, but as a potential source of enjoyment (*Freude*, in German). In the Netherlands this triggered the creation of *WaalWeelde*. Loosely based on the JPA approach, this integrated multi-actor programme aimed to develop a more natural river landscape enhancing economic performance at a higher level of protection. The programme connected public, private and societal organizations in the planning and implementation phase of multi-functional river management along the intensely navigated River Waal (Smits, 2009).

The JPA is an adaptive planning approach deviating from the top-down model practiced before the 1990s. Prior to this time, rivers were managed based on nationally developed blueprints which needed to be followed to the letter (Table 13.1). Adaptive management in dynamic environments seeks to learn and adjust, 'building the plane while flying it', rather than try to control the system at issue. We found much of the current 'Habermasian' participatory planning literature unrealistic, however. Starting from the community level, it assumes an underlying consensus that can be reached by deliberation (the argumentative turn) involving stakeholders at certain junctures to arrive at something that looks like a consensus – and by doing so this overcomes conflict. While attractive in theory, the deliberative turn is marred by social, practical institutional realities. We therefore contrast our approach with a deliberative design, as a more 'realistic', mixed-mode model (see Table 13.1).

Land-use planning, we find, involves both learning and fighting (Warner and Van Buuren, 2009); it is never entirely win-win. Land-use planning in a densely populated area with contrasting interests is very likely to lead to conflicts, all of which may not be bridgeable. Local interests may be fundamentally at odds with policy-makers' convenience, as well as with each other's (say, farmers vs. environmentalists). This means that reaching consensus is bound to be troublesome. If things go smoothly, a lot of 'social learning' and integrative negotiation will take place; if they don't, there will be 'distributive' phases in which each one fights for their piece of the cake.

People who will be expected to sell or lose their homes or lands may never really forgive planners for their loss. However, it is often possible to arrive at a truce, a *modus operandi*, an agreement to disagree, in which all agree that the procedure is fair even if they may not agree with the distributive outcome.

Despite these conflicting interests, therefore, it still makes sense to engage stakeholders in dialogue throughout the policy process. At worst,

Table 13.1 Comparative summary of approaches

Blueprint approach	Process (JPA) approach	Deliberative approach
Based on authority	Basic sense of trust and sense of interdependence	Shared problem
'Powering'	A mix of 'powering' and 'puzzling'	'Puzzling': power and politics are the problem
Rigid budget and time constraint	Flexible budget and time within limits	Flexible budget and time
Regulated by administrative contract	Regulated by voluntary agreement; adaptable agreement	Regulated by voluntary agreement; adaptable agreement
Output-oriented	Debate-oriented	Consensus-oriented
Rigid budget	Flexible budget	Flexible budget
Clear problem and goals, technical planning to tackle facts	Fuzzier problem and goals, social learning, agreement to disagree	Consensual goals, social learning to tackle (factual and) value differences

Note: This table compares the traditional blueprint approach to land-use planning, the currently popular deliberative ('Habermasian-Rousseauian') approach, and our proposals for a more 'realist' compromise between the two.

Source: After Verhallen and Warner (2007).

they will appreciate being heard and taken seriously, at best, they will feel 'ownership' of the proposed policy. If this leads to conflict, this is not always bad.

Surprisingly in light of the Dutch reputation for deliberative, inclusive planning, the Dutch system turns out not to be very participatory at all from a grass-roots perspective. Participation on policies and projects is usually the business of paid-up employees of NGOs and lobbyists (Wolsink, 2006). Public authorities tend to be unpleasantly surprised by local platforms (Community-Based Organizations) springing up and demanding a say, while they had spent most of their energies getting a range of formal stakeholders in line. These platforms have turned out to be savvy networkers in media, political, academic and bureaucratic circles and have developed successful PR strategies.

A lack of timely communication, consultation and adaptivity, on the part of both governments and local stakeholders have played an important part in conflicts over multi-functional river restoration projects (Warner, 2011). We also need to be mindful of the 'shadow of the past' as a potential conflict shaper and intensifier (Sebastian, 2009): if relations were seriously damaged before, even long ago, its overhang will deeply affect any future planning. For example, in the east Netherlands, conflict over the handling of Foot and Mouth disease in rural areas between public authorities and farmers at the turn of the millennium affected the legitimacy of interventions to Room for the River planned later. It is also not unusual for stakeholders at the implementation stage to keep coming back to discuss/question the principles of the plan while the project team wants to 'get on with it' (Warner, 2011).

Dissent, however, is not fatal to effective land-use planning. Conflict reveals the real state of play better than harmony, and as John Forester (2007) has noted, 'conflict is better than apathy'. Outright conflict may mean the temporary breakdown of communications between parties who see non-negotiation as their BATNA (Best Alternative to a Negotiated Agreement), but if there is a sufficient degree of interdependence between stakeholders, no one will pull out indefinitely (Verhallen et al., 2007; Warner, 2009).

As for deliberative planning, the literature and practice show that stakeholders do appreciate participation, but do not want to be consulted and made responsible for everything all of the time. The top rung on Arnstein's Ladder of Participation (1969), autonomy, is not necessarily considered an ideal end-point of participatory planning. Participation involves transaction and opportunity costs, bringing barriers to non-professional participants (Uphoff et al., 2002). As a fishing-sector stakeholder said in a hearing on the conflictive Jubilee River bypass project on the Thames: 'You are the authorities, tell us what you have in mind and we'll give you our opinion' (cited in Warner, 2011). Deliberative democracy only proves popular in limited doses. People do not want to deliberate about everything and anything: when issues are straightforward, they are likely to refer to the 'experts' and get on with their lives.

The modality of participation in this context is also important. Public participation was frequently translated into the devolution of responsibility to local actors and state retrenchment; the Netherlands is no exception. However, we find that despite a professed hands-off approach, the public sector in continental Europe is not quite prepared to let go, it hangs on to crucial aspects. As a result, multi-stakeholder platforms as a rule are not where decisions are made (Warner, 2007). Participatory processes are usually limited to one particular point in time: hearings after plans have already been developed, designed and costed. Then, after a lesser or greater degree of citizen consultation the project is implemented without further feedback. As a result, stakeholders may feel the participatory process is instrumentalized to further the interests of other actors (Dewan et al., 2014).

Finally, while potentially promoting social learning and dispute resolution and the generation of innovative ideas, a deliberative multi-stakeholder approach risks becoming a talking shop if it is not informed by expertise and linked to the formal decision-making process for resolving/managing intractable conflicts (Hisschemoller and Hoppe, 1998; Verhallen et al., 2007; Van Buuren et al., 2014). People may need some training to know what they are talking about in complex environments. Real-time scenarios and games may facilitate visualization of different alternatives.

Informed by Dutch, French and German experiences with joint planning gained in Freude am Fluss, the JPA team concluded therefore that conflict, some top-down steering and technocratic facilitation is considered inevitable. They propose that the customary deployment of technical expertise (puzzling about facts) needs to be complemented by deliberation over its underlying values and a strong anchoring (powering; Heclo, 1974; Van Buuren et al., 2014) in 'justifiable technocracy, desired collaboration and unavoidable conflict'.

This leads us to three complementary elements of 'joint planning' (De Groot and Warner, 2011):

1. Unavoidable top-down planning and technocracy.
2. Collaborative puzzling element.
3. Conflict management element.

We shall illustrate these elements in the context of maintaining the floodplains in the Dutch Rhine Delta.

Case Studies: History and Reconfiguration of Actors

The case studies *Munnikenland* and *Rijnwaarden* are projects within the *WaalWeelde* programme launched in 2006, in which 'Making Room for the River' and 'Joint Planning' were central concepts. However, *Rijnwaarden* covered a longer history of public-private collaboration. The planning process of this project started in 1996 with a new dynamic discourse emphasizing restoring riverine nature in the area (Table 13.2). Flood safety goals were added to the planning process later due to the near-floods of 1993 and 1995. In contrast, *Munnikenland* had an integrated plan to improve flood protection from the outset while restoring dynamic natural processes and safeguarding cultural interests.

In both cases the previous agricultural function of the floodplains was transformed to a combination of flood protection, nature and cultural functions – for instance constructing new side channels through the floodplain to increase the discharge capacity of the river and offering more space for natural values. In *Munnikenland*, the River Waal

Table 13.2 Characteristics of the 'WaalWeelde' *case studies* Munnikenland *and* Rijnwaarden

	Munnikenland:	*Rijnwaarden:*
Context of case study	*Munnikenland* was one of 39 projects in the 'Room for the River' programme	Autonomous development, but included in the 'Room for the River' programme
Start of planning	From 2006	From 1996; 1999: first draft of redevelopment plan, including a maintenance vision
Aim of project	To reduce the peak water levels (during high water) by 11 cm, in combination with nature restoration and the strengthening of cultural and historical values in the floodplain	To reduce the water levels (during high water) by 11 cm, while developing 500 hectares of new riverine nature, making the area accessible for recreation and allowing sand and clay mining
Measures	Dike relocation and lowering the floodplain (including construction of side channels)	Lowering the floodplain (including construction of side channels)
Total area size	700 hectares	590 hectares of land and 425 hectares of water

was given even more space through dike relocation. The regional Water Board and the Directorate for Public Works and Water Management (*Rijkswaterstaat*) coordinated the planning and implementation process at *Munnikenland* with a primary focus on flood safety objectives. The *Rijnwaarden* case was coordinated by the Government Service for Land and Water Management, a neutral governmental organization focused on coordinating land and water management. Additionally, many other governmental and non-governmental organizations were involved due to the JPA. Stakeholders were identified based on their position, their role in the decision process and their reputation, which resulted in the '4-B' concept: Directors (*Bestuurders*), Public officers (*Beambten*), Businesses (*Bedrijven*) and Citizens (*Burgers*) were all at the table. Directors represented the provincial government, *Rijkswaterstaat*, Water Management Board, municipalities and the State Forestry Service. Additionally, knowledge institutes, businesses such as sand, clay and gravel mining industries, nature organizations, consultancy firms, and representatives of civil platforms were part of the collaborative process in *WaalWeelde*. The express involvement of these groups was an advance over the ongoing Room for the River programme, where local interests at times felt sidelined. In particular, the activism of a local platform (*Hoogwaterplatform*) from 2002, successfully enlisting the other three 'Bs' in the Ooijpolder, an area slated for controlled flooding, had led to the shelving of the said plan (Roth et al., 2006). In other Room for the River projects, local activism led to considerable delays or modification of the intervention. It was realized that the early involvement of these groups could pre-empt later frustration, while planners could benefit from the knowledge and insights of these stakeholders, rather than fearing their power of obstruction.

As Room for the River terminated in 2015, river management in the Netherlands is shifting towards maintaining multi-functional floodplains. This implies a new focus for the current collaborative processes between public and private stakeholders and brings new collaborative challenges. Moreover, the shift implies a change in the geographical interests by adding a more local scale to the established multi-stakeholder groups. Additional interests in the maintenance of floodplains include local nature conservation organizations, agricultural nature stewardship associations and land owners. Especially in *Munnikenland* the municipal authority pushed to have maintenance activities incorporated for the local farmers, united in the agricultural nature stewardship association, *De Capreton*. This new configuration of actors will have to deal with challenges, such as a lack of long-term vision, fragmented maintenance policies, dispersal of land property rights and failure to catch the attention of directors. This makes the maintenance of multi-functional floodplains a complex issue. Table 13.2 provides some 'fast facts' about the two case studies, *Munnikenland* and *Rijnwaarden*. The next section will discuss how the JPA elements can be traced in these projects.

Top-down vs. Bottom-up (Powering)

The multi-functionality of floodplains leads to complex interdependence of stakeholders with respect to the different functions, especially concerning flood protection and nature restoration (Fliervoet et al., 2013; Schindler et al., 2013). A regional two-day conference in 2011 highlighted the perception of overdue maintenance, held by the Directorate for Public Works and Water Management (*Rijkswaterstaat*), of floodplains in the Dutch Rhine Delta. The success of river restoration programmes created an enormous increase in riverside softwood forests, which tend to reduce the river's peak discharge capacity. However agreed flood protection levels were not achieved, inciting *Rijkswaterstaat* to respond with a *top-down* maintenance programme called Streamline. The programme reduced flood risk to a single, conceivable and manageable physical problem, solvable by removing vegetation in the floodplains according to a baseline situation in 1997 (Van Soest, 2008). This top-down approach strongly contradicted the previously adopted multi-level and multi-stakeholder approach. Since the 1990s, public and private stakeholders had developed and implemented integrated plans to improve flood protection while restoring dynamic natural processes and safeguarding agriculture and recreational interests (Room for the River). A top-down approach would likely undo the spectacular increase in biodiversity achieved along the Dutch rivers and the new economic perspectives related to eco-tourism that also resulted from this transformation to more natural and multi-functional floodplains.

Finally, *Rijkswaterstaat* agreed to abandon 'resetting' the floodplains to the baseline situation of 1997. Like many Dutch planning policies and rules, the baseline reference was very static in relation to a dynamic, more natural floodplain environment. *Rijkswaterstaat* imposed upon land owners to maintain the floodplains as a steady-state area, as opposed to the provincial governments, which subsidize land owners to restore and develop new natural values in the floodplain. They adopted their approach by only removing vegetation in the so-called 'streamlines' of the floodplains: areas in the floodplain that will flood first during high peak discharges. However, this did not resolve the conflict on the maintenance of flood protection and natural values in a harmonized way.

Conflict Management

The Streamline approach accelerated the discussion on how to maintain the newly constructed multi-functional floodplains. As a result, not only physical problems (increase of vegetation) but also conflicting policy goals and collaborative challenges became clear (Fliervoet et al., 2013). As a water manager[3] explained: 'I have to request eight permits to remove one tree in the floodplain.' Moreover, water and nature policy are planned in isolation and implemented by two different authorities. The Ministry of Infrastructure is responsible for water and flood management policies, while the nature management policies are implemented by the provincial governments. The provincial governments plan and implement European Union Natura 2000 objectives based on the European legislation, and allocate subsidies for nature conservation. Natura 2000 is a network of protected natural areas in the European Union, encompassing the European Habitats Directive and the Birds Directive. This legislation demands for nature conservation and development of the European nature areas. The majority of natural values in the Dutch floodplains comes under Natura 2000, which implies compensation and mitigation efforts for every change in these floodplains, such as removing soft-wood forests to reach the flood safety levels. This might lead to frustrated water managers, as one

Rijkswaterstaat officer stated: 'compensation and mitigation: these concepts do not match our philosophy and cost too much money'.

For *Rijkswaterstaat*, the maintenance activities and decisions are hard to uphold, because of the huge number of land owners involved: 37,000 hectares out of the total 70,000 hectares are owned by 15,000 private land owners (Van Soest, 2008; interview June 2011). Therefore, collaboration between land owners, nature organizations and water agencies is stimulated.

The *Munnikenland* case (Figure 13.2) illustrates such a collaborative effort, whereby local farmers are involved in nature management in the floodplains together with the State Forestry Service and the Water Board (Luijt et al., 2012). *Munnikenland* is a floodplain along the Waal river and is situated in the middle of the Netherlands and part of the municipality of Zaltbommel. This floodplain area forms part of the Room for the River programme of work. The challenge was to reduce the peak flood level by 11 cm, in combination with nature restoration and the strengthening of cultural and historical values in the floodplain. These values included the castle of Loevestein and the New Dutch Waterline (in Dutch: *De Nieuwe Hollandse Waterlinie*), a former military line of defense based on controlled river inundation. After the planning process the local authority of Zaltbommel insisted on a vision of maintenance including 'agrarian stewardship': environmentally-minded farmers getting together to find ways of combining agricultural activities with nature conservation goals. This resulted in a partnership between the State Forestry Service, agricultural nature stewardship association De Capreton, a farmers' union and the regional Water Management Board. However, this collaboration was fraught, due to the wide variety of underlying landscape visions. After all, in addition to their different maintenance visions, it is important to understand the stakeholders' characteristics and motivating factors in order to reach joint action for floodplain management (Rosenberg and Margerum, 2008). In this case, for example, the agricultural stewardship associations, had a 'cultural landscape' vision as opposed to the natural dynamics or 'wilderness' river vision that the State Forestry Service cherished.

Collaborative Element (Puzzling)

To solve these conflicts and tensions stakeholders emphasized the importance of collaborative approaches to maintain the floodplains sustainably, despite the dominant role played by the Dutch governmental organizations (Fliervoet et al., 2016). Functionalist reasons given in favor of collaboration include the limited public resources available: government simply does not have all the information, power and funds necessary for environmental

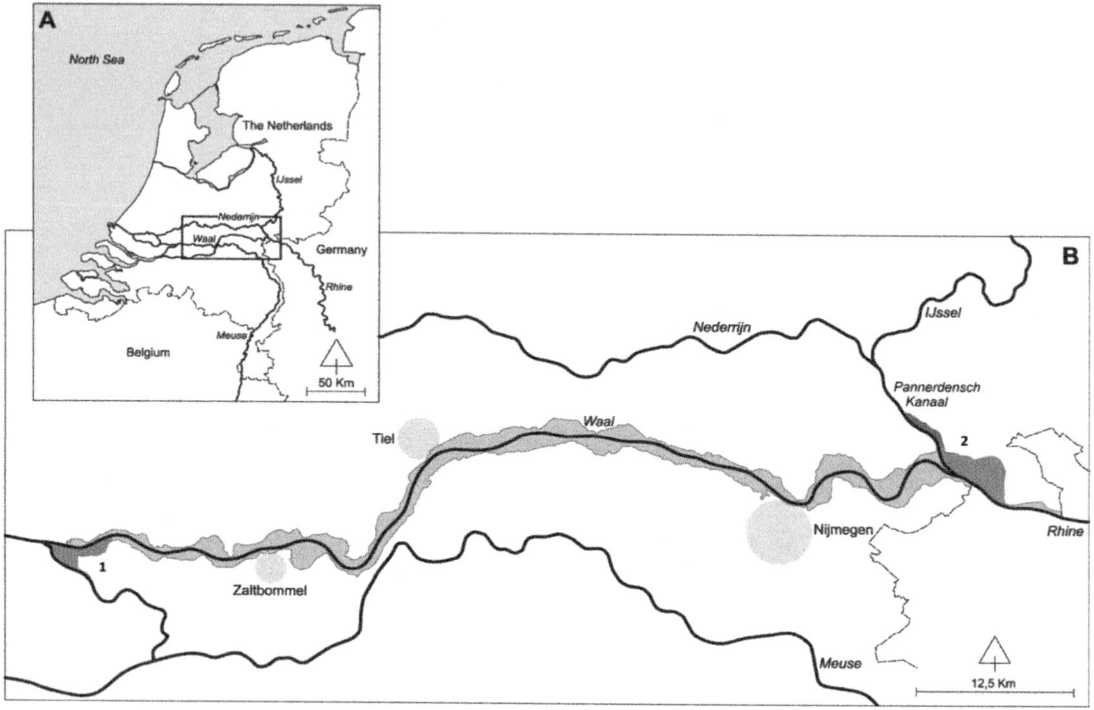

Note: *Munnikenland* (1) and *Rijnwaardense Uiterwaarden* (2) (dark grey). The floodplains along the Waal river are indicated in light grey, as well as some large cities (light grey circles).

Figure 13.2 The location of the case studies along the Waal and Rhine rivers

management, which makes the public sector dependent on other stakeholders (Gray, 1989; Huxham and Vangen, 2005). Budget cuts have only increased this dependence over the past few years. Moreover, involving diverse stakeholders can increase public support, reduce opposition and improve the implementation of government policy. Finally, there is a moral argument to say that involving stakeholders democratizes environmental management (Mostert et al., 2007).

We noted the fragmentation of Dutch maintenance activities above. However, collaborative initiatives regarding the maintenance of floodplains are observed at the policy, practitioner and scientific level. The actors' recognition that floodplain management has become a complex, dynamic and fragmented issue and the call for collaborative approaches resulted in the establishment of a temporary task force on floodplain management in 2011. The Task Force was tasked to find an integrated, multi-stakeholder approach to maintain the newly constructed multi-functional river landscapes. Late in 2013, the Task Force developed a joint governance structure, but without shared, formulated, collaborative objectives: only fuzzy objectives – such as efficiency – were identified, instead of a way to reconcile flood protection and nature goals. The envisioned governance structure consisted of a 'Waal Board', in which different public organizations had to cooperate, and new private-private partnerships between land owners and nature conservation organizations, called *Waardschappen* (stewardship councils). This governance structure at a previously unknown scale, the floodplain, first conceived of by a coalition of ministerial officers and environmentalists (De Bruin et al., 1987) but so far underdeveloped (Vreugdenhil et al., 2008), keeps alive the egalitarian ideal that everyone can contribute. But while the construction of a Waal Board and Waardschappen provides a platform for all stakeholders, it makes a clear distinction of responsibilities between public and private organizations, in contrast to the JPA of the *WaalWeelde* programme, in which a range of actors were involved in the redesign of floodplains based on a bottom-up approach and in public-private partnership.

By contrast, at the local, practitioner level a second case, *Rijnwaardense Uiterwaarden* (also shown in Figure 13.2) showed the opportunities for two partnerships between a group of land owners (initiators) and a group of nature conservation organizations. The group of land owners consisted of public and private organizations. The *Rijnwaardense Uiterwaarden* is a large floodplain area along the Rhine river located in the east of the Netherlands (Figure 13.2). The area is a strategic location regarding flood protection and nature objectives, because it is where the Rhine river divides into the Waal river and the Pannerdensch canal and its location is in the middle of a designated Natura 2000 area. The area has experienced a long history of designing redevelopment plans. The first redevelopment plan dates back to 1999. Finally, in 2012 the landowners committed themselves to develop an integrated design for the whole area by signing a collaborative agreement. In April 2013, this resulted in the development of a joint vision of maintenance (Willems, 2013). Soon the vision attracted the attention of three different organizations involved in nature management. With public sector support, the nature organizations decided to jointly construct a maintenance plan for the whole area instead of responding individually to the maintenance demand from landowners. Through highlighting their complementarity, dealing with expert knowledge, working with wild grazers and their experience with involving local volunteers and farmers, a collaboration was established between the State Forestry Service, an agricultural association for nature management and an organization for nature conservation called FREE Nature. Its director stated: 'the collaboration with the State Forestry Service and agricultural nature association was inspiring, but it was hard to reach agreement'.

At the time of writing the collaborative process had stopped due to the disintegration of the land owner group: 'The implementers (nature managers) are willing and able to collaborate, however the landowners and financiers are not free and fast to make choices for procedural reasons' (ibid.). While changing policies are indeed part of the issue, the diversity of land-owning interests is undeniable.

The maintenance of floodplains also attracted academic attention, especially from a management perspective. The collaborative element is observed in the funding of a national, interdisciplinary research programme, 'RiverCare: Towards Self-sustaining Rivers'. In this programme, a considerable number of Dutch universities and research institutes cooperate to improve predictive models and enhance river maintenance, meanwhile reducing river management costs by studying the interaction of hydraulic, morphological and ecological processes as well as governance issues. The researchers plan to monitor the effects of the Room for the River measures to enhance safety and reduce maintenance from a 'growing awareness that dynamic natural riverine processes should be better utilized (and restored) in order to comply with the multifunctional objectives of rivers' (Augustijn et al., 2014).

DISCUSSION: TENSIONS AND OPPORTUNITIES

The above has sketched three examples of environmentally-driven floodplain management: one unashamedly top-down and mono-functional, and two multi-stakeholder and multi-functional. The Saeftinghe case indicates that mono-sectorial top-down area management can work at a smaller scale. This relates to the issue Huxham and Vangen raise (2005, p. 13) advising practitioners and policy makers: 'don't collaborate unless you have to'. But the case also showed up ongoing tensions with other stakeholders and does not do the trick where multiple interests and functions are at play. Therefore, management of a multi-functional area clearly requires a different approach.

We suggest that joint planning as a working methodology could be introduced in the current collaborative processes to maintain multi-functional floodplains – in other words to apply a Joint Maintenance Approach (JMA) – because the two multi-stakeholder cases indicated the tension between a desire for multi-stakeholder participation and the reality of a fragmented and neglected maintenance process after the implementation of river widening programmes. This tension is analyzed by the top-down, conflict and collaborative elements of the process, resulting in challenges of collaboration for environmental case studies.

Despite integrated and collaborative approaches in the planning phase, organizations relapsed into top-down and single-objective strategies in the maintenance phase, especially when a shared vision for the maintenance of the floodplains is lacking. These single-objective measures show the difficulty of sustaining integrative and collaborative perspectives. However, top-down vs. bottom-up approaches are not the key determinant for the success of collaborative management (Koontz and Newig, 2014), as it shifts to a new phase. In Ohio, resources, willing land owners and networks were key factors promoting the implementation of successful collaborative watershed management. In our case, the conflicting, single-objective strategies brought the problem of joint floodplain maintenance back on the agendas of the directors.

Exploring the conflict element showed both the horizontal and vertical fragmentation of communities and governance institutions, but also the fragmented policy and political setting, which creates conflicts. For example, the Dutch flood safety and nature policies are very static in relation to a dynamic, more natural floodplain environment. These narrow single policies and responsibilities make it difficult to activate the right actors at the right moment and is a challenge for collaboration (Agranoff, 2007; Margerum, 2011). According to Rigg and O'Mahony (2013), it is hard to integrate at lower levels if there is no policy integration at higher levels, as illustrated by the conflicts in the case of *Munnikenland*. This case also showed the challenges of collaboration on the local scale – stakeholders frame the maintenance of floodplains to their own organizational interests (landscape vision). This challenge refers to the problem of path dependency (Watson, 2015), but also shows the importance of understanding each other's underlying frames and trying to reframe the problem towards a shared frame (Dewulf et al., 2011). Therefore, frames, motivations, time and unfamiliarity are all significant factors that raise conflicts in collaborative processes (i.e. Rosenberg and Margerum, 2008).

The collaborative element showed the presence of willingness to invest in new collaborative initiatives on diverse scales to maintain the floodplains in an integrated way, while the absence of willingness often prevents collaboration (Agranoff, 2007). At the national scale a multidisciplinary research programme was built to integrate disciplines, such as hydrology, morphology, ecology and social science, to sustainably maintaining rivers and their floodplains.[4]

At the regional level we found an institutional challenge with constructing an entity to maintain an integrated perspective, illustrated by the discussion on membership structures in the Task Force. The creation of 'stewardship councils' (Van Buuren et al., 2013) engaged all stakeholders, but needed to be better embedded in the preferences of local actors and contextual realities. Their set-up has promoted an ill-advised strict separation between public and private responsibilities, encumbering rather than promoting public-private collaboration regarding the maintenance of the floodplains. Public sector retrenchment is not matched by a hands-off approach in practice. At the local level the debate for new collaborative initiatives has started between landowners and nature managers (*Rijnwaarden*). However, the constraints of the funding procedures, the slowness of the process, and the power differences between the landowners prevented the implementation of shared maintenance activities (see also Lubell (2004) and Rigg and O'Mahony (2013) on such policy constraints and frustrations).

FURTHER IMPLICATIONS

How can we sustain collaborative initiatives, deal with previous relationships and improve the attractiveness of the collaborative process? Generating energy and enthusiasm can help accelerate a collaborative process. 'Serious games' visualizing alternatives are one way of doing this: if people can picture why something could or should be done, they are more likely to engage. For example, the floodplain management game by Stefanska et al. (2011), in which water managers and farmers interacted to manage a floodplain, proved a useful tool for stakeholders to experience the challenges of policy-making for river management regarding agricultural use of the floodplains. Furthermore, the decision-making process of the stakeholder could be analyzed with the help of the same game.

A pitfall here is decision-makers being tempted to delegate the tortuous process of convincing stakeholders to visual artists, whose rendering/ artists' impression of a development project may have strong power of persuasion, but also inevitably papers over very relevant cracks in the project (Hajer et al., 2006). A game or scenario session presenting and thinking through the consequences of alternatives may well provide a more 'objective' and informative setting for deliberation over a planned intervention.

A viable complement could be participatory monitoring to provide a common information base: without good-quality information, dialogue is uninformed and participants have no basis to challenge factually incorrect or biased positions and dispel myths on the causes, scale and severity of problems. Reliable information and training helps non-experts to build capacity and confidence so they can engage effectively in dialogue. This should include dealing with unwelcome information (corruption, political interference and linkages) and participatory monitoring in controversial policy issues: a 'safe space' for frank dispute without press interference (Cundill and Fabricius, 2009).

CONCLUSION

It is tempting to neglect the maintenance stage in any policy cycle. The present contribution has sought to remedy this lacuna, while recognizing the complexity of river management. The Dutch planning scene is fragmented, and densely populated by interested parties who are bound to encounter each other on various land-use issues. Where management is simple, a simple structure may suffice, although the case of Saeftinghe suggests this can still bring unease. Where the policy system is complex, Ashby's (1958) Law of Requisite Variety suggests a governance system that echoes this complexity. Based on our Dutch riverine cases, we see joint maintenance as a promising avenue for participatory river management. It can help develop a comprehensive perspective for floodplain management. Exploring the top-down, conflict and collaborative elements in the cooperative process of maintaining floodplains illustrated the increased complexity, which could not be addressed by a single organization or disciple. Therefore, we suggest applying a JMA to maintain multi-functional floodplains. This shift towards JMA creates collaborative challenges on the themes of fragmented policy and political setting; institutional innovation by building collaborative capacity; and participant factors, like organizational constraints and connecting fragmented frames. As maintenance in itself is not very 'sexy', serious games may help sustain enthusiasm and keep collaborative processes going. Stakeholders could start by setting up joint monitoring activities (participatory monitoring) to build trust and to find new collaborative relationships, before radically changing the institutional settings.

The 'puzzling' process facilitated by deliberative, participatory approaches to land-use planning may well need some 'powering' to bring results and continuity. Thus, bottom-up processes may still need to be complemented by top-down and technocratic elements to keep things moving.

In sum, 'joint maintenance' is an underexplored approach to multi-functional river management. There is still a lot to be learned before a JMA can really come into fruition. It may not be a bad idea to turn to experiences in non-water sectors – such as software development – for inspiration, where the need for maintenance-in-use as complementary to design-in-use is not unheard of (Marcolin et al., 2012). But the two *WaalWeelde* cases are a promising experiment.

NOTES

1. Source: see http://www.omroepzeeland.nl/nieuws/2013-11-05/561353/verdronken-land-saeftinghe-opgeknapt#.VcdHEGwVgdU.
2. See http://www.volkskrant.nl/archief/van-emmahaven-mogen-de-recreanten-wegblijven~a413393/, *De Volkskrant* daily newspaper, 3 March 1993.
3. Interviewed at Rijkswaterstaat, December 2011.
4. Likewise, in Australia five principles were defined to make interdisciplinary collaboration in research a success: forge a shared mission; develop 'T-shaped' researchers, i.e. with both sufficient breadth and depth; nurture constructive dialogue; give institutional support; and bridge research, policy and practice (Brown et al., 2015).

REFERENCES

Agranoff, R. (2007) *Managing within networks: adding value to public organizations*. Washington, DC: Georgetown University Press.

Ashby, W.R. (1958) Requisite variety and its implications for the control of complex systems. *Cybernetica* (Namur) 1(2): 83–99.

Augustijn, D., Schielen, R. and Hulscher, S. (2014) RiverCare: towards self-sustaining multifunctional rivers. *Geophysical Research Abstracts* 16, EGU2014.

Brown, R., Deletic, A. and Wong, T.H.F. (2015) How to catalyse collaboration. *Nature* 525: 315–317.

Cundill, G. and Fabricius, C. (2009) Monitoring in adaptive co-management: toward a learning based approach. *Journal of Environmental Management* 90: 3205–3211.

De Bruin, D., Hamhuis, D., Van Nieuwenhuijze, L., Overmars, W., Sijmons, D. and Vera, F. (1987) *Ooievaar. De toekomst van het rivierengebied*. Arnhem: Stichting Gelderse Milieufederatie.

De Groot, W. and Warner, J. (eds.) (2011) *The social side of river management*. New York: Nova Publishers.

De Kraker, A.J.M. (1997) *Landschap uit Balans: de invloed van de natuur, de economie en de politiek op de ontwikkeling van het landschap van de Vier Ambachten en het Land van Saeftinghe tussen 1488 en 1609*. Utrecht: Uitgeverij Matrijs.
Dewan, C., Buisson, M.-C. and Mukherji, A. (2014) The imposition of participation? The case of participatory water management in coastal Bangladesh. *Water Alternatives* 7(2): 342–366.
Dewulf, A., Mancero, M., Cardenas, G. and Sucozhanay, D. (2011) Fragmentation and connection of frames in collaborative water governance: a case study of river catchment management in Southern Ecuador. *International Review of Administrative Sciences* 77(1): 50–75.
Faysse, N. (2006) Troubles on the way: an analysis of the challenges faced by multi-stakeholder platforms. *Natural Resources Forum* 30(3): 219–229.
Fliervoet, J.M., Van den Born, R.J.G., Smits, A.J.M. and Knippenberg, L. (2013) Combining safety and nature: a multi-stakeholder perspective on integrated floodplain management. *Journal of Environmental Management* 128: 1033–1042.
Fliervoet, J.M., Geerling, G.W., Mostert, E. and Smits, A.J.M. (2016) Analyzing collaborative governance through social network analysis: a case study of river management along the Waal River in the Netherlands. *Environmental Management* 57(2): 355–367.
Forester, J. (2007) Public participation as mediated negotiation: entangled promises and practices. *International Journal of Public Participation* 1(1).
Gray, B. (1989) *Collaborating: finding common ground for multiparty problems*. San Francisco, CA: Jossey-Bass.
Hajer, M.A., Sijmonds, D.F. and Feddes, F. (2006) Inleiding. In *Een plan dat werkt. Ontwerp en Politiek in de Regionale Planvorming*. Rotterdam: Nai.
Healey, P. (1997) *Collaborative planning: shaping places in fragmented societies*. London: Macmillan.
Heclo, H. (1974) *Modern social politics in Britain and Sweden. From relief to income maintenance*. New Haven, CT: Yale University Press.
Hisschemoller, M. and Hoppe, R. (1998) Weerbarstige beleidscontroverses: een pleidooi voor probleemstructurering in beleidsontwerp en -analyse. In R. Hoppe and A. Pieterse (eds.) *Bouwstenen voor een argumentatieve beleidsanalyse*. Den Haag: Elsevier.
Huxham, C. and Vangen, S. (2005) *Managing to collaborate: the theory and practice of collaborative advantage*. London and New York: Routledge.
Immink, I. (2007) Established and recent policy arrangements for river management in the Netherlands: an analysis of discourses. Unpublished PhD dissertation.
Innes, J.E. and Booher, D.E. (2003) Collaborative policy making: governance through dialogue. In M. Hajer and H. Wagenaar (eds.) *Deliberative policy analysis: governance in the network society*. Cambridge, UK: Cambridge University Press, pp. 33–59.
Jacobusse, C. and Decleer, M. (2003) *Het Verdronken Land van Saeftinghe en de Westerschelde*. Leuven: Davidsfonds/De Koperen Tuin.
Kooiman, J. (ed.) (1993) *Modern governance*. London: SAGE.
Koontz, T.M. and Newig, J. (2014) From planning to implementation: top-down and bottom-up approaches for collaborative watershed management. *Policy Studies Journal* 42(3): 416–442.
Lubell, M. (2004) Collaborative environmental institutions: all talk and no action. *Journal of Policy Analysis and Management* 23(3): 549–573.

Luijt, J.K., Litjens, G. and van de Laar, R. (2012) Integrale Planstudie Munnikenland; Beheer en onderhoudsplan. Waterschap Rivierenland, Tiel (Report).

Marcolin, M., D'Andrea, V. and Hakken, D. (2012) Participatory maintenance-in-use: users' role in keeping systems alive. *Proceedings of the 12th Participatory Design Conference: Exploratory Papers, Workshop Descriptions, Industry Cases, Vol. 2*. Denmark: ACM, Roskilde, pp. 57–60.

Margerum, R.D. (2011) *Beyond consensus: improving collaborative planning and management*. Boston, MA: The MIT Press.

Mostert, E., Pahl-Wostl, C., Rees, Y., Searle, B., Tàbara, D. and Tippett, J. (2007) Social learning in European river basin management: barriers and supportive mechanisms from 10 river basins. *Ecology and Society* 12(1): 19.

Muhlig, I. (2011) Transboundary ecosystem services Scheldt River. Case study: Saeftinghe. MSc thesis. Earth Systems Sciences, Wageningen University.

Nienhuis, P.H. (2008) *Environmental history of the Rhine-Meuse Delta: an ecological story on evolving human-environmental relations coping with climate change and sea-level rise.* Berlin: Springer.

Rigg, C. and O'Mahony, N. (2013) Frustrations in collaborative working: insights from institutional theory. *Public Management Review* 15(1): 83–108.

Rijke, J., van Herk, S., Zevenbergen, C. and Ashley, R. (2012) Room for the river: delivering integrated river basin management in the Netherlands. *International Journal of River Basin Management* 10(4): 369–382.

Rosenberg, S. and Margerum, R.D. (2008) Landowner motivations for watershed restoration: lessons from five watersheds. *Journal of Environmental Planning and Management* 51(4): 477–496.

Roth, D., Warner, J. and Winnubst, M. (2006) Een noodverband tegen hoog water. Waterkennis, beleid en politiek rond noodoverloopgebieden. Boundary of Space Series. Wageningen University.

Schindler, S. et al. (2013) Floodplain management in temperate regions: is multi-functionality enhancing biodiversity? *Environmental Evidence* 2(1): 10.

Sebastian, A.G. (2009) Transboundary water politics: conflict, cooperation, and shadows of the past in the Okavango and Orange River Basins of Southern Africa. PhD dissertation, University of Maryland.

Smits, A.J.M. (2009) 'WaalWeelde': van onderaf werken aan ruimtelijke kwaliteit en duurzame veiligheid. *Vakblad Natuur Bos en Landschap* 6: 6–8.

Stefanska, J., Magnuszewski, P., Sendzimir, J., Romaniuk, P., Taillieu, T., Dubel, A., Flachner, Z. and Balogh, P. (2011) A gaming exercise to explore problem-solving versus relational activities for river floodplain management. *Environmental Policy and Governance* 21(6): 454–471.

Uphoff, N. et al. (2002) *Agroecological innovations. Increasing food production with participatory development*. London: Earthscan.

Van Buuren, A., Driessen, P., Teisman, G. and van Rijswick, M. (2013) Toward legitimate governance strategies for climate adaptation in the Netherlands: combining insights from a legal, planning, and network perspective. *Regional Environmental Change* 14(3): 1021–1033.

Van Buuren, A., Vink, M. and Warner, J. (2014) Constructing authoritative answers to a latent crisis? Strategies of puzzling, powering and framing in Dutch climate adaptation practices compared. *Journal of Comparative Policy Analysis: Research and Practice* 18(1): 70–87.

Van Soest, J. (2008) Stroomlijn. *Samen werken aan een veilig, natuurlijk en uitvoerbaar rivierbeheer*. Zwolle: Dienst Landelijk Gebied (Report).

Verhallen, A., Warner, J. and Santbergen, L. (2007) Towards evaluating MSPs for integrated catchment management. In J. Warner (ed.) *Multi-stakeholder platforms for integrated water management*. Aldershot: Ashgate.
Vreugdenhil, H.S.I., Slinger, J.H., Smits, A.J.M. and Kater, E. (2008) Tension bows as a tool to assess the impacts of institutional change: an example from Dutch floodplain management. International Association for Impact Assessment, 4–10 May, Perth, Australia.
Warner, J. (ed.) (2007) *Multi-stakeholder platforms for integrated catchment management*. Aldershot: Ashgate.
Warner, J. (2009) Negotiations in stakeholder platforms. In E. Chinyio and P. Olomolaiye (eds.) *Construction stakeholder management*. London: Wiley.
Warner, J. (2011) *Flood planning. The politics of water security*. London: IB Tauris.
Warner, J. and van Buuren, A. (2009) Multi-stakeholder learning and fighting on the river Scheldt. *International Negotiation* 14(2): 419–440.
Warner, J., Lulofs, K. and Bressers, H. (2010) The fine art of boundary spanning: making space for water in the East Netherlands. *Water Alternatives* 3(1): 137–153.
Warner, J., van Buuren, A. and Edelenbos, J. (2012) *Making space for the river. Governance experiences with multifunctional river flood management in the US and Europe*. London: IWA Press.
Watson, N. (2015) Factors Influencing the frames and approaches of host organizations for collaborative catchment management in England. *Society & Natural Resources* 28(4): 360–376.
Willems, L. (2013) Beheer Rijnwaardense uiterwaarden; Gezamenlijke basis voor het beheer. Dienst Landelijk Gebied, Arnhem (Report).
Wolsink, M. (2006) River basin approach and integrated water management: governance pitfalls for the Dutch Space-Water-Adjustment Management Principle. *Geoforum* 37(4): 473–487.

PART V

Process and participation

14. From the table to the street: strategies for building a more inclusive collaborative process

Jane Rongerude and Gerardo Francisco Sandoval

INTRODUCTION

The challenge of how to generate full representation and inclusion for disempowered populations has caused some theorists concerned with social justice to call into question the legitimacy of collaboration as a tool for planning. These critiques of collaborative planning tend to fall into two categories. The first focuses on representation. It asks whether there is enough room at the table for the groups that are often excluded from decision-making (Umemoto and Igarashi, 2009; Shilling et al., 2009). The second focuses on issues of power. This critique considers whether all voices are in fact equal around the table. It questions how differences in power beyond the table affect both the collaborative process at the table and the implementation of collaborative agreements after consensus has been reached (Huxley and Yiftachel, 2000; Lane, 2003; Weir et al., 2009; Purdy, 2012). Surprisingly, neither critique calls into question the idea of the table itself; in other words, the spaces and symbols of collaboration.

As long as collaborative processes are implemented through formal meetings that occur at times and places that are consistent with the logic and structures of privilege, then marginalized populations will never fully be able to exercise their voices as participants. This chapter investigates how collaborative processes can better involve the voices of marginalized populations. Rather than looking for ways to make more seats at the table, it argues that planners must challenge the metaphor of the table itself. Time, access, and mobility are critical dimensions of difference in the social and economic structure of communities (Young, 1990). True collaboration is not a table, but a street: a contested public space with open access, multiple points of entry and exit, complex movement, and self-organization. The metaphor of the street decenters collaborative processes, moving them to where the issues of concern are located and experienced rather than containing them in the rooms and seats of power. Just as the idea of "street science" (Corburn, 2005) brings together local knowledge with professional expertise to create "improved science and democracy" and better community outcomes, street collaboration envisions collaborative processes that incorporate marginalized groups as an essential voice that contributes to a more democratic process as well as better outcomes.

This chapter begins with a discussion of the barriers that limit the ability of marginalized populations to access and participate in collaborative decision-making processes. This overview focuses specifically on the structural challenges that preclude an ability to reach the table even when an invitation is openly extended with the intention to solicit input. Next the chapter challenges the metaphor of the table, arguing for a more flexible and adaptive metaphor for collaborative processes. A metaphor of the street is offered as an alternative because of its accessibility, flexibility, legibility, and its ability to accommodate opposition. We use case studies from practice to illustrate ways that practitioners have addressed the challenges of integration and inclusion in community-based collaborative processes. Finally, this chapter ends with suggestions for better integrating marginalized communities into collaborative processes and in doing so, bringing collaboration to the street.

COLLABORATING WITH MARGINALIZED POPULATIONS

Collaboration as it is understood in this volume is a civic activity that generates public involvement in decision-making (Margerum, 2011). In Arnstein's classic article on public participation (1969), this type of involvement occurs via partnerships that use negotiation as a way to redistribute power. The collaboration and collaborative governance literature conceptualizes this involvement in a slightly different way, by identifying participants as stakeholders that represent particular interests (Smutko et al., 2002; Ansell and Gash, 2008; Emerson et al., 2012). In this framework, stakeholder selection becomes a key technology for adequately representing a full range of perspectives and interests related to the issue at hand (Susskind and Cruikshank, 1989; Safford et al., 2009). Despite the critical importance of identifying all relevant stakeholder interests and the appropriate individuals to represent these interests (Innes, 1991), practitioners continue to find it difficult to identify stakeholders and to determine their relative importance within the process (Jepsen and Eskerod, 2009). Some critics suggest that these difficulties reveal deeper truths about the limits of collaborative processes, arguing that the purpose of such processes is to limit who participates in order to protect the interests of elites (Callon et al., 2009).

Despite this critique, the mandate for inclusion is clear. Ethical requirements for stakeholder analysis and communicative approaches to planning begin with a simple treatise, "No party affected by what is being discussed should be excluded from the discourse" (Flyvberg, 2001, 91). This ideal becomes complicated when seeking to involve marginalized populations. Although the nuances of the term have been subject to much scholarly debate, for the purposes of this discussion, marginality is defined as "a complex condition of disadvantage which individuals and communities experience as a result of vulnerabilities that may arise from unfavourable environmental, cultural, social, political and economic factors" (Mehretu et al., 2000, 90). Because marginalization contributes to both vulnerability and invisibility, many groups exist unseen while others have reasons to seek out invisibility. Furthermore, the experience of marginalization varies across space and time, affecting different populations in different ways and at different moments within a collaborative process.

Beyond learning to see invisible populations, planners must also learn to recognize culturally appropriate and meaningful representatives of marginalized groups. Outside interests, and in particular those affiliated with power or privilege, rarely understand the structure or cultural processes of these communities. As a result, practitioners struggle to know whether individuals who claim to represent the interests of a marginalized group do in fact represent that group's true interests or the complexity and variation of interests within the group. Without the legibility and legitimacy bestowed by formal institutional or organizational affiliation, individuals representing their own experiences as members of a marginalized group and leaders acknowledged within the community can both face mistrust or exclusion.

Stakeholder-based efforts are likely to mirror existing power structures in society and many exclude potential stakeholders who are not part of the structure of privilege (Lane and Hibbard, 2005; Callon et al., 2009; Margerum, 2011). In the event that racial and economic diversity are explicitly sought out in collaborative processes, participation tends to be tokenized, allowing organizers to claim representation, but not providing full voice to underrepresented communities (Umemoto and Igarashi, 2009). Self-designated representatives or grass-top leaders from community-based organizations may be recognizable representatives to outsiders, but fall short of representing the diverse interests within a marginalized group. "The risk of any stakeholder-led process is that the participants do not represent the range of perspectives in the community.

Choosing participants with extensive networks and linkages is more likely to exclude minorities isolated by community prejudice" (Margerum, 2011, 76). As a result, conveners may erroneously conflate network ties with contextual knowledge. While such ties may provide planners with access to a group, they cannot replace deep knowledge of the everyday lived experience of group members or the deliberative practices of the organizations that represent them.

Collaborative processes improve the technology of engagement by utilizing a systematic approach for recruiting and maintaining participants. Innes and Booher's DIAD (Diversity, Interdependence, Authentic Dialogue) theory of collaborative rationality speaks to the importance of both diversity and interdependence of interests among the participants of a collaborative process. However, the criteria of interdependency can also become a stumbling block for diverse participation. Marginalized groups exist outside structures of privilege, status, and recognition. In fact, for some groups, such as undocumented migrants, refugees, or indigenous peoples, their very right to occupy space is contested. Bringing marginalized groups into a process and recognizing their right to stake a claim in a shared common future despite their lack of formal status requires some parties to expand their view of who qualifies as a stakeholder. The challenge facing planners and other practitioners is how to create collaborative processes that also serve as spaces of inclusion.

THE PROBLEM WITH THE TABLE: FINDING A MORE INCLUSIVE METAPHOR

Inclusion provides necessary opportunities for situated learning (Friedmann, 1987; Healey, 2010) and facilitates a shared understanding among participants regarding the importance of context. It also reveals existing social capital among groups and plays a key role in building relationships among stakeholder groups, thereby changing the structures of social relations (Ostrom, 1986). In the metaphor of the table, inclusion equates being as open as possible to stakeholder involvement. Best practices for collaboration mandate hospitality and extensive invitations to join. If key stakeholders are excluded from a process, even unintentionally, the credibility of the collaborative is damaged. "The goal of a collaborative approach is to achieve consensus through information sharing and conflict resolution, which cannot happen if the full range of interest is not included" (Margerum, 2011, 69). This objective requires that processes err on the side of including too many participants rather than too few (Susskind and Cruikshank, 1989; Margerum, 2011) and extending invitations for participation with the intention of generating access for all stakeholders.

The imperative before planners is one of inclusion rather than one of invitation. While invitation leaves decisions regarding the form and location of an encounter with the entity that extends the invitation, inclusion opens up the possibility of socially situated participation that takes place at different locations and different scales. As Iris Marion Young argued in her classic text *Inclusion and Democracy* (2000), ". . . Socially situated interests, proposals, claims, and expressions of experience are often an important resource for democratic discussion and decision-making. Such situated knowledge can both pluralize and relativize hegemonic discourses, and offer otherwise unspoken knowledge to contribute to wise decisions" (7). Context is not an abstract backdrop against which life is experienced or a filter through which knowledge is gained. Context is a place. If the unspoken knowledge of marginalized populations is to be included in deliberative practices, the location of expression matters.

Marginality implies both proximity and exclusion. An attention to place situates the practice of collaboration and creates openings for both marginalized peoples and their systems of knowledge. In writing about indigenous planning, Hirini Matunga states that such an approach "requires that [planning] be done in/at the place *with* the people of the place" (2013, 5). Because marginalized groups may organize themselves differently than how power is organized, their knowledge challenges the boundaries by which collaboration is organized (Cornell, 2013). The situatedness of knowledge and peoples in terms of place and social structure requires that inclusive practice involves dynamic systems for engagement and two way exchanges of information where familiar problems can be reframed and new questions can be asked (Friedmann, 1987).

In a context of marginalization and unequal power, the question of why groups choose to participate is significant. The emancipatory potential of communicative planning and authentic dialogue (Forester, 2009; Innes and Booher, 2010) cannot be realized without meaningful spaces of engagement. Practitioners must take limits to mobility seriously, which requires more than transportation to an open and public location. It requires the ability to traverse structure and an invitation not to sit in a room, but to experience alternative perspectives from their location within the social structure. Structural barriers cannot be overcome in traditional meetings. "Thus, diverse representation may be a challenge not because a diverse array of participants was not invited. It may be a limitation because structural, societal, political and other factors make it very difficult for them to participate" (Margerum, 2011, 4). The transformative potential of dialogue is immediately constrained when a process becomes limited to a series of conversations held around a table.

Collaborative processes necessitate an inclusive convening process; however, when faced with marginalized groups that do not come to the table, planners tend to look for different ways to represent those imagined interests rather than different ways to generate access. This leads to a "power of representation dilemma" where well-meaning planners attempt to stand in for marginalized groups by championing social justice within a process (Uitermark and Nicholls, 2015). While planners and other practitioners may conceptualize their professional role in terms of furthering equity and social justice, their understanding of the imperatives generated by social justice is likely different than how communities understand their own needs and experiences. While social justice representatives or advocates may be well meaning and well informed, their perspective is ultimately one of privilege, missing the complexities and discontinuities of the lived experience of those within a marginalized group.

Collaborating with marginalized groups necessitates a view of inclusion that is focused on expanding representation and using planning processes to challenge current systems of power. This type of institutional amelioration is useful in reframing the collaborative charge in marginalized communities of color where relationships with power are a direct product of past discrimination that have cast a particular group into a subordinate position. Inclusive collaborative processes bring these relationships to the surface by meeting stakeholders where they are situated and taking seriously the content and framing of their concerns. They address conflicts over public space, rights to the city issues, social inequalities, institutional oppression, power imbalances, and structural barriers to participation. Political theorist Iris Marion Young advocates a paradigm of justice that addresses a politics of difference and directly tackles oppression and power imbalances (2000). In this framework inclusion is not an identical and simultaneous representation for everyone. Instead, it focuses on making amends for past institutional oppression and respecting group differences. In writing about indigenous planning, Robinson and Lane provide a further role for an inclusive process. It provides spaces where traditional "Western" planning is "decoded, recalled, and renegotiated on the ground" (Robinson and Lane, 2013, 406). The measure of voice for marginalized populations within a collaborative process then is not just the ability to change the outcome, but the ability to change the questions that are being asked. System change is accomplished by changing the frame.

True collaboration is better understood as a street: a public, multifaceted space with multiple and possibly contested meanings. Streets are civic spaces where public and private uses and public interests come together and where movement is directed by technology and human decision-making as well as heuristics and laws. Streets are recognizable with a form and meaning that is legible to users. At the same time, a street is a flexible space where both formal exchanges and the opportunity for chance encounters exist. Public struggles over space and resources, democratic protest, and co-creation all occur in the street. Taking collaborative processes into the streets provides an opportunity to hear marginalized voices that do not have the privilege or are structurally excluded from participating in collaborative processes around a "table." For example, it provides undocumented immigrants who are criminalized, have limited democratic rights, and are structurally excluded from otherwise participating in civic processes, with opportunities to be seen and to speak. In the street, marginalized groups can be both seen and heard not as separate and different, but as one thread of a complex social fabric.

CASE STUDIES: BUILDING MEANINGFUL ENGAGEMENT WITH MARGINALIZED COMMUNITIES

This section uses case studies from practice to illustrate steps that planners can take to create more inclusive collaborative processes. These steps involve recognizing emerging stakeholder groups, using research to learn about marginalized communities in the local context, starting with the grasstops, and using a variety of formats and multiple locations to engage in dialogue. These case studies were drawn from collaborative processes in Eugene and Medford, Oregon and Des Moines, Iowa. These two locations are useful to compare because they have similar population size and demographics; however, they face similar challenges to many urbanized areas across the country. The case studies presented here illustrate the possibility created when planners deepen the inclusion of marginalized populations, but they also illustrate the challenges of doing this work.

Collaborating with Undocumented Populations: The Oregon Experience

Outside of the Portland metropolitan area, Oregon is very much a rural state. Oregon's agricultural and forest industries are highly dependent on Latino immigrant labor and a significant portion of this labor force is undocumented (it is impossible to say exactly how much). Even though Latinos have been migrating to Oregon since World War II and there has been a dramatic increase in their numbers in the past 10 years, Latinos are largely excluded from formal political power and account for only 1 percent of elected officials. Much of the state's undocumented migrant population lives in a condition of invisibility and makes an effort to remain below the radar to minimize the risk of being deported. This represents a challenge to collaborative practice. Living in the shadows further perpetuates their marginalization and discourages undocumented immigrants from exercising their civic rights even within collaborative democratic processes. They have a real fear that just being at the table makes them vulnerable.

Before the formal engagement process began in the Oregon case, university researchers began studying the local context to learn where Latinos were already civically engaged. They asked questions such as: Are Latinos participating via community-based organizations or faith-based groups? What are the local community hubs: Community centers? Popular Latino small businesses in the areas where Latinos are increasingly present? Certain churches? What are the cultural events in the community such as multicultural festivals or fairs that draw people to public spaces?

Stories from the field: participatory workshops in Eugene and Medford, Oregon

The process described in this case study is structured around workshops that use a public participation model developed by artist and urban planner James Rojas. Mr. Rojas describes his method as one "that uses model-building workshops and on-site interactive models to help engage the public in the planning and design process." The goal of the method is to "translate conceptual planning ideas into physical forms, and learn about the value of planning and design in shaping how we live (placeit. org)." The method encourages participants to tell stories about their lived experience in cities. The open-ended nature of the workshops helps participants feel safe sharing their ideas and experiences.

The other component of the workshops uses a table-length replica of the city where the workshops are taking place. The model is taken into the streets and set up in front of Latino small business or at cultural fairs and in public spaces and people are encouraged to interact with it. For example, when we worked with the City of Eugene, Oregon to create more inclusive parks for marginalized Latinos, the model was placed at the Festival Latino where about 100 participants were encouraged to use the objects spread out across the model to illustrate their vision for the city's parks. Some examples of questions we used to initiate conversation were: "What's your favorite park in Eugene, and what do you like about it?" Or, "What would you change about the city's parks if you could?" The point was to get into a conversation with Latino participants and dive deeper into their recommendations for changing Eugene's public parks.

Using these participatory methods and workshops, the planning team was able to interact with about 400 Latinos in the City of Eugene. Two key findings emerged from the participatory workshops: The first was the need for the city to create an atmosphere of cultural inclusion and the need to shift to more "informal" park regulations. We heard from many Latinos that they did not feel their culture or ethnic history was represented in Eugene's public spaces. One 14-year-old girl told us that if the city really wanted to create more inclusive parks, they should name a park after a Latino historical figure. The planners that were present at that particular workshop thought it was a great idea and something that should be implemented in the near future.

The second recommendation for the city emerged from stories of frustrated Latinos who did not understand why there were so many regulations in local parks including rules for making reservations for parties and even rules for playing soccer. Latinos wanted to use the parks for their family parties and get-togethers but many times that led to conflicts with the white families who had made reservations. Many Latinos wanted to play soccer games but there were not many soccer fields available and those that did exist were taken by soccer leagues that were either too expensive to belong to or that Latinos did not know how to join or even feel comfortable joining. Hence, a major theme that emerged was the need to relax some regulations in order to accommodate more informal social and sporting events. The City of Eugene's Parks and Recreation staff have prioritized the outreach findings and are in the process of implementing the key recommendations. We believe the outreach findings resonated with city planning staff because they were included in the public outreach workshops. The planners were included in the inclusive collaborative process and a type of social learning took shape (Friedmann, 1987).

Another example comes from Medford, Oregon, a town in southern Oregon with a forest industry-based economy. Here we displayed the city model in front of a popular Latino grocery store. The store served as a community hub and received a lot of foot traffic. We spent the entire weekend speaking to people as they went inside and then came out of the grocery store. In that two-day period, we spoke to about 300 Latinos. Latinos wanted to feel more included in this southern Oregon city. They spoke about the need for more family activities for Latinos such as access to library services, youth education services, and youth recreational activities. Another major theme that emerged related to empowerment. There were no Latino city councilors or other elected officials, and Latinos also felt the city should support more Latino-owned businesses. There were also issues that emerged around strained Latino and police relations as a Latino youth had been killed by police a few years earlier. The final key issue that emerged related to cultural placemaking and the need to have more inclusive public spaces where the Latino population could feel more welcomed, which was similar to Eugene. These concrete issues were incorporated into a needs assessment and further explored by city leaders.

One very interesting interaction that occurred directly on the street was with a group of Pineros, Latino forest workers. After they interacted with the model and shared some of their suggestions, they began to have an informal conversation with researchers. They sat on the street and spoke about their experiences as Pineros traveling up and down the Pacific Northwest as they replanted trees. There were six of them, ranging from their early twenties to their mid-forties and they were a mixture of Mexican guest workers and undocumented workers. The Pineros described how they travel from town to town and live in hotels or guest houses organized by their contractors. They usually spend two weeks in each small town and work all day in the forest. When asked what they did in their free time, they laughed and said they did not really have any free time but when they did they liked to go shopping at the small Latino stores and buy Carne Asada and grill at the local parks and play pick up soccer games with other Pineros.

This interaction on the street demonstrated another spatial and temporal challenge facing collaborative processes seeking to include Latino communities: How to incorporate a key part of your town's labor force that is migratory and uses the housing and public spaces but remains invisible? The public input from these individuals would not have occurred at a meeting in a building outside of the public sphere; however, that changed when the participatory workshops took place out in the streets where everyone was visibly sharing and interacting. It is not possible to engage this invisible labor force in collaborative processes using the usual mechanism of engagement. Taking collaborative processes to the streets provided opportunities to incorporate marginalized voices that otherwise would have remained unnoticed and unheard.

Planning for Neighborhood Change: The Iowa Experience

Des Moines, Iowa has a unique system of neighborhood planning. The program is formally known as the Neighborhood Revitalization Program (NRP), and it began in 1990 based on the recommendations of a report from consultants Stockard and Engler who had been asked to evaluate the city's system of service provision (1989).

The NRP uses a strategy that calls for neighborhood residents, the City of Des Moines, Polk County, local business leaders, and the Neighborhood Finance Corporation to develop a public/private partnership that addresses revitalization issues within the Des Moines area. The NRP gives citizens the opportunity to organize and create neighborhood groups that can be officially recognized by the City Council and County Supervisors (Des Moines, https://www.dmgov.org/Departments/CommunityDevelopment/Pages/NeighborhoodDevelopment.aspx, 2015).

The program is intended to improve and stabilize the city's neighborhoods. It is also used to target and prioritize certain municipal resources including a one-time infusion of public works' monies that neighborhoods receive the first time they go through the planning process.

Neighborhoods are allowed to identify their own boundaries, create a neighborhood association, elect leadership for that association, and then apply for recognition from the city. Once a neighborhood has been recognized as a designated neighborhood, it can apply to participate in the neighborhood revitalization planning process. Currently, Des Moines has more than 50 recognized neighborhoods and approximately 26 of those have completed neighborhood action plans.

Beginning in 2011, the Neighborhood Planning Division of the city of Des Moines and the Department of Community and Regional Planning at Iowa State University formed a partnership to further the city's neighborhood planning efforts. It had been more than 20 years since the neighborhood program first began. Many of the first neighborhoods to go through the program had met their original goals and were ready to update their neighborhood plans. While the city supported their interests in doing this work, it was difficult to justify providing some neighborhoods with a second plan when many had yet to complete their first plan. This partnership provided a vehicle for stretching the city's limited resources, responding to neighborhood concerns, and providing graduate planning students with an opportunity to gain real-world experience.

In 2013, Iowa State University (ISU)'s graduate planning studio was charged with updating the neighborhood revitalization plans for two of the city's most distressed urban core neighborhoods: Capital East and Capital Park. While these communities had a long history of neighborhood-based activism and dedicated residents, the original community activists were aging at the same time that the demographics of these two communities were changing. Both neighborhoods were losing population and facing significant challenges with vacant properties, rent burden, unemployment, and low household incomes. These neighborhoods had become gateway communities as the white, working-class homesteaders of the previous generation were being replaced by households of new immigrants with young families. Both communities had become increasingly diverse over the last decade. While the largest single ethnic or racial group was still white, that number was shrinking. The largest demographic group in each neighborhood was households that were non-white and renters. However, the neighborhood associations remained dominated by white homeowners.

Monthly neighborhood association meetings never attracted more than a dozen people, and often only half that number would attend. If the neighborhood revitalization plan updates were to be based on community input and engagement, then the planning team was going to have to do more than rely on attendance at public meetings.

It was through this very common dilemma that the idea of "taking the meetings to the public" was created. A successful neighborhood revitalization plan had to meet three requirements: (1) it had to be based on the needs and objectives of the neighborhood; (2) it had to be legible to the residents of the neighborhood; (3) it had to provide access to resources. During the current era of constrained municipal budgets, the city was looking to do more with less. At the start of the project, there were few plans to make public resources available to implement these plans. The responsibility would rest with the neighborhood associations to complete the work unless potential partners could be identified to share in the work of implementation.

Stories from the field: taking the meeting to the public in Des Moines, Iowa

The process began the summer before the planning process was officially kicked off, as university researchers sought out knowledge about the emerging Latino community living in two neighborhoods. The objective of this research was to identify potential leaders as well as community gathering places and cultural practices. During this outreach, Latino community-based organizations talked about the deep distrust between the community and the city after the city ended funding for the Latino community center, causing it to close, and the city passed anti-food truck legislation that many felt was targeted at taco trucks. Through these conversations, the planning team was able to identify recognized leaders within the community as well as the places where many Latino families carried out their daily rounds: the schools, the markets, the churches. By working through social service agencies and building personal networks, researchers were able to move beyond organizations and talk to individuals about their hopes and dreams for their lives and their neighborhoods. Once the planning process began, these participants were invited to provide direct input into the planning process through an interview and/or survey, and also invited to attend either neighborhood association meetings and/or steering committee meetings. However, no one ever attended a formal meeting.

After the preliminary fieldwork, the outreach process began with short, structured surveys in the neighborhood. The teams went door to door, talking to individuals at their homes, in neighborhood parks, outside schools, and on the street. These surveys were conducted in both Spanish and English. Student researchers spent more than 200 person hours a week in the community, and collected approximately 150 completed surveys. They also canvassed many of the local businesses, talked to local church leaders, attended English Language Learner classes sponsored by a community-based organization and talked to passers-by outside high school football games, Latino markets, and gas stations. Latino business owners were engaged through individual outreach that included interviews and focus groups. This face-to-face interaction at the places where they carried out their daily rounds was essential for input. Business owners spoke of problems with crime, lighting issues that they felt contributed to the crime, and their reticence to contact the police. All of this work occurred through face-to-face conversations at the places where people were living their daily lives. In total they spoke to more than 600 people in the two neighborhoods. Once the data was analyzed, several key themes emerged in each community. These themes were first taken to the neighborhood association and then taken to a pre-established steering committee for further consideration.

Each neighborhood had a steering committee that met four times. The steering committees consisted of neighborhood residents, members of the neighborhood associations, city planning staff, other agency staff, local business owners, school administration, and representatives from community non-profit organizations. The steering committee was intended to provide the necessary resources to get the work done. After hearing the survey data and an overview of the demographics and challenges in each community, the steering committees prioritized themes and suggested four issues to be addressed in the plan. Then they identified programs to address those issues and committed resources to get the work done. Once the plan was finalized, the city went on to create a US$1.9 million program called Viva Each Bank that was intended as an implementation effort for these neighborhood plans.

Four Steps to More Inclusive Collaboration

1. Identify emerging stakeholder groups

Marginalization is not a static category. As communities change, the geography of inclusion and marginalization within a given place changes as well. In order to create inclusive processes, collaborative practitioners must learn to identify historically marginalized populations as well as emerging groups. For example, although Des Moines has long been a site of rural to urban migration within the state, the city is experiencing a new influx of global migrants, many of whom are refugees. This immigration has resulted in significant demographic changes in the city's urban core neighborhoods, and the membership of neighborhood associations did not reflect this diversity. The planning team recognized the need for a participatory process that more closely represented the demographics of the neighborhood and pushed to expand their outreach efforts beyond traditional neighborhood representatives. They reached out to neighborhood small businesses, non-profit organizations, and churches. In the absence of formal representative organizations, they went door to door in order to talk to residents face to face.

In the Oregon example, the Latino population increased by 26 percent from 2005 to 2014 and now comprises 12.5 percent of Oregon's total population (American Community Survey 2005, 2014). They are an emerging stakeholder group. The outreach methods presented in this case rely on understanding the Latino community context and the structural barriers that hamper their participation. For undocumented populations, these structural barriers include: the risks they face by making themselves visible, their limited time for participation, language barriers, their lack of resources for child care and transportation costs, and the limited experience they have in participating in collaborative processes.

2. Use research to learn about marginalized groups within the local context

The process should begin with learning the community. Often, this will require either practitioners or their university research partners to engage in research as a first step. This learning process is not open-ended, but rather focused on identifying organizations and individuals who can serve as legitimate voices for the community. Understanding the basic structure of the community is simply one technical problem out of many in a collaborative process and one that can be at least partially addressed through technical expertise and research. Utilize research to understand communities, not just "the problem." Expect to face distrust.

Research can help collaborative practitioners to identify who are the stakeholders, but also where to locate collaborative processes. In order to interact with marginalized groups, practitioners need to find ways to meet community members where they work, play, pray, shop—in other words, the places where they live their everyday lives. These may be known locations such as community centers or ethnic groceries, but also unexpected locations such as church-based tutoring programs, lots where pick up soccer games occur, or family picnic areas in regional parks. This research will facilitate successful recruitment for workshops, but also data gathering and feedback that can be analyzed and incorporated into the process.

3. Start with the grasstops

Deep engagement with marginalized communities requires engaging with both the grasstops and the grassroots. In other words, it requires engaging with individuals but also with the social service and cultural organizations that work with this population. Often these organizations have built trust with the community and can tap into the community's networks. Many already have relevant skills for collaboration and relationships with organizations that extend beyond the community (Takahashi and Smutny, 2001). In the Oregon example, outreach began with the grasstops because they served as visible and public representatives of the community. Because they provided services to undocumented Latinos, they had the trust of that community as well as familiarity with their issues and concerns. Their formal status as organizations allowed them to speak safely on the behalf of undocumented people.

In the Iowa case, the planning team engaged the grassroots through direct outreach that included knocking on doors, attending community events, and standing outside local markets, gas stations, and schools. They analyzed the information they gathered and used that data to inform the work of the stakeholder committee, which was comprised of the grasstops. While these organizations did not have identical views to those expressed by the grassroots, they were interested in knowing what grassroots individuals had to say. The result was a process where planners served as a bridge, bringing credibility to each and spurring action in between. It also meant that at times the planning team had to navigate differing opinions when formal organizations expressed different priorities than individuals. As the process continued over time, the grassroots outreach became focused on gathering feedback about the perspectives of the grasstops, both groundtruthing the priorities they expressed and sharing information about resource limitations and opportunities. The planning team engaged in their own reflective practice, both writing and problem-solving within the team of how best to address the challenges that came from serving as the bridge between two different groups who were speaking to one another, but not always face-to-face.

4. Use a variety of formats and locations to engage in dialogue

Inclusive collaborative practices require that practitioners identify neutral territory for engagement and utilize a deductive and formative approach to engagement. It requires that collaborative practitioners engage people in non-traditional places in order to do what in the Des Moines work we call, "taking the meeting to the public." It also requires utilizing flexible processes that allow participants to exercise their voice in a way that is meaningful and relevant to them rather than convenient and familiar to professionals and decision-makers. Non-traditional formats should apply to discursive elements of the process as well, allowing dialogue to be personal, iterative, and non-linear. This process should also engage the most marginalized stakeholders in problem identification, something that planning institutions do not do well (Lake and Zitcer, 2012; Kiisel, 2013). It is those in power who most often define problems for low-income people, not the people themselves.

These outreach methods rely on understanding the local community context and the structural barriers that hamper the participation of marginalized groups. Structural barriers include: the risks they face by making themselves visible, their limited time for participation, language barriers, their lack of resources for child care and transportation costs, and the limited experience they have in participating in collaborative processes. The outreach strategies discussed in this chapter directly address these barriers in the following ways: (1) by creating a process that is simple, open-ended, and non-coercive; (2) by not relying on language ability; (3) by creating a safe environment where participants can express their opinions; and (4) by creating events that are fun, family oriented, and interactive. These methods of public participation are non-coercive and safe for vulnerable participants, while still allowing them to interact with urban planners, city officials, and community leaders. These participatory outreach projects have reached about 1,000 Latinos in Oregon by engaging this population at cultural fairs, in public parks, in front of Latino businesses, and on the streets. In Des Moines, they engaged more than 600 individuals in two neighborhoods with a combined population of approximately 4,000 people. While participatory mapping or engagement efforts using art and other creative placemaking techniques are not new or unique to these examples (see for example, Robinson and Lane, 2013 or ArtPlace America http://www.artplaceamerica.org/), we are suggesting that practitioners include such activities within and as part of a collaborative process as a way of engaging marginalized populations who might otherwise be excluded from the process. They also help make the outreach process more engaging, interesting, creative, and democratic.

CONCLUSION: CONSTRUCTING INCLUSIVE DIALOGUE

Although planners and community practitioners have been asking the question of how to engage with marginalized populations for decades, the answer remains elusive. In conventional planning practice, participation is often assessed in terms of numbers or how many people show up for a particular event rather than who those people are or what sets of interests they represent. Public meetings remain the primary tool for engagement and participation is often low unless meetings are focused on particular matters of concern to a given constituency. For meetings regarding a controversial topic, large numbers of participants may attend, but a diversity of interests often continues to be absent.

In this chapter we have addressed a key debate within justice collaborative practice. That is, how to gain representation from populations that are excluded and marginalized. Taking collaborative methods to the streets opens up new opportunities for community engagement, dialogue, and inclusive democratic process. Moving away from the metaphor of the table enables collaborative practitioners to shape inclusive processes that utilize active, non-coercive, and creative techniques for exchanging information and for learning, both by planners, facilitators, and community participants. They attend to conflict and self-consciously address wicked problems and their roots in social inequality, racism, and oppression. They include marginalized and invisible populations as well as planners and public officials, uniting all stakeholder groups in a dynamic and iterative collaborative process that includes problem definition and authentic dialogue.

Ensuring that all stakeholders can exercise voice is the key to representation within inclusive collaboration. This requires doing more than simply valuing different perspectives. It requires actively opening a space within the process for those marginalized perspectives and allowing them to have impact within the process. Hence, collaborative processes need to encompass methods that legitimize narratives (Sandercock, 2003; Bulkens et al., 2015). That can be done through storytelling. In the Oregon case, planners, civic leaders, and others had the opportunity to hear powerful stories from undocumented Latino immigrants about their struggles in public spaces and the discrimination they felt in their community. Individuals with otherwise marginalized voices felt comfortable sharing their testimonies and voices with privileged stakeholders, which created a powerful transformative process as all stakeholders learned from each other about social justice concerns. This learning can produce powerful solutions, but more importantly lead to system change where new collective questions and new collective possibilities emerge (Innes and Booher, 2010).

Taking collaboration into the streets and seeking out the voices of marginalized populations also brings key challenges. While the techniques presented in this chapter allow practitioners to create more inclusive collaborative processes with better representation of marginalized communities and better integration of marginalized voices within a given place, we do not suggest they serve as a panacea for the enduring challenge of structural exclusion. Hence, we need to consider whether all voices are in fact equal and how relationships of power beyond the table affect both the collaborative process and the implementation of collaborative agreements.

Sustaining the engagement of marginalized voices and going beyond the representation debate is beyond the scope of this chapter but represents an important issue to tackle in the future. Sustaining marginalized voices within inclusive collaboratives demands that we connect these emerging voices to the halls of power. These methods also require a sustained involvement over time and resources. They often carry the heavy weight of mistrust and past exclusion and with them, the mandate to proceed differently. This requires that resources and relationships are sustained over time. The stakeholder process in Des Moines added a new twist to maintaining relationships with the community by engaging not just city planners and city agencies as stakeholders, but by building relationships among the many organizations doing relevant work around the city and connecting them to each other and the neighborhood. This more decentralized approach distributes relationships, resources, and institutional capacity rather than relying on a single relationship between the community and city planners or the community and the university.

The important role of the facilitator as expert continues to be a key challenge for inclusive collaboration and collaborative methods in general. Both of the leaders in these collaborative outreach projects were university professors who engaged their students in experiential learning opportunities to conduct the preliminary research as well as the outreach work. The university role provided legitimacy, it allowed them to be perceived as neutral facilitators, and it provided expertise regarding how to successfully reach marginalized populations using qualitative and ethnographic research methods. Because of the Institutional Review Board mandates that university researchers must address, it also required consideration of ethics and a careful attention to and mediation of the potential risks that vulnerable populations could face by participating in these efforts. Hence, it would be difficult for consultants or urban planners to take a similar research-based approach without a university partnership. Furthermore, the role of the planner as a collaborative practitioner is expanded in this approach. The planner no longer serves as merely a convener or a facilitator, but becomes a bridge, an advocate, a mediator, and a translator as well. Such a role requires a dynamic set of skills for future practitioners as well as grounding in reflective practice to enable individuals to navigate the uncharted territory of such engagement and the potential ethical dilemmas that are likely to arise.

Even though these are real challenges, and there is much research still to be done on inclusive collaboration, we have shown how important it is to break from the table metaphor and engage marginalized peoples on the streets. It is an important first step in this inclusive collaboration process that is now emerging and promises to tackle more structural barriers that ferment inequality in our cities and communities. It is also a call for collaborative practitioners to think more substantively about power, structural inequality and racism, and how a collaborative process can be a useful tool for increasing justice in our society.

REFERENCES

Ansell, C. and Gash, A. (2008). Collaborative Governance in Theory and Practice. *Journal of Public Administration Research and Theory*, 18(4), 543–571. doi: 10.1093/jopart/mum032

Arnstein, S. R. (1969). A Ladder of Citizen Participation. *Journal of the American Planning Association*, 35(4), 216–224.

Bulkens, M., Minca, C. and Muzaini, H. (2015). Storytelling as Method in Spatial Planning. *European Planning Studies*, 23(11), 2310–2326. doi: 10.1080/09654313.2014.942600.\

Callon, M., Lascoumes, P. and Barthe, Y. (2009). *Acting in an Uncertain World: An Essay on Technical Democracy*. Translated by Graham Burchell. Cambridge, MA: The MIT Press.

Corburn, J. (2005). *Street Science. Community Knowledge and Environmental Health Justice*. Cambridge, MA: The MIT Press.

Cornell, S. (2013). Reconstituting Native Nations: Colonial Boundaries and Institutional Innovation in Canada, Australia, and the United States. In R. Walker, T. Jojola and D. Natcher (eds.) *Reclaiming Indigenous Planning*. Montreal: McGill-Queens University Press.

Emerson, K., Nabatchi, T. and Balogh, S. (2012). An Integrative Framework for Collaborative Governance. *Journal of Public Administration Research and Theory*, 22(1), 1–29. doi: 10.1093/jopart/mur011

Flyvberg, B. (2001). *Making Social Science Matter: Why Social Inquiry Fails and How it Can Succeed Again*. Cambridge, MA: The MIT Press.

Forester, J. (2009). *Dealing with Differences: Dramas of Mediating Public Disputes*. Oxford: Oxford University Press.

Friedmann, J. (1987). *Planning in the Public Domain: From Knowledge to Action*. Princeton, NJ: Princeton University Press.

Healey, P. (2010). *Making Better Places: The Planning Project in the Twenty-First Century*. New York: Palgrave Macmillan.

Huxley, M. and Yiftachel, O. (2000). New Paradigm or Old Myopia? Unsettling the Communicative Turn in Planning Theory. *Journal of Planning Education and Research*, 19, 333–342.

Innes, J. (1991). Implementing State Growth Management in the U.S.: Strategies for Coordination, Working Paper 542, Institute of Urban and Regional Development, University of California, Berkeley.

Innes, J. and Booher, D. (2010). *Planning with Complexity: An Introduction to Collaborative Rationality for Public Policy*. London and New York: Routledge.

Jepsen, A. L. and Eskerod, P. (2009). Stakeholder Analysis in Projects: Challenges in Using Current Guidelines in the Real World. *International Journal of Project Management*, 27(4), 335–343. doi: 10.1016/j.ijproman.2008.04.002

Kiisel, M. (2013). Local Community Participation in the Planning Process: A Case of Bounded Communicative Rationality. European Planning Studies, 21(2), 232–250. http://dx.doi.org/10.1080/09654313.2012.722921

Lake, R. and Zitcer, A. (2012). Who Says? Authority, Voice, and Authorship in Narratives of Planning Research. *Journal of Planning Education and Research*, 32(4), 389–399. doi: 10.1177/0739456X12455666

Lane, M. (2003). Participation, Decentralization, and Civil Society: Indigenous Rights and Democracy in Environmental Planning. *Journal of Planning Education and Research*, 22(4), 360–373. doi: 10.1177/0739456X03022004003

Lane, M. and Hibbard, M. (2005). Doing it for Themselves: Transformative Planning by Indigenous Peoples. *Journal of Planning Education and Research*, 25, 172–184. doi: 10.1177/0739456X05278983

Margerum, R. D. (2011). *Beyond Consensus: Improving Collaboration to Solve Complex Public Problems*. Cambridge, MA: The MIT Press.

Matunga, H. (2013). Theorizing Indigenous Planning. In R. Walker, T. Jojola and D. Natcher (eds.) *Reclaiming Indigenous Planning*. Montreal: McGill-Queens University Press, pp. 3–34.

Mehretu, A., Pigozzi, B. W. and Sommers, L. M. (2000). Concepts in Social and Spatial Marginality. *Geografiska Annaler. Series B, Human Geography*, 82(2), Development of Settlements, pp. 89–101.

Ostrom, E. (1986). An Agenda for the Study of Institutions. *Public Choice*, 48, 3–25.

Purdy, J. M. (2012). A Framework for Assessing Power in Collaborative Governance Processes. *Public Administration Review*, 72(3), 409–417. doi: 10.111/j.1540-6210.2012.02525.x

Robinson, C. and Lane, M. (2013). Boundary-Riding: Indigenous Knowledge Contributions for Natural Resource Decision Making in Northern Australia Regions. In R. Walker, T. Jojola and D. Natcher (eds.) *Reclaiming Indigenous Planning*. Montreal: McGill-Queens University Press, pp. 396–413.

Safford, T. G., Carlson, M. L. and Hart, Z. H. (2009). Stakeholder Collaboration and Organizational Innovation in the Planning of the Deschutes Estuary Feasibility Study. *Coastal Management*, 37(6), 514–528.

Sandercock, L. (2003). Out of the Closet: The Importance of Stories and Storytelling in Planning Practice. *Planning Theory and Practice*, 4(1), 11–28. doi: 10.1080/1464935032000057209

Shilling, M. K., London, J. K. and Levanos, R. (2009). Marginalization by Collaboration: Environmental Justice as a Third Party In and Beyond CALFED. *Environmental Science & Policy*, 12, 694–709. doi:10.1016/j.envsci.2009.03.003.

Smutko, L. S., Klimek, S. H., Perrin, C. A. and Danielson, L. E. (2002). Involving Watershed Stakeholders: An Issue-Attribute Approach To Determine Willingness and Need. *Journal of the American Water Resources Association*, 38(4), 995–1006. doi: 10.1111/j.1752-1688.2002.tb05540.x

Stockard and Engler, Inc. (1989). *Housing Improvement and Neighborhood Revitalization: A Report Prepared for the Des Moines City Council and Polk County Board of Supervisors*. Cambridge, MA. Available at https://www.dmgov.org/Departments/CommunityDevelopment/PDF/Original1989SEReport.pdf

Susskind, J. and Cruikshank, L. (1989). *Breaking the Impasse: Consensual Approaches to Resolving Public Disputes*. New York: Basic Books.

Takahashi, G. and Smutny, G. (2001). Collaboration among Small, Community-based Organizations: Strategies and Challenges in Turbulent Environments.

Journal of Planning Education and Research, 21(2), 141–153. doi: 10.1177/0739456X0102100203

Uitermark, J. and Nicholls, W. (2015). Planning for Social Justice: Strategies, Dilemmas, Tradeoffs. *Planning Theory*, doi: 10.1177/1473095215599027. Available at http://plt.sagepub.com/content/early/2015/08/18/1473095215599027.full.pdf

Umemoto, K. and Igarashi, H. (2009). Deliberative Planning in a Multicultural Milieu. *Journal of Planning Education and Research*, 29(1), 39–53. doi: 10.1177/0739456X09338160

Weir, M., Rongerude, J. and Ansell, C. (2009). Collaboration is Not Enough: Virtuous Cycles of Reform in Transportation Policy. *Urban Affairs Review*, 44(4), 455–489. doi: 10.1177/1078087408322590

Young, I. M. (1990). *Justice and the Politics of Difference*. Princeton, NJ: Princeton University Press.

Young, I. M. (2001). *Inclusion and Democracy*. Oxford: Oxford University Press.

15. The challenge of transformative learning: mining practice stories to study collaboration and dispute resolution strategies

John Forester*

INTRODUCTION: A RESEARCH METHOD WITH SURPRISINGLY PRACTICAL RESULTS

How can we respond to the challenge of studying the nuts and bolts of environmental and broader public policy collaborations in a practically useful and a theoretically generative way? This chapter proposes a distinctive strategy—to produce detailed, narrative profiles of the facilitators of collaborations or the mediators of public disputes—so that we can study grounded, practical collaborative and dispute resolving practices in varied and complex public policy and institutional settings.

This strategy employs an innovative method that can help us to learn in ethnographically vivid, instructively engaged and practically grounded ways—while being theoretically generative as well.[1] If we ask good questions, we can explore the work of skilled practitioners as windows onto the world of collaborative and dispute resolution processes—even if the practitioners managing and facilitating these processes might simply call themselves not "mediators" but, more traditionally, "managers" or "engineers," "planners" or "administrators," for example.

We can begin with a wonderful saying from English philosopher John Austin, who anticipated post-modernism by 40 years or more. Austin once remarked, simply if quite wisely, "fact is richer than diction." Because our language of public policy dispute resolution and collaborative practices remains so often vague—"assessing," "convening," "fact-finding" and so on—we will see that the actual practice of "mediators," "facilitators," "consensus-builders" and their collaborative cousins involves far more interesting judgments and strategies, sensitivities and skills than our vague categories even begin to suggest. Practice, that is, often leads theory (see e.g. Schon 1983; Forester 1999, 2009, 2013)!

So if we wish to understand collaborative and dispute resolution practices better, we need refined research methods to see what "mediation," "collaboration," and "consensus-building," for example, might actually require as institutionally staged and responsive pragmatic actions, as thoughtfully and critically improvised, often innovative, organizational performances. Examining flows of practice in real cases, we must not be held hostage to our *presumptions* of what these practices "must" involve.

I wish to show, given five books mining such research materials (Forester 1999, 2009, 2013; Forester et al. 2001; Laws and Forester 2015), how we can produce richly detailed, analytically fertile accounts of both the difficulties and the opportunities of practical collaborative and dispute resolving work. We can do that by refining a fieldwork-based, oral history method to produce not autobiographical but case-focused narratives, "practice stories," practitioners' pragmatic accounts that can both (1) reveal efforts they consider central to their practice, and (2) richly illuminate topics of our interests. Such practice stories can teach us about the complexities and uncertainties, the formal obligations and the informal entanglements, the ambiguities and judgments, and the strategies and sensitivities involved in handling diverse practical collaborations and environmental disputes.

So consider an example of the kind of practice story we might produce followed by an initial analysis of this case material. For additional cases and rich teaching materials involving environmental, transportation, public health, land use planning, and urban design collaborations and practical urban, regional, and state-wide conflicts, see the fuller profiles in *Planning in the face of conflict* (Forester 2013), assessed at greater length analytically in *Dealing with differences: dramas of mediating public disputes* (Forester 2009), both premised on the basis of *The deliberative practitioner: encouraging participatory planning processes* (Forester 1999).

After considering lessons drawn from such accounts of grounded, even bureaucratically enmeshed deliberative practices, we turn to "how to" questions of method. Finally, we consider further substantive questions that a practice story focused research strategy might illuminate as we explore the challenges of learning from both emerging and existing forms of collaborative and dispute resolution practices.

A PRACTICE STORY EXCERPT FROM THE URBAN ENVIRONMENT OF CITY HALL

Consider several passages from the practice story of Richard Roberts, an experienced planner and consultant in New York State.[2] Roberts details how he learned as his work evolved as Deputy Director of a small western New York City's Department of Community Development:

> I started to manage the community development block grant projects, which was this new form of much more locally determined ways of using the federal support, so we had a lot more flexibility with it. And that's when I started using what ultimately we called "self-design," which was just to get people in the room. This is where I learned about the power of convening: Of just getting people in the room and saying, "What do you want? What would you like things to be like?" We would have our staff, our architects, our engineers and our design people in the room to support and give shape, to talk about the practicalities and the feasibilities of actualising their desires. This fundamentally reversed the design process. It started with what they wanted and would like to see happen, and then we used our resources to see if indeed that was possible—and how to make that happen.

He goes on,

> Before, the plans would have been made on the 4th floor of City Hall, in the suite of architectural and engineering offices, by civil engineers, architects and transportation engineers. And then they would have been presented to the parts of the city that they affected, and they would have been presented, using what, I'm sad to say, is still the most common technique—the design and defend mode. Meaning they say, "Here it is," and when people start asking questions about it, the designers defend their designs, and they say why it's that way and why it can't be changed. This is what sets up the loggerhead and conflictual situations between the professionals and the people, merchants or property owners, or whomever else.

He continues,

> It was my observation that the old process didn't work. They had been going for three and a half years trying to do a downtown development project and still didn't have anything going on the ground. Three and a half years of just going back and forth, and they couldn't get anything to happen because they were just constantly in conflict—back and forth.
>
> What this process did was basically start with the concept of the design from the values and perspectives of the people that were going to be affected by it, and then [it] used the technical resources to facilitate the actualization and operation of it. It was a complete reversal of the sequence. It made perfect use of those professional resources, but it subordinated them, in a way, to the values and interests of the people that were going to have to live with the results of the changes that were being made.

The big conceptual shift was in turning that around—and the only reason it happened was because we had the power; we were the Director and Deputy Director of the department. We could say, "We're going to do it this way."

He went on,

The professionals would not have done it this way. There was one architect that was happy to do it this way, and I think it's just because he had been beaten up so badly for so long that he just didn't want to do it the other way anymore. Thank God. He'd say, "Sure, I'll go in a room and sketch this stuff."

And that's literally what he would do. We would line the wall with paper and people would come in and he'd sketch. He loved it. It was very successful, but that actually set the stage for me to set the pattern to always think about starting from the values and interests of the parties as the foundation place to start, to use learning as the motivation for making change and to have the parties themselves do that learning. They themselves have to discover what they want to change—because once they do that, they are actually willing to change.

He summarized,

I would have to admit that it was a value of my own that led me to make these changes. I thought it was really quite arrogant for an architect or an engineer, or someone from any professional position, to presuppose that they knew what people wanted or needed in a neighborhood or in a business district. Or that they knew more about the neighborhood than the residents knew. I just thought there was something asymmetrical about that, but I saw nothing wrong with them collaborating and co-generating the plans. From a purely ethical and moral perspective, let alone a practical and pragmatic one, I thought it was wrong for them to overlay their "professional knowledge and expertise" onto people's lives and have those impacts occur on others *without others really having an initial way of helping to shape how that was going to happen*. This is what I've been doing ever since and the only difference was that, in that instance, the venue or application was at a community level. Eventually I brought it into individual organizational venues.

INTERPRETING THIS PRACTICE STORY: LESSONS AND IMPLICATIONS

This brief passage recounts a formative collaborative experience, in which a political opening—the support of the community development department's director—gave this practitioner the power not to implement results but to try a new process of public involvement and collaborative design. Roberts describes his own learning process here, and so we can come to learn with him too. Learning what *not* to do was crucial to learning what *to* do.

Roberts speaks early on of "learning about the power of *convening*," by which he obviously means much more than just getting people in the same room, though he means that too. He speaks immediately, significantly, of asking several future-oriented questions that both recognize and respect the participants ("What do *you* want?") and that draw them into a design process ("What would you like things to be like?"). Notice how these examples of questions speak not to past grievances but to future possibilities; they do not ask what you do *not* like (or *who* has done what damage to you) as much as they probe for practical proposals (cf. Susskind in Forester 2013).

Roberts speaks immediately to the place of expertise, practicality, and feasibility. He is no romantic, no ideologue. The architects and engineers must do their work, but he speaks of the design process now as being "fundamentally reversed." The experts can solve problems, but the affected city residents, the main street merchants and others, must be involved in defining and identifying the problems in the first place. Problem solution, he reminds us, can only be as good as problem formulation and problem identification (Rittel and Webber 1973).

Roberts assesses institutional history here in two significant ways. "They'd been going for three and a half years trying to do a downtown development project and still didn't have anything going on the ground," "three and a half years . . . just constantly in conflict" he says. So he's emphasizing problems of efficiency and effectiveness: "the old process didn't work," he suggests. But he teaches us more too: he identifies a traditional view of professional work that has often created problems: "*Before*, the plans would have been made on the 4th floor of City Hall, in the . . . offices . . . and then . . . presented *using what I'm sad to say is still the most common technique—the design and defend mode*" (emphasis added).

Roberts challenges us—and those we hope to collaborate with—to distinguish between what we know and how we express whatever we know. Let's not confuse the expertise of the architects and engineers—he clearly values making "perfect use of those professional resources"—with their timed performance and style of presentation, a "design and defend mode"—because that "common" mode, "decide, announce, defend," he suggests, often leads to impasse, not creative results.

How ironic, because surely the experts care deeply about their fields. Still, it's not expertise, but the *design and form of experts' interactions with affected publics* that has created "constant conflict," troubles of trust, accountability, and responsiveness—issues about which, of course, the experts suffer but are not expert at all. We see here no rejection of expertise and science, but an insistence to value process design: to promote the accountability of expertise, not its autonomy. Roerts warns that minimally consulted citizens can resist expert *autonomy* as presumptuous, poorly informed, and disrespectful, but, he argues, better process design can leverage expert knowledge accountably to respond to citizens' priorities, worries, and ignorance.

So Roberts acknowledges that "one architect" seemed "happy to do it this way," because, as he says, "he'd been beaten up so badly for so long that he just didn't want to do it the other way anymore." Roberts provides here, in part, a story of administrative innovation, an improvised way of using expertise to produce quicker results with no loss of professional quality!

Roberts suggests a fresh focus in our studies of collaboration when he says, "that actually set the stage for me . . . to always think about starting from the values and interests of the parties, as the foundation place *to start*"—to start, he says, not to end! Then he says, crucially, that he then came, "to use learning as the motivation for making change—and to have the parties themselves do that learning." And "This," he summarizes, "is what I've been doing ever since."

What can we learn from this fragment of Richard Roberts's practice story? We have a "story" here, one told not to entertain but to capture several practical themes. We see reference not only to constant, inherited conflict, but also to past and continuing institutional practices—both professional and administrative—that seem both inefficient and ineffective.

The planning staff looked for a better way. We learn of administrative and organizational innovation that did not seem to depend on substantial new resources. With his Director's support Roberts had the power to try a new process, but not the power to assure its success. So we see limits of conventional uses of professional expertise: limits of asking professional engineers and designers not only to solve problems but to diagnose them as well with little input from affected publics or their representatives. We see an improvised re-design of the use of expertise, so that "the design process" was, Roberts says, "fundamentally reversed": the professionals still speak to feasibility and practicality, but now they do it in collaboration with affected business owners and residents. We see what Roberts calls "the power of convening," following previous years spent with too little accomplished. We see Roberts struggling, too, to make sense of this new way of administering the planning process, as he tries to capture the lessons of this way of working which, he says, he has adopted "ever since": to use *learning as the motivation* for making change and to *have the parties themselves do that learning* (Forester 2009).

So this practice story suggests an emergent theory too—one that Roberts claims his whole career has corroborated: planning processes and governance can result in community change, at times, not because of raw power, but because community members can learn together, learn about threats and opportunities, learn "what they want to change" given the expertise at hand—because once community members, he says, "discover what they want to change" "they are actually willing to change" (cf. Adler's and Beutler's accounts in Forester 2013).

We also have here a grounded story that challenges popular suspicions that collaboration is inefficient, that it takes too long, that it must compromise or sacrifice quality, that it cannot be implemented within bureaucratic settings. To these prevailing theories that suspect, "If you find a swan, it will be white," Roberts provides a refutation; we have a healthy black swan.

So, I suggest, carefully gathered practice stories can be not only ethnographically vivid and rich, but scientifically useful, even generative. They provide far more than simple data points. They may challenge prevailing theories and assumptions. They may illuminate new practices and theoretical propositions to explore: here, for example, Roberts connects stakeholders' *learning* in the face of uncertainties and vulnerabilities to their willingness to act in new ways, their coming to decide to act now.

Notice that the work described here breaks the boundaries of the simple labels, "collaborative planning" or "convening stakeholders" or "co-generating knowledge" or "participatory action research." Generally, these labels work, but that's the problem—they *work too poorly*: our theories of practice tend to be quite impoverished relative to the complexities of practical judgment required. Likewise, in political science, public administration, planning and dispute resolution literatures, our language of process design does little justice to the complexity, richness, and subtleties of actually facilitated collaborative, dispute resolving processes (Forester 1999, 2009).

An Innovative Method: Assessing "Practice Stories" as Project-focused Oral Histories

How, then, might we gather and analyze such practice-focused oral histories or "practice stories"? I have mined the method that follows in six books and several dozen articles, along the way producing the most successful teaching materials I have ever used (Forester 1999, 2009, 2013; Forester et al. 2001; Laws and Forester 2015; Reardon and Forester 2016; for teaching materials, see especially Forester 2013).

It began in the classroom. I had applied for a small grant from a Cornell fund encouraging innovations in undergraduate education. My idea was very simple: let's try to connect the daily work or professional practice of our graduates—from ten years ago, let's say—to today's students sitting in those graduates' same seats. I wanted my students not only to consider my questions and arguments but also to confront more directly the kinds of practical challenges they might soon face "at work, after school."

I received the grant, but the idea was not nearly as simple as I had thought. Just how would I link the practice of our graduates back to the classroom? After several false starts, I luckily hired Linda Chu—a young journalist now studying for her master's in planning—as a research assistant.

I had asked Linda to interview a planning graduate, a transportation planner, then working to improve the connection between New York's two major airports, La Guardia and JFK International. A week later, Linda had written a clear three-and-a-half-page summary of our graduate's work. This was good, I thought, but somehow not good enough. Everything here was true, but somehow still too abstracted, too much Linda the outsider's version of the story.

So I gave Linda a book of Studs Terkel's, a well-known oral historian who had published the immensely popular *Working* (1974), in which people from all walks of life and occupation described candidly just what their being a priest, or a telephone operator, or a sex worker, or a car salesman was really like. Terkel briefly introduced and edited each account, but each person's story retained their own words, their own inflections and tone, their own senses of perspective, emotion, and emphasis.

So Linda returned a week later with 12 edited pages of transcript from her tape-recorded interview. Here now, in this transportation planner's own words, was his story of trying to connect the two airports, as he'd told it on the telephone to Linda who'd asked questions about how he did his work.

I distributed copies of those 12 pages to my third year undergraduate class as I told them what we'd done. Here, to supplement their earlier reading of case studies and negotiation practices, was this transportation planner's story, almost just as he'd told it to Linda. "It's optional," I said, "but this is his own story about what he does—it's not an academic article—so if you're curious, read it and we'll discuss it next week."

I didn't know what would happen. The next Tuesday, half the class had read Linda's transcript, half had not, and so I asked, "Well, what did you think?"

Marjorie raised her hand. "Yes?" I wondered, and she said in words I will never forget, "Now I know what to tell my mother when she asks, 'What do urban planners do?'"

I was surprised, and intrigued, too: this was a question that haunted our interdisciplinary program, and somehow this piece had given Marjorie the confidence to answer it.

Next to Marjorie sat Sean who had raised his hand too. He said next, simply, "This was the most practical thing I have read in this program in three years."

As I listened to their responses to this wholly experimental "practice story" that Linda had edited, I didn't know whether to laugh or to cry. They had just read a brilliant, award-winning economic development case study, grounded, vivid, politically and practically insightful, John Gaventa's wonderful *Power and powerlessness* (1980). They had just read Fisher and Ury's (1983) widely acclaimed negotiation primer, nothing if not immensely practical. What were Marjorie and Sean really saying? How could Marjorie now have the confidence to characterize what planners really did? How could Sean think that *this* was the most practical thing he had read in three years? I had no idea that their comments would foreshadow students' responses to "profiles of practitioners" that I would assign and explore in my classes for years to come!

Somehow Linda's transcript—crucially, in her interviewee's own distinctive words—had reached these two students in quite a profound way. Something pedagogically powerful had just taken place, but what? I really didn't get it—intellectually, morally, or practically.

But then I got lucky. A month later I came upon Martha Nussbaum's (1990) "Finely aware and richly responsible: literature and the moral imagination," and my interest in planning ethics led me to read the essay. That article, along with Linda's transcript and Sean's and Marjorie's comments, changed my life—for Nussbaum brilliantly and forcefully explained not just why, but in great detail how, my students had been so struck, so moved, and so impressed by such an ordinary, even somewhat messy, transcript, which turned out to be, of course, also quite extraordinary, once we read it closely (Nussbaum 1990; Forester 2012).

Nussbaum's question was this: How can we learn about ethics (the sensitive moral imagination of our practice and our options, their meaning and consequences) from novels? Novels after all are "made up," invented, fabricated, stories that are not even factual histories, so how could we learn about ethics—honesty, betrayal, generosity, callousness, respect, kindness and so on—from them?

I will not do violence (by overly quick summary) to Nussbaum's analysis, but most of my *Deliberative practitioner* rests upon her analysis of the demonstrative power of literature and, by extension, the power of narrative and story. I came to understand far better than I had how the-not-so-simple, detailed planner's story about his work of connecting the airports *showed* so much to my students, showed so much of the entangling responsibilities and complexities of his planning practice, showed so poignantly the challenges of perception and ambiguity and judgment that arose in such practical work—in this case, the work of planning and also collaborating with others.

The implications of all this reached far beyond the classroom, far beyond pedagogy, to both research and everyday professional practice, too. I had studied planners at work for many years, in part by being their "fly on the wall" in their staff meetings in City Hall. I was bound to secrecy and confidentiality, of course, but they appreciated having someone who cared about their work "sit in" and pay attention, and this was their way of helping academics appreciate the difficulties and opportunities of daily practice.

In the year after the classroom experience I described above, I came to realize that in the actual flow of planners' work, they had to gather and actually tell stories all the time, stories, again, not told for entertainment but to do real work. "What happened at the meeting last night?" they would ask one another, and they would hope to get a useful and perceptive account of who did what, so they might now know who to call, who to invite to a future meeting and, perhaps, who no longer to invite, and so on. I came to see that far from being confined to "novels" and "literature," stories were to practitioners a bit like water is to fish: if you try to get out of that water, you're not going to be doing good work for very long (Coles 1989). At work, the planners not only had to tell stories, but they had to become good listeners and analysts of others' stories as well, just as, in my students' own institutional, classroom, settings, the students had to become careful interpreters (of the meaning and significance!) of complex practice stories too (cf. Eckstein and Throgmorton 2003; Throgmorton 2003; Sandercock 2003, 2004).

Now this sensitivity to the ordinary challenges of everyday practice, including the everyday challenges of collaboration, had grown from my interest in the micro-politics of planning: the ways that selective attention and problem framing shaped who knew or even perceived what, and when, and how they did (Forester and Kreiswith 1993). So that interest now led me in two closely related directions, first to the essays on the practical work that stories do, essays that became *The deliberative practitioner* (Forester 1999). Second, though, I realized that by collecting and analyzing "practice stories"—refined descendants of Linda's early transcript produced from our transportation planner's account—I might now be able to do, just what I am suggesting that *readers of this volume can now do as well: explore the actual challenges and opportunities faced by participants in practical disputes, in collaborations and deliberations concerning environmental and other public policy concerns*. For the struggles of these engaged practitioners, who find themselves working "in between" multiple and conflicting stakeholders, promise to teach us not only about collaborative, deliberative, and dispute resolution practices but about encouraging public participation and even "managing" in organizations much more generally (Forester 2009; Laws and Forester 2015).

CO-GENERATING PROFILES OF PRACTITIONERS AS RESEARCH METHOD: PRACTICAL ADVICE

To produce rich, deep, and generative "practice stories" requires neither genius nor, of course, simply asking experienced practitioners, "Excuse me, what do you really do?" In what follows, I will explain how my students and a widening network of research colleagues have gathered and produced grounded, vivid, and rich practice stories relevant to dispute resolution and collaborative practices—for both research and classroom use—practice stories that explore the particular institutional contexts in which each interviewer, or you the reader, may be most interested. Because these practice accounts had been so useful in the classroom, Cornell Professor Scott Peters and I, with the help of then doctoral candidate Margo Hittleman, developed a practical guide to integrate the study of "profiles of practitioners" into undergraduate and graduate courses alike (see http://courses2.cit.cornell.edu/fit117/, or search via Google for, e.g. "Forester, practice stories"). Here's how to do it.

Collecting and Presenting Practice Stories for Analysis in Research and Teaching

We wish, first of all, to learn through the friction of actual practitioners' struggles. In whatever field of practice that we, or our students, wish to explore—environmental planning or urban design, transportation planning or city management, historic preservation or post-disaster response, for example, at neighborhood, urban, regional, or larger scales—we begin by identifying candidate interviewees. We look for practitioners who, by reputation, have been deeply immersed in the problems we wish to explore, practitioners who might be thoughtful, willing to speak about their own work, willing to discuss what they've tried, what they might have done differently, what they've found surprising, how they'd adapted and so on. We're not looking for heroes or incompetents, for ideologues, zealots, or salespeople; we want people who have spent years facing, handling, trying to do good work in a field of our interest.

Let's say I'm interested in exploring the character and handling of value-based or, perhaps, ethnic disputes (to take two examples explored in Forester (2009, 2013)). Then, when I identified (by reputation via networks) experienced mediators, for example, as candidates to interview, I asked, of course, if they would be willing to select and speak about a specific case that centrally involved one or the other of these kinds of disputes.

We select experienced practitioners, then, who might discuss (1) cases in which they have had deep experience, in which they've been "up to their eyeballs," really "in the thick of things," (2) cases that promise to align with our research interests, and, equally importantly, (3) cases that our interviewees consider really to reflect or show "the actual challenges and opportunities of their work." We *do not* ask for success stories. We ask for cases that the practitioner himself or herself finds fascinating, engaging, intriguing because in part it can teach us, again, about both the difficulties and obstacles, *the challenges*, and the openings and promises, *the opportunities*, of their actual work. Crucially, too, we do these interviews by asking (and not asking) some quite particular questions, as we shall soon see, persistent "how?" rather than "why?" questions (cf. Forester 2012).

So with a case selected by or with the practitioners, who often offer several cases that they might describe, we typically ask for one hour's conversation. We want ultimately, then, to follow the trajectory of their work on a real case. We want to save perhaps a quarter of an hour for their reflections about what they might have done differently, so that leaves us three-quarters of an hour for their story. But if we ask, as we usually do, for five to ten minutes of autobiographical history ("How did you come to do this kind of work?"), then we have thirty-five minutes or so left for the story of their work, and we try to begin *that* story by marking each case's *entry* and *outcome* points: "How did you get involved in this specific case?" "How did the case come out; what were you able to achieve?" So with that sense of origin and destination, our interview will work to "connect the dots," to connect entry to outcome—to connect "The mayor called and asked me to convene this group . . ." (their beginning) to "Nine months later we took an agreement to the City Council for ratification . . ." (their outcome).

But our interviews will connect beginnings to outcomes in two important ways that make these interviews quite practically different from those that social scientists ordinarily conduct. We wish, first of all, to learn about practice from the *actor's point of view*, not the spectator's. We want the account of the game from the player *on* the soccer field, not from the far less engaged spectator in the upper deck of the stadium. So how do we do that? Most of all, simply but essentially and quite practically, we do *not* ask, "What did you *think* about X," but we ask instead, "How did you *handle*, or *respond to*, X?"

Asking "What did you *think* about the pressure from the politician?" will give us the interviewee's views and perhaps theories about political pressure; but asking instead, "How did you *handle* the pressure from the politician?" will give us what we want, a story of engaged, politically sensitive practice, not political or psychological speculation or theory. This simple interviewing strategy makes a deep difference in what we can learn: asking not, "What did you think . . ." but, "How did you respond . . .?" for we want to learn about flows of practice in complex organizational and institutional contexts.

Because we want to understand such practical interactions, then, we also do *not* ask, "*Why* did you do X (call for a delay then)?" Instead we ask, "What did you see that led you to do X?" or "How did you come to do X (call for a delay then)?" If we ask the "why" question, the interviewee will often try to give us a rationale or justification for their action *to satisfy us*. If we ask "how" questions, instead, we learn about their perceptions of the setting and their practical judgments, without putting the interviewee on the defensive, having to justify themselves to us instead of explaining how they came to act as they did.

These interviews allow us to explore the kinds of issues that we, as researchers, find problematic, *as* these issues have been faced or experienced, as they have arisen or become problematic in a thoughtful and experienced practitioner's work. If we wish to learn about problems of "collaboration" or "adversarial science" or "fear" or "anger" or the relationship of dispute resolution to elected politicians, these interviews provide opportunities for us to ask, in specific settings, *how* experienced practitioners have handled and worked through just these questions.

Significantly, too, asking for *detail*, asking for *examples*, frees us from the interviewee's own shorthand, his or her own abstract summaries: "It's all a matter of building relationships," an interviewee might say. "Yes, surely," we should respond, "Building relationships: can you give me an example of what you mean?" Or the interviewee will say, "It all depends on respect," and we might ask simply, "Respect? Can you give me an example?" When we can prompt examples, we find they give us pictures worth far more than a thousand words, pictures of "respect" or "building relationships" that serve as *windows onto the practical worlds* we are exploring.

These interviews also provide the occasion to ask about surprises. What did these experienced planners—or managers or mediators—confront that they did not expect in the case at hand? What didn't they know to expect? Instances of surprise can teach us all, for surprise shows us the limits of our prior expectations, the limits of our operating theories, and so surprise and response teach us about what more refined theories and practical expectations we might need to bring to bear on cases in the future. As these practitioners learned from surprise, so might we, and so might our readers learn too (cf. Forester 1999 and Nussbaum's wonderful expression, "the moral relevance of surprise" (Nussbaum 1990)).

All through these interviews, we glimpse how our participant-interviewees built relationships with stakeholders, managed trust and suspicion, learned as they went, inquiring sometimes by themselves and sometimes facilitating inquiry by the stakeholders themselves too. As we see their stories of learning unfold, we may well expand our own sense of how we might learn too, in interviews, via argument, via site visits, from outside experts, or by being corrected by others in the flow of conversation and negotiation. All through these interviews we can recognize practical challenges of substantial theoretical interest: learning about interests, reconciling value differences, responding to posturing, strategies of joint fact-finding, ways of enabling venting and catharsis, modes of respecting deeply differing identities, strategies of representing stakeholders, and far more. In our excerpt from Richard Roberts, above, for example, we see no "last analysis" (no study gives us such closure), but we see both practically and theoretically intriguing issues emerge: the autonomy versus the accountability of relevant expertise, the timing of introducing answers to public problems, the difficulties not of expert knowing but of expert presumptuousness, the experience of citizens feeling disrespected or "done-to" rather than respected and listened to, the significance of alternative ways of convening and organizing process design, and far more.

CHALLENGES OF COLLABORATION AND PUBLIC DISPUTE RESOLUTION THAT WE MIGHT NOW EXPLORE

Consider, finally, just four challenges of collaboration and public dispute resolution practice that my interviews with planners and mediators, and their resulting practice stories (Forester 2009, 2013), suggest as opportunities for continuing research.

First, collaborative processes presume a constructed fabric of relationships making conversation, at times more formal argument, and creative negotiation possible. Richard Roberts assessed the power of convening, the conditions under which stakeholders and professionals actually meet. Although Americans may notoriously wish to "sit down and make a deal," many mediators have learned to "build relationships" first, to enable parties to "get to know each other"—whatever that really means. This raises more questions than it answers, but that's just the point: we need to understand better how such relationship building can encourage, or poison, joint learning and cooperative action—and explore how diverse socio-cultural rituals can play crucial facilitating roles.

Second, the presentation of self and the framing of contentious "issues" themselves need analysis, for we can often expect vulnerable stakeholders to be wary, guarded, selective about the information they reveal to each other. Mediators expect this, and they know to respect what's said initially even as they fully expect too that much more can—and will—be said, and that stakeholders will learn far more than they initially hear. Mediators know, too, that parties deserve respect not only, narrowly, for their opening statements but for their abilities to listen and learn, to consider today's information and tomorrow's options as well—and we can learn about collaborative possibilities from mediators' wisdom here (Forester 2009).

Third, many mediators know that when parties make demands—through the press, for example—that appear irreconcilable, many more options might still be found, even if the newspaper or media clips leave these nuances out. So mediators might ask to interview, and only then to convene, stakeholders at just those times when others, planners or managers or community leaders too, might think that only more antagonism can come from bringing together such adversaries (for an exemplary case, see Richardson's urban design/environment case in Forester 2013). The wisdom of mediation practice here might be put like this: parties might disagree deeply about fundamental doctrine or what their conception of the deity requires, but they might yet agree about where to put the traffic signs (Forester 2009, chapter 2). Parties might well disagree "fundamentally" about *these issues* and yet come to make important practical agreements on *those options*. They might disagree about abortion policy and yet agree to press for further funding for healthcare for small children. And so on.

Fourth, mediators' stories suggest that many people find the languages of "collaboration" and "dispute resolution" so abstract, vague, and ambiguous to be confusing if not badly misleading. In particular, students of collaboration and dispute resolution processes often confuse three kinds of stakeholders' interaction that need badly to be both *distinguished* and then carefully *re-integrated* practically. Processes of conversation and *dialogue* (1) differ from those of formal argument and *debate* (2), and both of those differ substantially, in kind, from creative, proposal-making processes of *negotiation* (3). Dialogue seeks understanding of significance and value; debate seeks justification via authoritative expertise; negotiation does still more as it seeks value-creating *commitment to a course of action* via the invention of interest-satisfying proposals (Forester 2009; Laws and Forester 2015). If we ignore dialogic processes, we risk solving the wrong problems. If we ignore expert debate, we may act on the right problems ineptly. If we ignore negotiations, we issue report after report on important problems and do nothing more. We need to understand each of these processes (and their relationships!) better than we do.

As importantly, these three processes require different forms of skilled intervention if they are to succeed, and each may be important in any given case. Dialogue requires the work of a skilled *facilitator*; in contrast, debate requires the work of a skilled *moderator*; and negotiation, if it is not to produce lose-lose outcomes typified by the tragedy of the commons, requires the work of a skilled *mediator*—a mediator encouraging not only dialogic clarifications or the sharper arguments of debates but far more: creative, responsive, workable proposals not for endless talk or argument but for future action.

We began here with a lengthy excerpt from Richard Roberts's practice story—to provide an example of richly grounded material suggesting both the *difficulties* (of traditional roles of experts for example) and the *opportunities* of public collaboration and dispute resolution strategies too (Roberts's fundamentally reversing what he called the overall "design process"). I have argued that collaborative and dispute resolving practices are emergent, ambiguous, and fascinating, and that if we listen closely, if we bother to gather and assess practitioner-focused profiles, if we examine such "practice stories" addressing the challenges and opportunities of actual collaborative and dispute resolving efforts, we stand to learn a great deal about emergent possibilities of practice across a range of legal and institutional settings. We can recognize new opportunities; we can develop powerful research (Forester 2009; Laws and Forester 2015) and teaching materials (Forester 2013) too. We will also be able—if we develop careful practitioner profiles—to connect our theoretical work on collaborative challenges ever more closely to actual collaborative practices and possibilities.

NOTES

* Author's note: this chapter has been revised and adapted from a keynote lecture prepared for the International Workshop on Comparative Public Conflict Resolution: Development of public policy consensus building theory and practice in Asia that took place on November 15–16, 2007, in Seoul, South Korea.

1. That we gather practice accounts in the language of the practitioners themselves creates not simply a quaint flavor of local scenery but what Seyla Benhabib (1990), following Hannah Arendt, has called the moral resonance of our analysis with the character of the case material at hand.
2. The profile of Richard Roberts (a pseudonym) was created by Cornell master's student Renee Hill as a project for my course, City and Regionals Planning 546, "Introduction to Environmental and Community Dispute Resolution," given at Cornell University in the Fall term of 2006.

REFERENCES

Benhabib, S. 1990. Hannah Arendt and the redemptive power of narrative. *Social Research*, 57: 1.

Coles, R. 1989. *The call of stories*. Boston: Houghton Mifflin.

Eckstein, B. and J. Throgmorton (eds.). 2003. *Story and sustainability: planning, practice and possibility for American cities*. Boston: The MIT Press.

Fisher, R. and W. Ury. 1983. *Getting to yes*. New York: Penguin.
Forester, J. 1999. *The deliberative practitioner: encouraging participatory planning processes*. Cambridge, MA: The MIT Press.
Forester, J. 2009. *Dealing with differences: dramas of mediating public disputes*. New York: Oxford University Press.
Forester, J. 2012. Learning to improve practice: lessons from practice stories and practitioners' own discourse analyses (or why only the loons show up). *Planning Theory and Practice*, 13(1): 11–26.
Forester, J. 2013. *Planning in the face of conflict: surprising possibilities of facilitative leadership*. Chicago: American Planning Association Press.
Forester, J. and B. Kreiswith. 1993. Profiles of planners in housing and community development, in land use and the environment, in historic preservation, in participatory action research, and women in planning. (Spiral bound, City and Regional Planning Department, Cornell University.)
Forester, J., R. Fischler and D. Shmueli (eds.). 2001. *The community builders: profiles of Israeli planners and designers*. Albany: SUNY Press.
Gaventa, J. 1980. *Power and powerlessness*. Urbana: University of Illinois Press.
Hill, R. "Profile of Richard Roberts on community development and organizational consulting." Available via John Forester, Department of City and Regional Planning, Cornell University.
Laws, D. and J. Forester. 2015. *Conflict, improvisation, governance: street level practices for urban democracy*. New York: Routledge.
Nussbaum, M. 1990. "Finely aware and richly responsible: literature and the moral imagination." In Martha Nussbaum *Love's knowledge*. New York: Oxford, pp. 148–167.
Reardon, K. and J. Forester (eds.). 2016. *Rebuilding community after Katrina: transformative education in the New Orleans Planning Initiative*. Philadelphia, PA: Temple University Press.
Rittel, H. R. and M. M. Webber. 1973. Dilemmas in a general theory of planning. *Policy Sciences*, 4: 155–169.
Sandercock, L. 2003. Out of the closet: The importance of story in planning practice. *Planning Theory and Practice*, 4(1): 11–28.
Sandercock, L. 2004. *Cosmopolis 2: Mongrel cities of the 21st century*. New York: Continuum.
Schon, D. 1983. *The reflective practitioner*. New York: Basic Books.
Terkel, S. 1974. *Working: people talk about what they do all day and how they feel about what they do*. New York: New Press.
Throgmorton, J. 2003. "Planning as persuasive storytelling in a global-scale web of relationships." *Planning Theory*, 2(2):125–153.

16. Hunting for country and culture: the challenges surrounding Indigenous collaborative partnerships on the coast of northern Australia

Cathy J. Robinson

> We used to hunt buffalo and dugong back in those mission days . . . We were used to sell the meat . . . I rode on the horse . . . I was a good hunter! Now government mob says buffalo is feral and we have to shoot it . . . government mob says dugong is rare and we shouldn't hunt it . . . but both animals are important for local Aboriginal people and culture . . . I still hunt these animals to care for my country . . . this needs to be respected today. (Jacob Nayinggal, interview with author)

One of the most significant issues facing collaborative wildlife management with Indigenous peoples today is the legal recognition of Indigenous rights to coastal areas, including the right to hunt and manage biological resources (Havemann et al., 2005; Robinson and Mercer, 2000). This issue has sparked considerable interest in the cultural, legal aspects of Indigenous hunting, the ecological impacts of Indigenous people's use and management of animals, and the rights Indigenous communities have to ocean areas and resources. This chapter draws on Jacob's buffalo (*Bubalus bubalis*), sea turtle and dugong history to reflect efforts made by coastal Indigenous communities in Australia's Northern Territory (NT) to establish collaborative agreements that recognise and engage with their native title rights and management responsibilities. Similar to other parts of the world the Australian courts have established that native title is grounded in the history of Indigenous peoples, their legal systems, and their connections to their traditional lands. Accordingly, non-Indigenous people and nation states are obliged to reassess some of the deep inequalities that have resulted from the long experience of colonial encounter and to attempt to consider opportunities for social justice and reconciliation (Hibbard et al., 2008; Walker et al., 2013).

Jacob's history demonstrates the complexity of ideas and behaviours associated with colonialism and the collaborative process. Coastal zones are a complex planning locale to examine these issues because they are the sites of extreme colonial rupture of cultural and ecological terrains. Although the coast forms a theatre for the interaction of salt and freshwater ecological processes and a fulcrum for Indigenous people's community lives and identity, the coast has suggested certain other cultural and physical landscapes to the colonial mind (Sharp, 2002). In this perspective, the sea remained essentially free, common and untransformed, while settler changes on land underpinned the contemporary ideal: interaction with the land defined the state between 'savage' and 'civil' society, proving the settler's worth and providing the justification for taking Indigenous 'waste' land for the production of 'proper' agrarian-based societies (Sharp, 1996). As a result, the perceived ecological effects of colonisation and attendant conceptualisations of Aboriginality and their relationship to animal species often changed at the shoreline.

The chapter begins by briefly explaining 'looking after country' – a phrase used as a holistic reference to the social, cultural and economic values of the environment embraced within Indigenous people's relationships to their traditional estates. This includes rights, relationships and responsibilities to animals that move within and between Indigenous countries, including dugong and turtle in the sea and water buffalo that travel across the massive NT floodplains. The Indigenous-settler-animal histories that intertwine along this frontier coastal zone are then summarised. The chapter concludes by drawing together the threads of the previous discussions to reflect on how legacies of past inter-species interactions continue to frustrate Indigenous people in their efforts to negotiate a set of principles for cross-cultural collaboration that values cultural tolerance and sustainable co-existence. Indigenous and non-Indigenous groups and community members are now working towards ways to collaboratively co-manage coastal areas and species that ensure native title rights and responsibilities are respected. It is within the philosophy and practices of these community initiatives that innovative and equitable collaborative frameworks and outcomes may be found.

LOOKING AFTER COUNTRY

Like many Indigenous people in Australia, Jacob Nayinggal and his community 'look after' his country by looking after the relationships to which they are legally and morally bound. From this perspective, management is not so much about controlling the sacred or physical elements of country but managing the Indigenous knowledge and relationships to this system (Morphy, 1990; Rose, 1992). If social relations, rights and responsibilities to country are maintained, the system is balanced and the country and life will continue to flourish. Balanced through this cultural-legal framework, Indigenous people's decisions about wildlife are carefully controlled to ensure that Indigenous input and knowledge are appropriate for the place or purpose and to give power and context to Indigenous law and interpretation.

Across Indigenous Australia, ancestral songs and stories (sometimes called Dreamings) connect country with people (Rose, 1996). As he recounted these Aboriginal histories, Jacob described how Dreamings were expressions of his country and how his country was governed by a complex regime of law. Within this cultural-legal system, people, country and natural resources are linked by powerful spiritual creatures, defined as essence created by the travels of spirit-being Dreamings which are classified and ordered into groups (Morphy, 1993). Indigenous people inherit membership to these moiety groups which in turn affects the way Indigenous groups' social, ecological and spiritual rights and relationships are categorised and expressed.

In the nearby northern coastal region near the remote community of Borroloola, Yanyuwa Elder, Mussolini Harvey, describes how the travels of Dreamings moving through country provide the framework through which Yanyuwa relationships to country are expressed. Yanyuwa life and land histories are organised around these places; they provide the 'mapped' boundaries of rights and responsibilities determining protocols and the permissions required when Yanyuwa people move through country, stay in places, or use and manage the resources:

> These songs tell the story of the Dreaming as they travelled over the country, everything the Dreaming did is in the songs, the country is in songs, the naming of people are in the songs . . . These songs are like maps, they tell us about the country, they are maps which we carry in our heads. (Harvey, 1988)

Indigenous communities whose homeland territories lie along the northern Australian coast do not separate spiritual, social, ecological or economic aspects of country or its management, and they do not divide rights and responsibilities to country at the shoreline (Sharp, 1996; Smyth, 2001). Instead, they assert that resources, like land and sea country, are not common or free because resources have owners and because these owners are governed by laws (Bradley, 1998; Robinson and Munungguritj, 2001). These laws determine who has the right to do what – including rights to and protocols for hunting animals (such as dugong) and rights to exclude or access territory. Laws also frame the ways in which Indigenous peoples' rights and responsibilities are conceived. As Rose asserts, rights are given by birth and locality, and are embedded in an identifiable group collective. These rights inform Aboriginal people and priorities about their responsibilities to country, each other, and past and future generations (Rose, 1995).

Across northern Australia, dugong and turtle and their sea grass bed and reef habitats have been incorporated into the activities of Dreaming Ancestors, which are known and owned by many coastal Aboriginal people according to Aboriginal law (Bradley, 1998). The names and classification systems for dugong and marine turtles are different in each of the more than 100 Aboriginal and Torres Strait Islander languages of northern Australia. This knowledge is embedded within cultural structures and processes, providing the foundations for Aboriginal people's behaviour when hunting dugong and turtle within coastal-marine territories (Kennett et al., 2010).

Water buffalo has also had a positive role in the historical and contemporary economy and culture of many Aboriginal communities since they were first introduced to Australia between 1822 and 1866 (Altman et al., 1996; McKnight, 1971). Many Aboriginal people call buffalo *Nganabbarru* and believe that the buffalo is a manifestation of the 'Rainbow Serpent', an enormously significant creature in Aboriginal religious life, and therefore buffalo are an animal that still belongs to Aboriginal people's country (Bowman and Robinson, 2002).

The deep and complex relationships Aboriginal people have with their surroundings is also grounded by practical activity and ongoing interaction with country. Hunting is one practical expression of this connection which is celebrated and communicated with ancestral songs, stories and paintings. Jacob's account of hunting buffalo, turtle and dugong reflected a form of dialogue between his people and country – and is therefore reciprocated and embedded in each other, and both are vital for the sustainability of life and the land. He described severe personal sickness if country or sites to which they are spiritually linked are mismanaged, damaged or disturbed. With the appropriate categorisation of social relations, cultural-ecological knowledge, and use of country, he argued, the system is balanced and the country responds.

In more recent centuries, Aboriginal knowledge and tenure systems have had to find new ways to interpret the experience of contact and changes imposed by external agents. To do this, coastal Indigenous communities across the NT have drawn on their discrete and shared rights and responsibilities to the area to negotiate and establish various mechanisms by which non-Indigenous people, procedures and laws might be understood within their communities. As Yolngu elder Raymatja Marirka-Munungguritj explained:

> The past, present and future of Yolngu community life at Yirrkala is not a linear story . . . our view of history is not a movement away from the present towards a distant future. History stays in the place where it has been made. It stays and becomes the foundation of the present and the future. (Marika-Mununggurritj, cited in Robinson and Mununggurritj, 2001, 98)

COLONISING THE BEACH

British settlers who arrived to Australia over two hundred years ago viewed the continent as a 'frontier' where a new colonial identity could be carved from the bush, and in the process the Indigenous landscape and people were supposed to fade away. Interaction with land defined the relationship between the natural environment and civil society, proving the settler's worth and justifying the transformation of Indigenous 'waste' land into 'proper' agrarian-based colonies and societies. Aboriginal communal relationships with nature were seen as indicators of a society in an 'unevolved' state before rights became individual and secure (Morphy, 1993). Since local law went unrecognised, the law of England became the law of the Australian colony. Neither civilised nor in legal possession of the land, 'wild' and 'savage' natives were conflated with the natural artefact of the bush; thus, they could be transformed by the process of encounter.

Indigenous people in Australia were hunter-gatherers, who, perhaps more than any other Indigenous people around the world, have been until very recently disregarded as land and resource owners and managers. This colonial view decreed that Australia's Aboriginal people were parasites on nature – as Australia's influential anthropologist Elkin (1954: 15) put it: 'The food-gathering life is parasitical; the Aborigines are absolutely dependent on what nature produces without any practical assistance on their part.' The idea that the land was untransformed led directly to the idea that land was unowned and was intricately connected to the view that colonisers had arrived to a country that was terra nullius (land belonging to no one). As Rose argues, closer analysis of the impact this ideal had on local Aboriginal people and their country reveals the ruptured effect colonisation had on much older interconnections throughout the continent:

> The specific place approach tends to marginalise the understanding that many of the processes particular to a given place were repeated over and over across the continent, and thus the devastation was continent-wide and was the result of cultural practices that continue to this day. On the other hand . . . the devastation of this continent includes the loss of coherence, and thus the breaking up of the links that articulated a continent-wide system is fundamental to and

> inseparable from the devastation of conquest. It thus raises for the reader questions of rupture of human systems and of ecological systems as well. (Rose, 1995, 192)

Colonial rupture of cultural and ecological terrains is particularly evident in the case of the coastal zone. While forming a central location for the interaction of salt and freshwater ecological processes and a focus for Indigenous people's domestic and cultural lives, the beach suggested certain cultural and physical landscapes to the colonial mind. Ecological effects of colonisation and attendant ideas on Aboriginality often changed at the shoreline. In metaphor and reality the sea was essentially empty as the colonial vision stayed fixed on the land beyond the shoreline.

Yet the NT was a rather unique frontier experience. Over the decades colonial improvers 'fought' with a deficient outback, colonial settlers remained a minority, their hopes for the land continued to be dashed. Australia's North soon became known as the place of the 'black man's climate', where nature triumphed over community development and settler citizenship (e.g. see Robinson, 2005). Describing the Territory in the 1920s, one settler wrote:

> What can a white man do in absence of good soil,
> Except bemoan and look upon his fate?
> To carry on and labour is to spoil
> And drag his status to the black man's state. ('North Australia', *NT Times*, 20 January 1928)

Relegation to the black man's status conjured powerful images for settlers who were constantly struggling to prove their worth in what they considered to be a hostile environment. In its state, contemporary life in the North remained 'uncivilised'. This dual notion of deficiencies in space and community continued through early settlement as both governments and the (white) communities they served struggled to find a vision suited to the Territory's terrains. Northern colonial ownership, citizenship and the transforming frontier were all being seriously questioned (Powell, 1996).

Coastal wildlife industries emerged as a small yet important part of Australia's 'made in the North' adapted frontier policy. A central aspect underpinning this imperative was the type of human–environment relationship that denied or justified who had the right to be a citizen of Australia. As Jacob recalled:

> We were told to hunt to become part of whitefella culture . . . to make money out of him [buffalo, turtle and dugong] . . . and be part of Australia.

Jacob recalled his experience working in the northern Australia's Gunbalanya (Oenpelli) mission during the 1950s and 1960s when coastal Indigenous communities, buffalo, turtle and dugong were all treated as a coastal 'resource' as part of the mission enterprise. These coastal wildlife industries were seasonal and valued by Aboriginal people because they enabled them to sustain their economic, ceremonial and social responsibilities to their traditional estates and maintain social and ceremonial links with neighbouring groups (cf. Robinson, 2005). Yet Jacob's animal histories highlight the power of a planning regime that enabled land and seascape rights and meanings of Euro-Australians to gain prominence over those of Indigenous peoples. Land surveys, settlement schemes, Aboriginal reserves and colonial resource and cultural management regimes were not simply implemented to appropriate Indigenous cultures and take their resources and land. They were also ways to delineate the *differences* between Indigenous and non-Indigenous societies and geographies. Those divisions were expected to be eradicated in the making of the frontier and signified a robust imperative underpinning a belief that Indigenous people would 'assimilate or perish'.

TOWARDS CROSS-CULTURAL COLLABORATION

In Australia's NT, control and management of land and marine areas and resources is an important legal and political issue, particularly since the Commonwealth Aboriginal Land Rights (Northern Territory) Act 1976 officially converted around 75% of the land along the Territory's coastline to Indigenous communal ownership. Despite land claim testimonies repeatedly detailing how the sea is an integral part of Indigenous traditional country, the legislation (Section 73) only allows two kilometres of the sea to be enclosed from the low water mark. Few sea closures have been granted and the process is generally criticised as failing to provide adequate mechanisms to enable Indigenous perspectives or participation to be incorporated into the control and management of the coastal-marine area. Meanwhile native title claims are currently being tested nearby in coastal-marine areas under the Commonwealth Native Title Act 1993, including some community demands to have their system of coastal-marine management recognised and implemented in the waters around Northern Territory Islands. Federal Court rulings have shown that in some cases native title sea rights do exist but these rights do not totally override, nor extinguish, the existing rights of other stakeholders with valid, pre-existing permits or lease, be they fishers, mining corporations or pearling companies.

Many Indigenous groups are now joining together to form community management organisations to respond to government management programmes and to ensure native law and responsibility provide the template for contemporary collaborative agreements (Hill et al., 2012; Ross et al., 2009; Smyth, 2001) and wildlife-based enterprises (Zander et al., 2014). This echoes developments across the globe as the contest over Indigenous and environmental rights has erupted in earnest and generated international support for the achievement of guarantees of sustainable cultural and ecological biodiversity (Anaya, 1995). While different countries have reflected on an array of different legal and settlement histories to guide the restructuring of colonial-Indigenous relations, the sharpened profile of Indigenous rights within the international arena has helped to clarify the 'official' thinking on rights to, and appraisals of, environments and resources (Walker et al., 2013).

In Australia there is now a range of formal co-management and other planning agreements which have offered a spectrum of opportunities to engage Indigenous communities in wildlife and environmental management decisions across Australia (Hill et al., 2012; Ross et al., 2009). This has included a range of collaborative partnerships that have been brokered between Indigenous Traditional Owners and government agencies, conservation groups and industry (Baker et al., 2001). Jacob Nayinggal was engaged in the co-management agreement established in Kakadu National Park which is also nominated as a World Heritage Area for its natural and cultural values. The co-management agreement for Kakadu is governed under the terms of the Environment Protection and Biodiversity Act 1999 (Cth) which gives statutory recognition to an Aboriginal majority on the Kakadu Board of Management. In conjunction with the Direction of National Parks and Wildlife, the Board is responsible for preparing and overseeing decisions under a Plan of Management (Lawrence, 2000).

The sharing of power and responsibility between the government and local Indigenous communities is at the core of collaborative agreements with Indigenous communities, enabled through institutionalised arrangements for the active participation of Indigenous communities in making decisions (Berkes, 2009; Davies and Young, 2001). Collaboration through formal co-management agreements has emerged as a popular approach, particularly for enabling Indigenous communities to participate in environmental and wildlife management decisions (Hill et al., 2012; Ross et al., 2009). In such cross-cultural contexts collaboration often involves different Indigenous and non-Indigenous actors working together to make sense of knowledge from different sources or to generate new knowledge (Berkes, 2009; Folke, 2004; Robinson and Wallington, 2012).

There is now a growing field of scholarship focused on Indigenous collaborative planning approaches and practice (Roux et al., 2006). In part this reflects the growing agency of Indigenous planning agendas that seeks to explore if and how environmental planning can enhance (or frustrate) Indigenous community goals, including claims for self-determination and resource sovereignty rights (e.g. Lane and Hibbard, 2005). Indigenous leaders and scholars have recognised that while effective and culturally appropriate modes of collaboration are important and necessary, the difficulties involved should not be underestimated. Barriers to cross-cultural collaboration include power imbalances (Hill et al., 2012; Lane and Hibbard, 2005), lack of respect for Indigenous knowledge (Agrawal, 2002; Davies et al., 2013) and the absence of a common language and a shared worldview (Bowman and Robinson, 2002; Memon and Kirk, 2012).

When tens of thousands of buffalo were culled in northern Australia's Kakadu National Park as part of a 1990s national feral animal programme it tested cross-cultural relations and the widespread government-sponsored hunting of these animals sparked considerable dispute between officials and Indigenous and non-Indigenous interests about the risks posed by buffalo relative to their value as a potential resource (Robinson and Whitehead, 2003). Sea turtle and dugong are now subject to conservation plans and agreements under the Territory Parks and Wildlife Conservation Act 2001 (TPWCA). This includes ongoing discussions about limiting Aboriginal hunting of these species which have support from local communities if these efforts are embedded in broader regional efforts which empower Indigenous people (Kennett et al., 2004). Similar to other efforts to build Indigenous–conservation alliances, efforts to build effective collaborative conservation partnerships are sometimes an aspiration that is still being worked toward, rather than something that has already been achieved (cf. Nadasdy, 2003; Peterson et al., 2005).

Today the small buffalo populations that are left are highly valued by Aboriginal communities because, as Jacob put it, there is always 'plenty of meat on buffalo – feed everyone . . .'. Rather than simply being a feral animal requiring eradication 'he [buffalo] has an aboriginal name . . . as long as not too many – buffalo can stay' (cf. Robinson et al., 2005). Jacob's responsibilities for his traditional estate includes Kakadu National Park and he was active in conservation efforts to engage in collaborative conservation of turtle and dugong in the Northern Territory coastal-marine area (cf. Kennett et al., 2004; Kennett et al., 2010). Like many Indigenous communities across northern Australia Jacob was worried about seeing less turtle and dugong on his territories. There is a growing awareness that many areas returned or owned by Aboriginal communities have been substantially modified, including habitats that have suffered from a loss of biodiversity and a degree of degradation. Even so, Jacob was adamant that these efforts had to be couched in regional efforts of shared responsibilities for these habitats and species amongst all northern coastal and Arafura sea stakeholders (Ginytirrang Mala, 1994) and that cross-cultural consensus building efforts would be respectful so as to enable biodiversity objectives and Indigenous cultural aspirations to be met in a socially just and environmentally sustainable way (cf. Nursey-Bray et al., 2010).

Local and purpose-built knowledge partnerships have offered important bridges to the challenges surrounding cross-cultural collaborations on these land and sea borderlands. One key challenge facing dugong, turtle and buffalo management partnership is to ensure that Indigenous people and their unique knowledge contributions are integral to the ongoing negotiation of collaborative agendas and arrangements. Such knowledge partnerships need to enable local people to use and refine their knowledge systems in ways that maintain the integrity of knowledge practices as well as provide coast-scape and Indigenous benefits. Integral to such knowledge partnerships is a requirement that collaborators work to build the trust and interactional expertise needed to test and co-produce knowledge that is meaningful, relevant and robust enough to maintain co-operation for sustainable joint management action.

CONCLUSION

Past outback myths are sometimes carried into the present, directing the interaction of people and environment and allowing some cultural spaces to be washed away from colonial memory and knowledge. But the myth is becoming increasingly shaky as contemporary partnerships with Indigenous communities recognise that localised collaborative dialogue and knowledge building efforts offer one key to a sustainable reconciliation with the land and its people. Indigenous people's claims to country insist that conventional environmental and cultural understandings and interactions be decolonised and localised. Slowly, relationships blended into a mythologised 'frontier' are being decoded, recalled and re-negotiated on the ground; and, necessarily, that re-introduces Indigenous people's interpretations and expressions of their relationships to country.

Yet the colonial myth continues to die hard, as the ingrained outback frontier ideology sometimes resists local responsibilities and realities and remains reluctant to concede its co-existence with Indigenous environments and people. Australia's northern beach lingers on as a frontier, spatialising improved co-legal and collaborative dialogue to envisage and resolve cultural and environmental interaction. Beyond the colonial beach, the sea remains empty space – devoid of 'improvement' and therefore continuing to remain homogeneous, common and unowned. Rather than the beach acting as a possible connecting environment of diverse past and present human interactions and environmental understanding, coastal space continues to loosen entwined cultural and ecological systems.

Recent contact with non-Indigenous people who have re-categorised coastal landscapes into land and sea and buffalo, turtle, dugong into shifting categories of feral, resource and wild animals has led to confusion concerning their status and created challenges for cross-cultural collaborative efforts. A significant issue facing efforts to negotiate and implement collaborative management agreements with local Indigenous people today is the recognition of Aboriginal people's rights to use and be involved in decisions about how these coastal species and geographies ought to be managed. Established policies and procedures limit the formal institutional capacity for innovation and for supporting cross-cultural collaborative efforts and contemporary consensus building efforts occur amid the history of prior agreements these policies represent. This historical legacy can act to constrain cross-cultural collaboration because new solutions displace the authoritative voice of these established institutions and the land and seascapes that these institutions have created. This includes challenges to contemporary interpretations about the ways in which Aboriginal hunting is an expression of Aboriginal management and traditional ecological knowledge and the rights Indigenous people have to care for country through hunting these animals.

So how might collaborative agreements provide new approaches to wildlife use and environmental management based on genuine partnerships founded on respect for cultural difference? The Indigenous claim for country is a straightforward one. It is a claim for the recognition of the discrete and shared responsibilities of a collective group and implies reciprocal relations of care between Indigenous people and their ecosystems. In recent years, coastal Indigenous communities across northern Australia have established community management organisations to respond to government management regimes and resource allocation programmes and to ensure that native law and responsibility enter into the collaborative process. In each case, Indigenous people insist that collaborative interactions and outcomes must no longer allow or promote loss of locality. Instead, collaborative agreements and relationships must be re-imagined to offer partnerships which draw upon and reinforce Indigenous people's distinct and extant relationships with their coastal homeland territories.

Obviously, but importantly, each collaborative effort and agreement is locally and regionally special. A turtle is not a salmon; nor is it a caribou, and coasts around the world reflect the product of an elaborate web of distinct, shared and continuing Indigenous and non-Indigenous perspectives and experiences. Recent local efforts to establish cross-cultural collaborative partnerships around shared Indigenous and other notions of place offer insights into how sustainable reconciliation with the coast and its people might be achieved. While the result of this process is far from clear, Indigenous people are certain about one end point: future collaborative governance systems will be devised from Indigenous relationships with their geographies, and they will endure in their places of origin.

REFERENCES

Agrawal, A. (2002). Indigenous knowledge and the politics of classification. *International Social Science Journal*, 54(173), 277–281. doi:10.1111/1468-2451.00380

Altman, J. C., Bek, H. and Roach, L. M. (1996). Use of wildlife by indigenous Australians: economic and policy perspectives. In M. Bomford and J. Caughley (eds), *Sustainable use of wildlife by Aboriginal peoples and Torres Strait Islanders* (pp. 77–94). Canberra: AGPS.

Anaya, S. J. (1995). *Indigenous peoples in international law*. New York: Oxford University Press.

Baker, R., Davies, J. and Young, E. (2001). Managing country: an overview of the prime issues. In R. Baker, J. Davies and E. Young (eds), *Working on country: contemporary Indigenous management of Australia's lands and coastal regions* (pp. 3–19). Melbourne: Oxford University Press.

Berkes, F. (2009). Evolution of co-management: role of knowledge generation, bridging organizations and social learning. *Journal of Environmental Management*, 90(5), 1692–1702.

Bowman, D. M. J. S. and Robinson, C. J. (2002). The getting of the Nganabbarru: observations and reflections on Aboriginal buffalo hunting in Northern Australia. *Australian Geographer*, 33(2), 191–206. doi:10.1080/00049180220151007

Bradley, J. (1998). We always look North. Yanyuwa identity and the maritime environment. In N. Peterson and B. Rigsby (eds), *Customary marine tenure in Australia* (pp. 125–141). Sydney: Oceania Publications Monograph No. 48.

Davies, J. and Young, E. (eds) (2001). *Working on country: contemporary Indigenous management of Australia's lands and coastal regions*. Melbourne: Oxford University Press.

Davies, J., Hill, R., Walsh, F. J., Sandford, M., Smyth, D. and Holmes, M. C. (2013). Innovation in management plans for community conserved areas: experiences from Australian Indigenous protected areas. *Ecology and Society*, 18(2), 14. doi:10.5751/ES-05404-180214

Elkin, A. ([1938] 1954). *The Australian Aborigines: how to understand them*. Sydney: Angus & Robertson.

Folke, C. (2004). Traditional knowledge in social-ecological systems. *Ecology and Society*, 9(3), 7. Online at http://www.ecologyandsociety.org/vol9/iss3/art7/

Ginytjirrang Mala (1994). *An Indigenous marine protection strategy for Manbuynga ga Rulyapa (Arafura Sea)*. Darwin: Northern Land Council and Ocean Rescue 2000.

Harvey, M. (1988). *The Dreaming*. In J. Bradley, *Yanyuwa country: the Yanyuwa people of Borroloola tell the history of their land* (p. xi). Richmond, Australia: Greenhouse Publications.

Havemann, P., Thiriet, D., Marsh, H. and Jones, C. (2005). Traditional use of marine resources agreements and dugong hunting in the Great Barrier Reef World Heritage Area. *Environmental and Planning Law Journal*, 22(4), 258–280.

Hibbard, M., Lane, M. B. and Rasmussen, K. (2008). The split personality of planning: Indigenous peoples and planning for land and resource management. *Journal of Planning Literature*, 23(2), 136–151. doi:10.1177/0885412208322922

Hill, R., Grant, C., George, M., Robinson, C. J., Jackson, S. and Abel, N. (2012). A typology of Indigenous engagement in Australian environmental management: implications for knowledge integration and social-ecological system sustainability. *Ecology and Society*, 17(1), 23. doi:10.5751/ES-04587-170123

Kennett, R., Robinson, C. J., Kiessling, I., Yunupingu, D., Munungurritj Mr and Yunupingu, D. (2004). Indigenous initiatives for co-management of Miyapunu/Sea Turtle. *Ecological Management and Restoration*, 5(3), 159–166. doi:10.1111/j.1442-8903.2004.00204.x

Kennett, R., Jackson, M., Morrison, J. and Kitchens, J. (2010). Indigenous rights and obligations to manage traditional land and sea estates in North Australia: the role of Indigenous rangers and the I-Tracker Project. *Policy Matters*, 17, 135–142.

Lane, M. B. and Hibbard, M. (2005). Doing it for themselves: Transformative planning by Indigenous peoples. *Journal of Planning Education and Research*, 25(2), 172–184.

Lawrence, D. (2000). *Kakadu: the making of a national park*. Melbourne: Melbourne University Press, Melbourne.

McKnight, T. L. (1971). Australia's buffalo dilemma. *Annals of the Association of American Geographers*, 61(4), 759–773. doi:10.1111/j.1467-8306.1971.tb00824.x

Memon, P. A. and Kirk, N. (2012). Role of indigenous Māori people in collaborative water governance in Aotearoa/New Zealand. *Journal of Environmental Planning and Management*, 55(7), 941–959.

Morphy, H. (1990). Myth, totemism, and the creation of clans. *Oceania*, 60(4), 312–328. doi:10.1002/j.1834-4461.1990.tb01558.x

Morphy, H. (1993). Colonialism, history, and the construction of place: the politics of landscape in Northern Australia. In B. Bender (ed.), *Landscape: politics and perspectives* (pp. 205–244). Oxford: Berg Publishers.

Nadasdy, P. (2003). *Hunters and bureaucrats: power, knowledge, and Aboriginal-State relations in the Southwest Yukon*. Vancouver, BC: UBC Press.

Nursey-Bray, M., Marsh, H. and Ross, H. (2010). Exploring discourses in environmental decision making: an Indigenous hunting case study. *Society & Natural Resources*, 23(4), 366–382. doi:10.1080/08941920903468621

Peterson, M. N., Peterson, M. J. and Peterson, T. R. (2005). Conservation and the myth of consensus. *Conservation Biology*, 19(3), 762–767.

Powell, A. (1996). *Far country. a short history of the Northern Territory*. Melbourne: Melbourne University Press.

Robinson, C. J. (2005). Buffalo hunting and the feral frontier of Australia's Northern Territory. *Social and Cultural Geography*, 6(6), 885–901. doi:10.1080/14649360500353285

Robinson, C. and Mercer, D. (2000). Reconciliation in troubled waters? Australian oceans policy and offshore native title rights. *Marine Policy*, 24(4), 349–360. doi:10.1016/S0308-597X(00)00011-7

Robinson, C. J. and Munungguritj, Mr. (2001). Sustainable balance: a Yolngu framework for cross-cultural collaborative management. In R. Baker, J. Davies and E. Young (eds), *Working on country: contemporary Indigenous management of Australia's lands and coastal regions* (pp. 92–107). Melbourne: Oxford University Press.

Robinson, C. J. and Wallington, T. J. (2012). Boundary work: engaging knowledge systems in co-management of feral animals on Indigenous lands. *Ecology and Society*, 17(2), 16. doi:10.5751/ES-04836-170216

Robinson, C. J. and Whitehead, P. (2003). Cross-cultural management of pest animal damage: a case study of feral buffalo control in Australia's Kakadu National Park. *Environmental Management*, 32(4), 445–458. doi:10.1007/s00267-003-0013-6

Robinson, C. J., Smyth, D. and Whitehead, P. J. (2005). Bush tucker, bush pets, and bush threats: cooperative management of feral animals in Australia's Kakadu National Park. *Conservation Biology*, 19(5), 1385–1391. doi:10.1111/j.1523-1739.2005.00196.x

Rose, D. B. (1992). *Dingo makes us human. Life and land in an Australian Aboriginal culture*. Melbourne: Cambridge University Press.

Rose, D. B. (1995). Rupture and the ethics of care in colonised space. In T. Bonyhady and T. Griffiths (eds), *Prehistory to politics: John Mulvaney, the humanities and the public intellectual* (pp. 190–216). Melbourne: Melbourne University Press.

Rose, D. B. (1996). *Nourishing terrains: Australian Aboriginal views of landscape*. Canberra: Australia Heritage Commission.

Ross, H., Grant, C., Robinson, C. J., Izurieta, A., Smyth, D. and Rist, P. (2009). Co-management and Indigenous Protected Areas in Australia: achievements and ways forward. *Australasian Journal of Environmental Management*, 16(4), 242–252. doi:10.1080/14486563.2009.9725240

Roux, D. J., Rogers, K. H., Biggs, H. C., Ashton, P. J. and Sergeant, A. (2006). Bridging the science-management divide: moving from unidirectional knowledge transfer to knowledge interfacing and sharing. *Ecology and Society*, 11(1), 4. Available at http://hdl.handle.net/10204/953

Sharp, N. (1996). *No ordinary judgement. Mabo, the Murray Islanders land case*. Canberra: Aboriginal Studies Press.

Sharp, N. (2002). *Saltwater people*. Melbourne: Allen & Unwin.

Smyth, D. (2001). Management of sea country: Indigenous people's use and management of marine environments. In R. Baker, J. Davies and E. Young (eds), *Working on country: contemporary Indigenous management of Australia's lands and coastal regions* (pp. 60–74). Melbourne: Oxford University Press.

Walker, B., Jojola, T. and Natcher, D. (2013). *Reclaiming Indigenous approaches to community and land-use planning in the twenty-first century*. Montreal: McGill-Queen's University Press.

Zander, K. K., Austin, B. A. and Garnett, S. K. (2014). Indigenous peoples' interest in wildlife-based enterprises in the Northern Territory, Australia. *Human Ecology*, 42, 115–126. doi:10.1007/s10745-013-9627-3

PART VI

Conclusions

17. The challenges of collaborative governance: towards a new research agenda

Richard D. Margerum, Cathy J. Robinson and Ken Genskow

The Challenges of Collaboration in Environmental Governance grew out of a series of discussions, forums and conference roundtables addressing the issues facing collaboration and the critical concerns moving forward. The chapters in this book demonstrate that collaboration has been adopted across the globe as governments, non-governmental organizations and communities agree on how to share responsibility and concern for complex and wicked environmental problems. It is safe to say that collaboration is transitioning from an emerging idea to the norm of policy, management and planning practice. It is also safe to say that collaboration is not waning in its application. If anything, increasing problem complexity, diffusion of responsibility, internationalization of environmental problems and the increasing role of citizens and non-governmental organizations point to a growing role for collaboration.

However, as models and frameworks for collaboration mature there is a need to move beyond current practice to more closely investigate the challenges. This book focuses on the difficulties, weaknesses and limits of collaboration—not with a view towards an overhaul, but with a view towards improving practice to better address the urgent environmental issues facing us today. A consistent underlying theme raised throughout this book is that the challenges are varied and considerable, complex and multifaceted, and the challenges raise new questions and issues for collaborative practitioners and scholars. This final chapter revisits the ongoing challenges of collaboration presented throughout this book and outlines an agenda for the next wave of collaboration research.

REVIEWING THE CHALLENGES DEFINED IN THIS BOOK

As authors in this volume highlight, collaboration encompasses the process of facilitating and operating in multi-organizational arrangements to solve problems that are not easily solved by single organizations (Margerum, Chapter 2; Koontz, Chapter 3; Agranoff, Chapter 4). Collaboration can be attractive for politicians to provide customized, lower-cost outcomes (Weber, Chapter 10) and to help enable effective and legitimate policies required to handle complex environmental issues such as climate change and large river-estuary ecosystems (Koontz, Chapter 3; van Buuren and van Popering-Verkerk, Chapter 7; Wondolleck and Lurie, Chapter 9). Collaboration can also enable local voices to be heard, although unfair power dynamics and incompatible value systems can marginalize some groups such as Indigenous and rural communities (Purdy, Chapter 11; Rongerude and Sandoval, Chapter 14; Robinson, Chapter 16).

Effective collaboration often relies on planning structures and logistical solutions combined with the roles of key leaders, knowledge brokers and facilitators to build trust, share knowledge and enable learning for improved outcomes (Ross et al., Chapter 8). It is important to understand that the practice of collaborative membership entails creative process and facilitative leadership (Forester, Chapter 15). This includes the work of process experts, scientists, community members and collaborative group members who share, co-produce and sometimes restrict knowledge being brought to the collaborative planning table (Gilfedder et al., Chapter 6; Warner et al., Chapter 13). It is also important to understand the decision-making level in which collaboration occurs because regional or national policy-level collaboratives have different mandates and operational norms and procedures compared to local on-the-ground collaborative groups (Margerum, Chapter 2).

Across scales, the complexity and 'wickedness' of some environmental problems can overwhelm collaborative efforts particularly when solutions require long-term, large-scale responses that go beyond program funding or political cycles (van Buuren and van Popering-Verkerk, Chapter 7; Wondolleck and Lurie, Chapter 9). Various authors in this book discuss issues of utilizing collaboration to address climate change adaptation (van Buuren and van Popering-Verkerk, Chapter 7), diffuse water quality management issues (Wondolleck and Lurie, Chapter 9), large-scale land degradation (Gilfedder et al., Chapter 6) and species conservation and recovery (Weber, Chapter 10; Robinson, Chapter 16) among other complex environmental issues. In some contexts the gravity of the profound environmental issues puts additional pressure on collaborators to reach consensus that will deliver desired and sustainable outcomes.

Collaborative governance arrangements and processes now exist across the world as government agencies, non-governmental organizations, local communities and corporate bodies trial, adapt and refine consensus building efforts to manage these and other complex natural resource management issues. Several authors in this book highlight the maturity, diversity and evolution of collaboration as it has emerged from a new paradigm to a central concept of practice (Margerum, Chapter 2; Koontz, Chapter 3; Agranoff, Chapter 4; and Edelenbos and van Meerkerk, Chapter 5). In some cases governments have mandated bold experiments to tackle large basin partnerships—such as CALFED in the United States or Dutch efforts to manage their Delta program (van Buuren and van Popering-Verkerk, Chapter 7; Wondolleck and Lurie, Chapter 9, Warner et al., Chapter 13) or Australia's experiment with a regional approach to coordinate local collaborative and voluntary efforts (Gilfedder et al., Chapter 6; Ross et al., Chapter 8). In other cases collaboration has emerged from grass-roots engagement and strategies (Rongerude and Sandoval, Chapter 14) and from efforts to address power imbalances that are created by policy issues or even the collaborative processes (Agranoff, Chapter 4; Purdy, Chapter 11). As such as there are different pedigrees of collaborative arrangements and planning practice and each test consensus building efforts in different ways—whether to sustain buy-in from partners engaged in mandated efforts to reach a common goal (Wondolleck and Lurie, Chapter 9) or to disrupt deeply entrenched views about how consensus is best achieved and who can (and cannot) be at the collaborative planning table (Robinson, Chapter 16). Often controversy forms the roots of collaboration, and the environmental, political, racial and other causes of this conflict can linger into ongoing efforts to build robust and effective partnerships.

Tracing the evolution of collaboration in different countries shows the messy politics, unexpected failures and maladaptations that sit alongside the extraordinary success and innovation involved in collaborative arrangements and efforts. Maturity in research and practice of collaboration has pinpointed key attributes of effective collaborative structures and processes. These include vitality in leadership, knowledge brokering, dialogue and deliberation (Edelenbos and van Meerkerk, Chapter 5). Social and policy networks that form and shadow the collaborative partnership can influence and add complexity to formal and informal relationships used in problem solving and decision-making (Agranoff, Chapter 4). Contributions from science, local and other forms of knowledge need to inform efforts to resolve differences and coordinate action (Gilfedder et al., Chapter 6; Robinson, Chapter 16). Leaders, champions, facilitators and knowledge brokers become critical nodes to dynamic (and sometimes unstable) collaborative networks (Agranoff, Chapter 4; Weber,

Chapter 10). As Forester (Chapter 15) observes, the *practices* of these actors are key in the collective effort to negotiate stakeholder accountability for decisions, manage unequal or hidden power dynamics and agendas between participating collaborators, and build trust in the process and outcomes of consensus building efforts.

REFINING THE COLLABORATION RESEARCH AGENDA

In his chapter exploring the emergence of collaborative environmental governance, Tomas Koontz (Chapter 3) refers to the first and second waves of scholarship. The first wave he defines as normative and prescriptive research that highlights the failings of top-down approaches, makes normative claims about collaborative practice and presents best practices. The second wave built on this first generation by presenting typologies, addressing new research questions, focusing on the issue of outcomes, and integrating research beyond the environmental realm to broader collaborative public management. The second wave of scholarship has been able to cast a critical eye on the architecture and attributes of collaboration and expose the cultural barriers and conflicting values that can inhibit the development or achievement of shared goals and the resistance to adaptation and long-term commitment—particularly when there is a mismatch between political cycles and the resources and efforts required to tackle large and long-term environmental issues. These multiple waves of research have also been noted by authors reviewing the scholarship on networks (Sørensen and Torfing, 2008).

The notion that there are weaknesses in the current research agenda focused on collaboration is not a new one. For example, Sørensen and Torfing (2008, p. 6) note that research on network governance is still young and has not yet become fully "sedimented" into a well-developed paradigm with its own clear-cut definitions, taxonomies and methods. Similarly, O'Leary and Vij (2012) highlight the need for a consistent overarching theory, the need for greater integration and depth across the different theories incorporated into the field, the need for more real-time tracking of collaboration and longitudinal studies, and more work on the role of mandates in collaboration. A number of researchers have acknowledged both the progress of collaboration-related scholarship and the need for a new agenda that addresses the current shortcomings. These include conceptual weaknesses, methodological weaknesses, limited attention to addressing globalization, issues related to information technology and social media, and the need to address the issue of accountability, performance and outcomes (Layzer, 2008; O'Leary and Vij, 2012; Sørensen and Torfing, 2008; Sullivan and Skelcher, 2002; Weber, 2003).

Also important are weaknesses revealed directly and indirectly in the research presented in this volume. First, there needs to be more collective learning to build on the previous generations of collaboration research. Rigor is required to examine the history of scholarship into collaborative environmental governance and to exchange information among practitioners and scholars. There continues to be considerable scholarship that attempts to reinvent or design new wheels when numerous others are already available that could be reviewed, tested and improved.

Second, in our effort to seek out a range of authors across different fields and countries it became apparent that there is a need for more interdisciplinary and comparative research. Cross-fertilization of research approaches and findings need to be shared among those working in public policy, public administration, planning, geography, conflict resolution, political science and other related fields. Much can be learned from practice and scholarship in different countries and comparative research could distil common and unique features of effective collaborative regimes.

Third, there is a need to consider what future collaborative partnerships may need and what challenges they may face. New global knowledge sharing systems, sophisticated community engagement mechanisms and networks, shifting demographics, dynamic political priorities and tensions, pressing environmental issues, and increased complexity and competition will affect collaborations across scales. Those that are here already and those on the horizon create very different planning conditions than those that sparked the first era of collaborative watershed and environmental management efforts.

A continuing challenge across the generations of collaboration research relates to the inadequate funding to support this kind of work. In the United States, foundations supported some of the early emerging research (e.g., The William and Flora Hewlett Foundation and the Amherst H. Wilder Foundation), but there have been few long-term sustained research efforts. Federal agencies continue to support applied research, but this is often focused on specific agency projects and constrained by time frames. Agencies such as the U.S. National Science Foundation have been somewhat indifferent to research related to collaborative governance and management, preferring narrower disciplinary approaches to the complex, multifaceted questions arising in practice. In contrast, the European and Australian government funding agencies have been more innovative in supporting multi-year, interdisciplinary research agendas related to governance. Addressing many of the key research needs listed below will require the kind of long-term and comparative monitoring and evaluation approaches often championed in the physical sciences.

A COLLABORATION RESEARCH AGENDA

Collaboration has evolved from an emerging concept to a central tenet of modern planning, management and governance. Its evolution is not driven by theory or management trends, but by contexts, problems and participants that demand an interactive approach. It has evolved because the complexity of governance demands multiple participants and multiple voices. It has also evolved rapidly in part because practitioners and researchers have documented its successes and achievements. However, as it assumes a mantle of mainstream practice, collaboration must also look more critically at the challenges it faces in relation to context, process, participation and outcomes.

Towards this end, we sought to outline a clear research agenda for collaboration. We started with the concepts and themes that appeared across the chapters in this book, identifying research needs related to time scale, politics and governance, collaborative practice, public roles, individual roles, science and complexity, external pressures, management relationships. We asked the authors contributing to this volume to help elaborate on this agenda and flesh out some of the key questions moving forward.

We then cast our net more widely, reaching out to almost fifty additional leading researchers from a wide range of fields to peer review this list and help refine the categories and questions. We received feedback from twenty-one researchers and combined them with the feedback from our contributing authors to present a refined collaboration research agenda. While not a definitive list of all research needs, the result is a robust agenda that advances our goal of cataylzing the next generation of research to further our understanding and development of collaborative governance.

Longitudinal Research

Most of the research on collaboration to date has relied on one-off studies or analysis of collaboration at single points in time. There has been some research examining consistent themes and practice over longer periods of time (Cheng et al., 2015; Curtis et al., 2014; Lange et al., 2013; Schuett et al., 2001; Selin and Chavez, 1994; Yabes and Goldstein, 2015; Yaffee and Wondolleck, 1994), but little longitudinal research that allows understanding of its application to ongoing management and governance. In many settings, collaboration confronts complex problems that require ongoing intervention. As some peer reviewers pointed out, the call for longitudinal research on collaborative governance assumes that partnerships or arrangements *should* endure over time—instead of being reoriented, recreated or redeployed. However, many of our authors and peer reviewers believed a longitudinal perspective is critical for understanding success, because outputs and outcomes take so long to manifest themselves. Furthermore, a longitudinal analysis provides an opportunity to examine the many layers of collaborative process, design and practice. This includes the need to consider how collaborative capacities of individuals and institutions evolve over time, and how approaches evolve in response to internal learning and the external environment.

Key research needs

- Understanding the nuances of collaborative practice evolves over time.
- Understanding how collaborative approaches respond to environmental, social and political change, and why some collaborative bodies are dynamic and resilient over time while others tend to buckle or collapse.
- Evaluating collaborative governance in relation to long-term outputs and outcomes to better relate alternative structures and processes to effectiveness.
- Understanding the issues related to sustaining collaborative governance over the long term in relation to relationships, trust, networks and structures.
- Empirical reinvestigation of case studies from the 1980s and 1990s to determine the long-term lessons that can be drawn from success, failure or redirection.

Politics and Governance

While collaboration has evolved in many contexts to resolve differences between political ideologies and perspectives, elected officials and high-level bureaucrats play an important direct and indirect role in collaboration practice (Beierle and Cayford, 2002; Keast et al., 2007; Koontz et al., 2004; Layzer, 2008; Lubell et al., 2010; McAllister et al., 2015; Sørensen and Torfing, 2008; Sullivan and Skelcher, 2002; Tatenhove and Leroy, 2000; Thomas, 2003). This is particularly true for collaborative governance problems involving large-scale problems and major policy debates (Gerlak, 2005; Heikkila, 2006; Lurie, 2011). In developing countries and contexts, collaboration faces even greater challenges where there is a little history of power-sharing and governance systems are still strongly influenced by central control (Dore, 2007; Warner, 2007; Wegerich, 2007).

Our contributing authors and peer reviewers noted that power is an inherent aspect of collaboration and should not be valued as negative.

Elected officials and bureaucrats have the power to support or derail collaboration through such levers as their control over information, interpersonal relationships and resource allocation. Importantly, these individuals are exposed to a wide range of decisional processes ranging from local elites to non-local interest groups. Real-world problems often involve sets of sub-problems where collaboration may be used for some and more command and control approaches used for others. This raises a number of issues about the factors that lead stakeholders to prefer certain strategies over others and how collaboration works in parallel to traditional political and governance decision-making.

Key research needs

- What are the specific challenges of governance in the face of political turnover?
- Effective approaches to building trust among stakeholders, agencies and elected officials in different contexts.
- The role of elected officials and high-level bureaucrats as advocates, leaders, participants—and the challenges of sustaining these roles over time.
- The role of elected officials and high-level bureaucrats as opponents to collaborative governance efforts.
- The politics of consensus building in cross-cultural settings.
- The influence of informal networks on the efforts of formal collaborative organizations to build and sustain legitimacy to reaching and delivering on agreements.
- The role of parallel political and bureaucratic processes in offering alternative venues for change or inducing participation in collaborative venues.

The Art and Nuance of Collaborative Practice

In addition to the calls for more rigorous science and empirical work, there is also an equally strong call for understanding the nuanced art of practice (Forester, 2013; Innes and Booher, 1999, 2009; Laws and Forester, 2015). Insight might also be provided by incorporating the views of embedded researchers who can gather information throughout the process as practice changes and adjusts over time (Lurie, 2011). An underlying theme emerging from many of these researchers is that our understanding of practice may be best served by understanding the stories of the practice told by collaborative leaders, facilitators and knowledge brokers. From this perspective, addressing the challenges of collaboration is not resolved through just best practices, typologies or performance measures. Instead, a research agenda needs to provide practitioners and participants with a greater appreciation of the complex adaptations, improvisations and dynamics of collaborative practice as it plays out around the tables, streets and fields in different contexts.

Key research needs

- How does the role of researcher as convener or participant in the day-to-day practice of collaborative agreements and processes translate experiences into findings that can be used by practitioners to improve future collaborative efforts?
- How do we identify and break down barriers to allow researchers to co-produce knowledge and findings with participants?
- What guidance can be provided in terms of structuring the collaborative arrangement, and how do these arrangements evolve from scratch?
- What are the implications for professionals in collaborative practice when they engage in research to explore the nuances of collaboration?
- What is the tacit knowledge that repeat practitioners have developed through experience that goes beyond simple "how to" advice?
- How do we translate the many stories of practice into lessons and training for researchers and research practice—to add to theory, methods and professional skills of researchers engaged in the study of collaborative environmental governance regimes?

The Role of Community and the Public

There has been considerable research focused on the role of the stakeholders at the table. However, there has been far less attention paid to a broader view of participation that takes into account community perceptions. One set of contributions in this area addresses the role of community-based or grass-roots collaboration efforts, which are exemplified by watershed and ecosystem partnership organizations (Benson et al., 2013; Campbell, 1994; Curtis, 1998; Curtis et al., 2002; Curtis et al., 2014; Hahn, 2011; Nickelsburg, 1998; Robins and Dovers, 2007; van Meerkerk et al., 2013; Weber, 2003). Another set of contributions—occurring largely outside environmental fields—has examined non-profit organizations involved in community-based efforts to address topics such as health, social services and substance abuse (Colby and Murrell, 1998; Cooper et al., 2008; Darlington et al., 2005; Grengs, 2002; Israel and Schulz, 1998; Mandell,

2001; Marans and Schaefer, 1998; Rich et al., 2001). A third set of contributions, which include several authors in this book, is examining strategies to empower urban, minority and/or Indigenous communities in addressing local concerns (Main and Sandoval, 2015; Sandoval and Maldonado, 2012). This work also captures growing popular interest in identifying how these communities can take greater charge of governance, exemplified by the Black Lives Matter movement in urban U.S. cities or Aboriginal self-governance efforts in Australia. These trends challenge the traditional approaches to initiating and convening collaborative efforts, because they tend to induce participation among those who already have access and power and may accentuate distrust of governing organizations by disaffected minority groups. In particular, there are significant challenges of engaging a broad cross-section of potentially affected individuals.

Key research needs

- The strategies and approaches for integrating broad-based engagement that extends the table or integrates the table with the community.
- The relationship between community outreach efforts and political participation and roles.
- The long-term satisfaction, strategies and sustainability of community and public engagement efforts that operate in parallel to traditional stakeholder approaches.
- The settings and conditions under which public-oriented empowerment methods may be more effective than stakeholder-oriented methods.
- The tensions and synergy between government-led efforts and those led by other stakeholders.
- The interplay between collaboration for environmental governance and movements for empowerment and social justice.

The Role of Individual Participants

A number of researchers cite the role of trust, relationships and understanding as keys to collaborative practice (Beierle and Konisky, 2000; Chrislip and Larson, 1994; Huxham, 2003; Huxham and Vangen, 2005; O'Leary and Bingham, 2009). Participants are engaged in collaborative processes for a variety of reasons, including: governance responsibilities, individual or organizational power, personal stake, representational role, and providing a community or cultural perspective. This diversity of reasons creates a diversity of roles and unique challenges to participation. Furthermore, individuals are often asked to engage in intensive communication, deliberation and conflict resolution that may be challenging or create disparities of experience. There have been important contributions to the role of leaders and how they can support or constrain collaborative management (Chrislip and Larson, 1994; Forester, 2013; Linden, 2008; Sullivan et al., 2012). There has been less work on the personal characteristics, the transformational processes, the representative-organization relations that help collaborative practice (Huxham and Vangen, 2005; O'Leary and Bingham, 2008).

Key research needs

- How are participant relationships created and sustained over time?
- How are participant relationships framed and reframed over time to sustain collaborative governance?
- What are the approaches to addressing destructive individuals or those whose goals are to overtly or covertly destabilize collaborative efforts?
- What are the different types of leadership practices needed in collaborative governance?
- What are the key competencies of relationship builders and boundary spanners and how do these competencies evolve over time in response to changing collaborative governance dynamics?
- What are the requirements and practices of individuals representing organizations in collaboration, including issues of adequate participation, sufficient decision-making power and credible commitment?
- What are the conditions and contextual factors that allow mutual relationships to develop?
- How are collaborative governance processes sustained in the face of changing participants?
- What is the configuration of informal settings, boundary spanning activities, deliberations, trust building and institutional relations required to sustain governance networks over time?
- How do configurations of participant dynamics and vitality relate to outcomes over time?

Science and Problem Complexity

The governance of environmental problems often involves multiple stakeholders with different perspectives, different knowledge bases and different goals. Effective collaboration demands the reconciliation of these differences and expects that partners can provide a formal space in which to negotiate a common understanding of the environmental problem and an agreed course of action based on a broad set of knowledge contributions. While researchers have addressed the normative conditions for successful knowledge sharing, considerable challenges remain involving the negotiation, production and application of knowledge for collaboration (Gerlak, 2005). This work suggests that there is merit in investing in analytical descriptions of the way knowledge is "worked" into decision-making and action on the ground. There has also been considerable work in the literature on conflict resolution, science policy and science engagement that has not been widely accessed in the collaborative governance literature (Ascher et al., 2002; Bobker, 2009; Ehrmann and Stinson, 1999; Failing et al., 2007; Gerlak, 2005; Goldstein, 2010; Goldstein and Butler, 2010; Kallis et al., 2010; Ozawa, 2005).

Key research needs

- What collaborative mechanisms are used to collect, critique and use different types (local, scientific and other) of knowledge?
- Understanding the characteristics of scientific knowledge that is used (or not) in collaborative decision-making.
- Understanding the characteristics of Indigenous and local knowledge that is used (or not) in collaborative decision-making and how it can be utilized without requiring transformation or adoption of a "westernized" knowledge framework.
- What are the institutional conditions that are required to ensure collaborative partners have adequate knowledge to make and evaluate decisions?
- How is new knowledge co-produced and created when there is (real or perceived) power imbalances amongst stakeholders and differing opinions about the validity of each knowledge type?
- What are the systemic biases against non-scientific knowledge in decision-making?
- How can communities of practice emerge as a domain of knowledge production for collaborative governance?

External Pressures

Collaborative governance has emerged in part in response to tensions, conflict and pressures to address environmental problems that are not easily solved. Collaborative efforts occur alongside these external pressures, which not only affect negotiation and power balance within the collaborative process, but also offer parallel venues and strategies for those within the process whose power is challenged (Lubell et al., 2010).

Even when collaborative approaches lead to agreements, frameworks and new governance approaches, the external pressures do not dissolve. These pressures may be important for maintaining stakeholder commitment and focus on outcomes, but they may also lead stakeholders to seek new forums, alternative venues, or abandon a collaborative approach (Layzer, 2008; Sullivan et al., 2012). Researchers have examined many issues related to these external pressures, including alternative venues, power balances, cross-scale pressures and issues of power (Ansell, 2011; Brisbois and Loë, 2015; Cheng et al., 2015; Conrad, 2015; Edelenbos et al., 2013; Emerson et al., 2012; Martin and Guarneros-Meza, 2013; Moseley and Charnley, 2014).

Key research needs

- How does mandated collaboration compare to settings in which participants engage voluntarily?
- Under what conditions do external pressures lead to stronger commitment to collaboration?
- How do external pressures—including those seeking alternative strategies and venues—affect negotiations and power balance within collaborative governance arrangements?
- How does the presence of alternative strategies and venues affect collaborative problem framing, convening and processes?
- What is the role of elite access, lobbying and political influence in supporting or undermining collaborative governance?
- How are the tensions between collaborative and hierarchical governance modes resolved?
- What are the cross-scale pressures and interplay that affect collaborative governance?

Management Relationships

Collaboration in many settings requires an ongoing set of arrangements to govern complex problems, often organized in the form of network structures. Researchers have explored different forms of these arrangements, the varying roles of management organizations, and the new challenges this places on traditional organizations (Agranoff, 2007; Benjamin et al., 2011; Butler and Goldstein, 2010; Gray, 1989; Kickert et al., 1997; Koontz et al., 2004; Mandell, 2001; O'Leary and Bingham, 2008; O'Leary and Vij, 2012; O'Toole, 1997; O'Toole and Montjoy, 1984; Provan and Kenis, 2008). A key aspect of this is also measuring performance and accountability in a shared decision making environment (Head, 2008; Hertting and

Vedung, 2012; Imperial and Hennessey, 2000; Imperial and Kauneckis, 2003; Ingraham and Getha-Taylor, 2008; Koontz et al., 2004; Koppenjan, 2008; Weber and Khademian, 2008; Weber, 2003). Many issues remain regarding accountability, effectiveness and governance arrangements.

Key research needs

- What are the strategies and approaches for balancing individual accountability related to agency missions and mandates with shared accountability in multi-party governance arrangements?
- What is the role of performance and accountability frameworks in revitalizing or disbanding unproductive collaborative governance arrangements?
- What are the most effective means for sustaining ongoing multi-party management arrangements?
- What are the most effective reward systems for organizations which recognize the new expectations of multi-party management arrangements?

Scale and Level of Collaboration

A final set of research needs that appeared in some of the chapters in this book, and were also noted by our peer reviewers, were issues of scale and level of collaboration. A number of researchers have highlighted issues related to action-level, local scale or community-based collaboration (Gray et al., 2001; Mandell, 2001; Margerum, 2007; McAllister, 1999; Nickelsburg, 1998; Robins and Dovers, 2007; Thomas and Koontz, 2011). Others highlight the unique challenges confronting policy-level, large-scale collaborative efforts (Cheng and Daniels, 2005; Gerlak, 2005; Heikkila, 2006; Heikkila and Gerlak, 2005; Lurie, 2011; Robinson et al., 2011). There has also been some attention directed to the relationships or nesting of collaborative efforts at different scales (Margerum, 2011; Marshall, 2008; Wyborn and Bixler, 2013).

Key research needs

- How do collaborative governance efforts at similar scales align efforts to address cross-cutting policy and management issues?
- What are the potential nesting relationships and mechanisms for collaborative strategies at different levels—for example, watershed efforts within a larger river basin or river basin work within the European Union?

- What are the shortcomings of local-scale and action-level collaboration efforts, and how do larger-scale or higher-level governance mechanisms respond to address these shortcomings?
- What is the future role of transnational collaboration to address complex and urgent global issues such as climate change?

CONCLUSION

One of the other goals of this book has been to profile the range of researchers from different disciplines, methodological backgrounds, contexts and countries to highlight the potential for collaboration on a collaborative governance research agenda. There is clearly much more to be explored, but we hope this provides future researchers with new ideas and a basis from which to build on previous work. Perhaps most importantly, we hope this research agenda helps address two trends related to the lack of collaboration in collaboration research.

One of the trends in current scholarship is to focus on a domestic or regional agenda (North America, Europe, Australia) at the expense of comparative international research. Research funders tend to reinforce this focus, and comparative work is complicated by funding, language barriers and the complexity of multi-institution research. In fact, many of the complexities of collaborative governance cited in this book are present in collaborative research. The chapters presented here only scratch the surface of the breadth of international research, but there is much to be learned in comparing findings from countries such as the United States, the Netherlands, Australia and India.

Another trend is the tendency for researchers to focus within their disciplinary homes. This focus is often embedded in our academic training and reinforced by the conferences we attend, the journals we read, and the citations we use and expect to see. This book sought to encourage greater cross-disciplinary collaboration. We have authors whose training is in geography, urban planning, political science, public policy, public administration, business administration, and natural resources management. Furthermore, our authors draw on an even wider range of theoretical homes, including institutional analysis, conflict resolution, collaborative governance, networks, communicative planning, or resilience. By necessity we have had to limit our focus and we are thus missing perspectives from anthropology and sociology, theorists focused on social networks and leadership, and researchers working in community health and non-profit management among others. Even so, a quick review of the citations and references throughout this book should lead readers to new research, new sources and new areas of scholarship they have not explored before.

The problems and issues being addressed through collaborative governance defy simple solutions and are clearly not going away. In some respects they are the wicked problems and issues that have been confounding scholars for decades. In other respects the stakes are much higher because population pressures, resource use, diffusion of problems, climate change and many other factors have made the issues even more complex and more difficult to address. Effectively using collaboration in practice faces many challenges, but researchers make clear that the need for collaboration is unavoidable for addressing many vexing real-world problems. The challenge is to build a research agenda that works to improve how collaboration is understood and practiced, and ultimately to produce better governance that helps improve environmental outcomes.

REFERENCES

Agranoff, R. (2007). *Managing within networks: adding value to public organizations*. Washington, DC: Georgetown University Press. Retrieved from http://www.loc.gov/catdir/toc/ecip071/2006031171.html

Ansell, C. K. (2011). *Pragmatist democracy: evolutionary learning as public philosophy*. Oxford and New York: Oxford University Press.

Ascher, W., Steelman, T. A., and Healy, R. G. (2002). *Knowledge and environmental policy: re-imagining the boundaries of science and politics*. Cambridge, MA: The MIT Press.

Beierle, T. C., and Cayford, J. (2002). *Democracy in practice: public participation in environmental decisions*. Washington, DC: Resources for the Future.

Beierle, T. C., and Konisky, D. M. (2000). Values, conflict, and trust in participatory environmental planning. *Journal of Policy Analysis and Management: [The Journal of the Association for Public Policy Analysis and Management]*, *19*(4), 16.

Benjamin, C. E., Brechin, S. R., and Thoms, C. A. (2011). Introduction to the special issue: organizational networks and environmental governance. *Journal of Natural Resources Policy Research*, *3*(3), 211–222.

Benson, D., Jordan, A., Cook, H., and Smith, L. (2013). Collaborative environmental governance: are watershed partnerships swimming or are they sinking? *Land Use Policy*, *30*(1), 748–757. Retrieved from http://doi.org/10.1016/j.landusepol.2012.05.016

Bobker, G. (2009). The means do not justify the ends: a comment on CALFED. *Environmental Science and Policy*, *12*(6), 726–728.

Brisbois, M. C., and Loë, R. C. de. (2015). Power in collaborative approaches to governance for water: a systematic review. *Society & Natural Resources*, *29*(7), 775–790. Retrieved from http://doi.org/10.1080/08941920.2015.1080339

Butler, W. H., and Goldstein, B. E. (2010). The US fire learning network: springing a rigidity trap through multi-scalar collaborative networks. *Ecology and Society*, *15*(3), 21.

Campbell, A. (1994). *Community first: landcare in Australia*. London: International Institute for Environment and Development.
Cheng, A. S., and Daniels, S. E. (2005). Getting to the "we": examining the relationship between geographic scale and ingroup emergence in collaborative watershed planning. *Human Ecology Review*, *12*(1), 30–43.
Cheng, A. S., Gerlak, A. K., Dale, L., and Mattor, K. (2015). Examining the adaptability of collaborative governance associated with publicly managed ecosystems over time: insights from the Front Range Roundtable, Colorado, USA. *Ecology and Society*, *20*(1). Retrieved from http://doi.org/10.5751/ES-07187-200135
Chrislip, D. D., and Larson, C. E. (1994). *Collaborative leadership: how citizens and civic leaders can make a difference*. San Francisco, CA: Jossey-Bass.
Colby, S. M., and Murrell, W. (1998). Child welfare and substance abuse services: from barriers to collaboration. In R. L. Hampton, V. Senatore, and T. P. Gullotta (eds.), *Substance abuse, family violence and child welfare. Bridging perspectives* (pp. 188–219). Thousand Oaks, CA: Sage.
Conrad, E. (2015). Bridging the hierarchical and collaborative divide: the role of network managers in scaling up a network approach to water governance in California. *Policy & Politics*, *43*(3), 349–366. Retrieved from http://doi.org/10.1332/030557315X14350819637950
Cooper, T. L., Bryer, T. A., and Meek, J. W. (2008). Outcomes achieved through citizen-centered collaborative public management. In L. B. Bingham and R. O'Leary (eds.), *Big ideas in collaborative public management* (pp. 211–229). New York: M. E. Sharpe.
Curtis, A. (1998). Agency-community partnerships in landcare: lessons for state-sponsored resource management. *Environmental Management*, *22*(4), 563–574.
Curtis, A., Shindler, B., and Wright, A. (2002). Sustaining local watershed initiatives: lessons from landcare and watershed councils. *Journal of the American Water Resources Association*, *38*(5), 1207–1216.
Curtis, A., Ross, H., Marshall, G. R., Baldwin, C., Cavaye, J., Freeman, C., Carr, A., and Syme, G. J. (2014). The great experiment with devolved NRM governance: lessons from community engagement in Australia and New Zealand since the 1980s. *Australasian Journal of Environmental Management*, *21*(2), 175–199.
Darlington, Y., Feeney, J. A., and Rixon, K. (2005). Interagency collaboration between child protection and mental health services: practices, attitudes and barriers. *Child Abuse & Neglect*, *29*(10), 14.
Dore, J. (2007). Mekong region water-related MSPs–unfilled potential. In J. Warner (ed.), *Multi-stakeholder platforms for integrated water management* (pp. 205–234). Aldershot, England: Ashgate Publishing.
Edelenbos, J., Bressers, N., and Scholten, P. (eds.). (2013). *Water governance as connective capacity*. Aldershot, England: Ashgate Publishing.
Ehrmann, J. R., and Stinson, B. L. (1999). Joint fact-finding and the use of technical experts. In L. Susskind, S. McKearnon, and S. Carpenter (eds.), *Consensus building handbook: a comprehensive guide to reaching agreement* (pp. 375–399). Thousand Oaks, CA: Sage.
Emerson, K., Nabatchi, T., and Balogh, S. (2012). An integrative framework for collaborative governance. *Journal of Public Administration Research and Theory*, *22*(1), 1–29.
Failing, L., Gregory, R., and Harstone, M. (2007). Integrating science and local knowledge in environmental risk management: a decision-focused approach. *Ecological Economics*, *64*(1), 47–60.

Forester, J. F. (2013). *Planning in the face of conflict: the surprising possibilities of facilitative leadership* (1st Edition). Chicago, IL: APA Planners Press.

Gerlak, A. K. (2005). The formation of large-scale collaborative resource management institutions: clarifying the roles of stakeholders, science, and institutions. *Policy Studies Journal*, *33*(4), 30. Retrieved from http://doi.org/10.1111/j.1541-0072.2005.00134.x

Goldstein, B. E. (2010). The weakness of tight ties: why scientists almost destroyed the Coachella Valley multispecies habitat conservation plan in order to save it. *Environmental Management*, *46*(2), 268–284.

Goldstein, B. E., and Butler, W. H. (2010). Expanding the scope and impact of collaborative planning: combining multi-stakeholder collaboration and communities of practice in a learning network. *Journal of the American Planning Association*, *76*(2), 238–249.

Gray, B. (1989). *Collaborating: finding common ground for multiparty problems*. San Francisco, CA: Jossey-Bass.

Gray, G. J., Enzer, M. J., and Kusel, J. (eds.). (2001). *Understanding community-based forest ecosystem management*. Binghamton, NY: Food Products Press.

Grengs, J. (2002). Community-based planning as a source of political change - the transit equity movement of Los Angeles' Bus Riders Union. *Journal of the American Planning Association*, *68*(2), 165–178.

Hahn, T. (2011). Ecology and society: self-organized governance networks for ecosystem management: who is accountable? *Ecology & Society*, *16*(2), 18.

Head, B. W. (2008). Assessing network-based collaborations: effectiveness for whom? *Public Management Review*, *10*(6), 733–749.

Heikkila, T. (2006). Comparing collaborative mechanisms in large-scale ecosystem governance. *Natural Resources Journal*, *46*(3), 657–707.

Heikkila, T., and Gerlak, A. K. (2005). The formation of large-scale collaborative resource management institutions: clarifying the roles of stakeholders, science, and institutions. *Policy Studies Journal*, *33*(4), 583–612.

Hertting, N., and Vedung, E. (2012). Purposes and criteria in network governance evaluation: how far does standard evaluation vocabulary takes us? *Evaluation*, *18*(1), 27–46. Retrieved from http://doi.org/10.1177/1356389011431021

Huxham, C. (2003). Theorizing collaboration practice. *Public Management Review*, *5*(3), 401–423.

Huxham, C., and Vangen, S. (2005). *Managing to collaborate: the theory and practice of collaborative advantage*. London and New York: Routledge. Retrieved from http://www.loc.gov/catdir/toc/ecip0418/2004013650.html

Imperial, M. T., and Hennessey, T. (2000). Improving watershed governance: collaboration, public value, and accountability. Presented at the American Political Science Association, 31 August–3 September.

Imperial, M. T., and Kauneckis, D. (2003). Moving from conflict to collaboration: watershed governance in Lake Tahoe. *Natural Resources Journal*, *43* (4), 1009–1055.

Ingraham, P. W., and Getha-Taylor, H. (2008). Incentivizing collaborative performance: aligning policy intent, design and impact. In L. Bingham and R. O'Leary (eds.), *Big ideas in collaborative public management* (pp. 79–96). Armonk, NY: M. E. Sharpe.

Innes, J. E., and Booher, D. E. (1999). Consensus building as role playing and bricolage: toward a theory of collaborative planning. *Journal of the American Planning Association*, *65*(1), 9–26.

Innes, J. E., and Booher, D. E. (2009). *Planning with complexity: an introduction to collaborative rationality for public policy*. New York: Routledge.
Israel, B. A., and Schulz, A. J. (1998). Review of community-based research: assessing partnership approaches to improve public health. *Annual Review of Public Health, 19*, 173–202.
Kallis, G., Kiparsky, M., and Norgaard, R. (2010). Collaborative governance and adaptive management: lessons from California's CALFED water program. *Environmental Science and Policy, 12*(6), 631–643.
Keast, R., Brown, K., and Mandell, M. (2007). Getting the right mix: unpacking integration meanings and strategies. *International Public Management Journal, 10*(1), 9–33.
Kickert, W. J. M., Klijn, E.-H., and Koppenjan, J. F. M. (1997). *Managing complex networks: strategies for the public sector*. London: Sage. Retrieved from http://knowledge.sagepub.com/view/managing-complex-networks/SAGE.xml
Koontz, T. M., Steelman, T. A., Carmin, J., Korfmacher, K. S., Moseley, C., and Thomas, C. W. (2004). *Collaborative environmental management: what roles for government?* Washington, DC: Resources for the Future. Retrieved from http://www.loc.gov/catdir/toc/ecip0419/2004014207.html
Koppenjan, J. (2008). Creating a playing field for assessing the effectiveness of network collaboration by performance measures. *Public Management Review, 10*(6), 699–714.
Lange, P., Driessen, P. P. J., Sauer, A., Bornemann, B., and Burger, P. (2013). Governing towards sustainability—conceptualizing modes of governance. *Journal of Environmental Policy & Planning, 15*(3), 403–425. Retrieved from http://doi.org/10.1080/1523908X.2013.769414
Laws, D., and Forester, J. (2015). *Conflict, improvisation, governance: street level practices for urban democracy*. New York and London: Routledge.
Layzer, J. A. (2008). *Natural experiments: ecosystem-based management and the environment*. Cambridge, MA: The MIT Press.
Linden, R. (2008). Collaborating across organizational boundaries. In T. Newell, G. Reeher, and P. Ronayne (eds.), *The trusted leader: building the relationships that make government work* (pp. 156–180). Washington, DC: CQ Press.
Lubell, M., Henry, A. D., and McCoy, M. (2010). Collaborative institutions in an ecology of games. *American Journal of Political Science, 54*(2), 287–300.
Lurie, S. D. (2011). The CALFED Bay-Delta Program: lessons from the rise and fall of a large-scale ecosystem management network. *Journal of Natural Resources Policy Research, 3*(3), 251–262.
Main, K., and Sandoval, G. F. (2015). Placemaking in a translocal receiving community: the relevance of place to identity and agency. *Urban Studies, 52*(1), 71–86. Retrieved from http://doi.org/10.1177/0042098014522720
Mandell, M. P. (2001). Collaboration through network structures for community building efforts. *National Civic Review, 90*(3), 10.
Marans, S., and Schaefer, M. (1998). Community policing, schools and mental health: the challenge of collaboration. In D. S. Elliott, B. A. Hamburg, and K. R. Williams (eds.), *Violence in American schools: a new perspective* (pp. 312–347). Cambridge, UK and New York: Cambridge University Press.
Margerum, R. D. (2007). Overcoming locally based collaboration constraints. *Society & Natural Resources, 20*(2), 135–152. http://doi.org/10.1080/08941920601052404
Margerum, R. D. (2011). *Beyond consensus: improving collaborative planning and management*. Boston, MA: The MIT Press.

Marshall, G. R. (2008). Nesting, subsidiarity, and community-based environmental governance beyond the local level. *International Journal of the Commons*, *2*(1), 75–97.

Martin, S., and Guarneros-Meza, V. (2013). Governing local partnerships: does external steering help local agencies address wicked problems? *Policy & Politics*, *41*(4), 585–603. Retrieved from http://doi.org/10.1332/030557312X655819

McAllister, R. R. J., Taylor, B. M., and Harman, B. P. (2015). Partnership networks for urban development: how structure is shaped by risk. *Policy Studies Journal*, *43*(3), 379–398. Retrieved from http://doi.org/10.1111/psj.12103

McAllister, S. T. (1999). Community based conservation: restructuring institutions to involve local communities in a meaningful way. *Colorado Journal of International Law and Policy*, *10*, 195–225.

Moseley, C., and Charnley, S. (2014). Understanding micro-processes of institutionalization: stewardship contracting and national forest management. *Policy Sciences*, *47*(1), 69–98.

Nickelsburg, S. M. (1998). Mere volunteers? The promise and limits of community-based environmental protection. *Virginia Law Review*, *84*, 1371–1409.

O'Leary, R., and Bingham, L. (2008). Surprising findings, paradoxes, and thoughts on the future of collaborative public management research. In R. O'Leary and L. Bingham (eds.), *The collaborative public manager: new ideas for the twenty-first century* (pp. 255–269). Washington, DC: Georgetown University Press.

O'Leary, R., and Bingham, L. (2009). *The collaborative public manager: new ideas for the twenty-first century*. Washington, DC: Georgetown University Press.

O'Leary, R., and Vij, N. (2012). Collaborative public management: where have we been and where are we going? *The American Review of Public Administration*, *42*(5), 507–522. Retrieved from http://doi.org/10.1177/0275074012445780

O'Toole, L. J., Jr. (1997). Treating networks seriously: practical and research-based agendas in public administration. *Public Administration Review*, *57*(1), 45–52.

O'Toole, L. J., and Montjoy, J. R. S. (1984). Interorganizational policy implementation: a theoretical perspective. *Public Administration Review*, *44*(6), 491–503.

Ozawa, C. (2005). Putting science in its place. In J. T. Scholz and B. Stiftel (eds.), *Adaptive governance and water conflict. New institutions for collaborative planning* (pp. 185–195). Washington, DC: Resources for the Future.

Provan, K. G., and Kenis, P. (2008). Modes of network governance: structure, management, and effectiveness. *Journal of Public Administration Research and Theory*, *18*(2), 229–252. Retrieved from http://doi.org/10.1093/jopart/mum015

Rich, M. J., Giles, M. W., and Stern, E. (2001). Collaborating to reduce poverty: views from city halls and community-based organizations. *Urban Affairs Review*, *37*(2), 184–204.

Robins, L., and Dovers, S. (2007). Community-based NRM boards of management: are they up to the task? *Australian Journal of Environmental Management*, *14*(June), 111–122.

Robinson, C., Margerum, R., Koontz, T., Moseley, C., and Lurie, S. (2011). Policy-level collaboratives for environmental management at the regional scale: lessons and challenges from Australia and the United States. *Society & Natural Resources*, *24*(8), 849–859.

Sandoval, G. F., and Maldonado, M. M. (2012). Latino urbanism revisited: place-making in new gateways and the urban-rural interface. *Journal of Urbanism:*

International Research on Placemaking and Urban Sustainability, *5*(2–3), 193–218. Retrieved from http://doi.org/10.1080/17549175.2012.693123

Schuett, M. A., Selin, S. W., and Carr, D. S. (2001). Making it work: keys to successful collaboration in natural resource management. *Environmental Management*, *27*(4), 587–593. Retrieved from http://doi.org/10.1007/s002670010172

Selin, S., and Chavez, D. (1994). Characteristics of successful tourism partnerships: a multiple case study design. *Journal of Park and Recreation Administration*, *12*(2), 51–61.

Sørensen, E., and Torfing, J. (2008). *Theories of democratic network governance*. New York: Palgrave Macmillan.

Sullivan, H., and Skelcher, C. (2002). *Working across boundaries: collaboration in public services*. Basingstoke: Palgrave Macmillan.

Sullivan, H., Williams, P., and Jeffares, S. (2012). Leadership for collaboration. *Public Management Review*, *14*(1), 41–66. Retrieved from http://doi.org/10.1080/14719037.2011.589617

Tatenhove, J. van, and Leroy, P. (2000). The institutionalisation of environmental politics. In J. van Tatenhove, B. Arts, and P. Leroy (eds.), *Political modernisation and the environment* (pp. 17–33). The Netherlands: Springer. Retrieved from http://link.springer.com/chapter/10.1007/978-94-015-9524-7_2

Thomas, C. W. (2003). *Bureaucratic landscapes: interagency cooperation and the preservation of biodiversity*. Cambridge, MA: The MIT Press. Retrieved from http://www.loc.gov/catdir/toc/fy035/2002071779.html

Thomas, C. W., and Koontz, T. M. (2011). Research designs for evaluating the impact of community-based management on natural resource conservation. *Journal of Natural Resources Policy Research*, *3*(2), 97–111.

Van Meerkerk, I., Boonstra, B., and Edelenbos, J. (2013). Self-organization in urban regeneration: a two-case comparative research. *European Planning Studies*, *21*(10), 1630–1652.

Warner, J. (2007). *Multi-stakeholder platforms for integrated water management*. Aldershot, England and Burlington, VT: Ashgate Publishing. Retrieved from http://www.loc.gov/catdir/toc/ecip078/2006103144.html

Weber, E. P. (2003). *Bringing society back in: grassroots ecosystem management, accountability, and sustainable communities*. Cambridge, MA: The MIT Press.

Weber, E., and Khademian, A. M. (2008). Managing collaborative processes: common practices, uncommon circumstances. *Administration Society*, *40*(5), 431–464. Retrieved from http://doi.org/10.1177/0095399708320181

Wegerich, K. (2007). Against the conventional wisdom: why sector reallocation of water and multi-stakeholder platforms do not take place in Uzbekistan. In J. Warner (ed.), *Multi-stakeholder platforms for integrated water management* (pp. xvi, 281). Aldershot, England: Ashgate Publishing. Retrieved from http://www.loc.gov/catdir/toc/ecip078/2006103144.html

Wyborn, C., and Bixler, R. P. (2013). Collaboration and nested environmental governance: scale dependency, scale framing, and cross-scale interactions in collaborative conservation. *Journal of Environmental Management*, *123*, 58–67. Retrieved from http://doi.org/10.1016/j.jenvman.2013.03.014

Yabes, R., and Goldstein, B. E. (2015). Collaborative resilience to episodic shocks and surprises: a very long-term case study of Zanjera irrigation in the Philippines 1979–2010. *Social Sciences*, *4*(3), 469–498. Retrieved from http://doi.org/10.3390/socsci4030469

Yaffee, S. L., and Wondolleck, J. M. (1994). *Building bridges across agency boundaries: in search of excellence in the United States Forest Service*. Research report for USDA Forest Service Pacific Northwest Research Station. Ann Arbor, MI: School of Natural Resources and Environment, University of Michigan.

Index